冨樫義博

Yoshihiro Togashi here. I'm back to doing a weekly serial, and here I am publishing the first volume already. Thanks to all my readers for their support. I am entirely indebted to you. I took this picture at a certain party, by the way, not at a shady membership club. I'll work hard to crank out dozens of volumes. I promise not to complain. I won't run away. I won't lose it. I think. Maybe.

Yoshihiro Togashi

Yoshihiro Togashi's manga career began in 1986 at the age of 20, when he won the coveted Osamu Tezuka Award for new manga artists. He debuted in the Japanese **Weekly Shonen Jump** magazine in 1989 with the romantic comedy **Tende Shôwaru Cupid**. From 1990 to 1994 he wrote and drew the hit manga **YuYu Hakusho**, which was followed by the dark comedy science-fiction series **Level E** and the adventure series **Hunter x Hunter**. In 1999 he married the manga artist Naoko Takeuchi.

HUNTER X HUNTER Volume 1
SHONEN JUMP Manga Edition

STORY AND ART BY
YOSHIHIRO TOGASHI

English Adaptation/Gary Leach
Translation/Lillian Olsen
Touch-up Art & Lettering/Mark Griffin
Design/Amy Martin
Editor/Pancha Diaz

Printed in the U.S.A.

Published by VIZ Media, LLC
P.O. Box 77010
San Francisco, CA 94107

10
First printing, March 2005
Tenth printing, May 2019

PARENTAL ADVISORY
HUNTER X HUNTER is rated T+ for Older Teen and is recommended for ages 16 and up. It contains realistic violence and mature language.

viz.com

shonenjump.com

HUNTER × HUNTER

ハンター ハンター

Story & Art by
Yoshihiro Togashi

Volume 1

Volume 1

CONTENTS

Chapter 1
The Day of Departure   5

Chapter 2
An Encounter in the Storm   39

Chapter 3
The Ultimate Choice   63

Chapter 4
Kiriko: Wicked Magical Vulpes   83

Chapter 5
The First Phase Begins, part 1   105

Chapter 6
The First Phase Begins, part 2   125

Chapter 7
Respective Reasons   145

Chapter 8
The Other Enemy   165

Hunter x Hunter

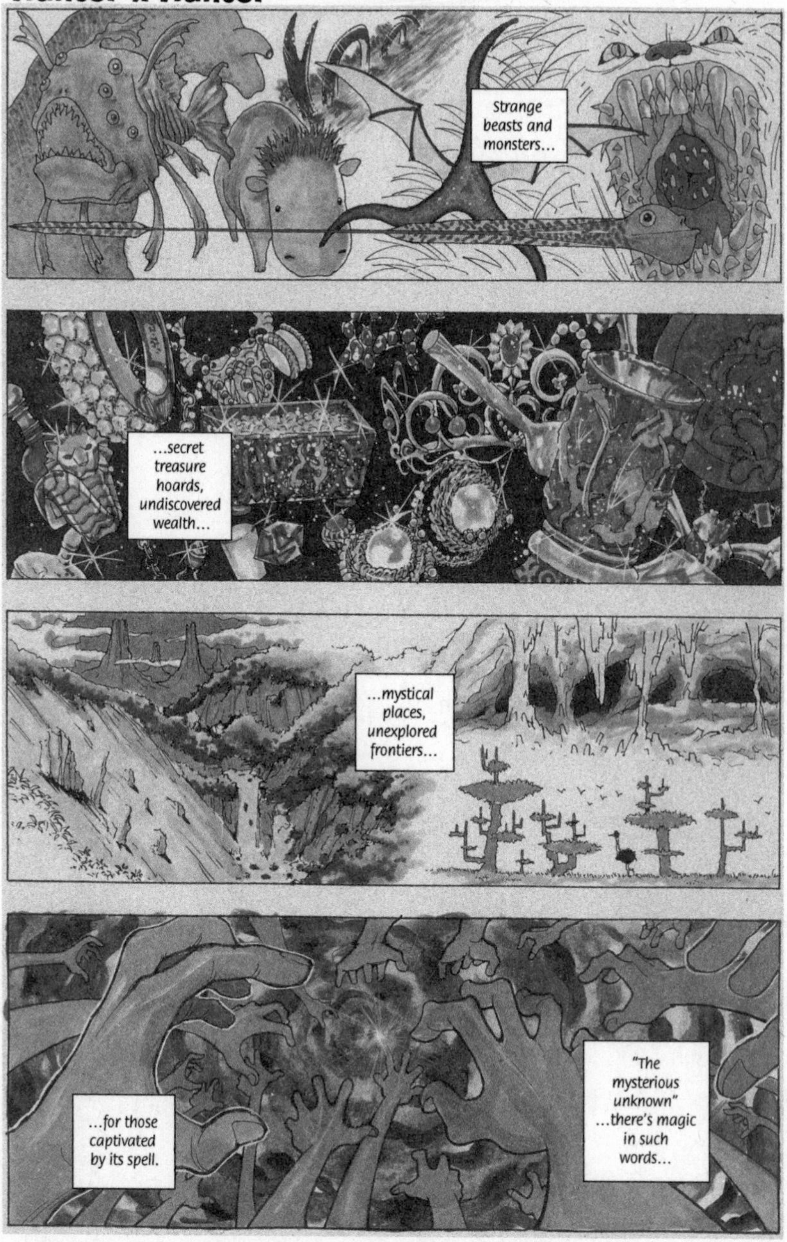
Strange beasts and monsters...
...secret treasure hoards, undiscovered wealth...
...mystical places, unexplored frontiers...
"The mysterious unknown" ...there's magic in such words...
...for those captivated by its spell.

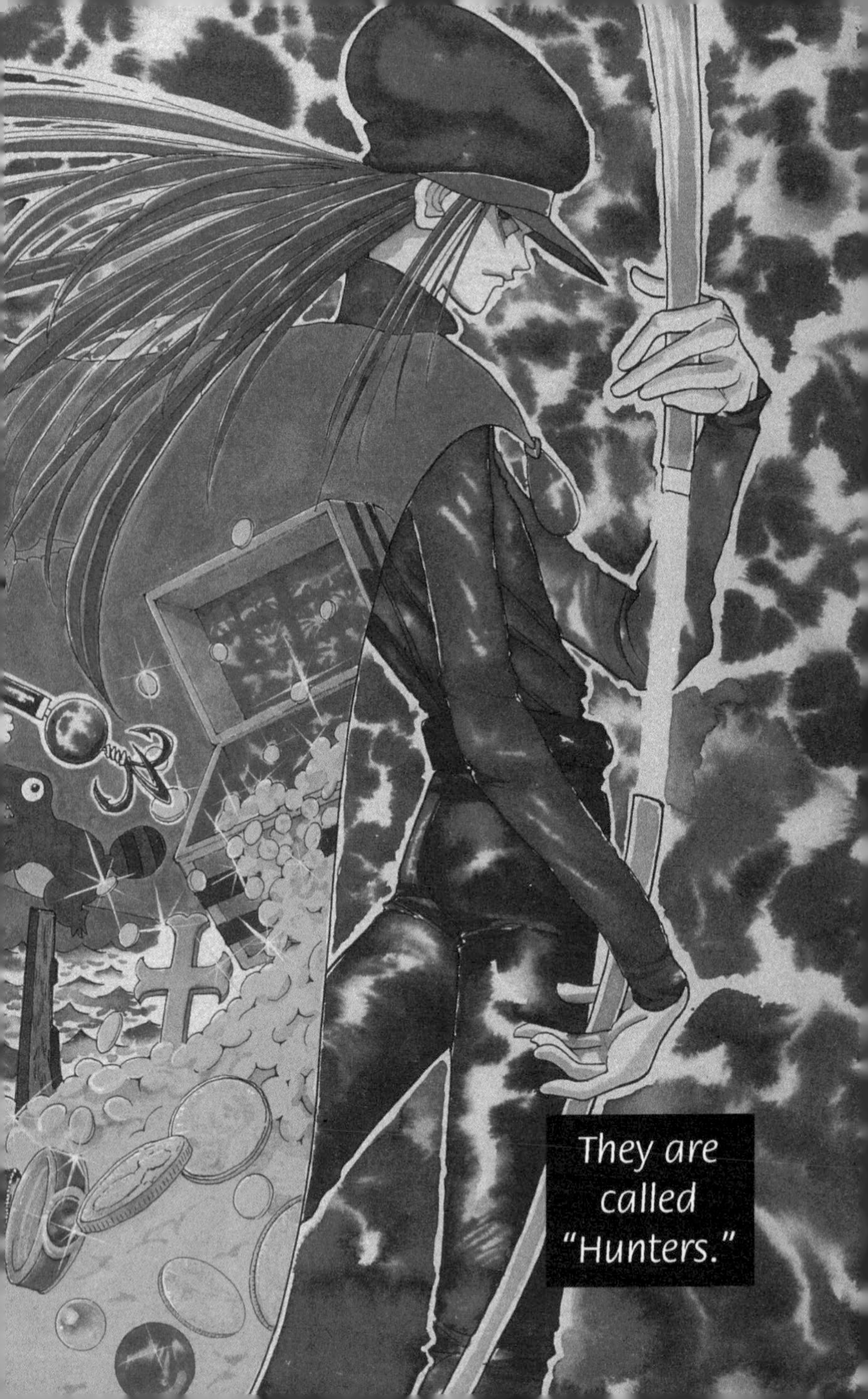
They are called "Hunters."

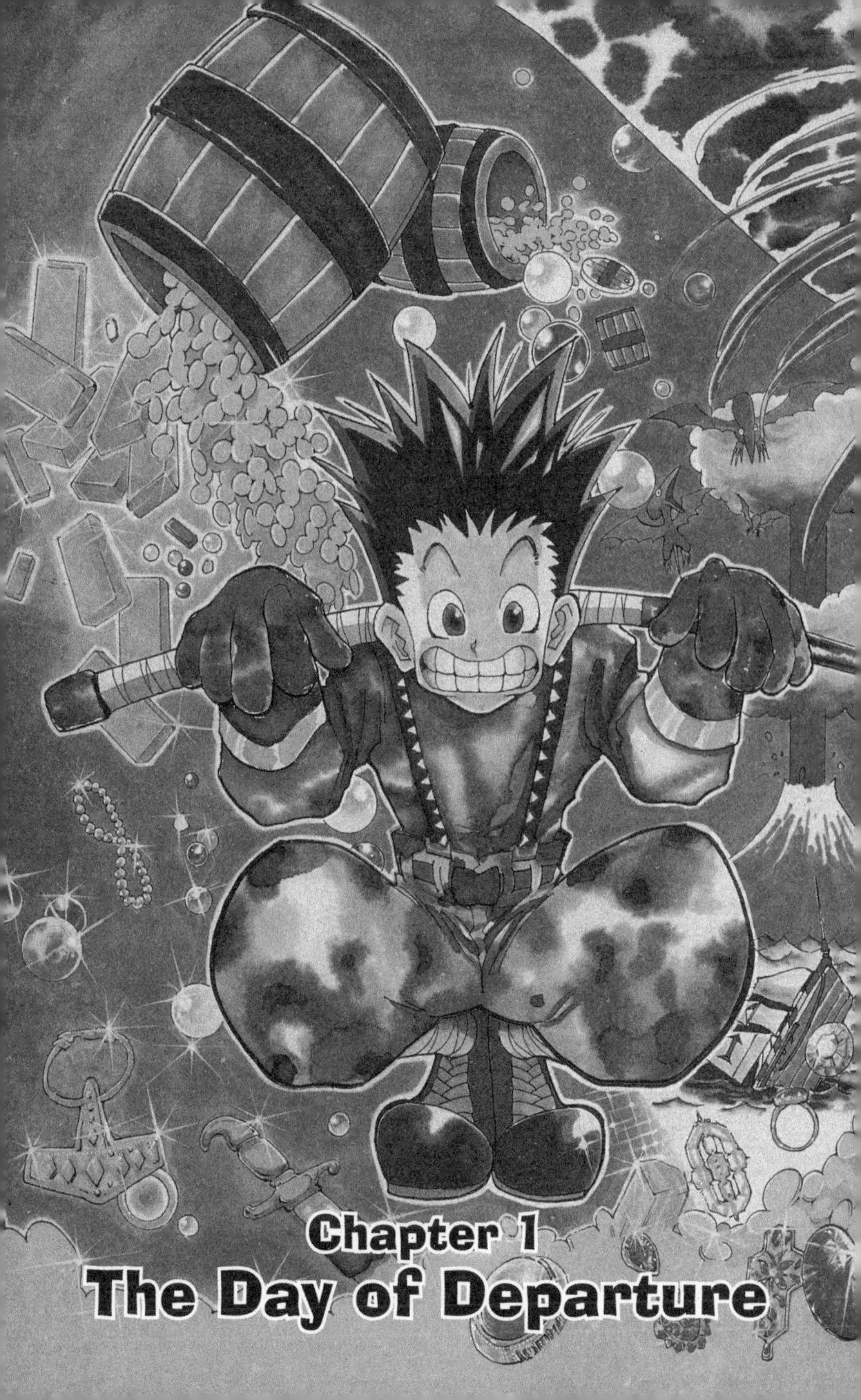
Chapter 1
The Day of Departure

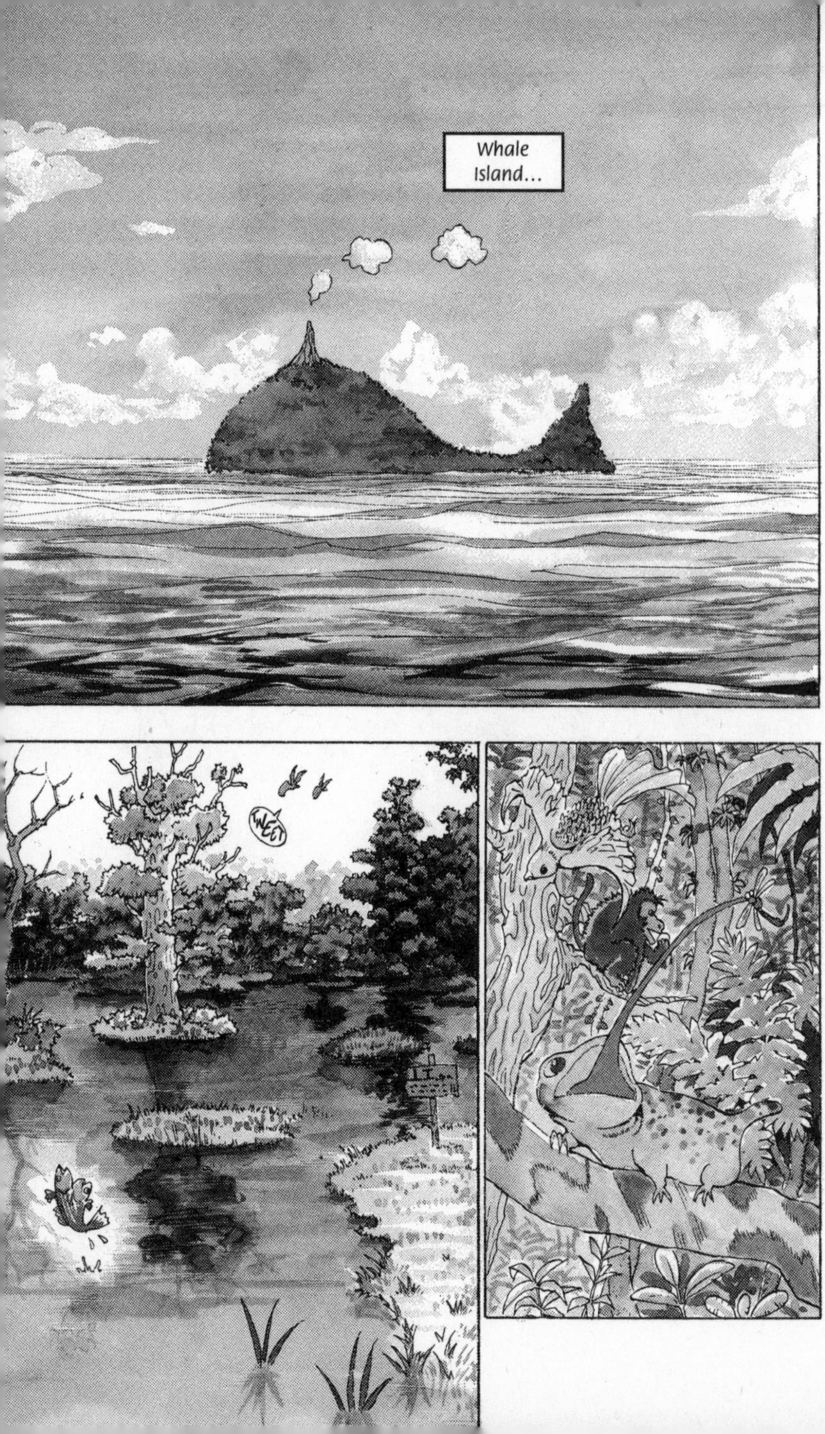
Whale Island...
TWEET

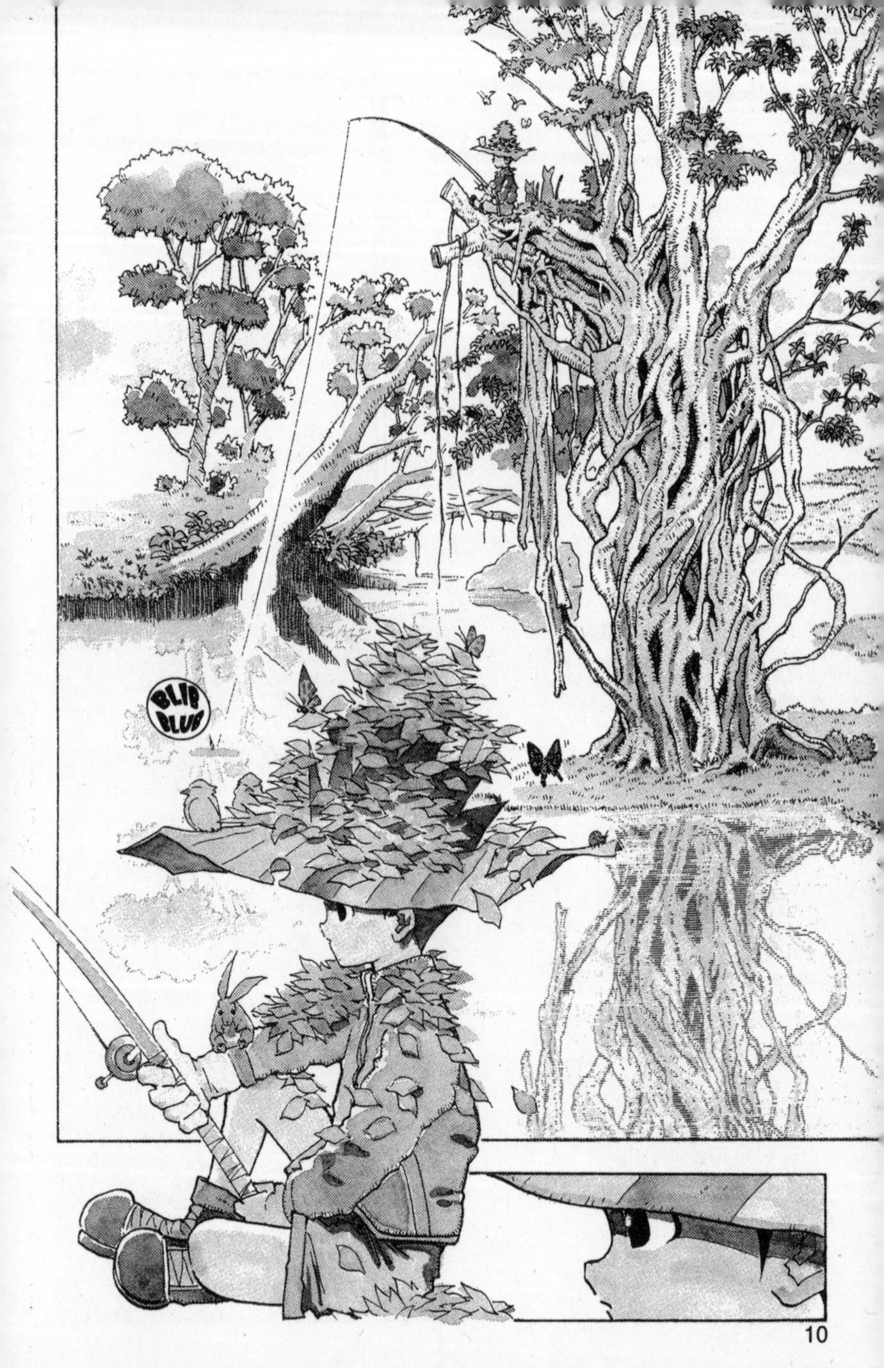
BLIB BLUB

READ THIS WAY

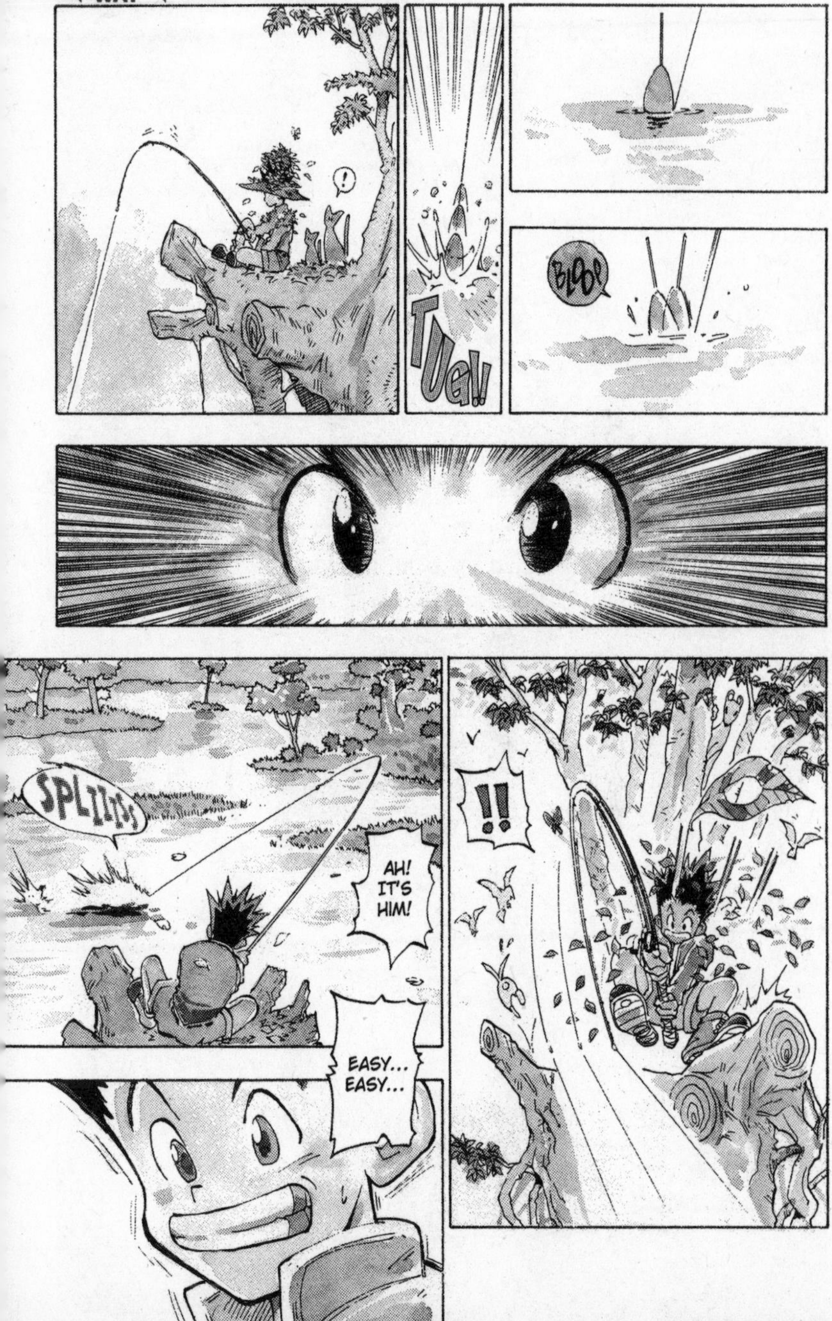
BLOOP
TUG!!
!
!!
SPLIIISH
AH! IT'S HIM!
EASY... EASY...

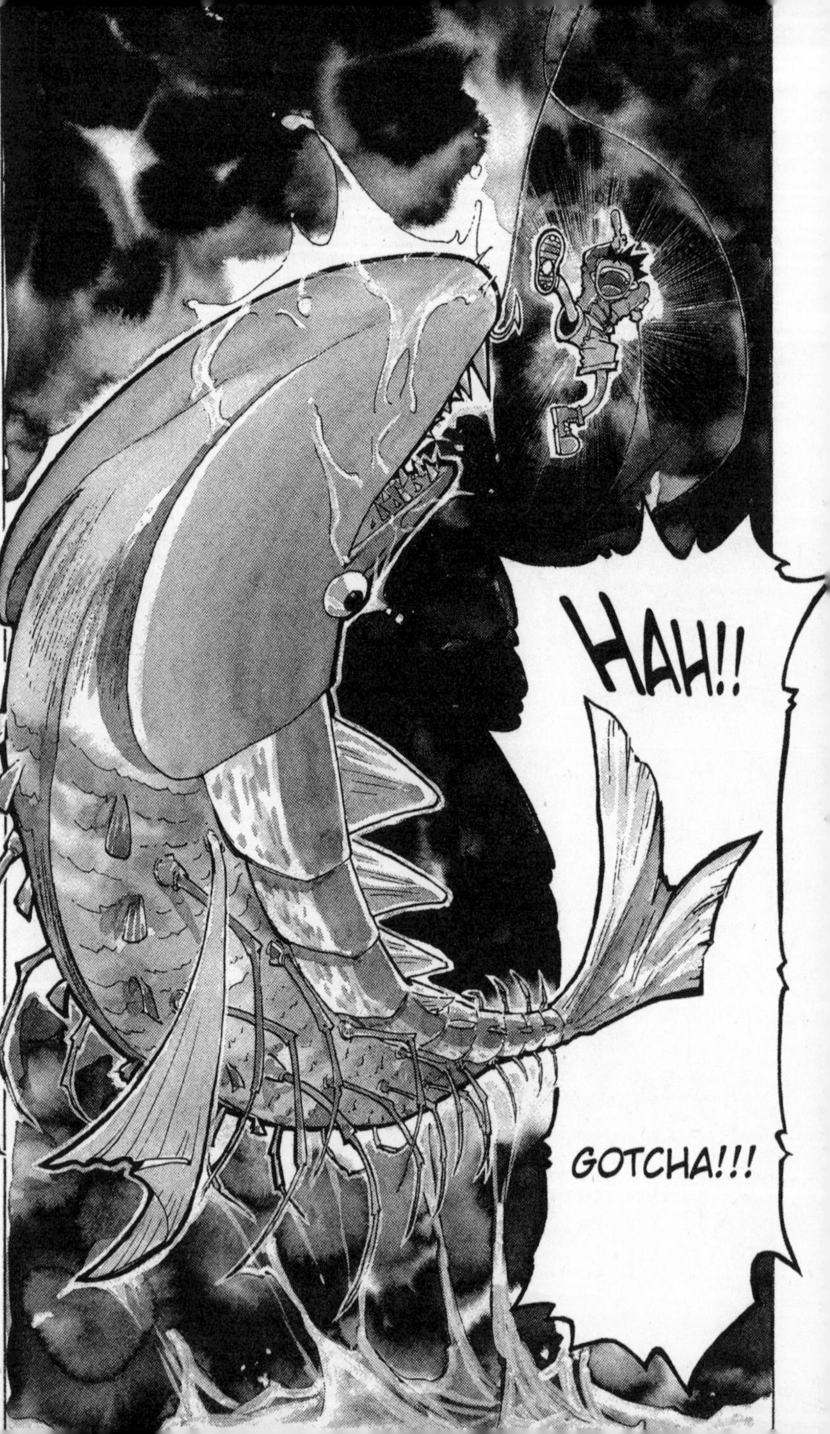
HAH!!
GOTCHA!!!

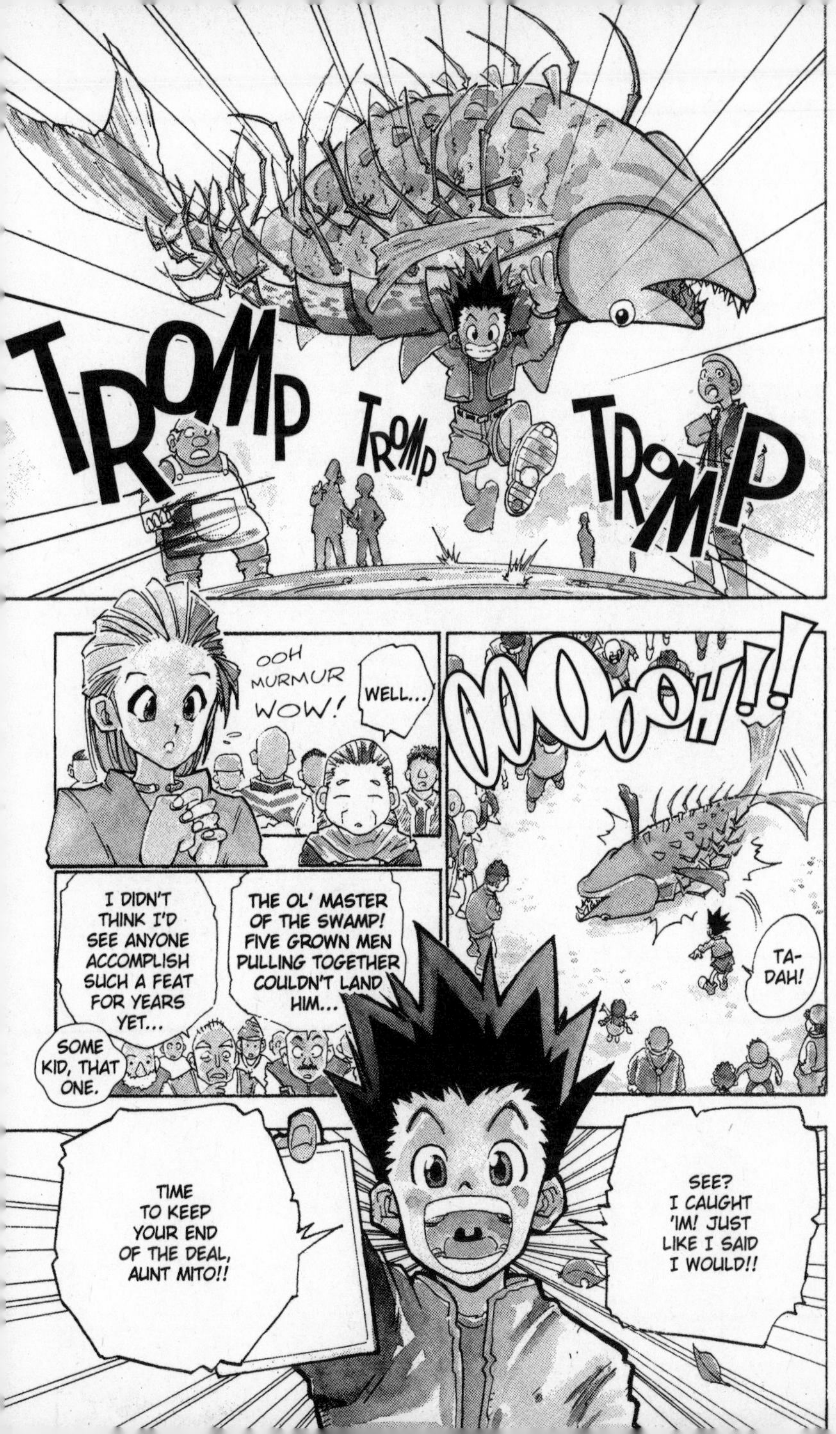
TROMP
TROMP
TROMP
OOOOOH!!
TA-DAH!
WELL...
OOH
MURMUR
WOW!
THE OL' MASTER OF THE SWAMP! FIVE GROWN MEN PULLING TOGETHER COULDN'T LAND HIM...
I DIDN'T THINK I'D SEE ANYONE ACCOMPLISH SUCH A FEAT FOR YEARS YET...
SOME KID, THAT ONE.
SEE? I CAUGHT 'IM! JUST LIKE I SAID I WOULD!!
TIME TO KEEP YOUR END OF THE DEAL, AUNT MITO!!

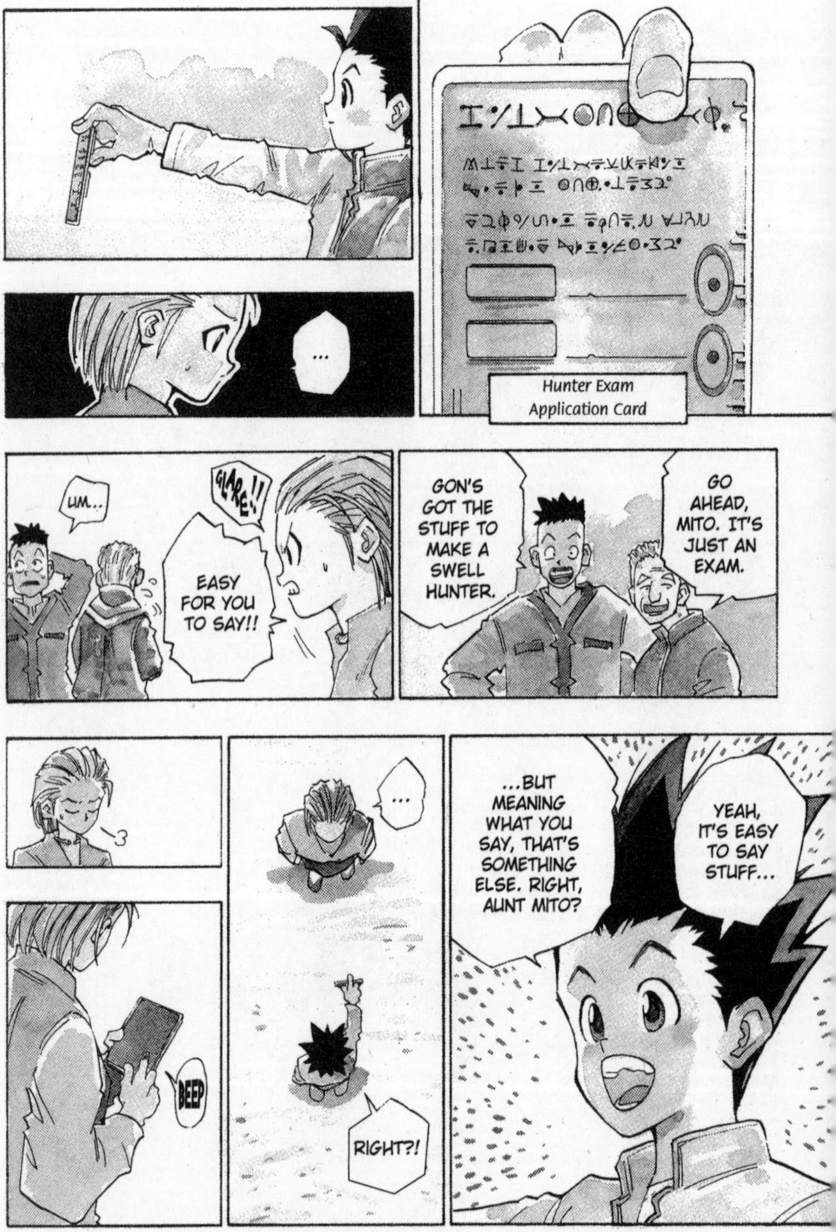
Hunter Exam
Application Card
...
GO AHEAD, MITO. IT'S JUST AN EXAM.
GON'S GOT THE STUFF TO MAKE A SWELL HUNTER.
GLARE!!
EASY FOR YOU TO SAY!!
UM...
YEAH, IT'S EASY TO SAY STUFF...
...BUT MEANING WHAT YOU SAY, THAT'S SOMETHING ELSE. RIGHT, AUNT MITO?
...
RIGHT?!
BEEP

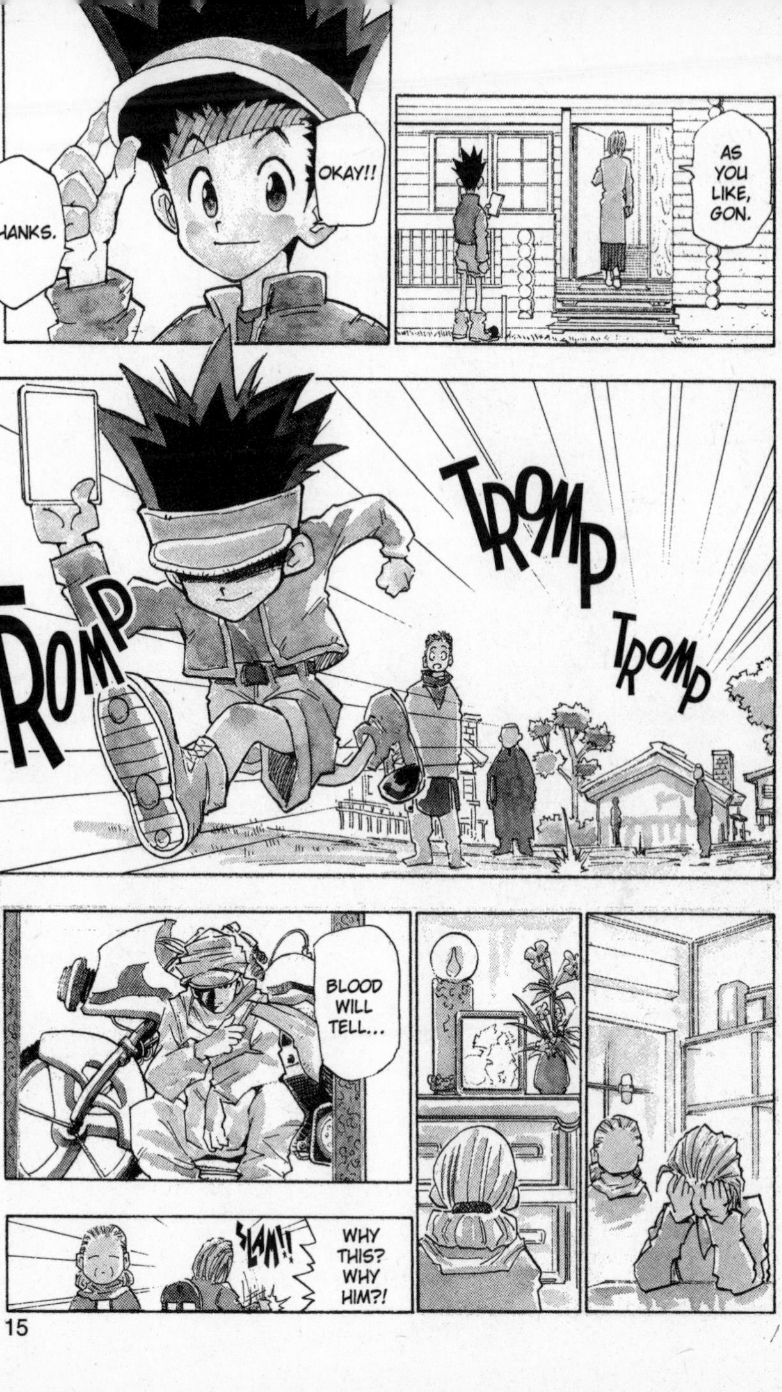
AS YOU LIKE, GON.
OKAY!!
THANKS.
TROMP
TROMP
TROMP
BLOOD WILL TELL...
WHY THIS? WHY HIM?!
SLAM!!

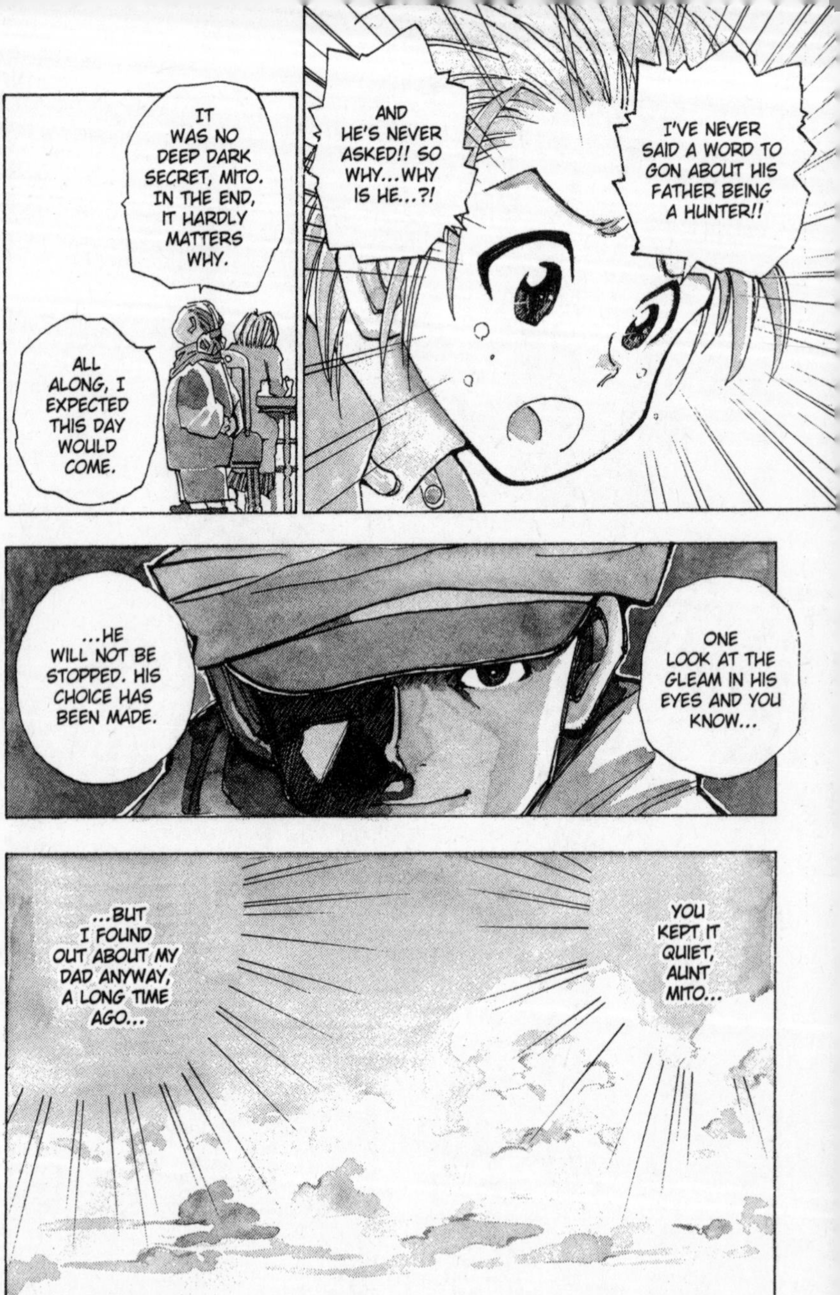
I'VE NEVER SAID A WORD TO GON ABOUT HIS FATHER BEING A HUNTER!!
AND HE'S NEVER ASKED!! SO WHY...WHY IS HE...?!
IT WAS NO DEEP DARK SECRET, MITO. IN THE END, IT HARDLY MATTERS WHY.
ALL ALONG, I EXPECTED THIS DAY WOULD COME.
ONE LOOK AT THE GLEAM IN HIS EYES AND YOU KNOW...
...HE WILL NOT BE STOPPED. HIS CHOICE HAS BEEN MADE.
YOU KEPT IT QUIET, AUNT MITO...
...BUT I FOUND OUT ABOUT MY DAD ANYWAY, A LONG TIME AGO...

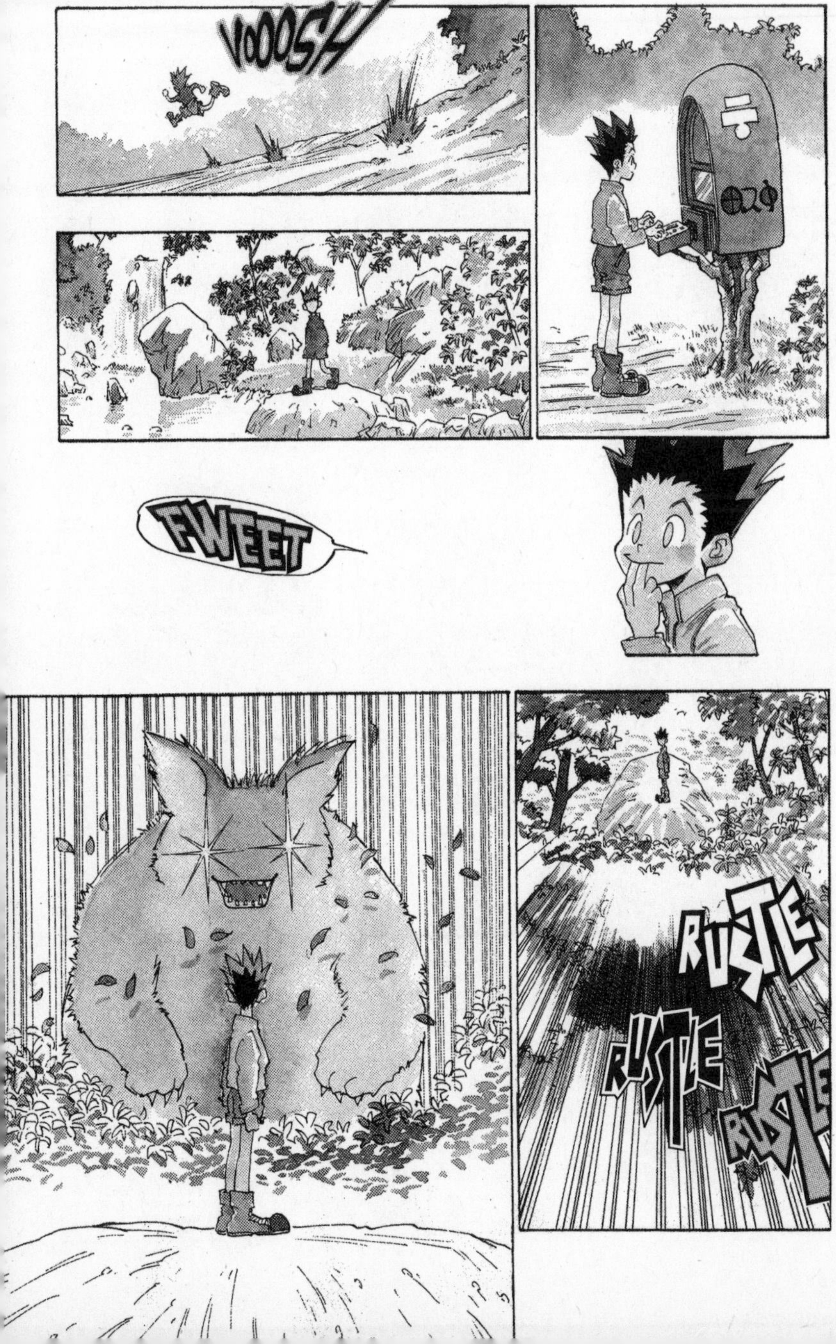
VOOOSH
FWEET
RUSTLE
RUSTLE
RUSTLE

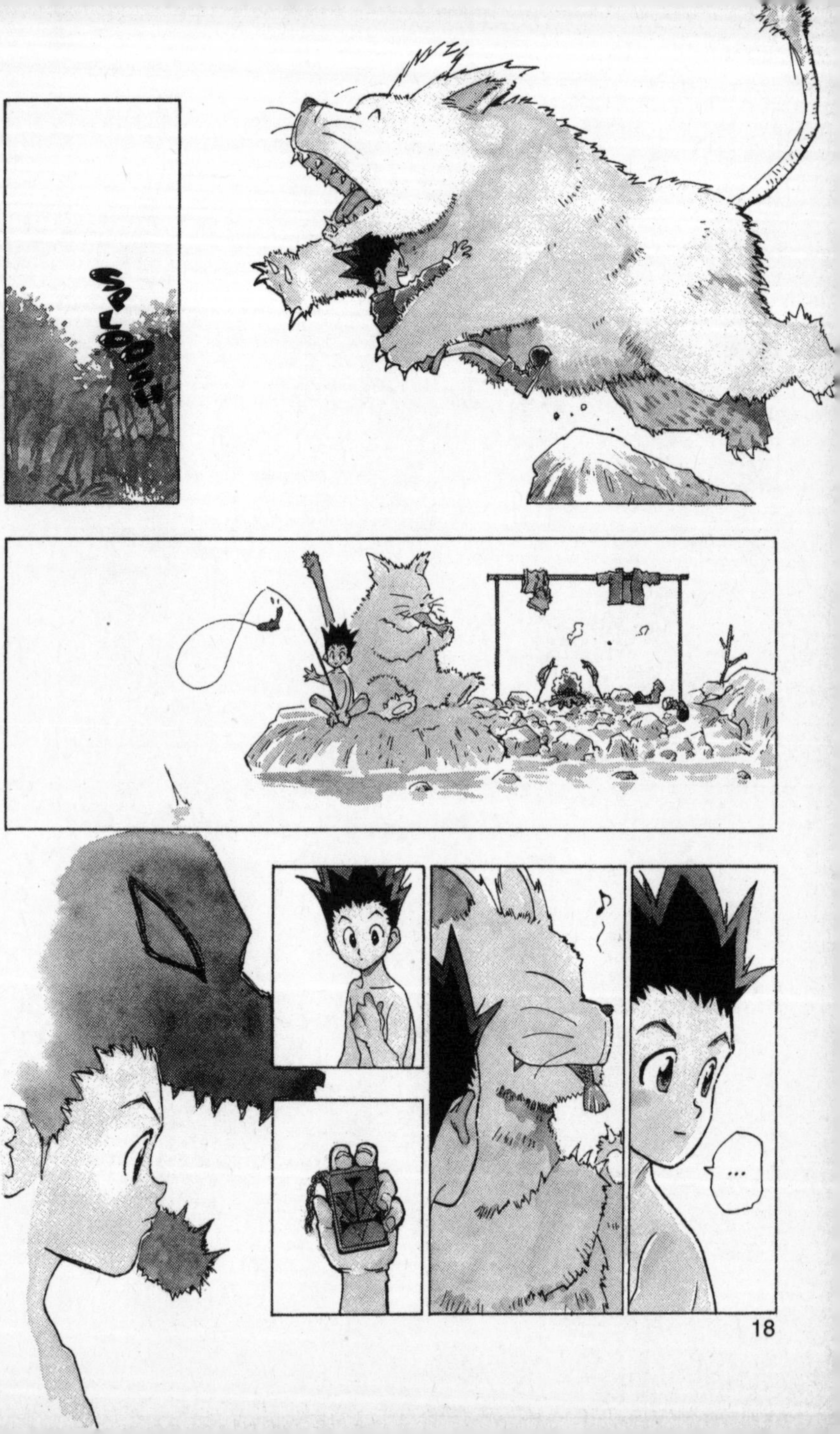
SPLOOSH
♪~
...

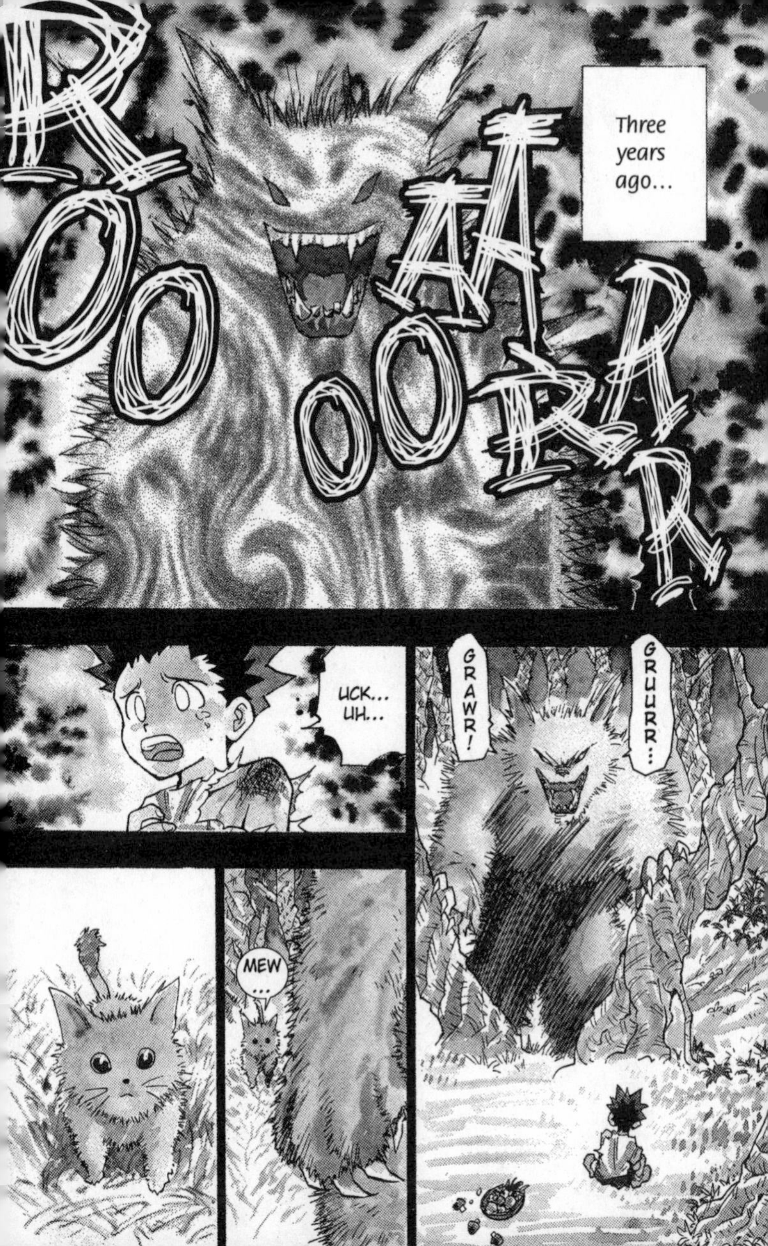
Three years ago…
GRUURR…
GRAWR!
UCK… UH…
MEW…

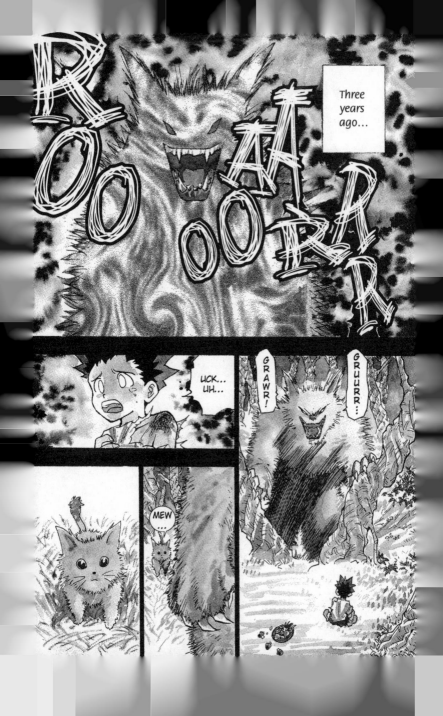

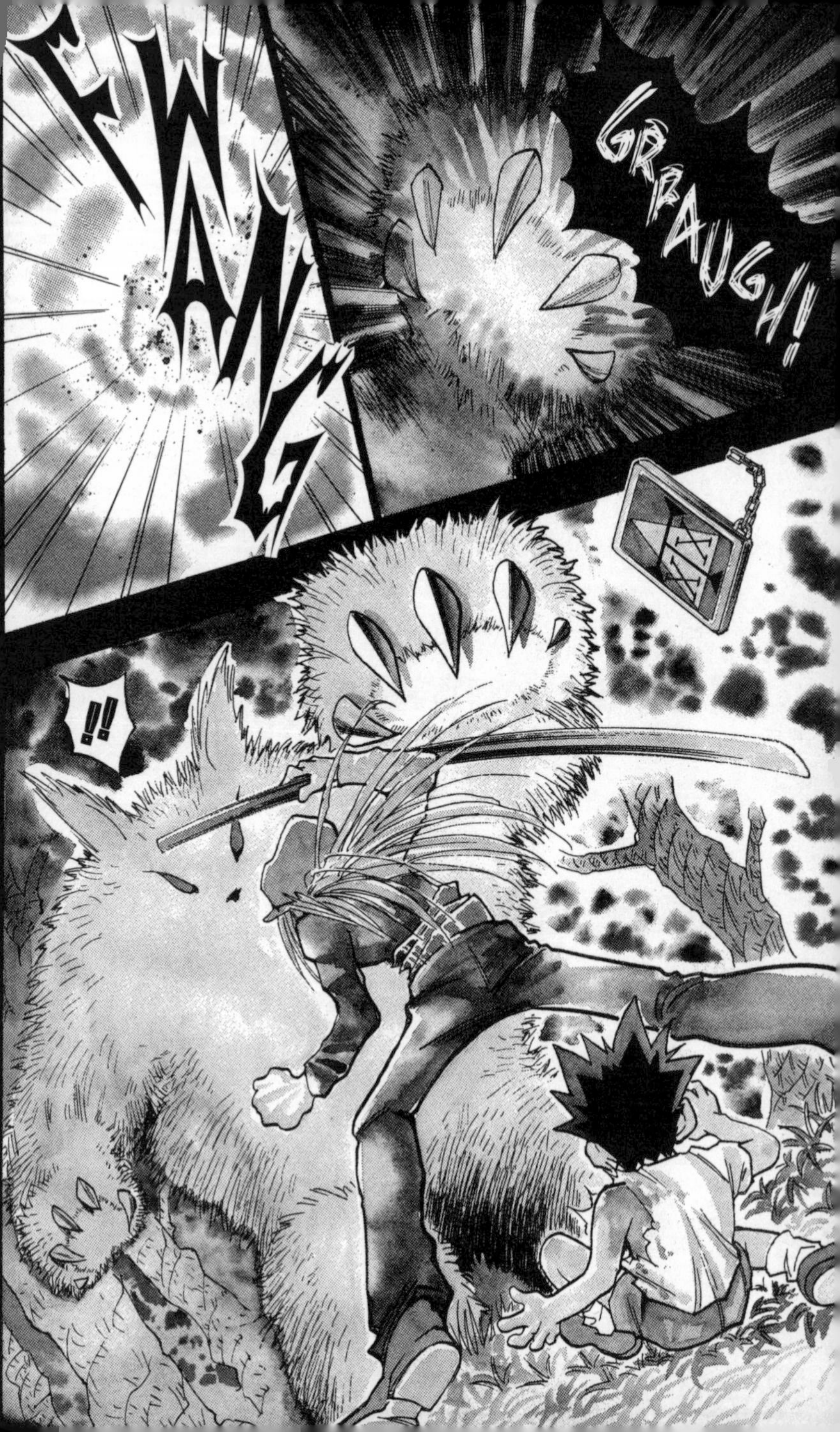
GRRAUGH!
FWANG
!!

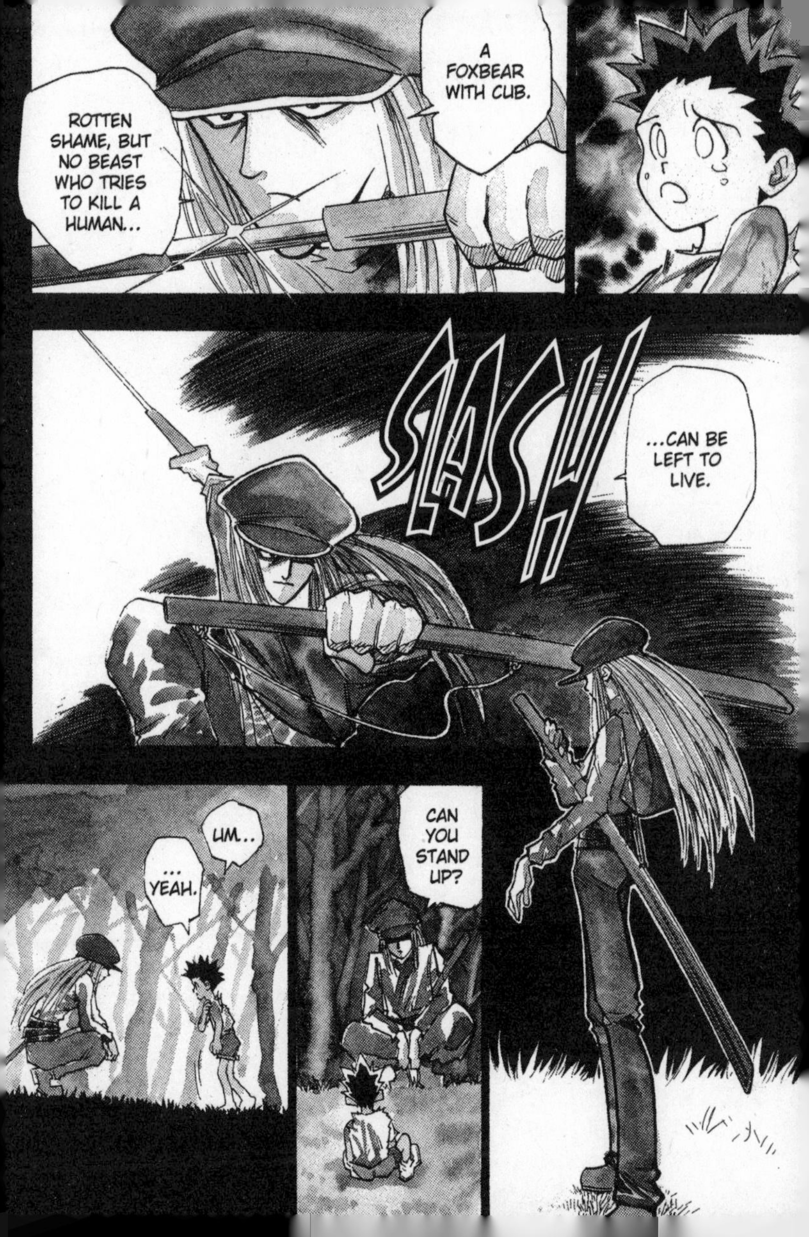
A FOXBEAR WITH CUB.
ROTTEN SHAME, BUT NO BEAST WHO TRIES TO KILL A HUMAN...
...CAN BE LEFT TO LIVE.
SLASH
CAN YOU STAND UP?
UM...
...YEAH.

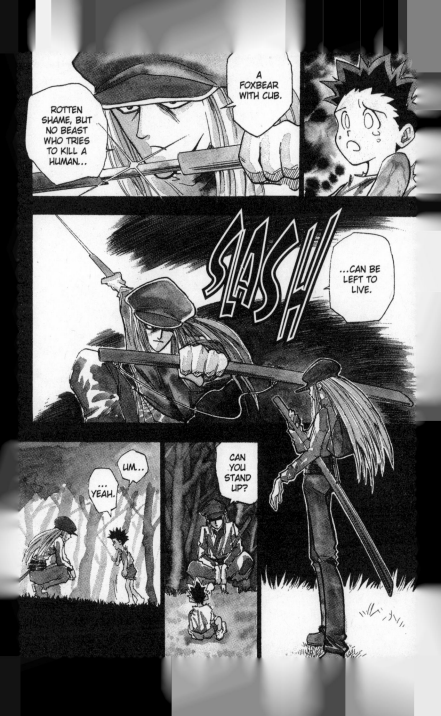

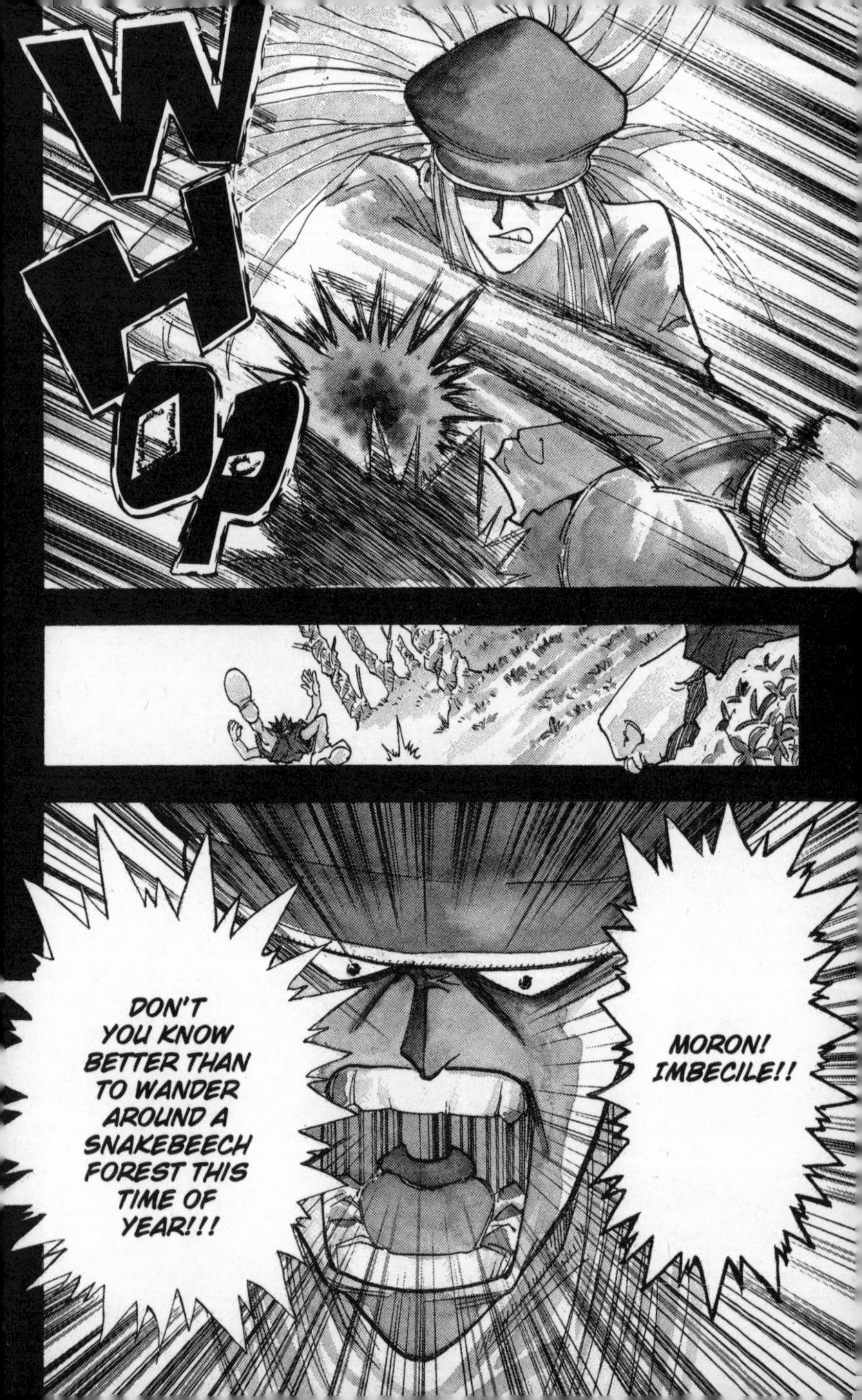
WHOP
MORON! IMBECILE!!
DON'T YOU KNOW BETTER THAN TO WANDER AROUND A SNAKEBEECH FOREST THIS TIME OF YEAR!!!

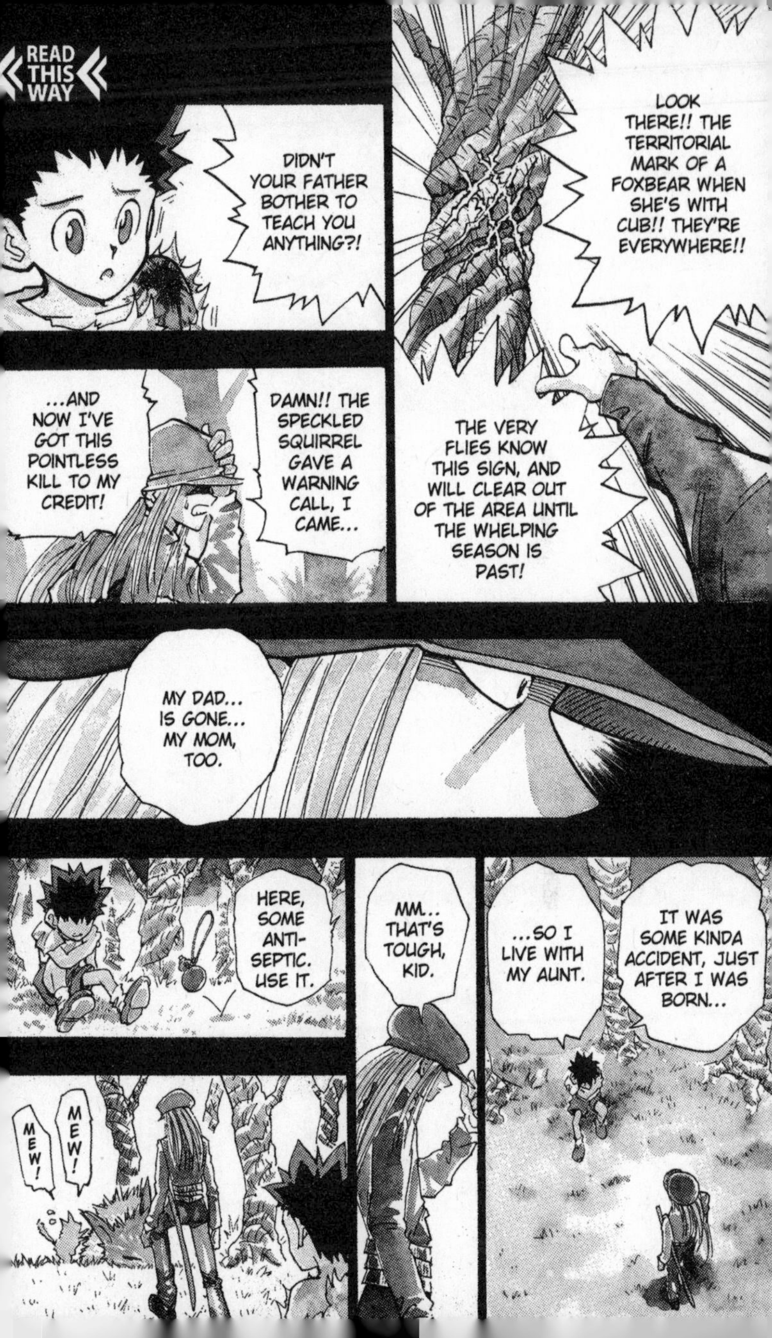
READ THIS WAY
LOOK THERE!! THE TERRITORIAL MARK OF A FOXBEAR WHEN SHE'S WITH CUB!! THEY'RE EVERYWHERE!!
THE VERY FLIES KNOW THIS SIGN, AND WILL CLEAR OUT OF THE AREA UNTIL THE WHELPING SEASON IS PAST!
DIDN'T YOUR FATHER BOTHER TO TEACH YOU ANYTHING?!
DAMN!! THE SPECKLED SQUIRREL GAVE A WARNING CALL, I CAME...
...AND NOW I'VE GOT THIS POINTLESS KILL TO MY CREDIT!
MY DAD... IS GONE... MY MOM, TOO.
IT WAS SOME KINDA ACCIDENT, JUST AFTER I WAS BORN...
...SO I LIVE WITH MY AUNT.
MM... THAT'S TOUGH, KID.
HERE, SOME ANTI-SEPTIC. USE IT.
MEW!
MEW!

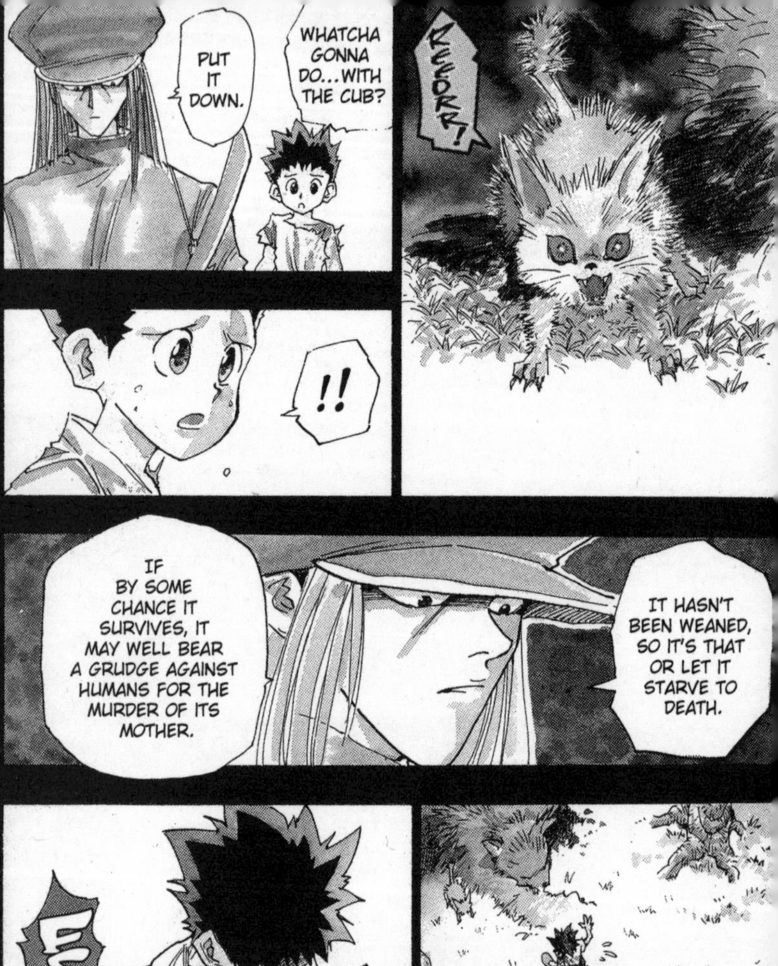
REEORR!
WHATCHA GONNA DO...WITH THE CUB?
PUT IT DOWN.
!!
IT HASN'T BEEN WEANED, SO IT'S THAT OR LET IT STARVE TO DEATH.
IF BY SOME CHANCE IT SURVIVES, IT MAY WELL BEAR A GRUDGE AGAINST HUMANS FOR THE MURDER OF ITS MOTHER.
?
DASH
HUG
FWST!

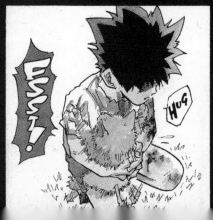

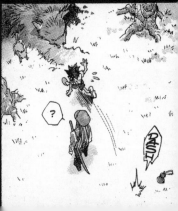

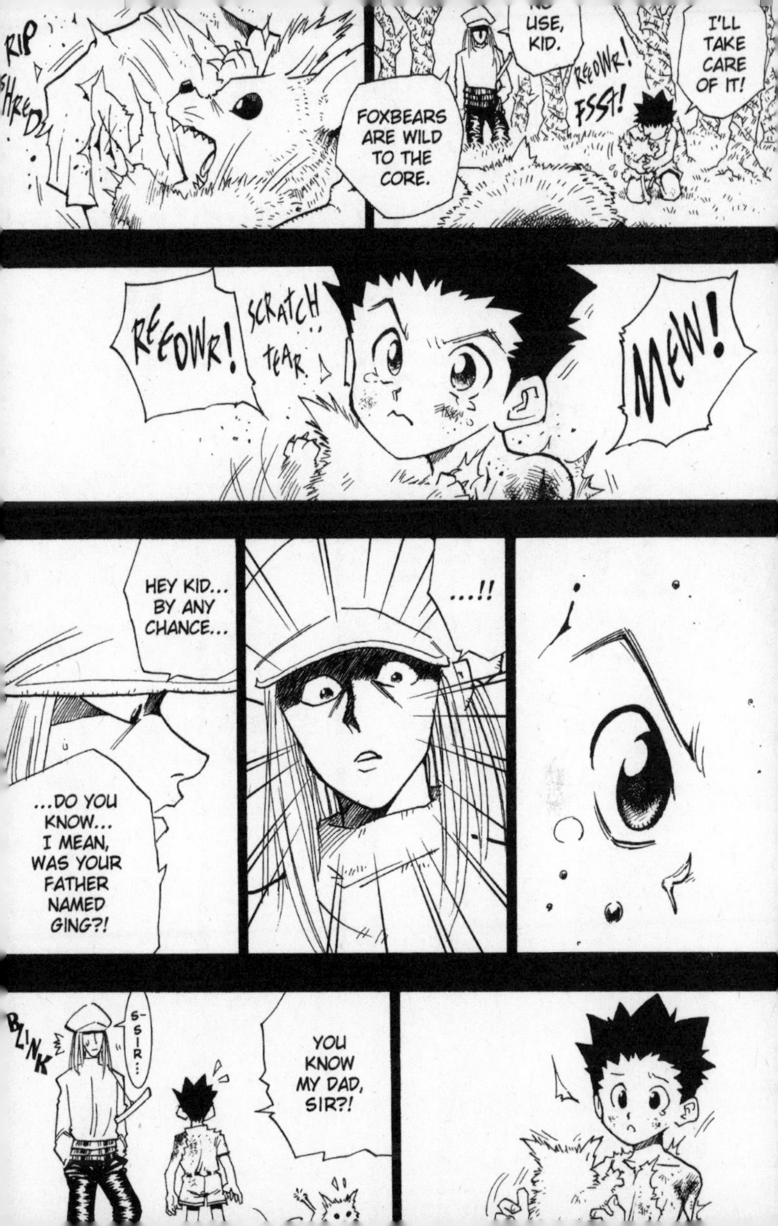
I'LL TAKE CARE OF IT!
USE, KID.
REEOWR!
FSST!
FOXBEARS ARE WILD TO THE CORE.
RIP
SHRED
MEW!
SCRATCH
TEAR
REEOWR!
...!!
HEY KID... BY ANY CHANCE...
...DO YOU KNOW... I MEAN, WAS YOUR FATHER NAMED GING?!
YOU KNOW MY DAD, SIR?!
S-SIR...
BLINK

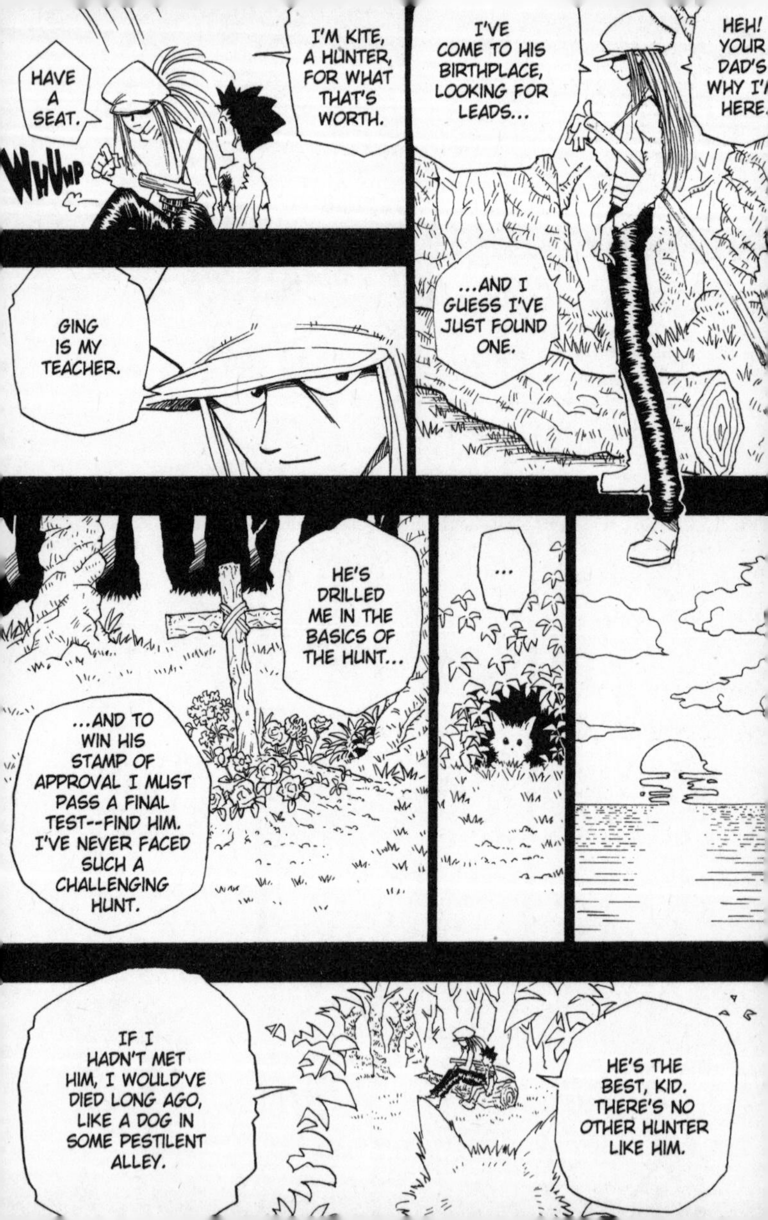
HEH! YOUR DAD'S WHY I' HERE.
I'VE COME TO HIS BIRTHPLACE, LOOKING FOR LEADS...
...AND I GUESS I'VE JUST FOUND ONE.
I'M KITE, A HUNTER, FOR WHAT THAT'S WORTH.
HAVE A SEAT.
WHUMP
GING IS MY TEACHER.
...
HE'S DRILLED ME IN THE BASICS OF THE HUNT...
...AND TO WIN HIS STAMP OF APPROVAL I MUST PASS A FINAL TEST--FIND HIM. I'VE NEVER FACED SUCH A CHALLENGING HUNT.
HE'S THE BEST, KID. THERE'S NO OTHER HUNTER LIKE HIM.
IF I HADN'T MET HIM, I WOULD'VE DIED LONG AGO, LIKE A DOG IN SOME PESTILENT ALLEY.

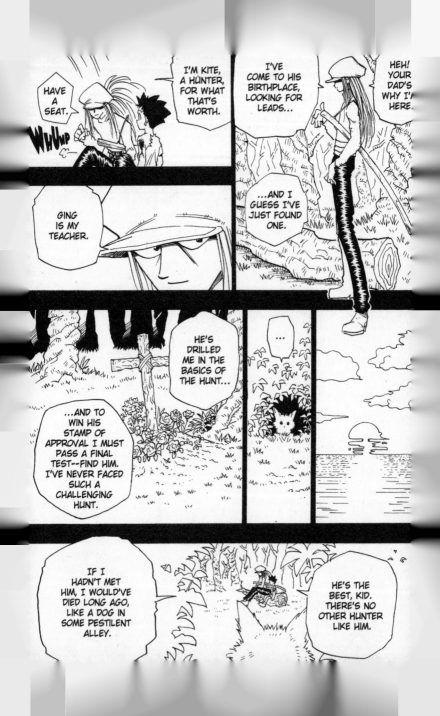

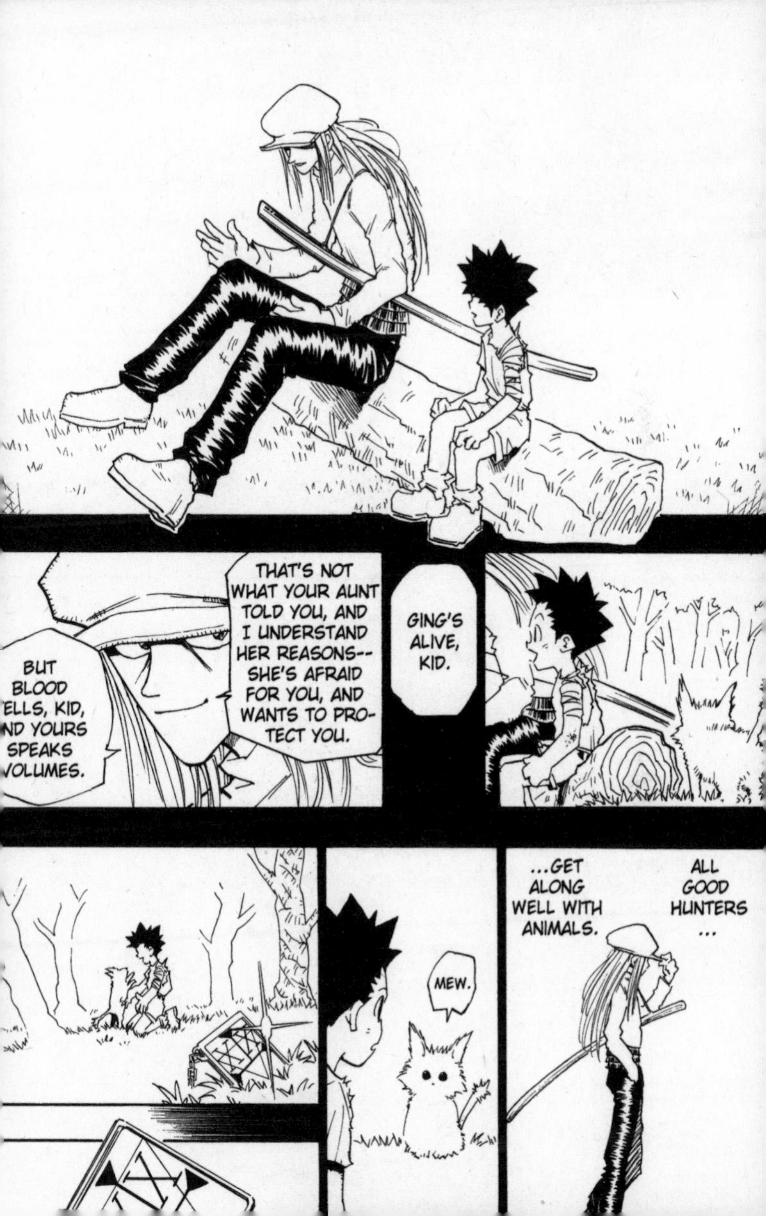
GING'S ALIVE, KID.
THAT'S NOT WHAT YOUR AUNT TOLD YOU, AND I UNDERSTAND HER REASONS-- SHE'S AFRAID FOR YOU, AND WANTS TO PRO-TECT YOU.
BUT BLOOD ELLS, KID, ND YOURS SPEAKS VOLUMES.
ALL GOOD HUNTERS ...
...GET ALONG WELL WITH ANIMALS.
MEW.

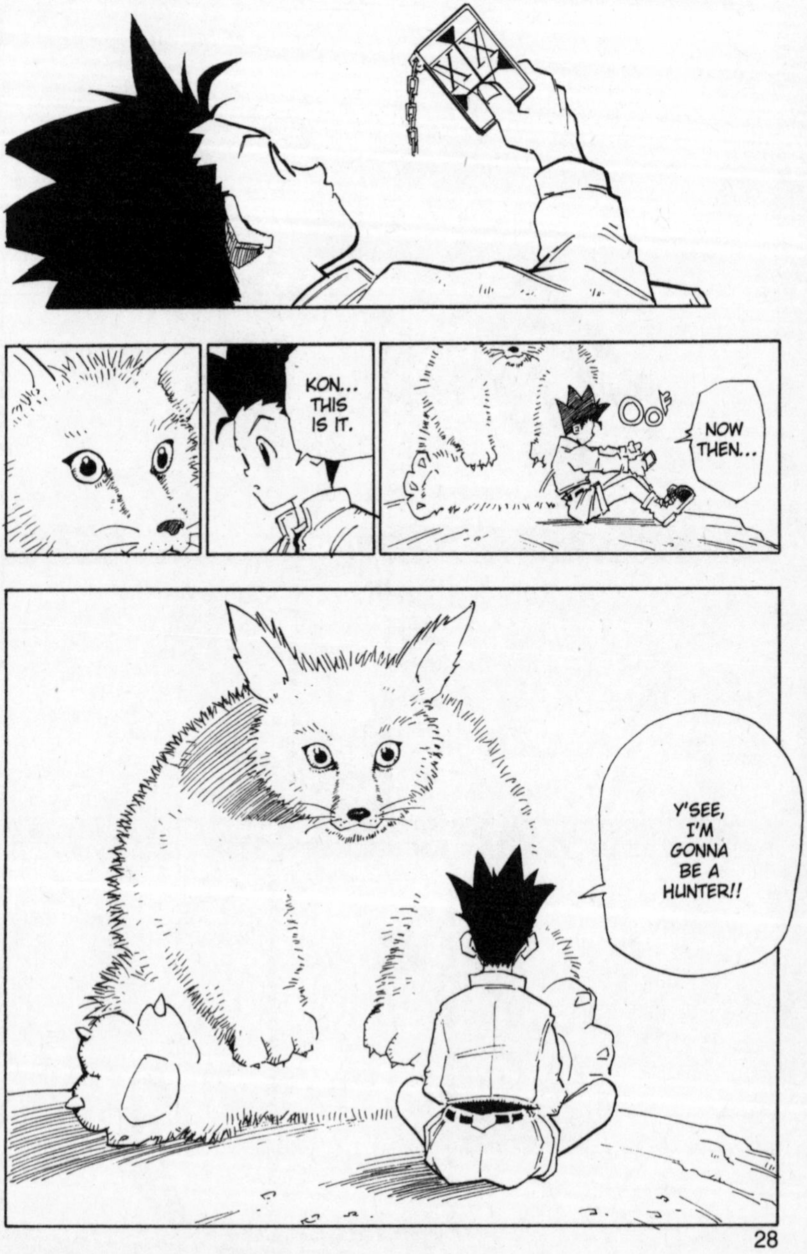
NOW THEN...
Oof
KON... THIS IS IT.
Y'SEE, I'M GONNA BE A HUNTER!!

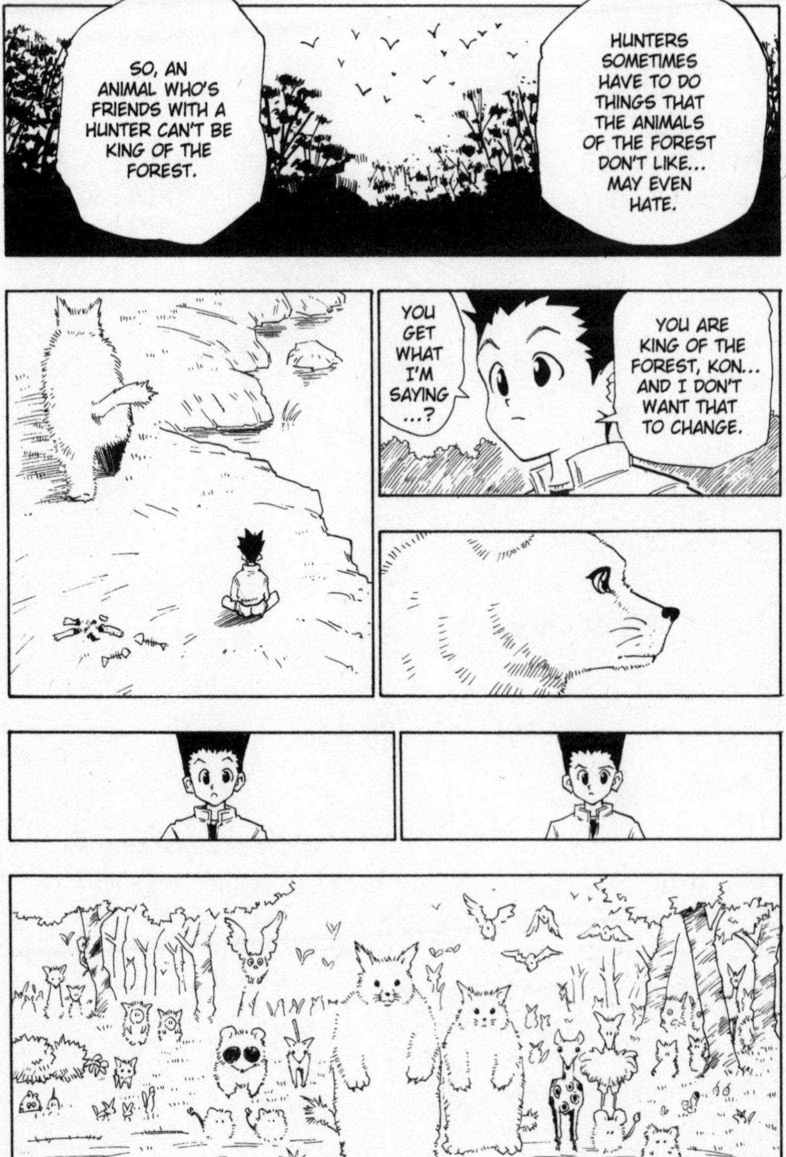
HUNTERS SOMETIMES HAVE TO DO THINGS THAT THE ANIMALS OF THE FOREST DON'T LIKE... MAY EVEN HATE.
SO, AN ANIMAL WHO'S FRIENDS WITH A HUNTER CAN'T BE KING OF THE FOREST.
YOU ARE KING OF THE FOREST, KON... AND I DON'T WANT THAT TO CHANGE.
YOU GET WHAT I'M SAYING ...?

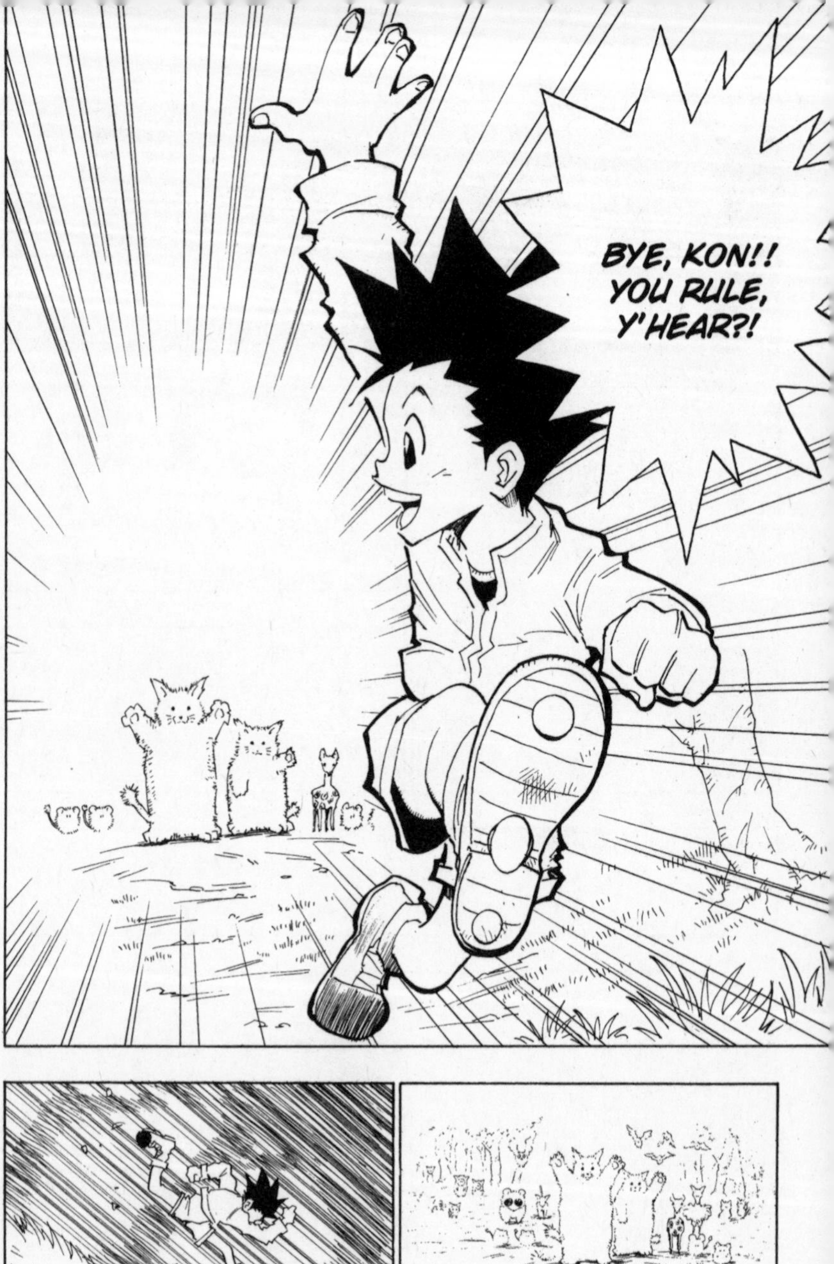
BYE, KON!!
YOU RULE,
Y'HEAR?!

READ THIS WAY

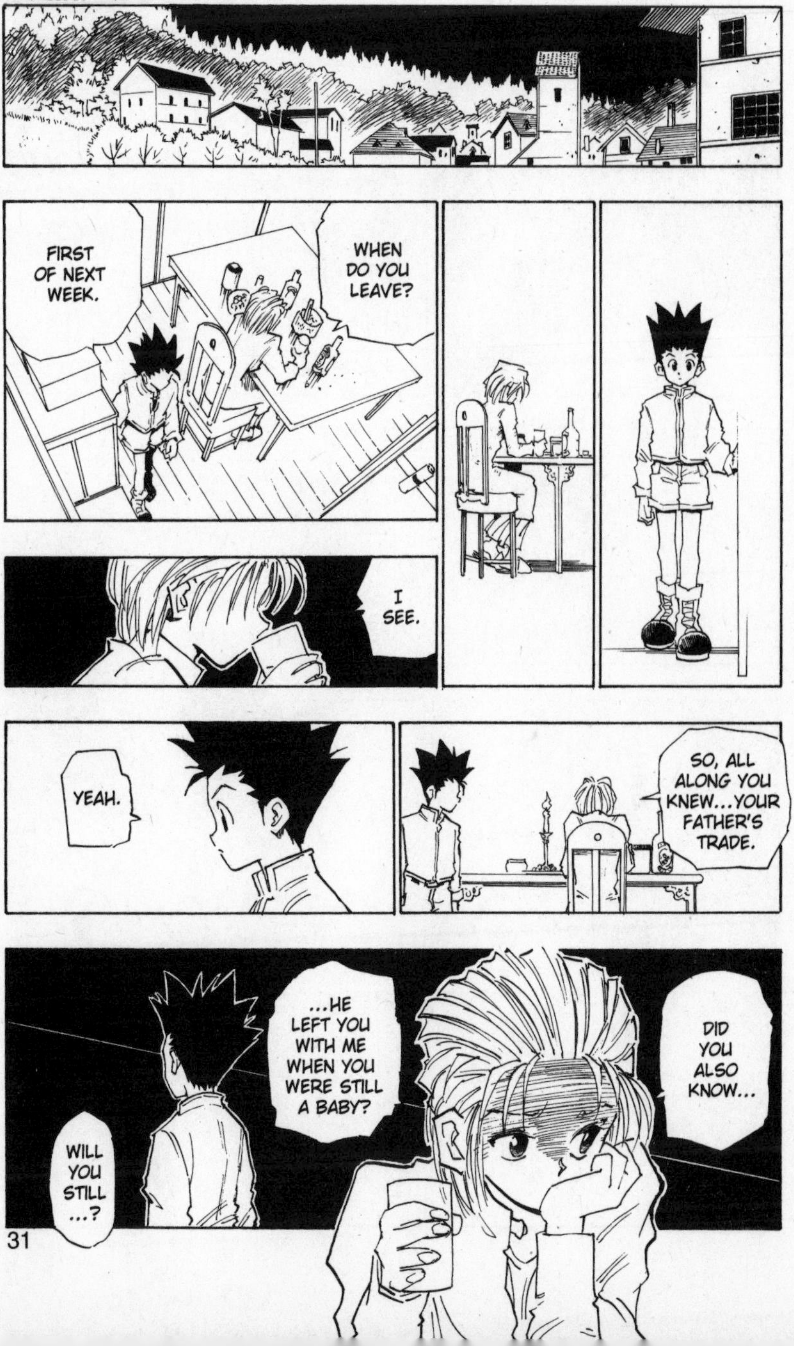

WHEN DO YOU LEAVE?
FIRST OF NEXT WEEK.
I SEE.
SO, ALL ALONG YOU KNEW...YOUR FATHER'S TRADE.
YEAH.
DID YOU ALSO KNOW...
...HE LEFT YOU WITH ME WHEN YOU WERE STILL A BABY?
WILL YOU STILL ...?

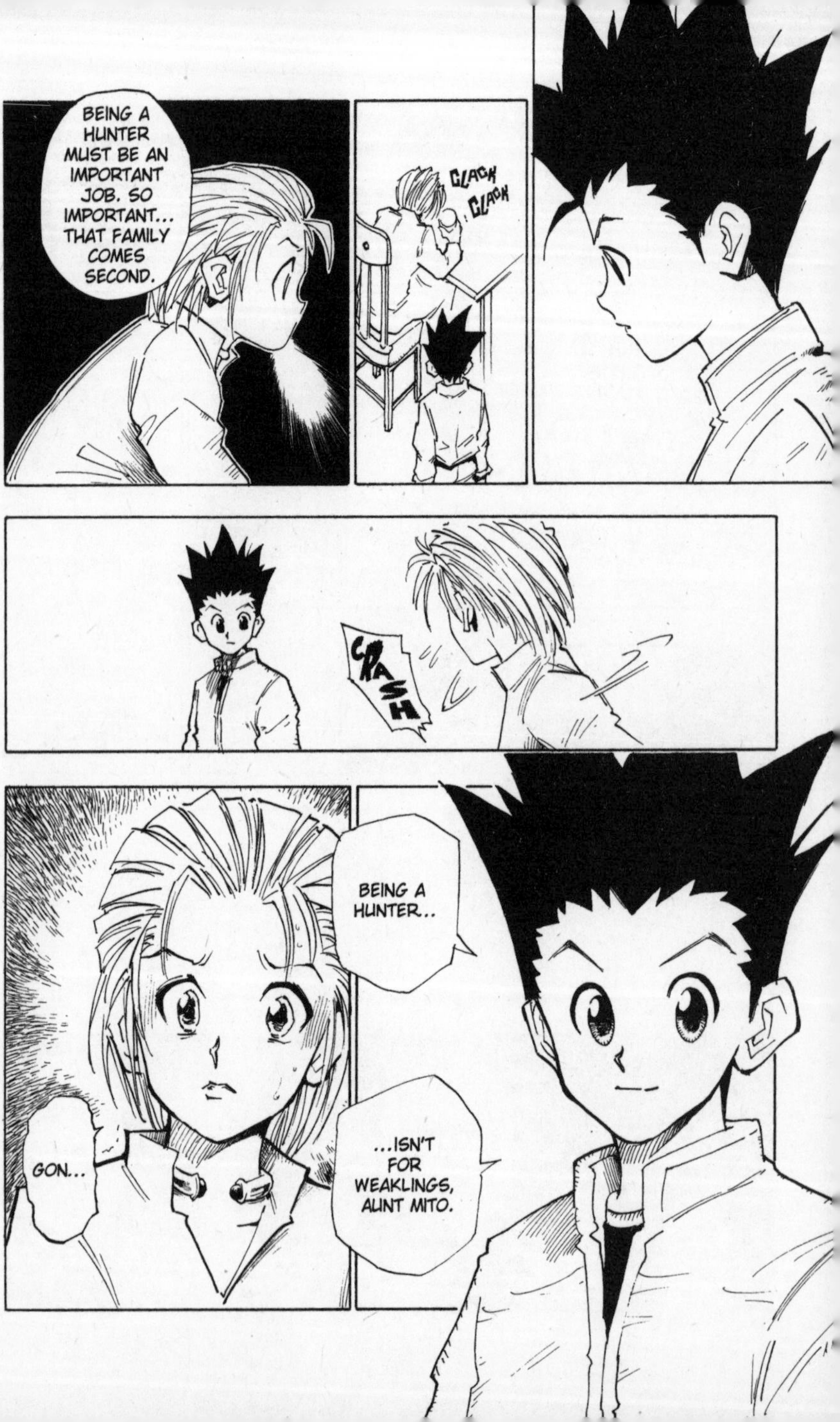
CLACK
CLACK
BEING A HUNTER MUST BE AN IMPORTANT JOB. SO IMPORTANT... THAT FAMILY COMES SECOND.
CRASH
BEING A HUNTER...
...ISN'T FOR WEAKLINGS, AUNT MITO.
GON...

READ THIS WAY

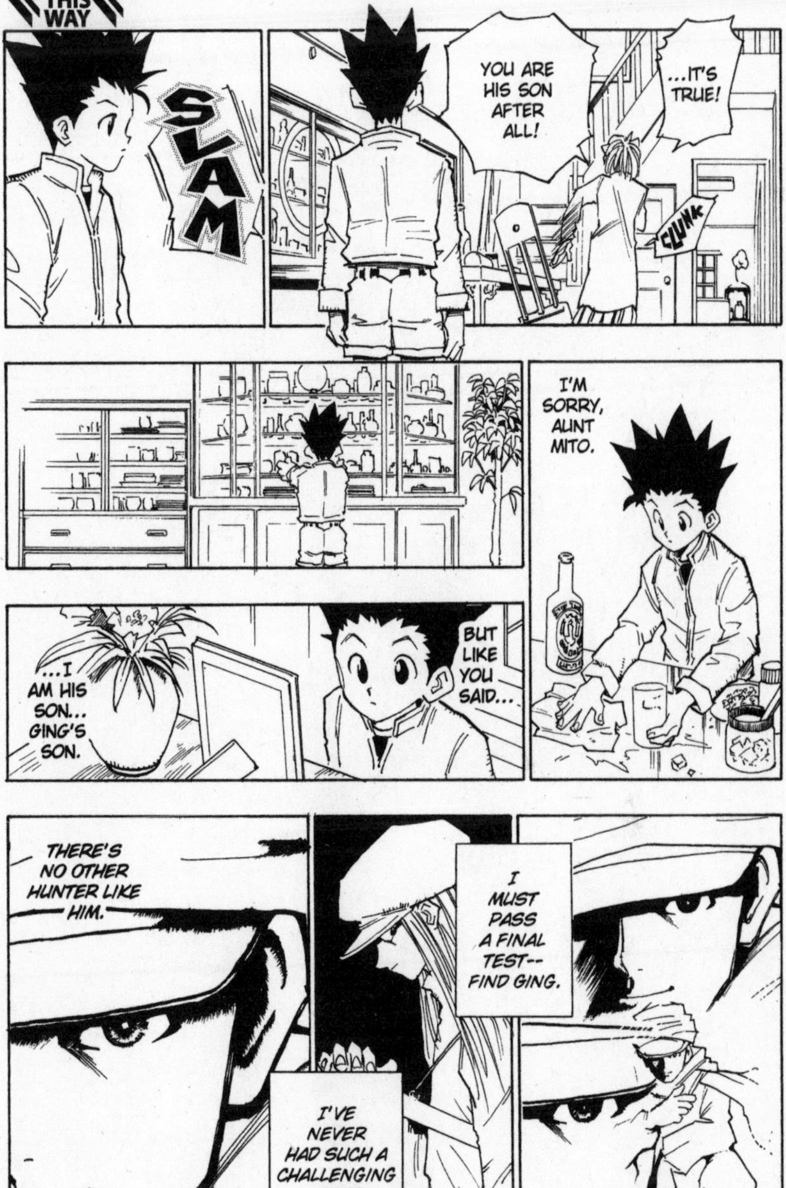
...IT'S TRUE!
YOU ARE HIS SON AFTER ALL!
CLUNK
SLAM
I'M SORRY, AUNT MITO.
BUT LIKE YOU SAID...
...I AM HIS SON... GING'S SON.
I MUST PASS A FINAL TEST-- FIND GING.
I'VE NEVER HAD SUCH A CHALLENGING HUNT.
THERE'S NO OTHER HUNTER LIKE HIM.

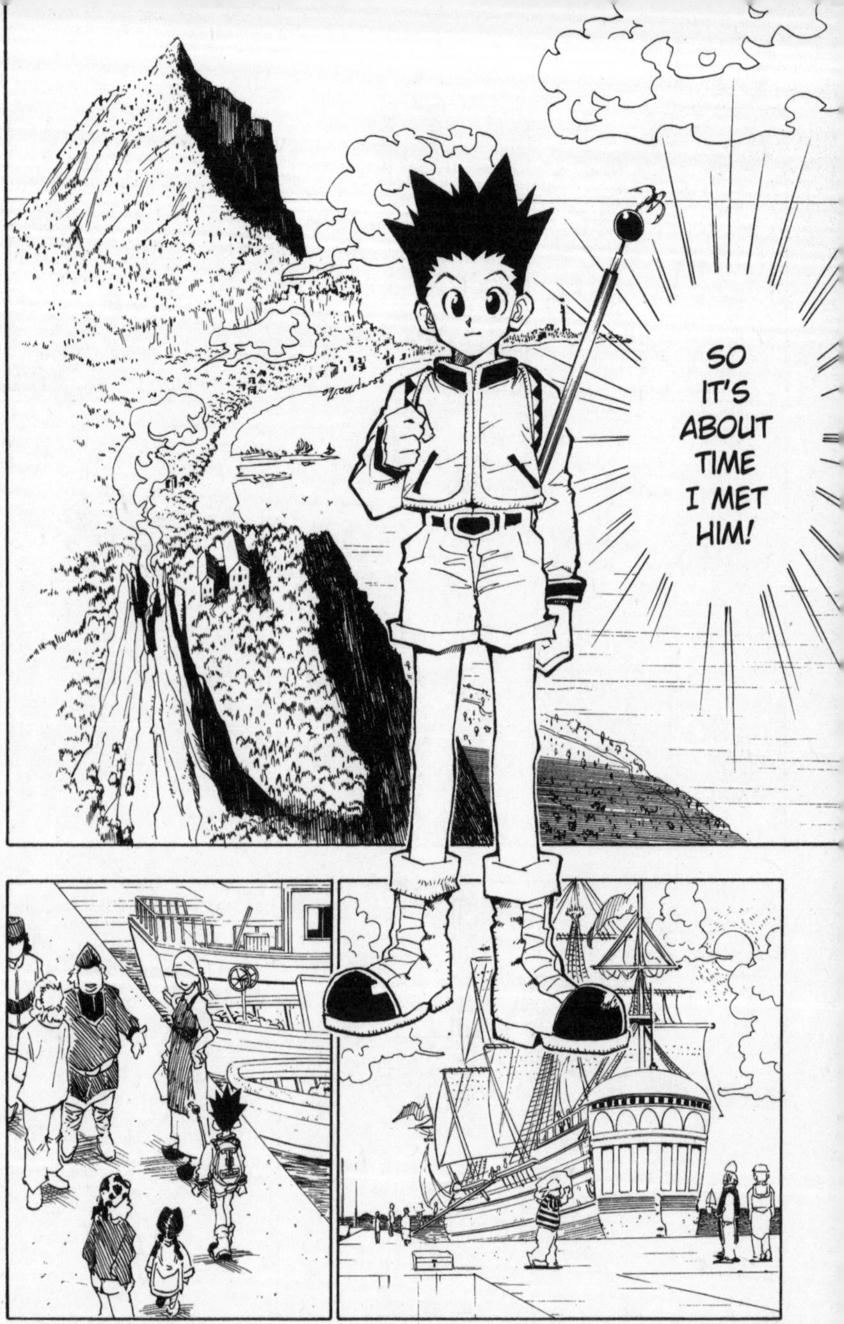
SO IT'S ABOUT TIME I MET HIM!

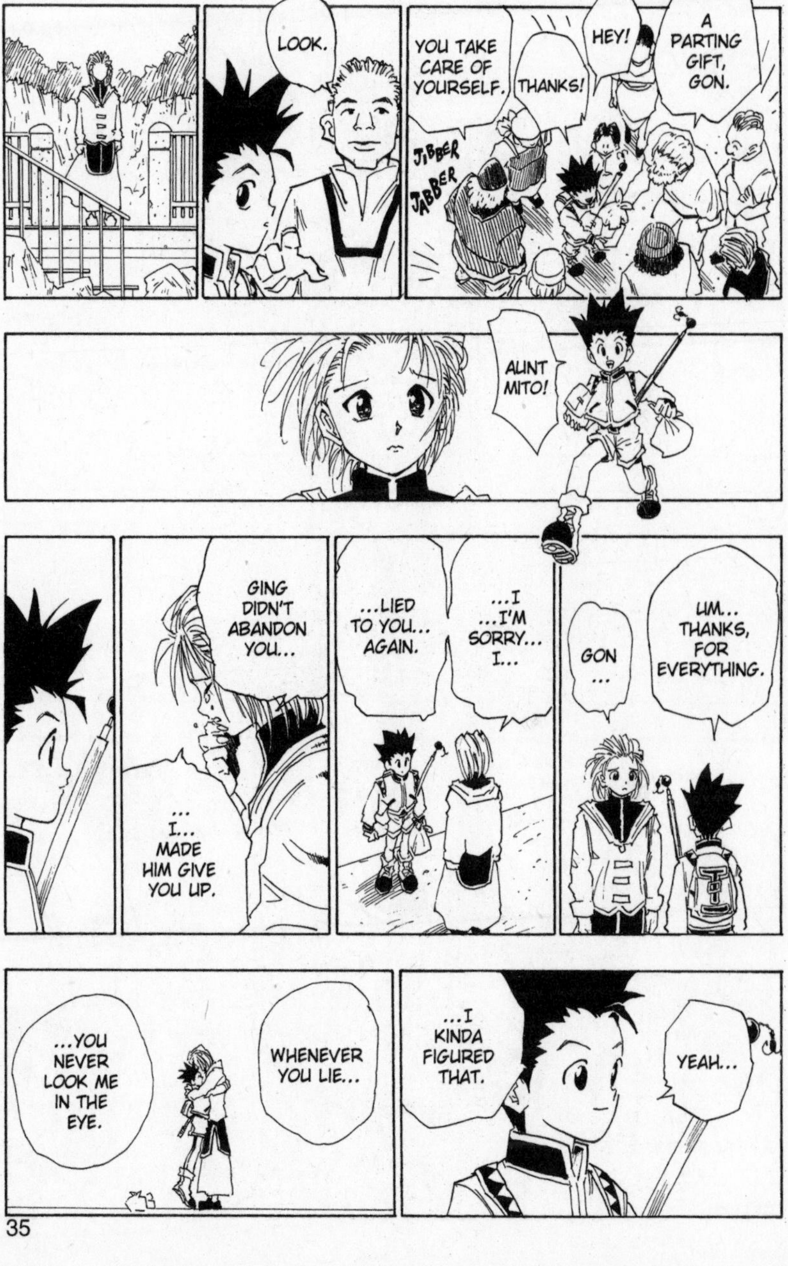
A PARTING GIFT, GON.
HEY!
THANKS!
YOU TAKE CARE OF YOURSELF.
JIBBER JABBER
LOOK.
AUNT MITO!
UM... THANKS, FOR EVERYTHING.
GON ...
...I ...I'M SORRY... I...
...LIED TO YOU... AGAIN.
GING DIDN'T ABANDON YOU...
... I... MADE HIM GIVE YOU UP.
YEAH...
...I KINDA FIGURED THAT.
WHENEVER YOU LIE...
...YOU NEVER LOOK ME IN THE EYE.

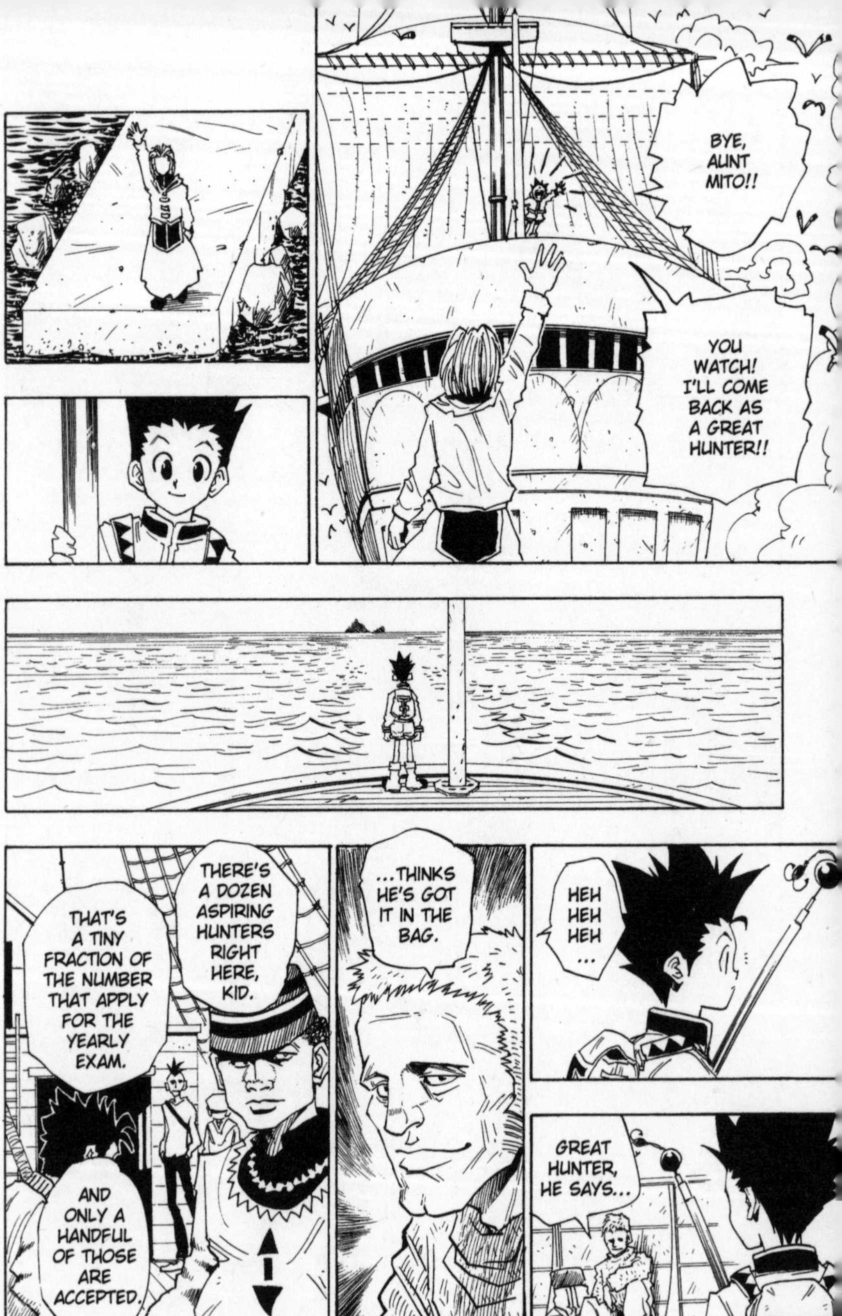
BYE, AUNT MITO!!
YOU WATCH! I'LL COME BACK AS A GREAT HUNTER!!
HEH HEH HEH ...
GREAT HUNTER, HE SAYS...
...THINKS HE'S GOT IT IN THE BAG.
THERE'S A DOZEN ASPIRING HUNTERS RIGHT HERE, KID.
THAT'S A TINY FRACTION OF THE NUMBER THAT APPLY FOR THE YEARLY EXAM.
AND ONLY A HANDFUL OF THOSE ARE ACCEPTED.

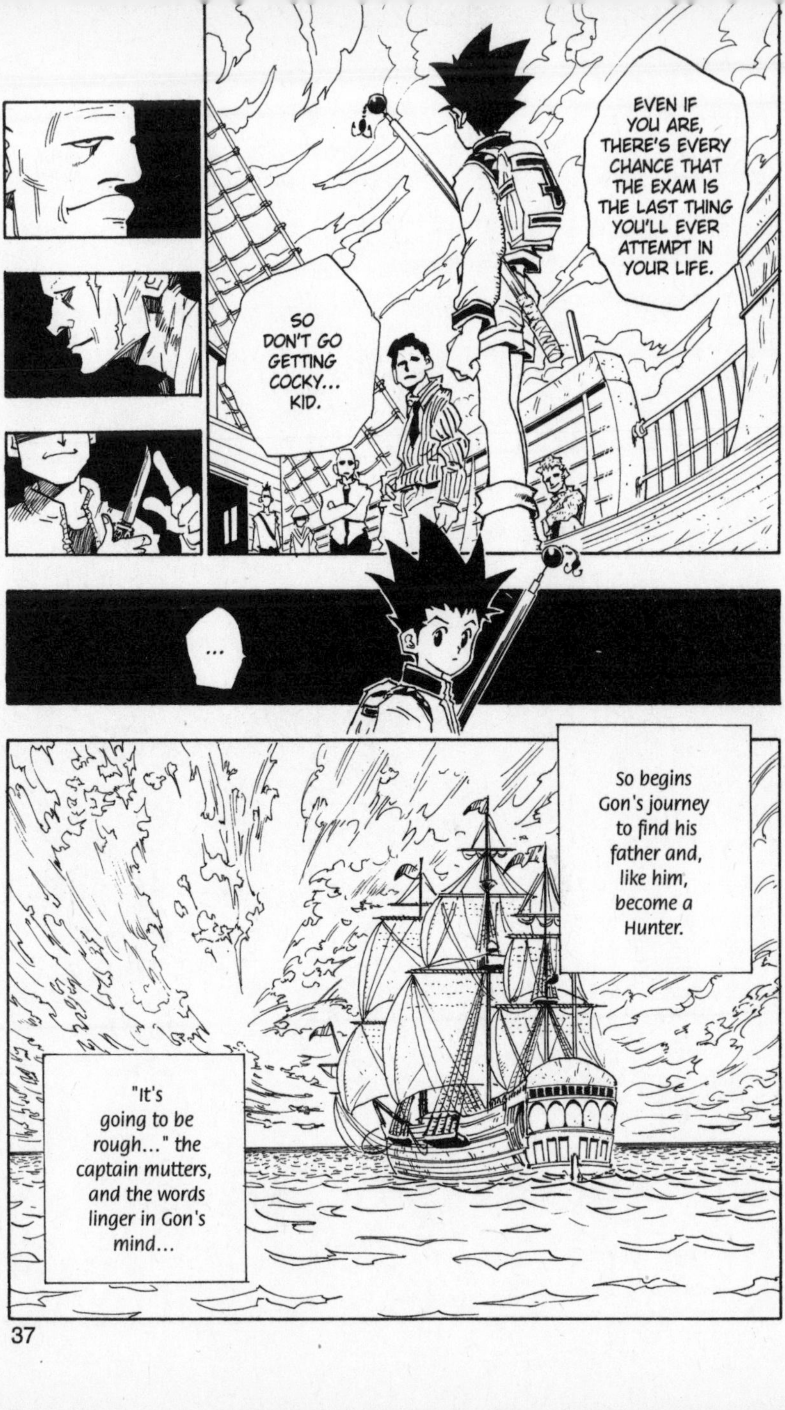
EVEN IF YOU ARE, THERE'S EVERY CHANCE THAT THE EXAM IS THE LAST THING YOU'LL EVER ATTEMPT IN YOUR LIFE.
SO DON'T GO GETTING COCKY... KID.
...
So begins Gon's journey to find his father and, like him, become a Hunter.
"It's going to be rough..." the captain mutters, and the words linger in Gon's mind...

Gon

Chapter 2
An Encounter in the Storm

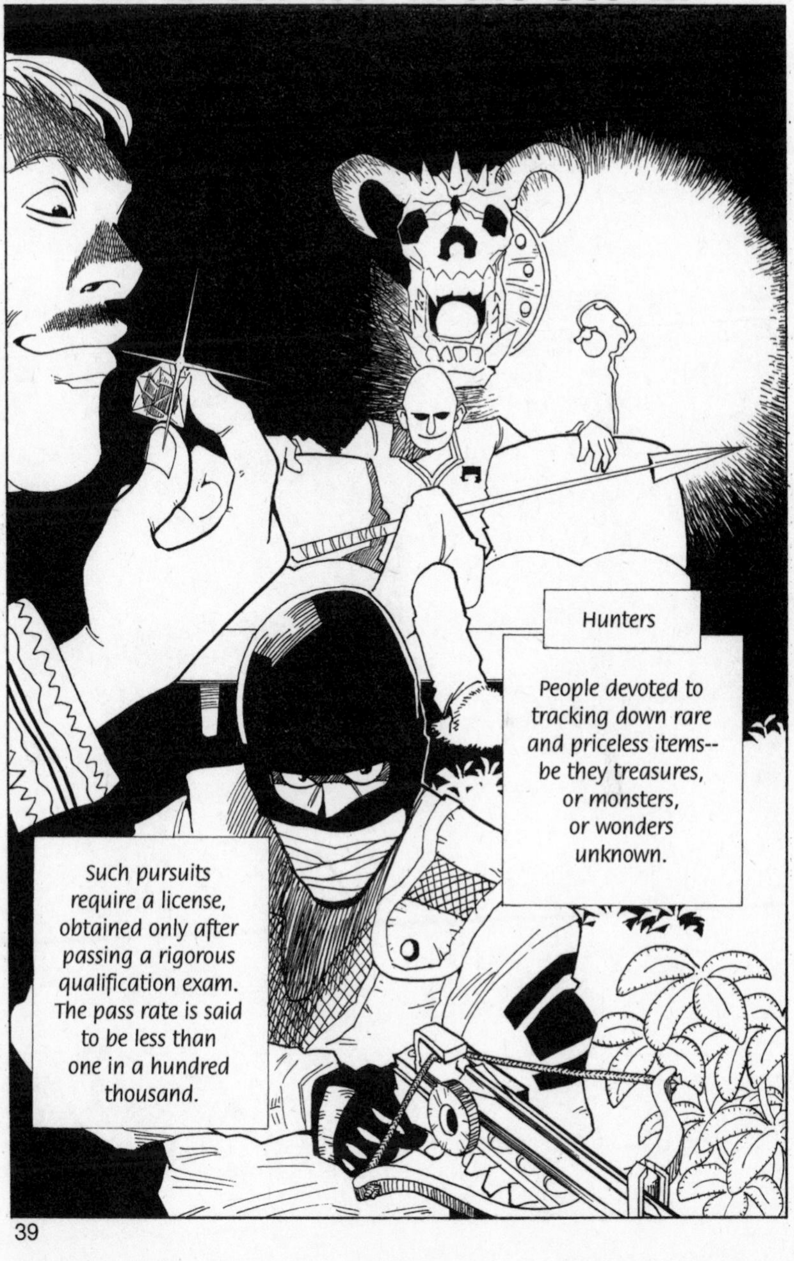
Hunters
People devoted to tracking down rare and priceless items--be they treasures, or monsters, or wonders unknown.
Such pursuits require a license, obtained only after passing a rigorous qualification exam. The pass rate is said to be less than one in a hundred thousand.

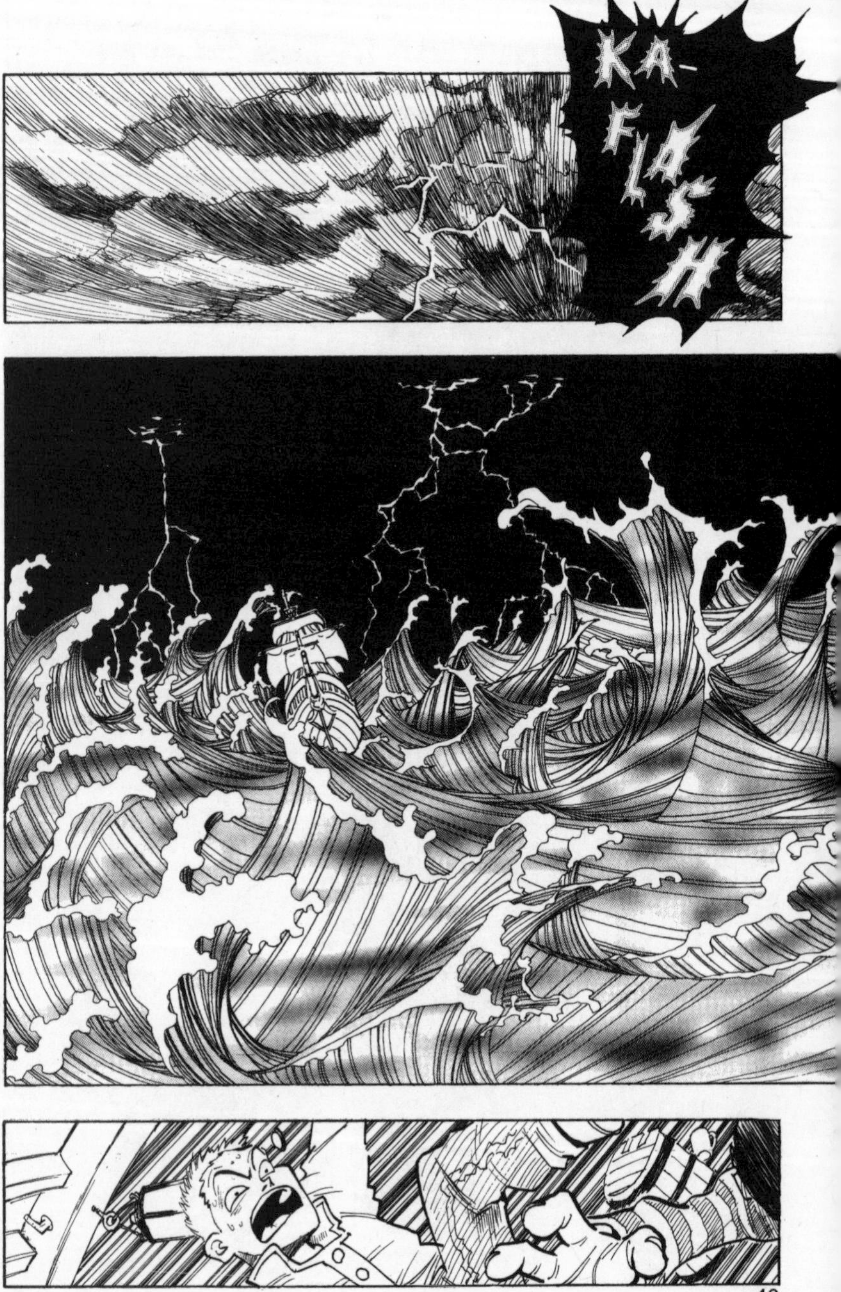
KA-FLASH

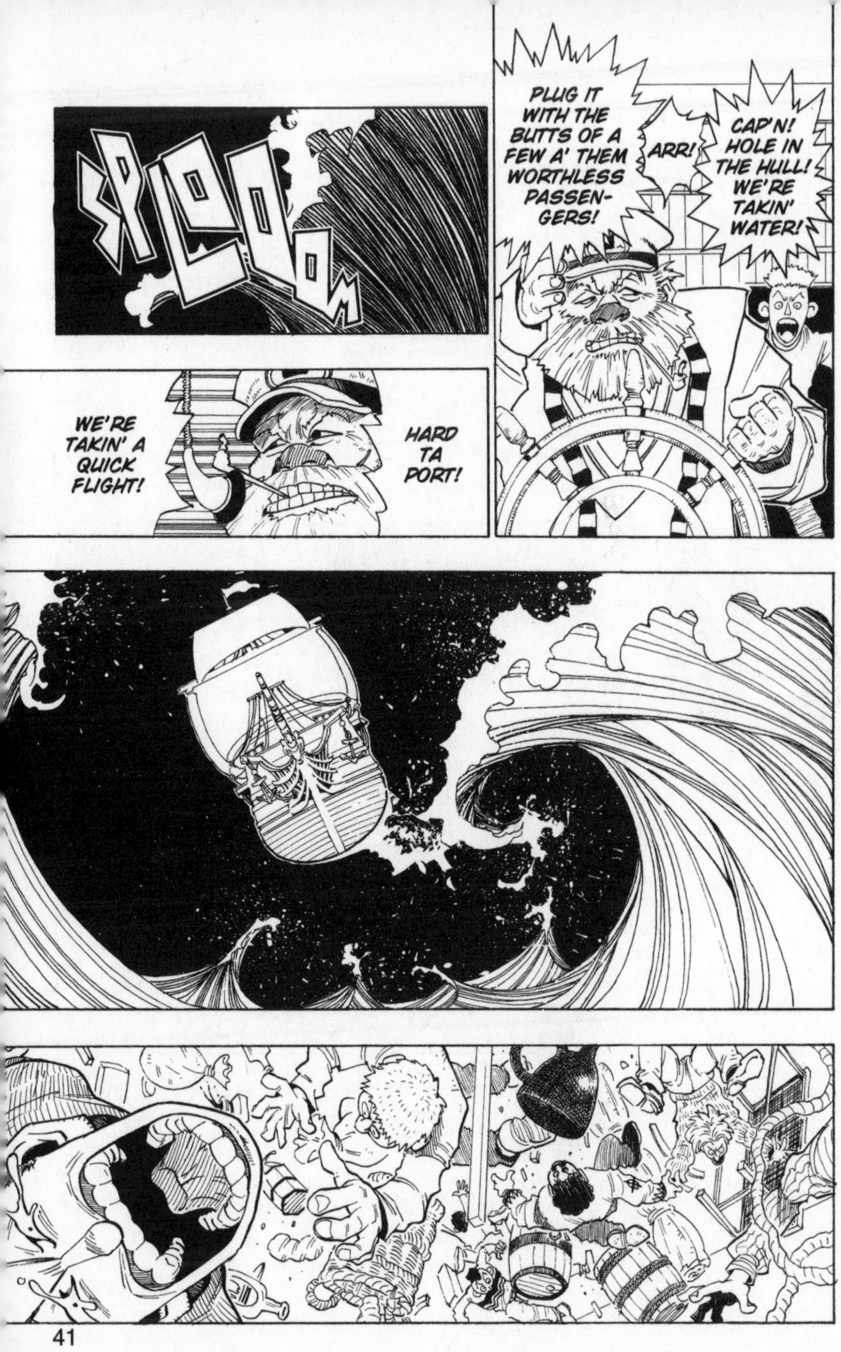
CAP'N! HOLE IN THE HULL! WE'RE TAKIN' WATER!
ARR!
PLUG IT WITH THE BUTTS OF A FEW A' THEM WORTHLESS PASSENGERS!
SPLOOOM
HARD TA PORT!
WE'RE TAKIN' A QUICK FLIGHT!

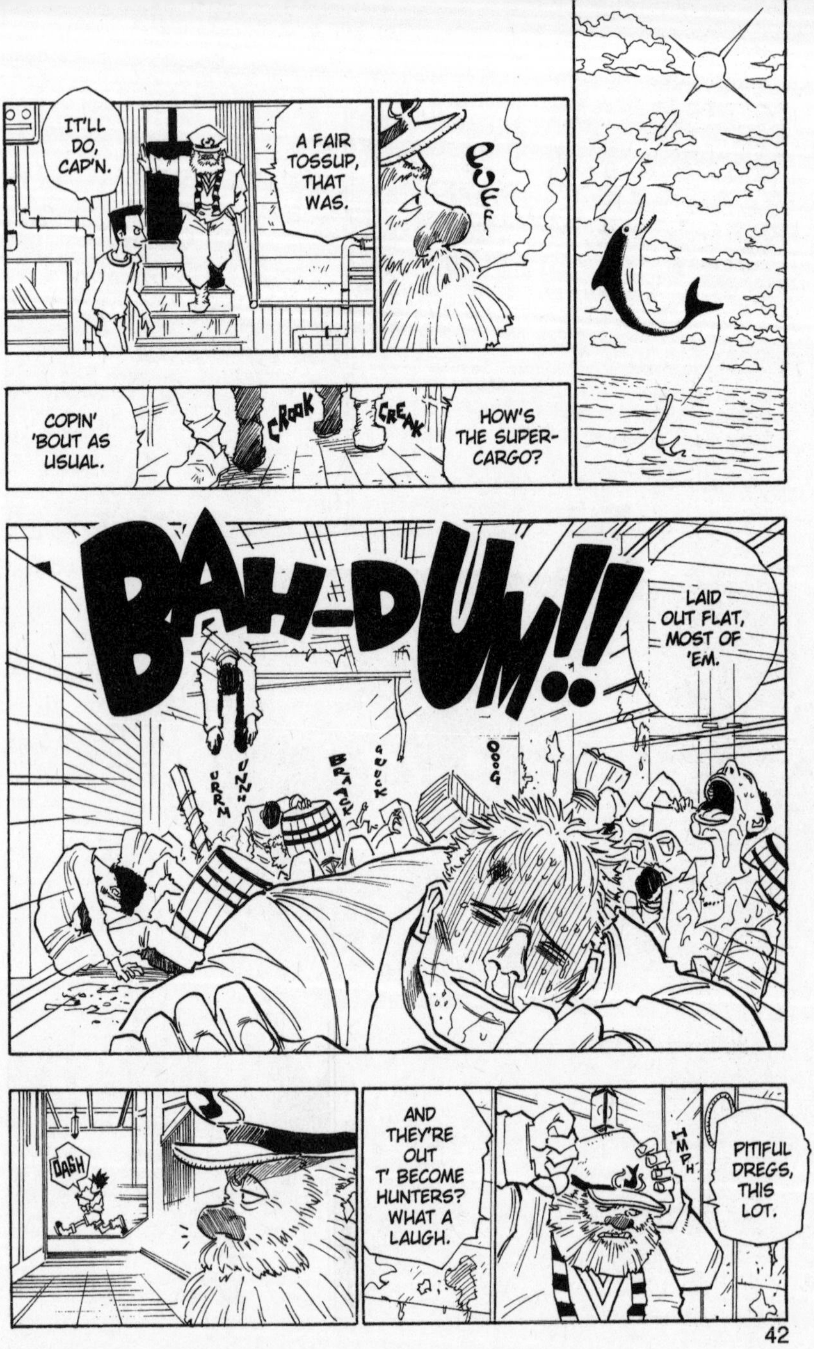

EUFF
A FAIR TOSSUP, THAT WAS.
IT'LL DO, CAP'N.
HOW'S THE SUPER-CARGO?
CREAK
CROOK
COPIN' 'BOUT AS USUAL.
LAID OUT FLAT, MOST OF 'EM.
BAH-DUM!!
OOOG
GUUCK
BRATCK
UNNH
URRM
PITIFUL DREGS, THIS LOT.
IMPH
AND THEY'RE OUT T' BECOME HUNTERS? WHAT A LAUGH.
DASH

READ THIS WAY

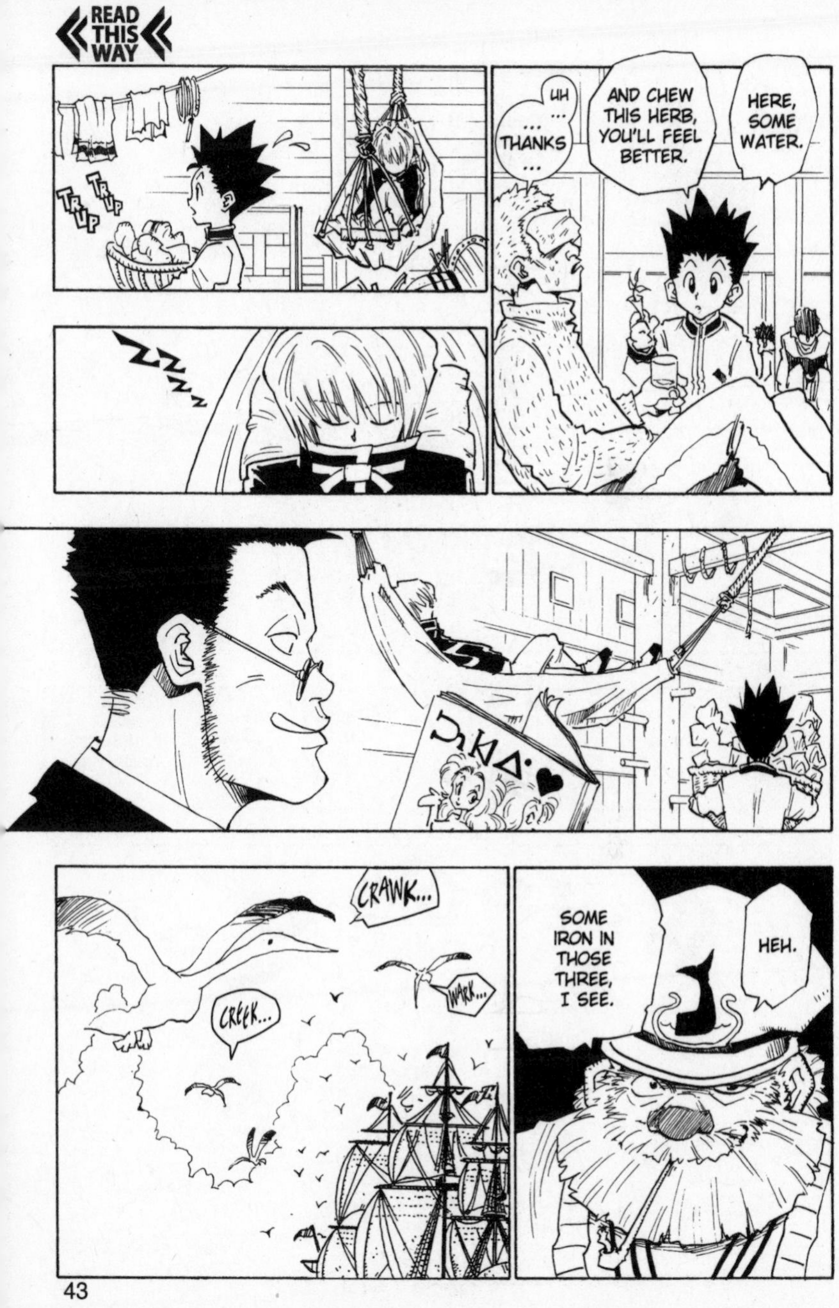
HERE, SOME WATER.
AND CHEW THIS HERB, YOU'LL FEEL BETTER.
UH ... ... THANKS ...
TRUP TRUP
Z Z Z Z
HEH.
SOME IRON IN THOSE THREE, I SEE.
CRAWK...
WARK...
CREEK...

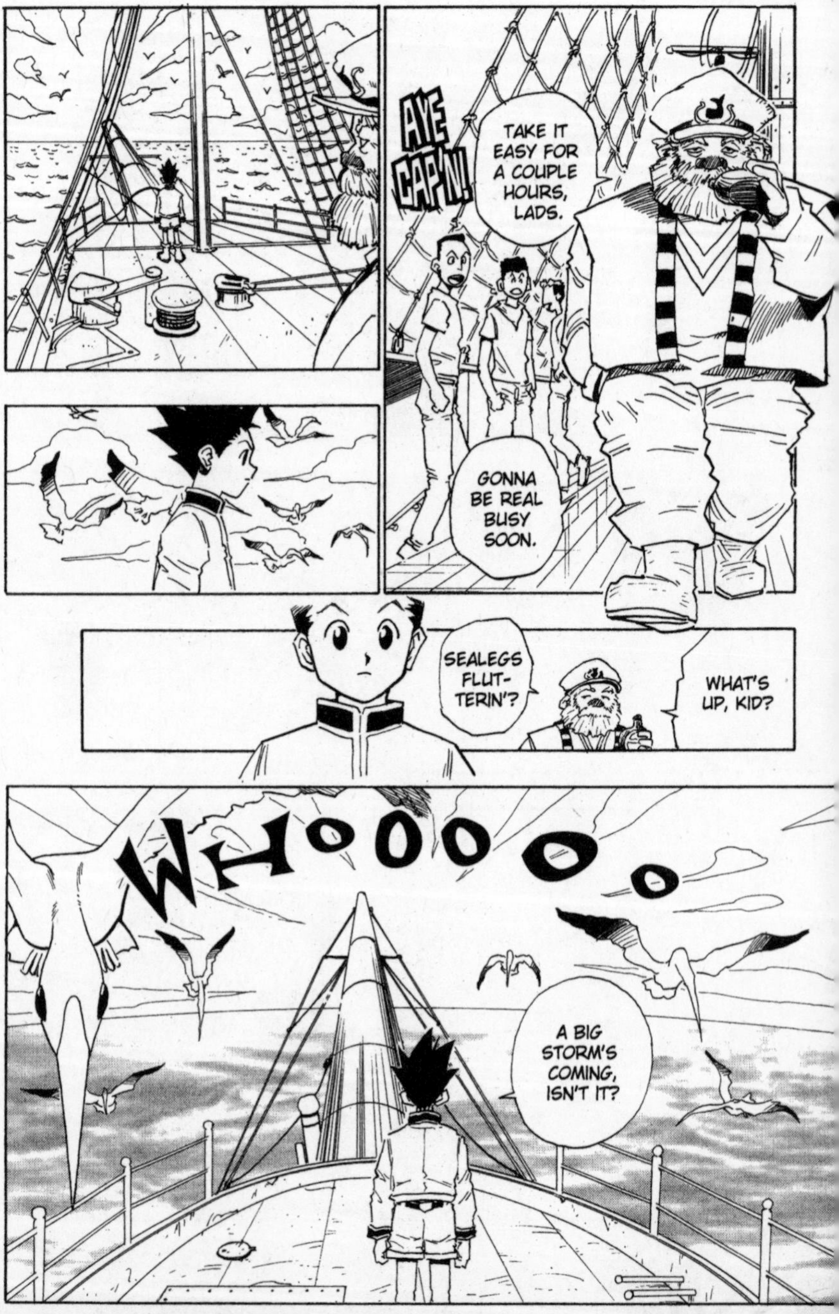
TAKE IT EASY FOR A COUPLE HOURS, LADS.
AYE CAP'N!
GONNA BE REAL BUSY SOON.
WHAT'S UP, KID?
SEALEGS FLUT-TERIN'?
WHOOOOO
A BIG STORM'S COMING, ISN'T IT?

READ THIS WAY

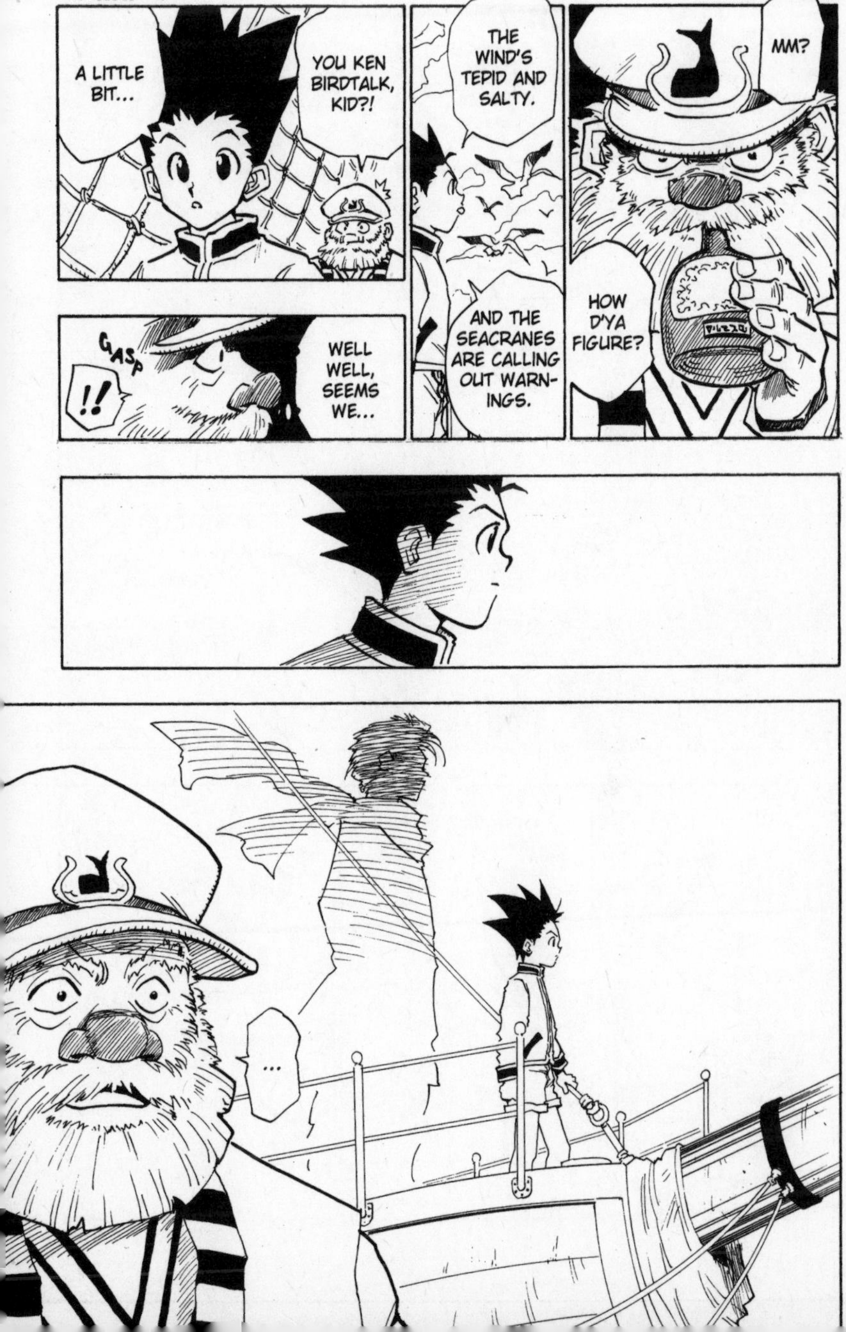
MM?
HOW D'YA FIGURE?
THE WIND'S TEPID AND SALTY.
AND THE SEACRANES ARE CALLING OUT WARNINGS.
YOU KEN BIRDTALK, KID?!
A LITTLE BIT...
WELL WELL, SEEMS WE...
GASP
!!
...

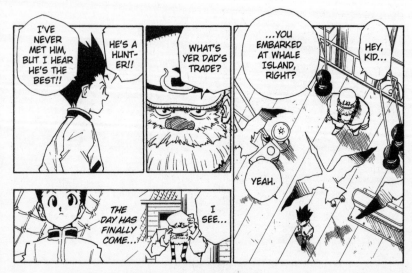

HEY, KID...
...YOU EMBARKED AT WHALE ISLAND, RIGHT?
YEAH.
WHAT'S YER DAD'S TRADE?
HE'S A HUNTER!!
I'VE NEVER MET HIM, BUT I HEAR HE'S THE BEST!!
I SEE...
THE DAY HAS FINALLY COME...
SO, CAN YOU TELL ME THE STORM'S SIZE AND WHEN WE'LL HIT IT?
IT'S TWICE AS BIG AND VIOLENT AS THE LAST ONE.
AT OUR CURRENT SPEED, WE'LL BE IN IT IN SAY...THREE HOURS.
'BOUT RIGHT...
...AND NOT SOME LANDLUBBER'S LUCKY GUESS, EITHER...
HEH!
C'MON, I'LL SHOW YOU HOW TO STEER A SHIP.
WOW!!

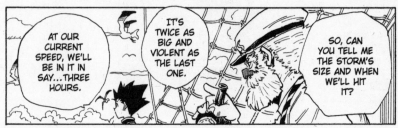

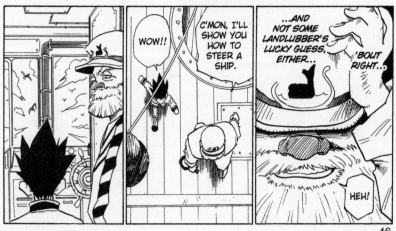

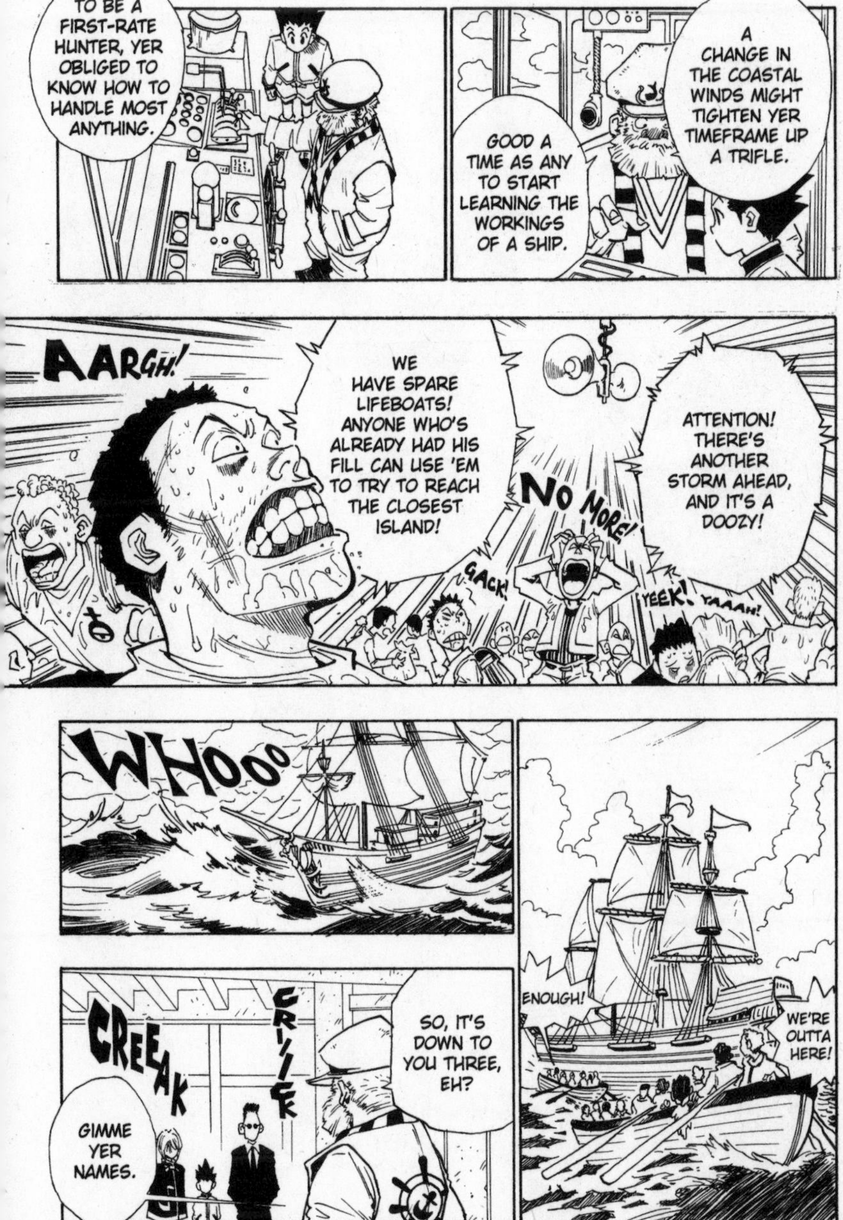
A CHANGE IN THE COASTAL WINDS MIGHT TIGHTEN YER TIMEFRAME UP A TRIFLE.
GOOD A TIME AS ANY TO START LEARNING THE WORKINGS OF A SHIP.
TO BE A FIRST-RATE HUNTER, YER OBLIGED TO KNOW HOW TO HANDLE MOST ANYTHING.
ATTENTION! THERE'S ANOTHER STORM AHEAD, AND IT'S A DOOZY!
WE HAVE SPARE LIFEBOATS! ANYONE WHO'S ALREADY HAD HIS FILL CAN USE 'EM TO TRY TO REACH THE CLOSEST ISLAND!
NO MORE!
YAAAH!
YEEK!
GACK!
AARGH!
WE'RE OUTTA HERE!
ENOUGH!
WHOOO
SO, IT'S DOWN TO YOU THREE, EH?
CRIIICK
CREEAK
GIMME YER NAMES.

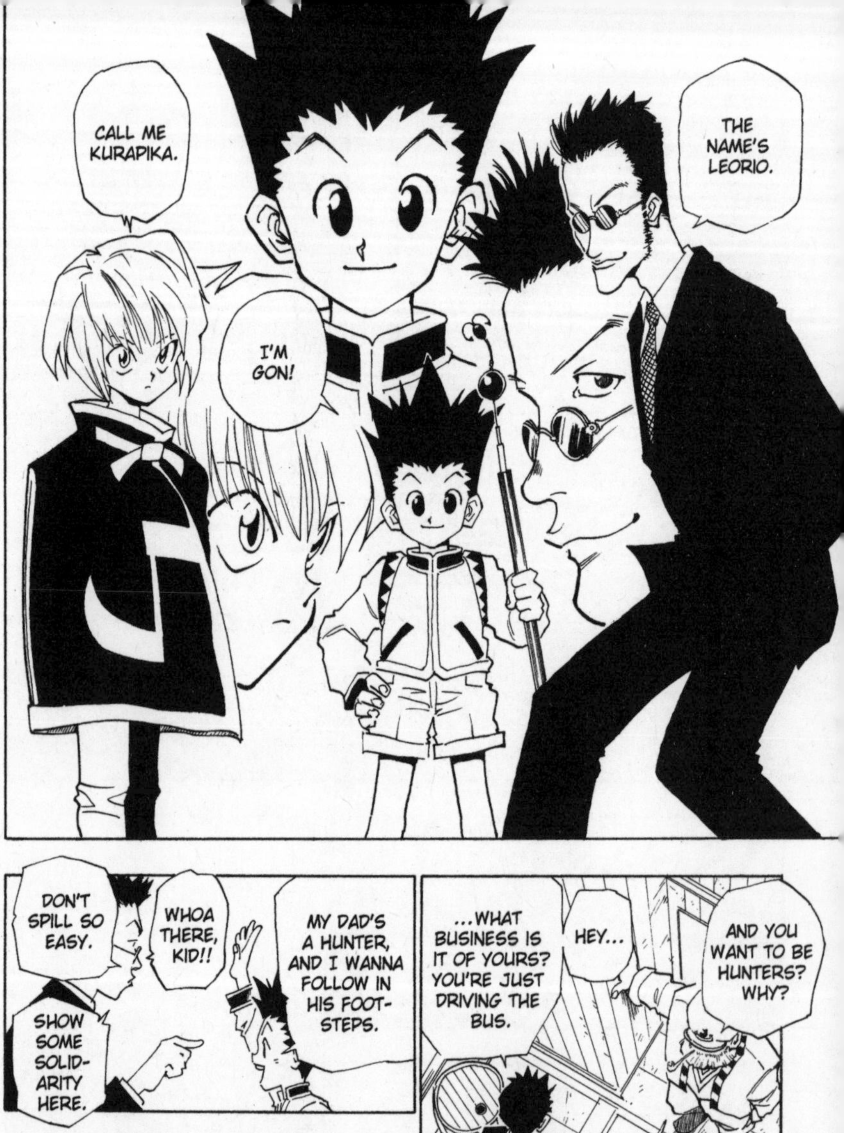
THE NAME'S LEORIO.
CALL ME KURAPIKA.
I'M GON!
AND YOU WANT TO BE HUNTERS? WHY?
HEY...
...WHAT BUSINESS IS IT OF YOURS? YOU'RE JUST DRIVING THE BUS.
THAT A FACT?
YOU KNOW IT!
MY DAD'S A HUNTER, AND I WANNA FOLLOW IN HIS FOOT-STEPS.
WHOA THERE, KID!!
DON'T SPILL SO EASY.
SHOW SOME SOLID-ARITY HERE.
WHY? WHAT'S THE BIG SECRET?
NEVER YOU MIND.
I DON'T JUMP WHEN SOMEONE SAYS "BOO!"

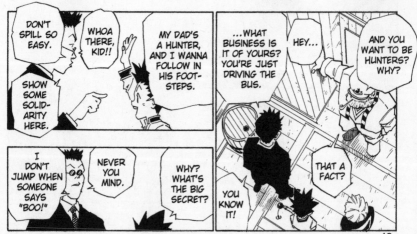

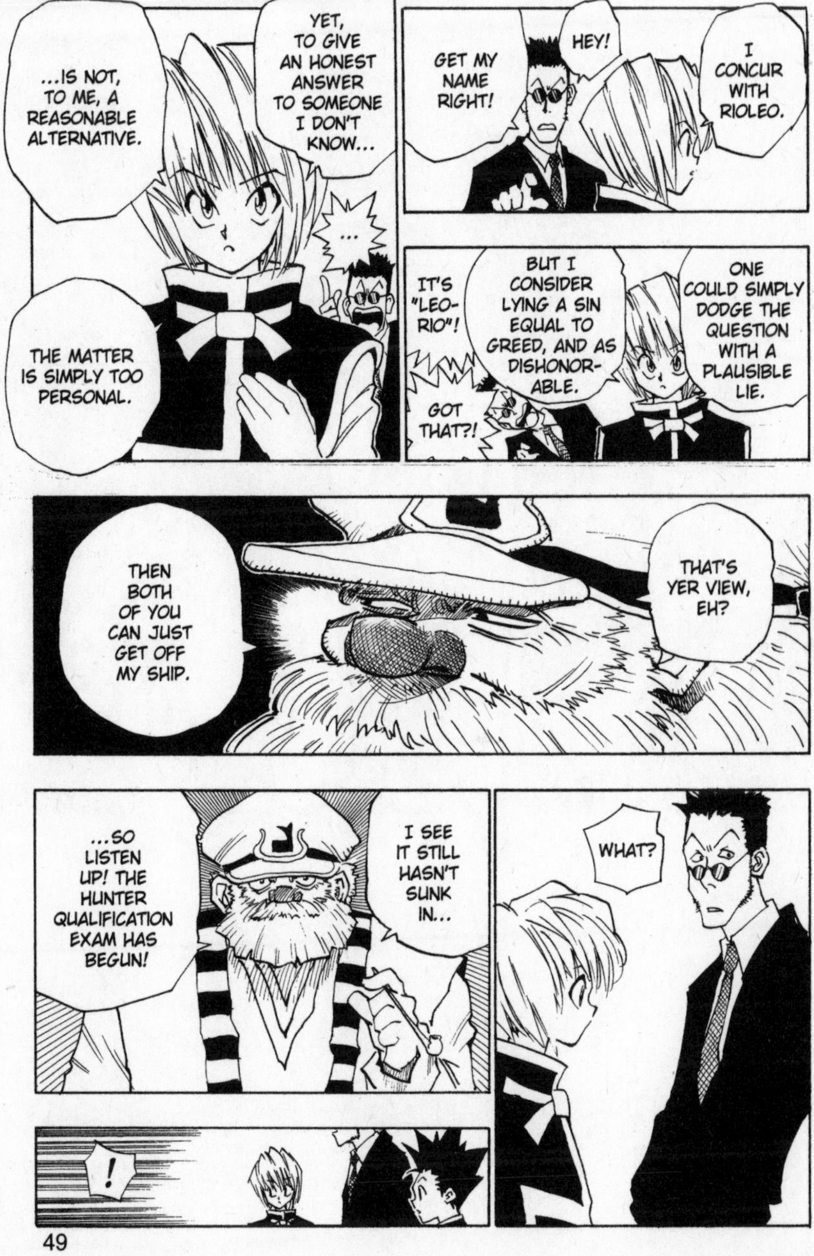
I CONCUR WITH RIOLEO.
HEY!
GET MY NAME RIGHT!
ONE COULD SIMPLY DODGE THE QUESTION WITH A PLAUSIBLE LIE.
BUT I CONSIDER LYING A SIN EQUAL TO GREED, AND AS DISHONOR-ABLE.
IT'S "LEO-RIO"!
GOT THAT?!
YET, TO GIVE AN HONEST ANSWER TO SOMEONE I DON'T KNOW...
...IS NOT, TO ME, A REASONABLE ALTERNATIVE.
...
THE MATTER IS SIMPLY TOO PERSONAL.
THAT'S YER VIEW, EH?
THEN BOTH OF YOU CAN JUST GET OFF MY SHIP.
WHAT?
I SEE IT STILL HASN'T SUNK IN...
...SO LISTEN UP! THE HUNTER QUALIFICATION EXAM HAS BEGUN!
!

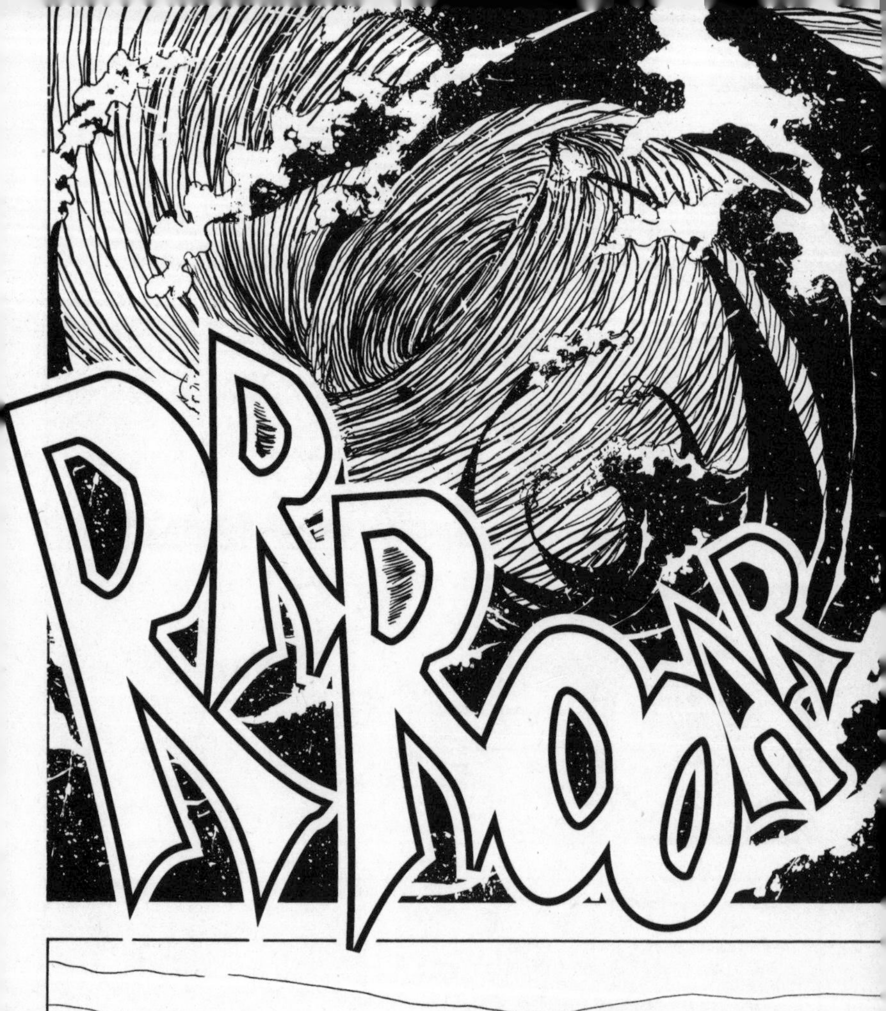
RRROOAR
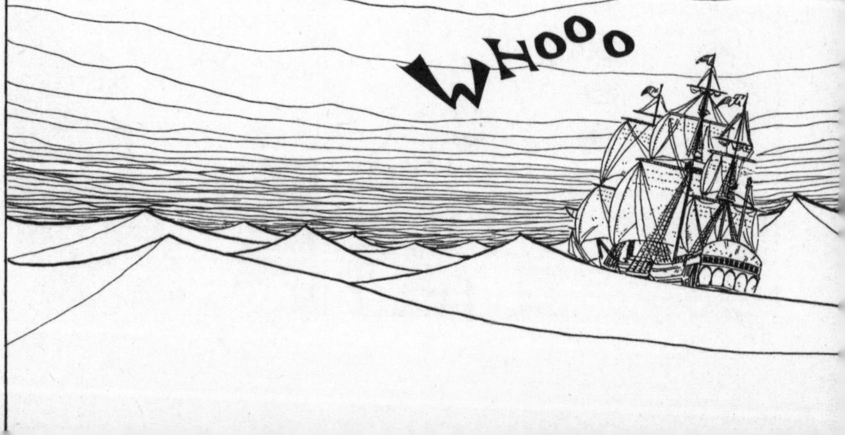
WHOOO

READ THIS WAY

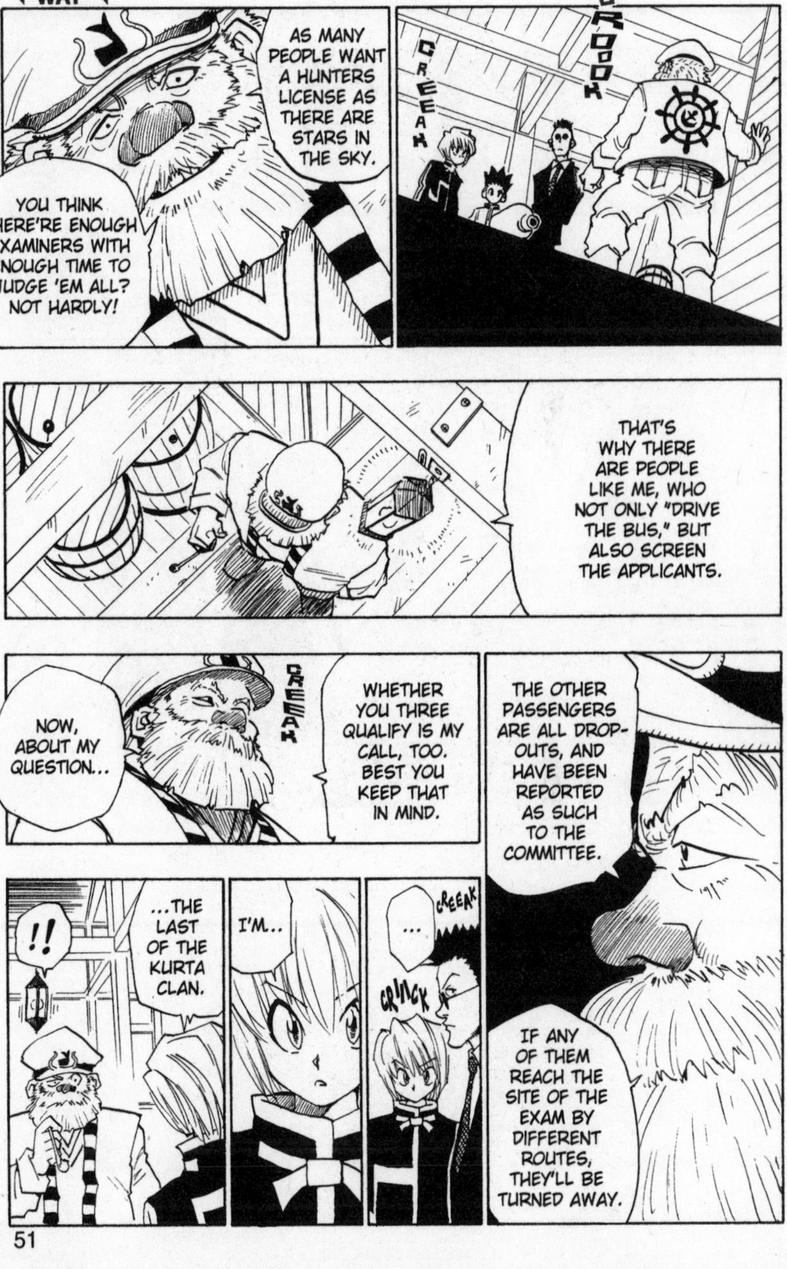
CROOOK
CREEAK
AS MANY PEOPLE WANT A HUNTERS LICENSE AS THERE ARE STARS IN THE SKY.
YOU THINK THERE'RE ENOUGH EXAMINERS WITH ENOUGH TIME TO JUDGE 'EM ALL? NOT HARDLY!
THAT'S WHY THERE ARE PEOPLE LIKE ME, WHO NOT ONLY "DRIVE THE BUS," BUT ALSO SCREEN THE APPLICANTS.
THE OTHER PASSENGERS ARE ALL DROP-OUTS, AND HAVE BEEN REPORTED AS SUCH TO THE COMMITTEE.
IF ANY OF THEM REACH THE SITE OF THE EXAM BY DIFFERENT ROUTES, THEY'LL BE TURNED AWAY.
WHETHER YOU THREE QUALIFY IS MY CALL, TOO. BEST YOU KEEP THAT IN MIND.
CREEAK
NOW, ABOUT MY QUESTION...
...
CREEAK
CRINCK
I'M...
...THE LAST OF THE KURTA CLAN.
!!

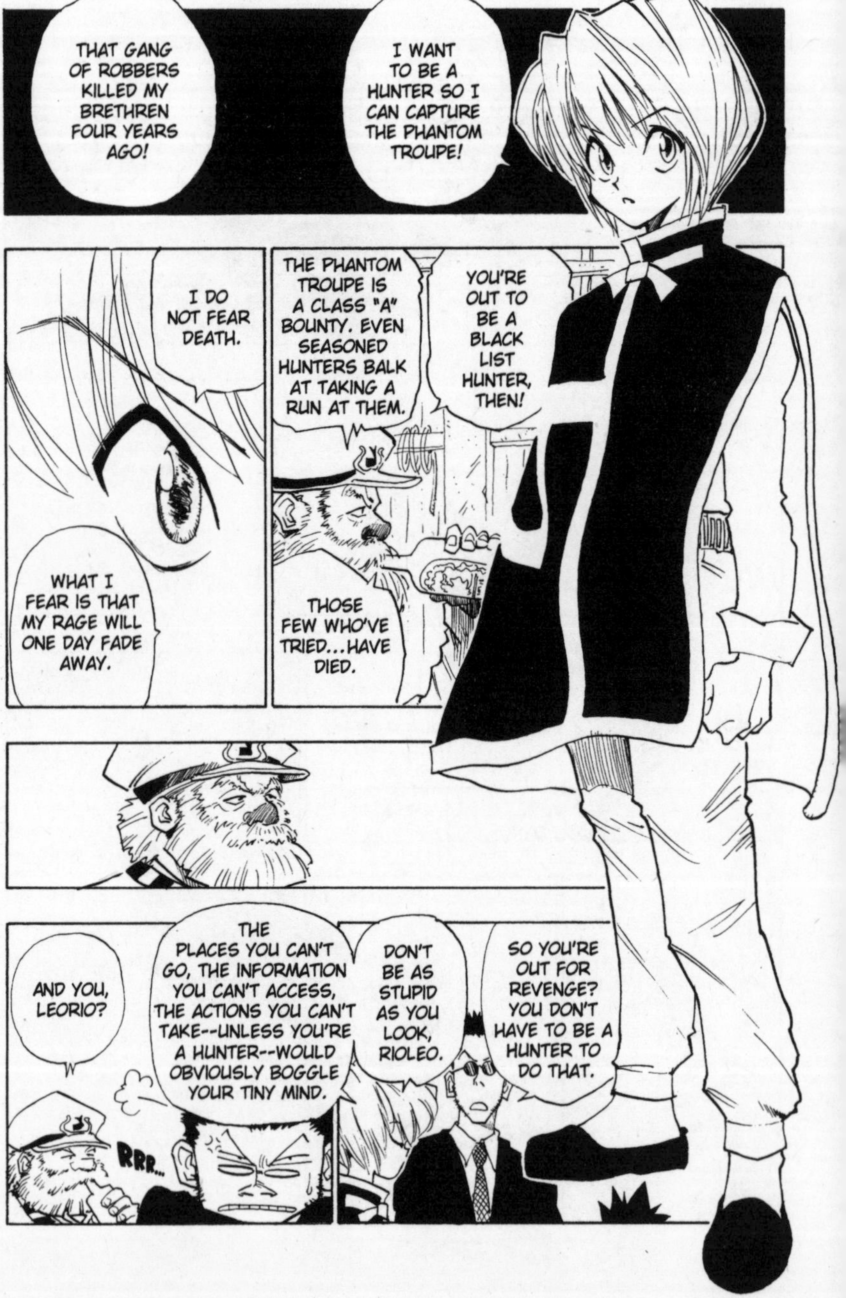
I WANT TO BE A HUNTER SO I CAN CAPTURE THE PHANTOM TROUPE!
THAT GANG OF ROBBERS KILLED MY BRETHREN FOUR YEARS AGO!
YOU'RE OUT TO BE A BLACK LIST HUNTER, THEN!
THE PHANTOM TROUPE IS A CLASS "A" BOUNTY. EVEN SEASONED HUNTERS BALK AT TAKING A RUN AT THEM.
THOSE FEW WHO'VE TRIED...HAVE DIED.
I DO NOT FEAR DEATH.
WHAT I FEAR IS THAT MY RAGE WILL ONE DAY FADE AWAY.
SO YOU'RE OUT FOR REVENGE? YOU DON'T HAVE TO BE A HUNTER TO DO THAT.
DON'T BE AS STUPID AS YOU LOOK, RIOLEO.
THE PLACES YOU CAN'T GO, THE INFORMATION YOU CAN'T ACCESS, THE ACTIONS YOU CAN'T TAKE--UNLESS YOU'RE A HUNTER--WOULD OBVIOUSLY BOGGLE YOUR TINY MIND.
RRR...
AND YOU, LEORIO?

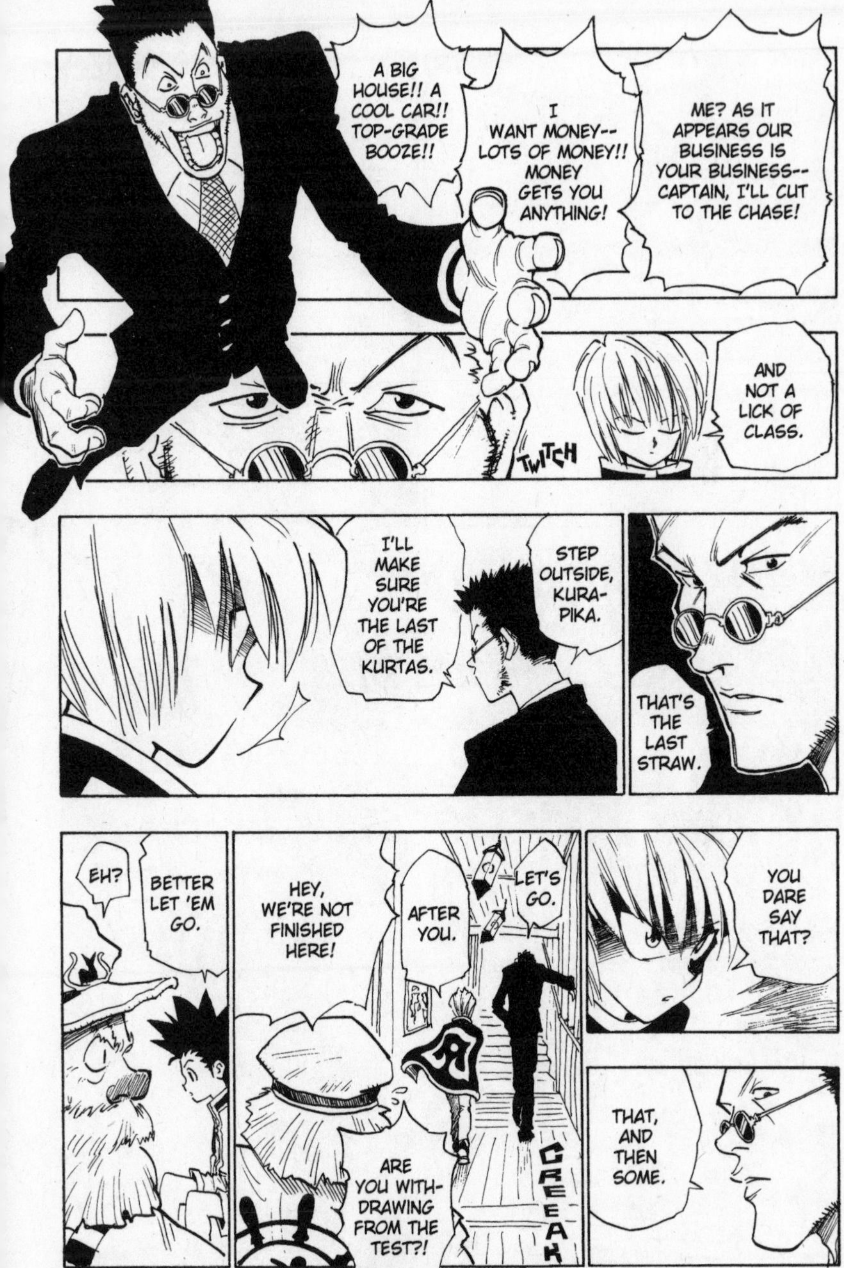
ME? AS IT APPEARS OUR BUSINESS IS YOUR BUSINESS-- CAPTAIN, I'LL CUT TO THE CHASE!
I WANT MONEY-- LOTS OF MONEY!! MONEY GETS YOU ANYTHING!
A BIG HOUSE!! A COOL CAR!! TOP-GRADE BOOZE!!
AND NOT A LICK OF CLASS.
TWITCH
THAT'S THE LAST STRAW.
STEP OUTSIDE, KURA-PIKA.
I'LL MAKE SURE YOU'RE THE LAST OF THE KURTAS.
YOU DARE SAY THAT?
THAT, AND THEN SOME.
LET'S GO.
AFTER YOU.
HEY, WE'RE NOT FINISHED HERE!
ARE YOU WITH-DRAWING FROM THE TEST?!
CREEAK
BETTER LET 'EM GO.
EH?

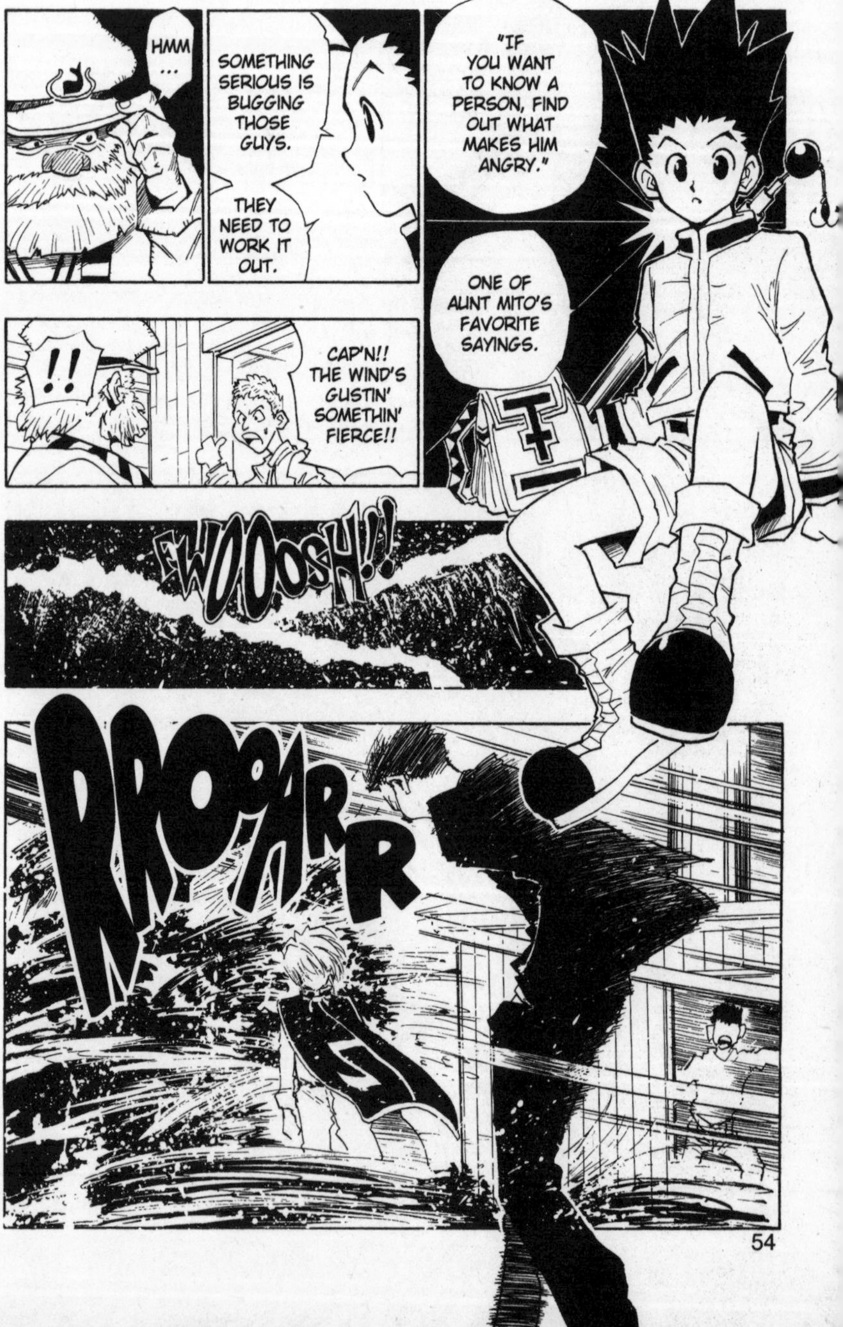
"IF YOU WANT TO KNOW A PERSON, FIND OUT WHAT MAKES HIM ANGRY."
ONE OF AUNT MITO'S FAVORITE SAYINGS.
SOMETHING SERIOUS IS BUGGING THOSE GUYS.
THEY NEED TO WORK IT OUT.
HMM ...
CAP'N!! THE WIND'S GUSTIN' SOMETHIN' FIERCE!!
!!
FWOOSH!!
RROOARR

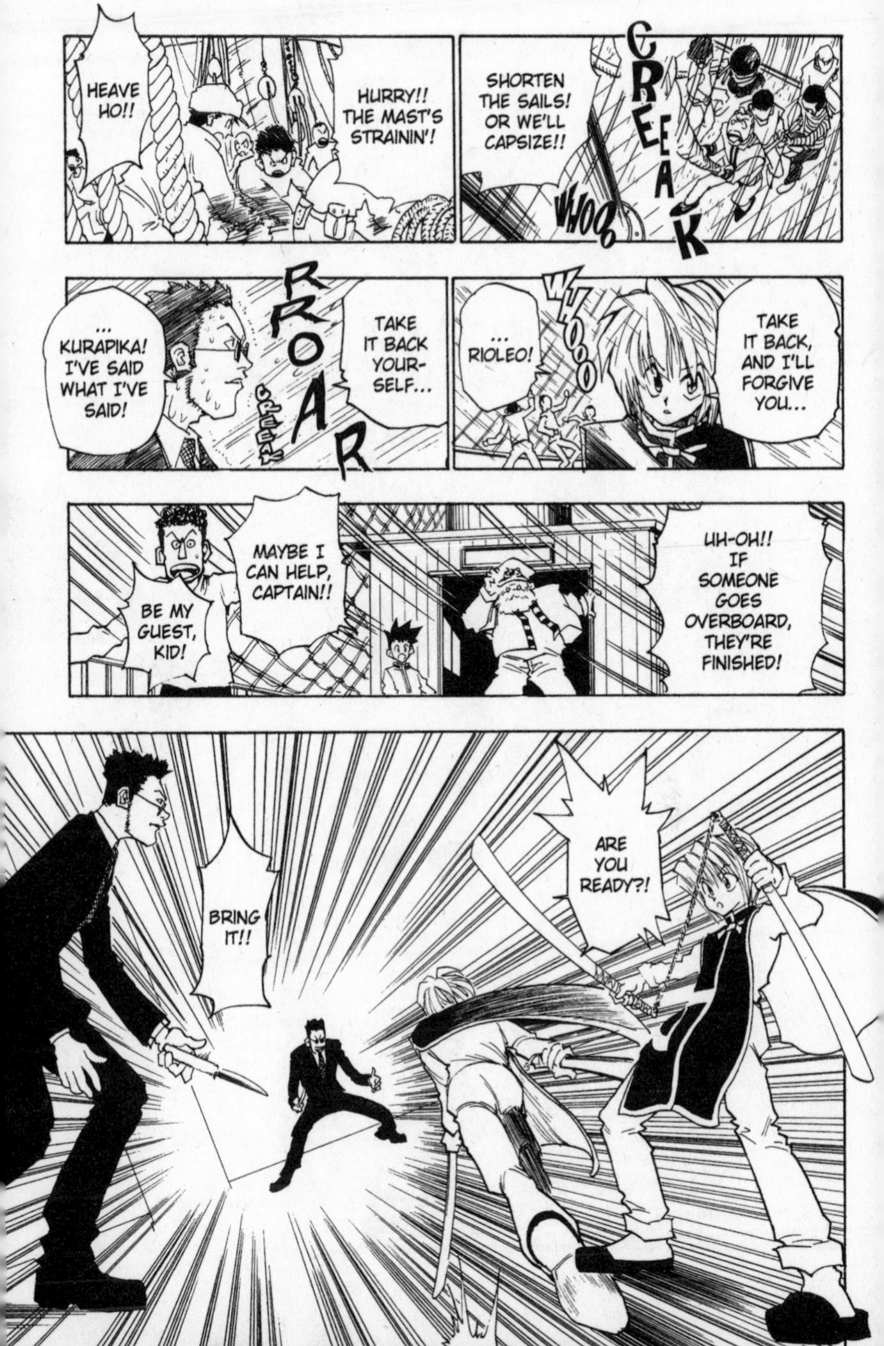
CREAK
SHORTEN THE SAILS! OR WE'LL CAPSIZE!!
WHOOO
HURRY!! THE MAST'S STRAININ'!
HEAVE HO!!
TAKE IT BACK, AND I'LL FORGIVE YOU...
WHOOOO
... RIOLEO!
TAKE IT BACK YOURSELF...
RROAR
... KURAPIKA! I'VE SAID WHAT I'VE SAID!
UH-OH!! IF SOMEONE GOES OVERBOARD, THEY'RE FINISHED!
MAYBE I CAN HELP, CAPTAIN!!
BE MY GUEST, KID!
ARE YOU READY?!
BRING IT!!

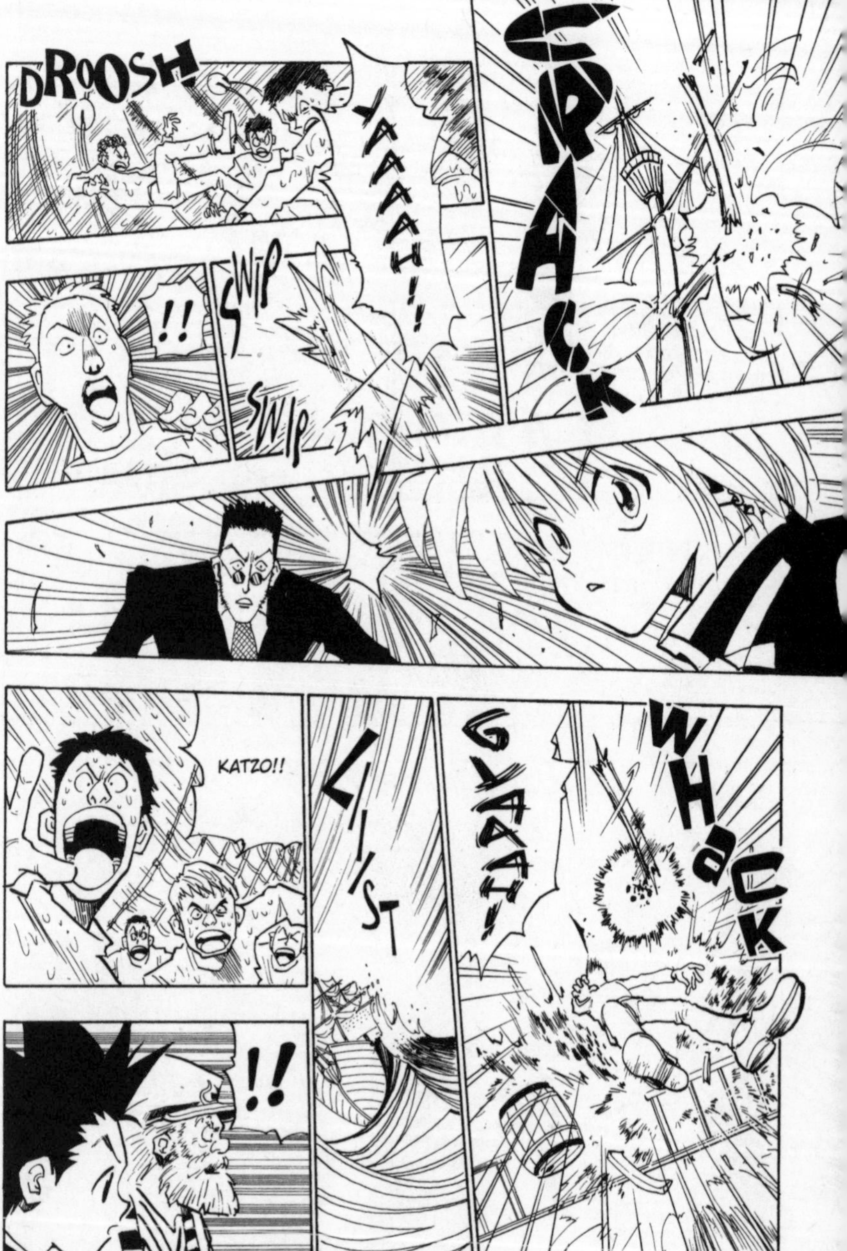
CRAACK
DROOSH
YAAAAAH!!
SWIP
SWIP
!!
WHaCK
GYAAAH!!
LIIIST
KATZO!!
!!

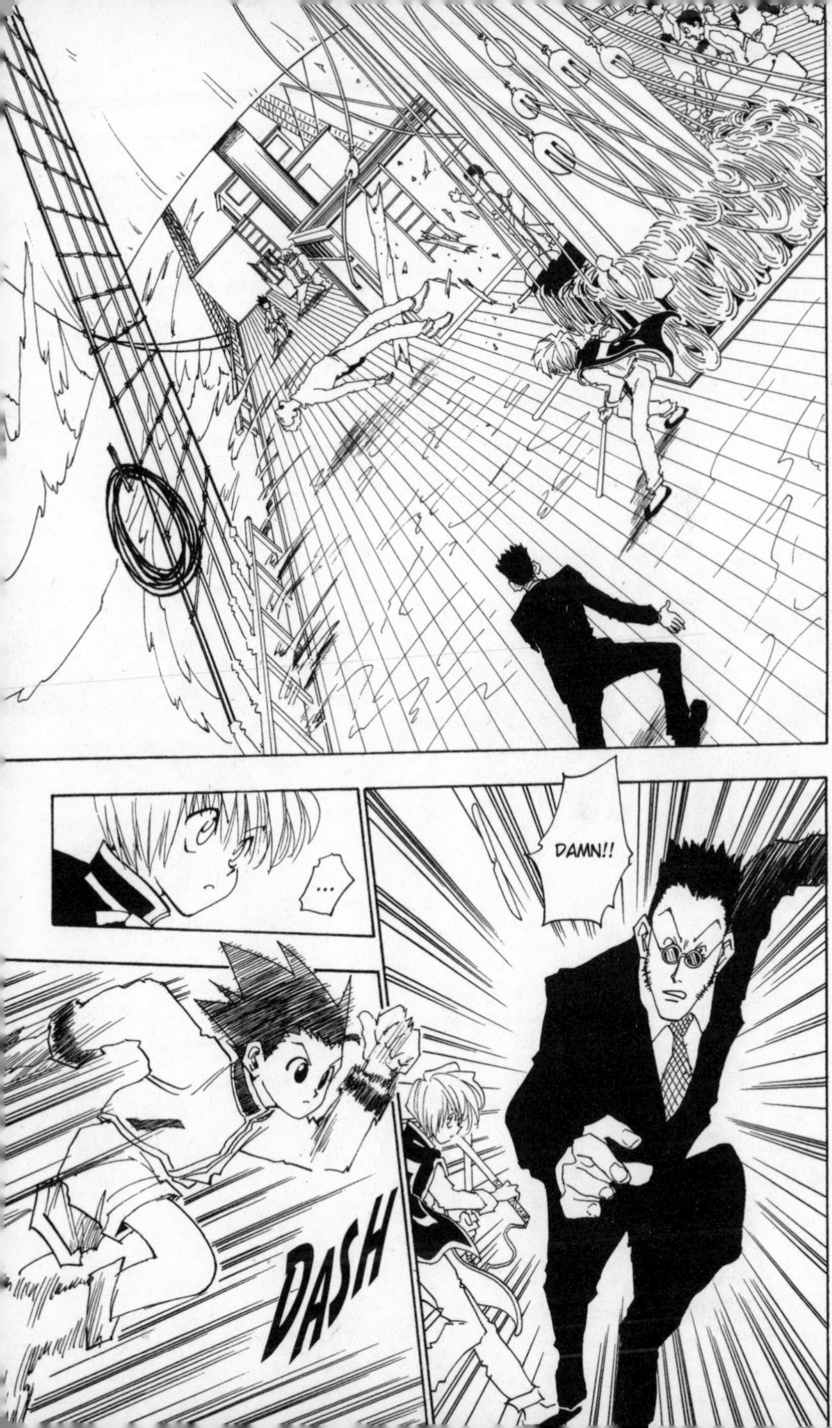
DAMN!!
...
DASH

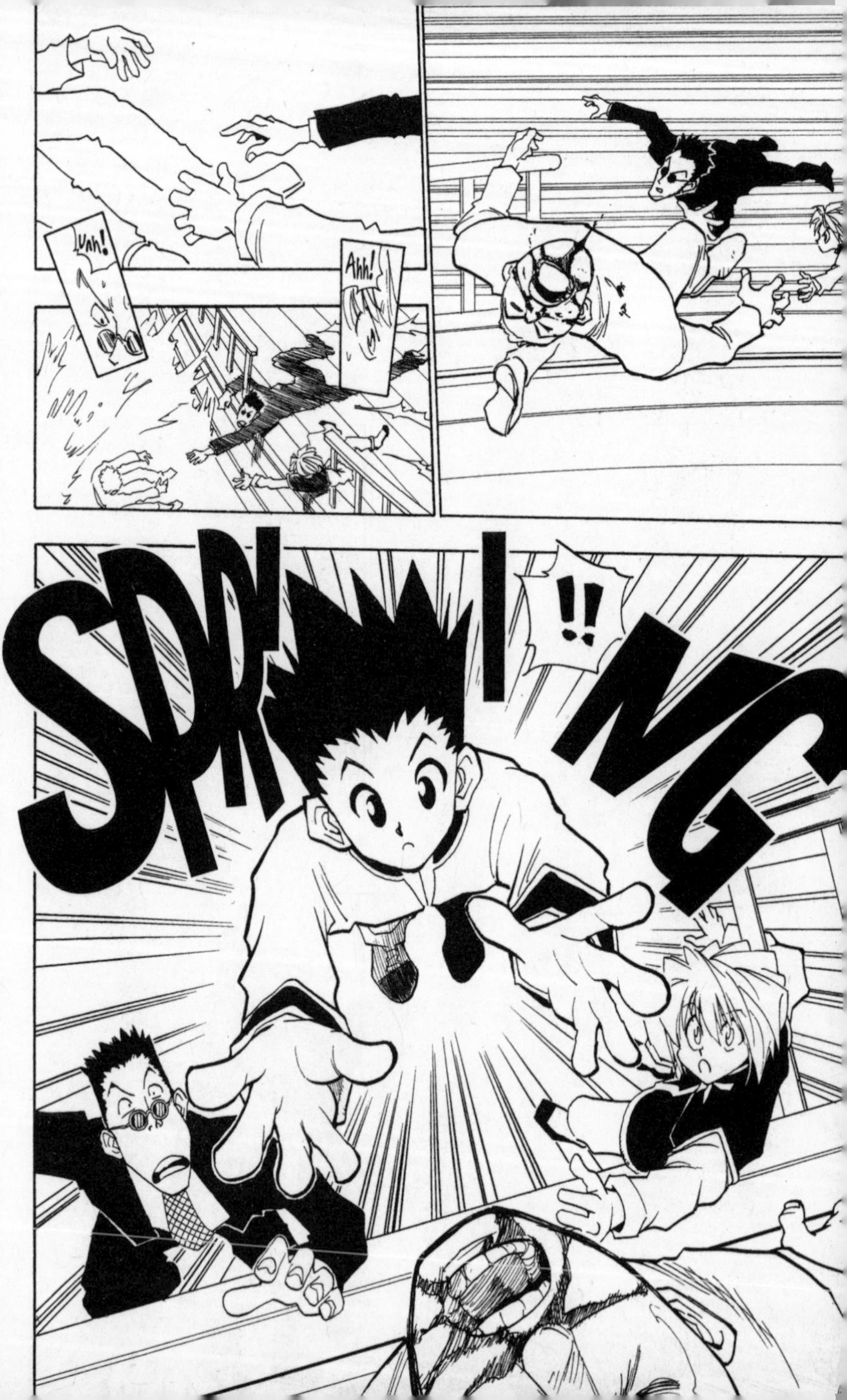
Ahh!
Unh!
SPRING
!!

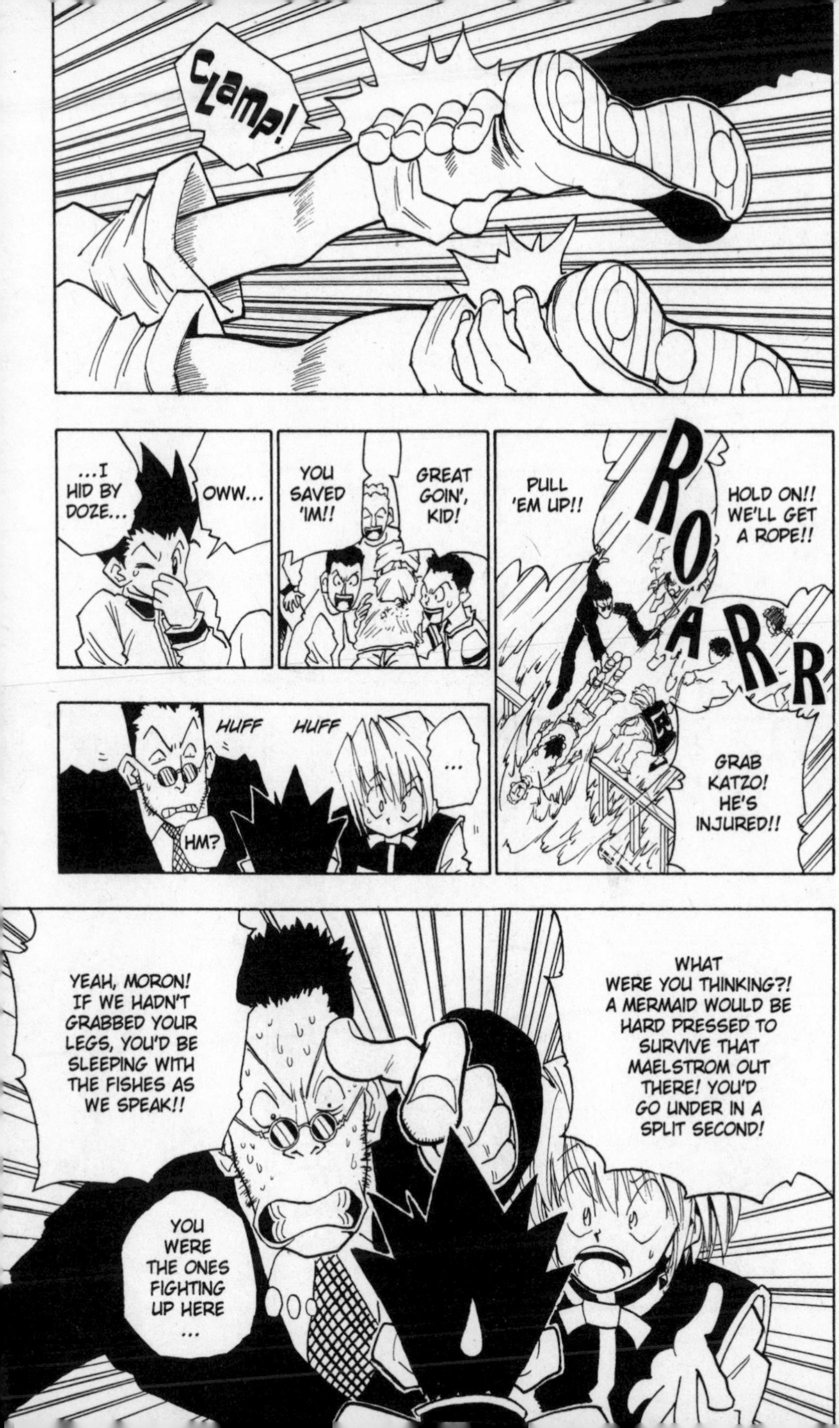
CLAMP!
HOLD ON!! WE'LL GET A ROPE!!
ROARR
PULL 'EM UP!!
GRAB KATZO! HE'S INJURED!!
GREAT GOIN', KID!
YOU SAVED 'IM!!
OWW...
...I HID BY DOZE...
...
HUFF HUFF
HM?
WHAT WERE YOU THINKING?! A MERMAID WOULD BE HARD PRESSED TO SURVIVE THAT MAELSTROM OUT THERE! YOU'D GO UNDER IN A SPLIT SECOND!
YEAH, MORON! IF WE HADN'T GRABBED YOUR LEGS, YOU'D BE SLEEPING WITH THE FISHES AS WE SPEAK!!
YOU WERE THE ONES FIGHTING UP HERE ...

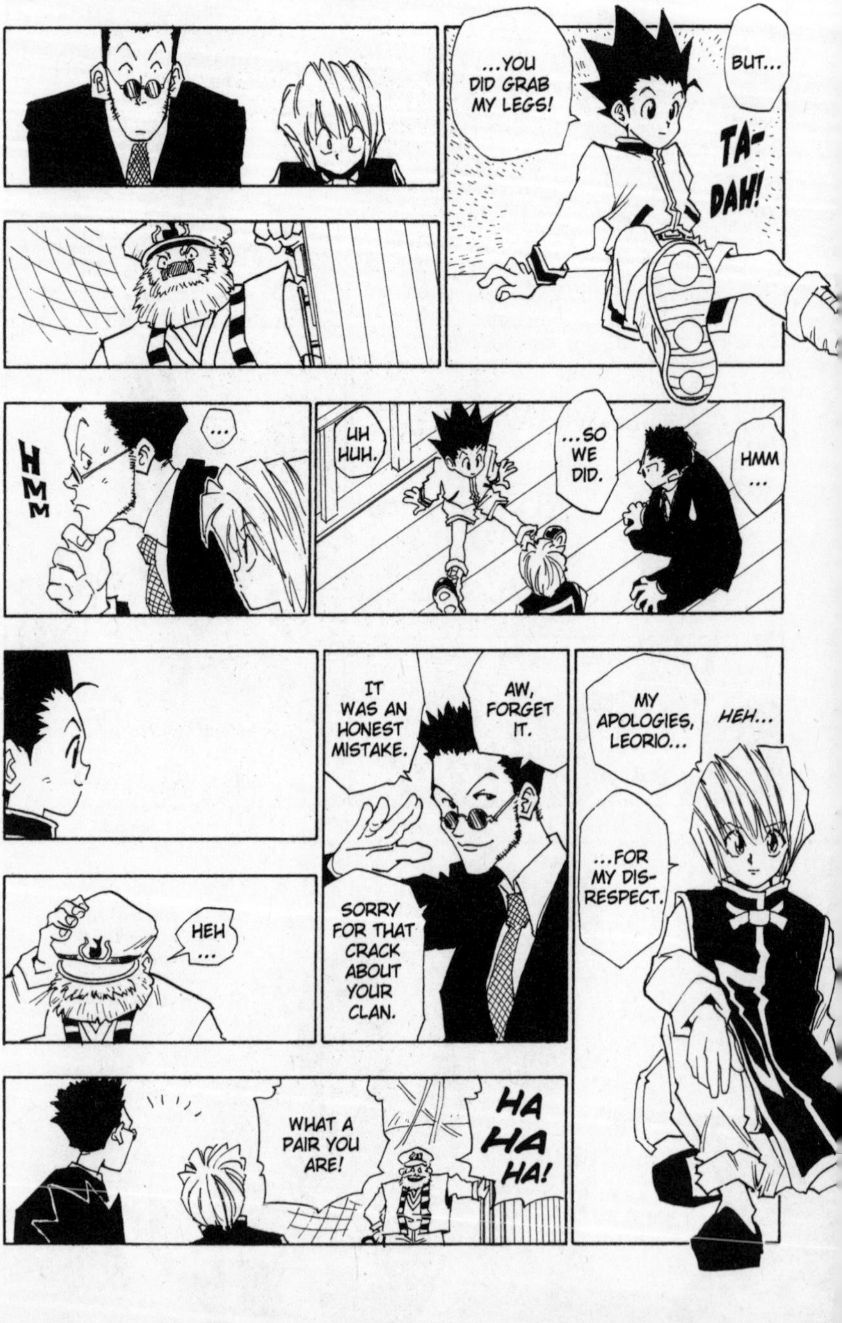
BUT...
TA-DAH!
...YOU DID GRAB MY LEGS!
HMM...
...SO WE DID.
UH HUH.
...
HMM
HEH...
MY APOLOGIES, LEORIO...
...FOR MY DIS-RESPECT.
AW, FORGET IT.
IT WAS AN HONEST MISTAKE.
SORRY FOR THAT CRACK ABOUT YOUR CLAN.
HEH...
HA HA HA!
WHAT A PAIR YOU ARE!

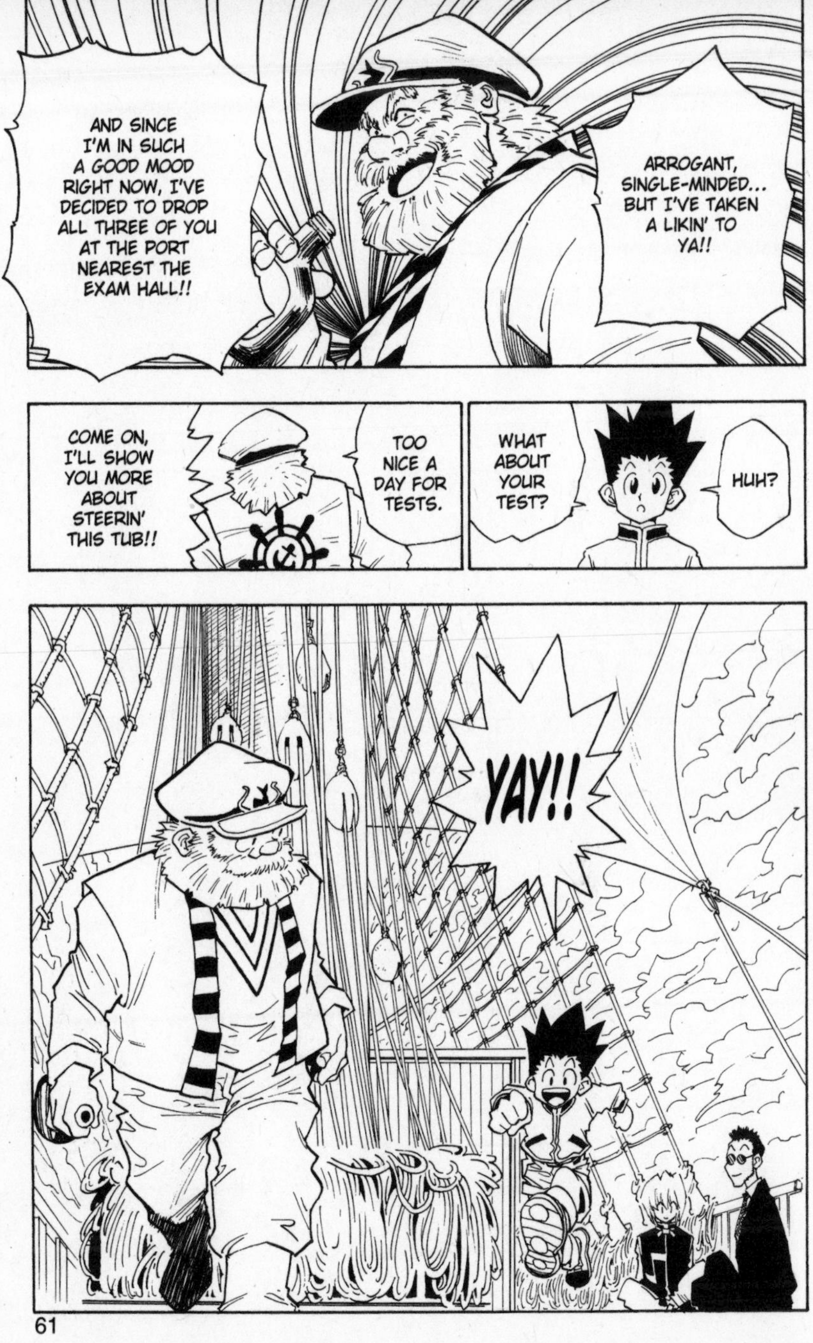
ARROGANT, SINGLE-MINDED... BUT I'VE TAKEN A LIKIN' TO YA!!
AND SINCE I'M IN SUCH A GOOD MOOD RIGHT NOW, I'VE DECIDED TO DROP ALL THREE OF YOU AT THE PORT NEAREST THE EXAM HALL!!
HUH?
WHAT ABOUT YOUR TEST?
TOO NICE A DAY FOR TESTS.
COME ON, I'LL SHOW YOU MORE ABOUT STEERIN' THIS TUB!!
YAY!!

Kurapika

Chapter 3

The Ultimate Choice

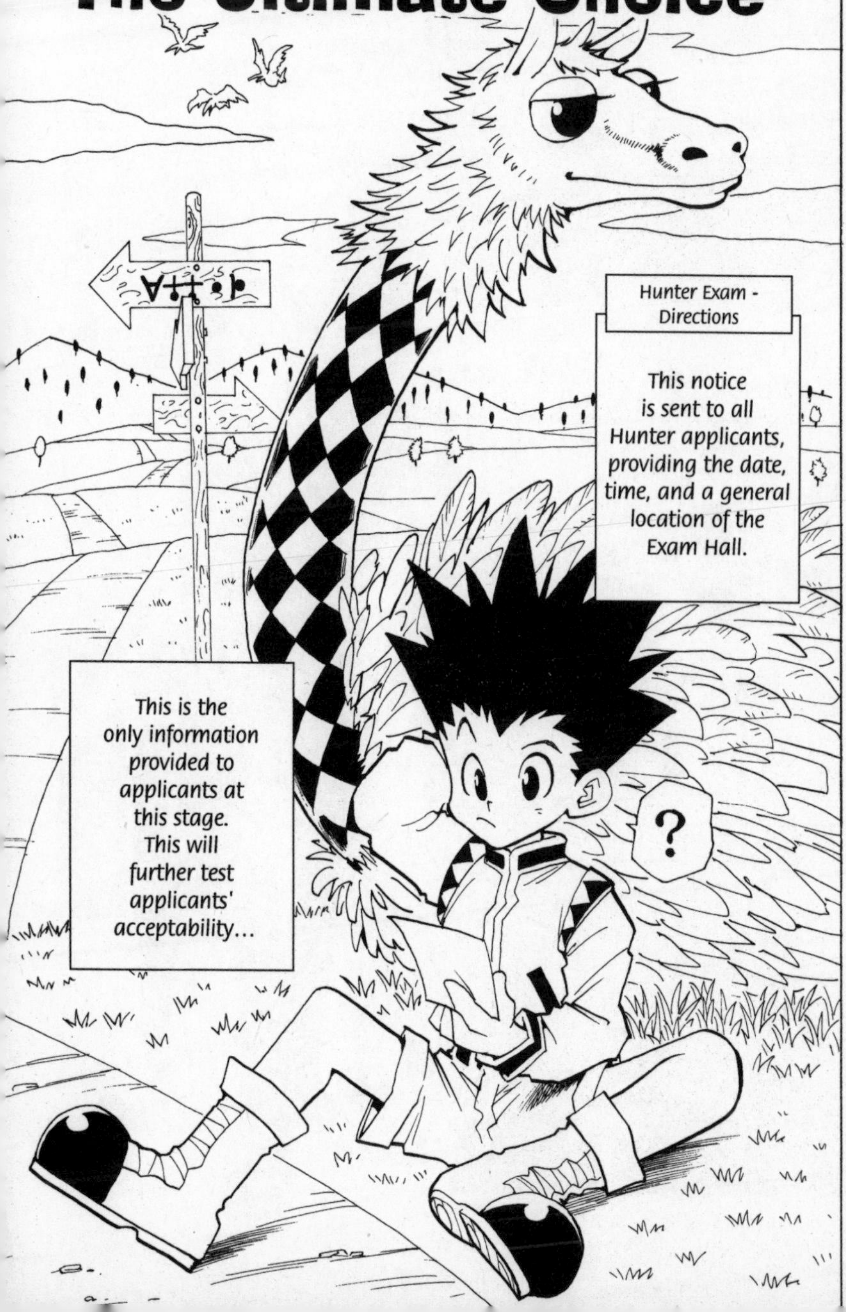

Hunter Exam - Directions
This notice is sent to all Hunter applicants, providing the date, time, and a general location of the Exam Hall.
This is the only information provided to applicants at this stage. This will further test applicants' acceptability...
?

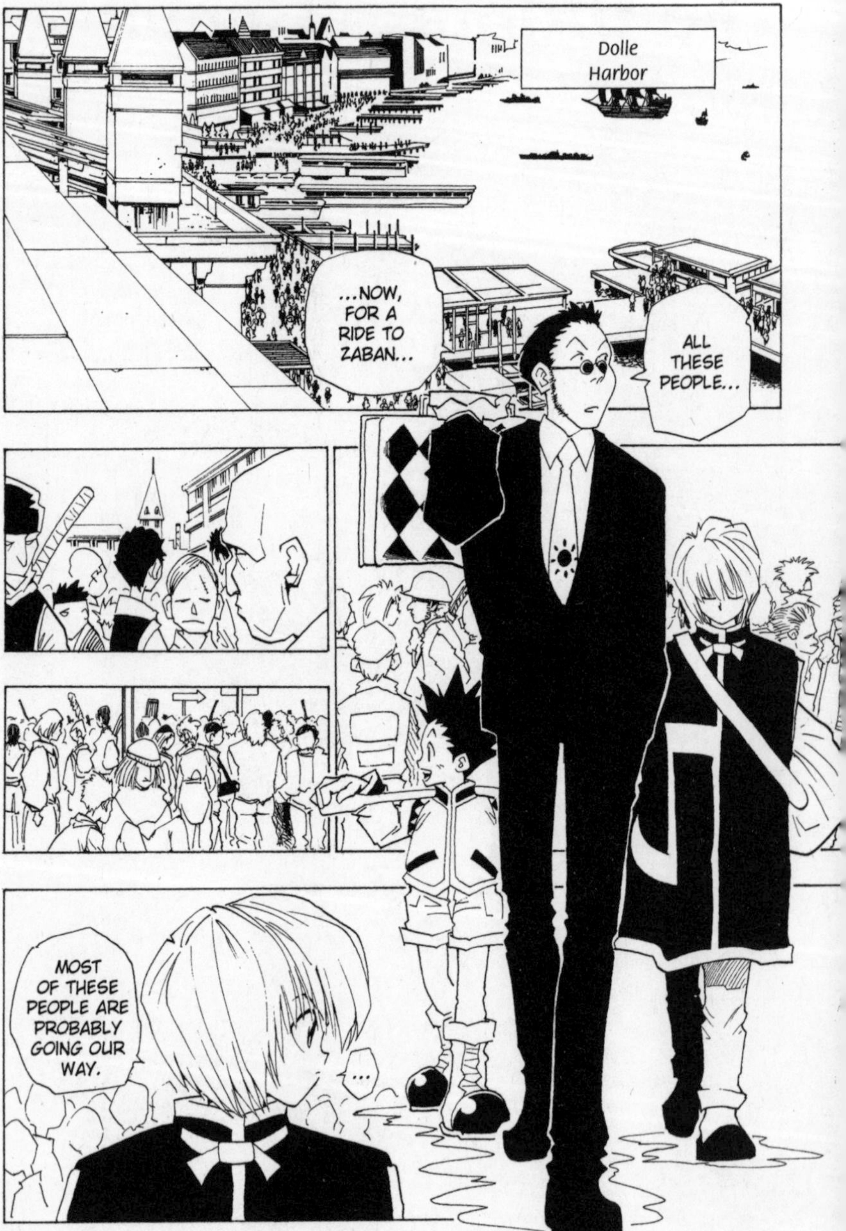
Dolle Harbor
ALL THESE PEOPLE...
...NOW, FOR A RIDE TO ZABAN...
...
MOST OF THESE PEOPLE ARE PROBABLY GOING OUR WAY.

READ THIS WAY

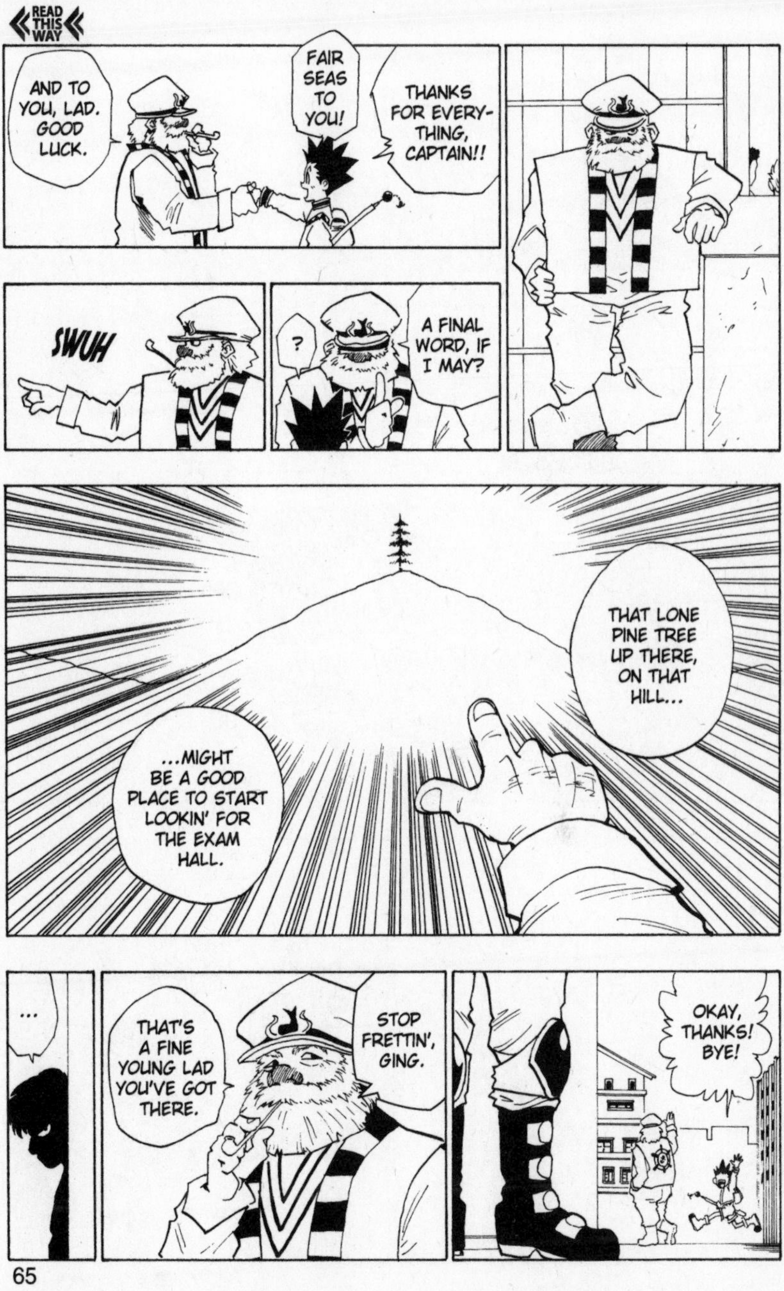
THANKS FOR EVERY-THING, CAPTAIN!!
FAIR SEAS TO YOU!
AND TO YOU, LAD. GOOD LUCK.
A FINAL WORD, IF I MAY?
?
SWUH
THAT LONE PINE TREE UP THERE, ON THAT HILL...
...MIGHT BE A GOOD PLACE TO START LOOKIN' FOR THE EXAM HALL.
OKAY, THANKS! BYE!
STOP FRETTIN', GING.
THAT'S A FINE YOUNG LAD YOU'VE GOT THERE.
...

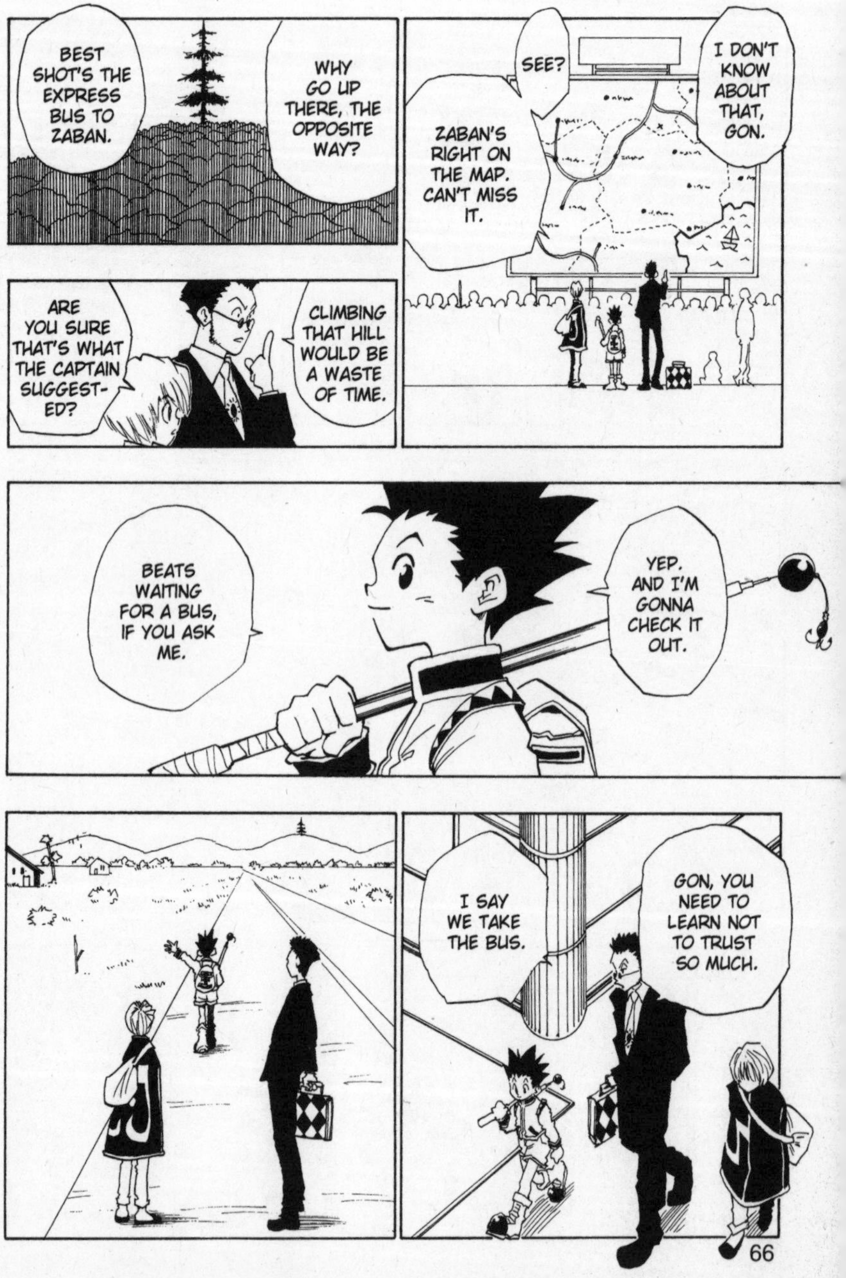
I DON'T KNOW ABOUT THAT, GON.
SEE?
ZABAN'S RIGHT ON THE MAP. CAN'T MISS IT.
WHY GO UP THERE, THE OPPOSITE WAY?
BEST SHOT'S THE EXPRESS BUS TO ZABAN.
CLIMBING THAT HILL WOULD BE A WASTE OF TIME.
ARE YOU SURE THAT'S WHAT THE CAPTAIN SUGGEST-ED?
YEP. AND I'M GONNA CHECK IT OUT.
BEATS WAITING FOR A BUS, IF YOU ASK ME.
GON, YOU NEED TO LEARN NOT TO TRUST SO MUCH.
I SAY WE TAKE THE BUS.

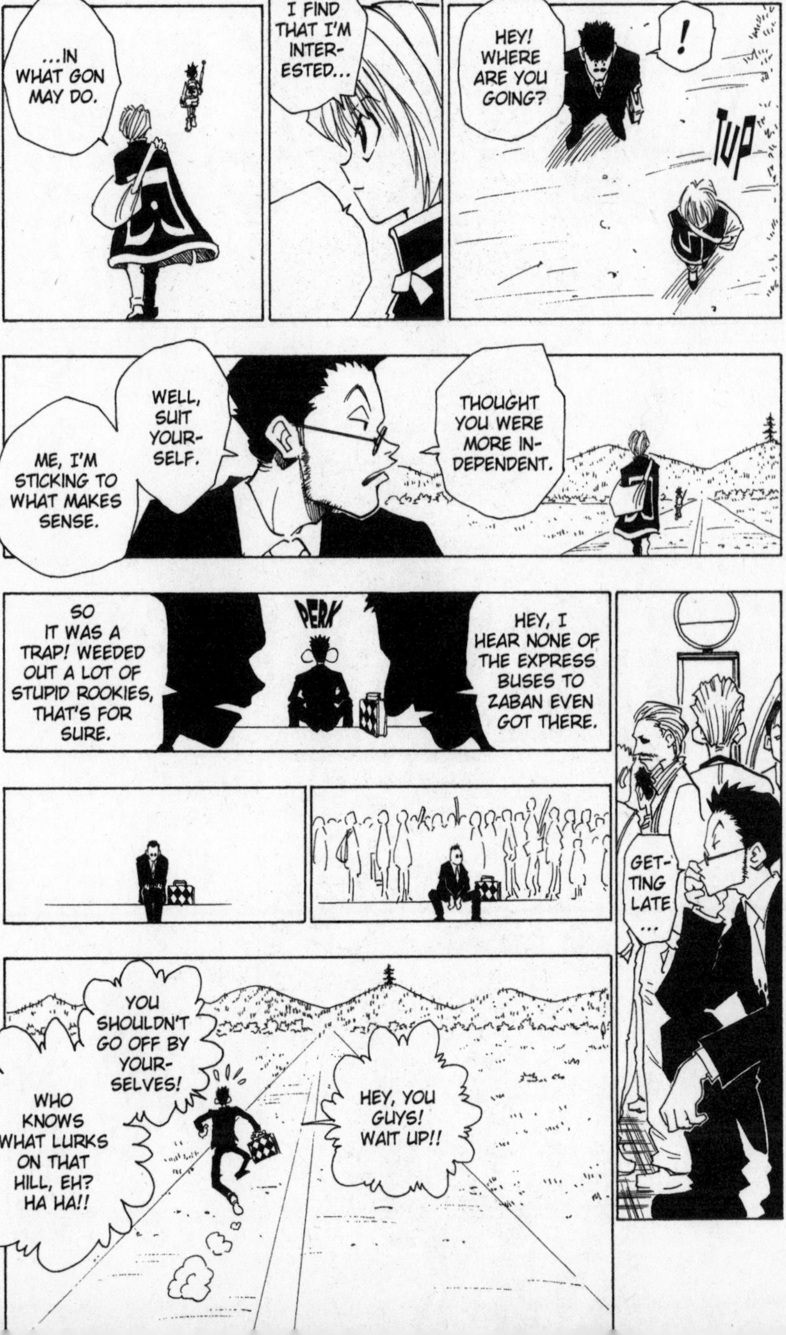
HEY! WHERE ARE YOU GOING?
!
TUP
I FIND THAT I'M INTER-ESTED...
...IN WHAT GON MAY DO.
THOUGHT YOU WERE MORE IN-DEPENDENT.
WELL, SUIT YOUR-SELF.
ME, I'M STICKING TO WHAT MAKES SENSE.
GET-TING LATE ...
HEY, I HEAR NONE OF THE EXPRESS BUSES TO ZABAN EVEN GOT THERE.
PERK
SO IT WAS A TRAP! WEEDED OUT A LOT OF STUPID ROOKIES, THAT'S FOR SURE.
HEY, YOU GUYS! WAIT UP!!
YOU SHOULDN'T GO OFF BY YOUR-SELVES!
WHO KNOWS WHAT LURKS ON THAT HILL, EH? HA HA!!

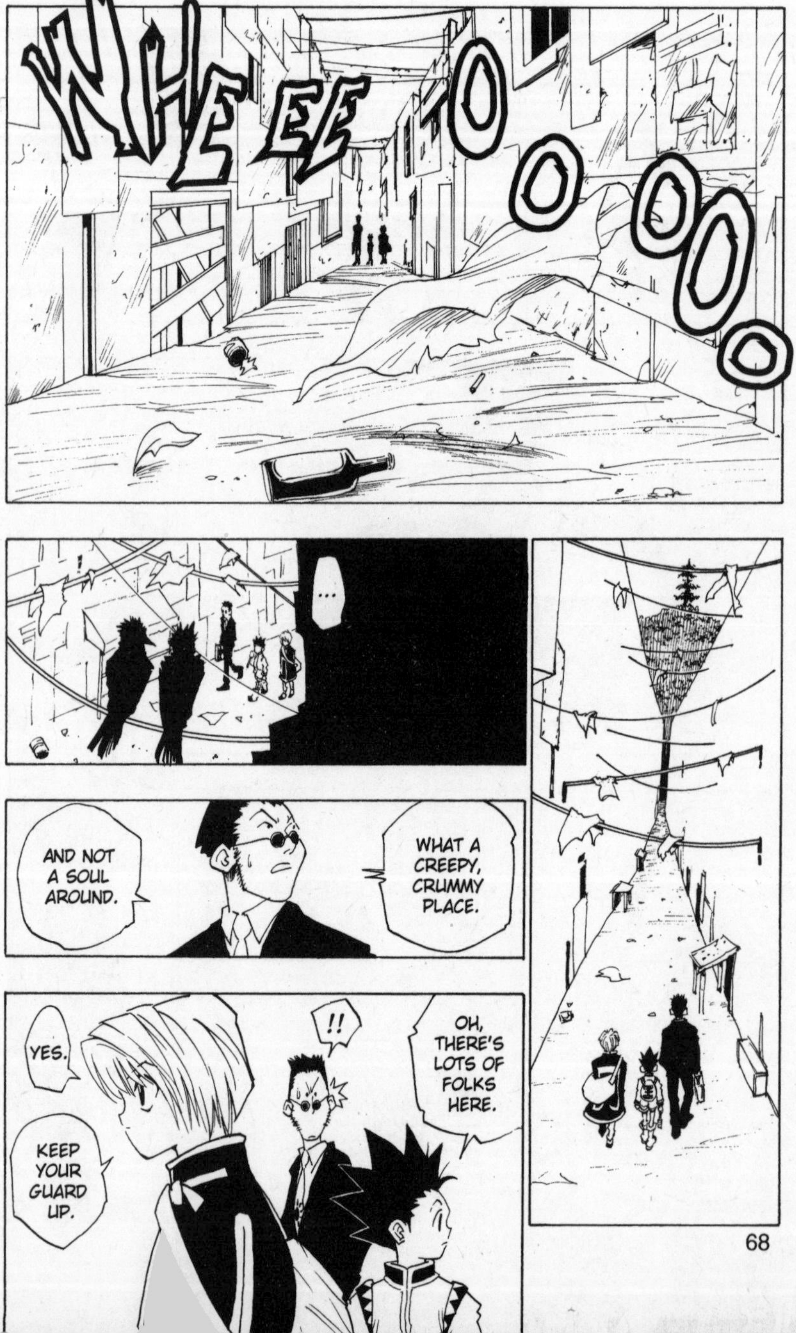
WHEEOOOOO
...
WHAT A CREEPY, CRUMMY PLACE.
AND NOT A SOUL AROUND.
OH, THERE'S LOTS OF FOLKS HERE.
!!
YES.
KEEP YOUR GUARD UP.

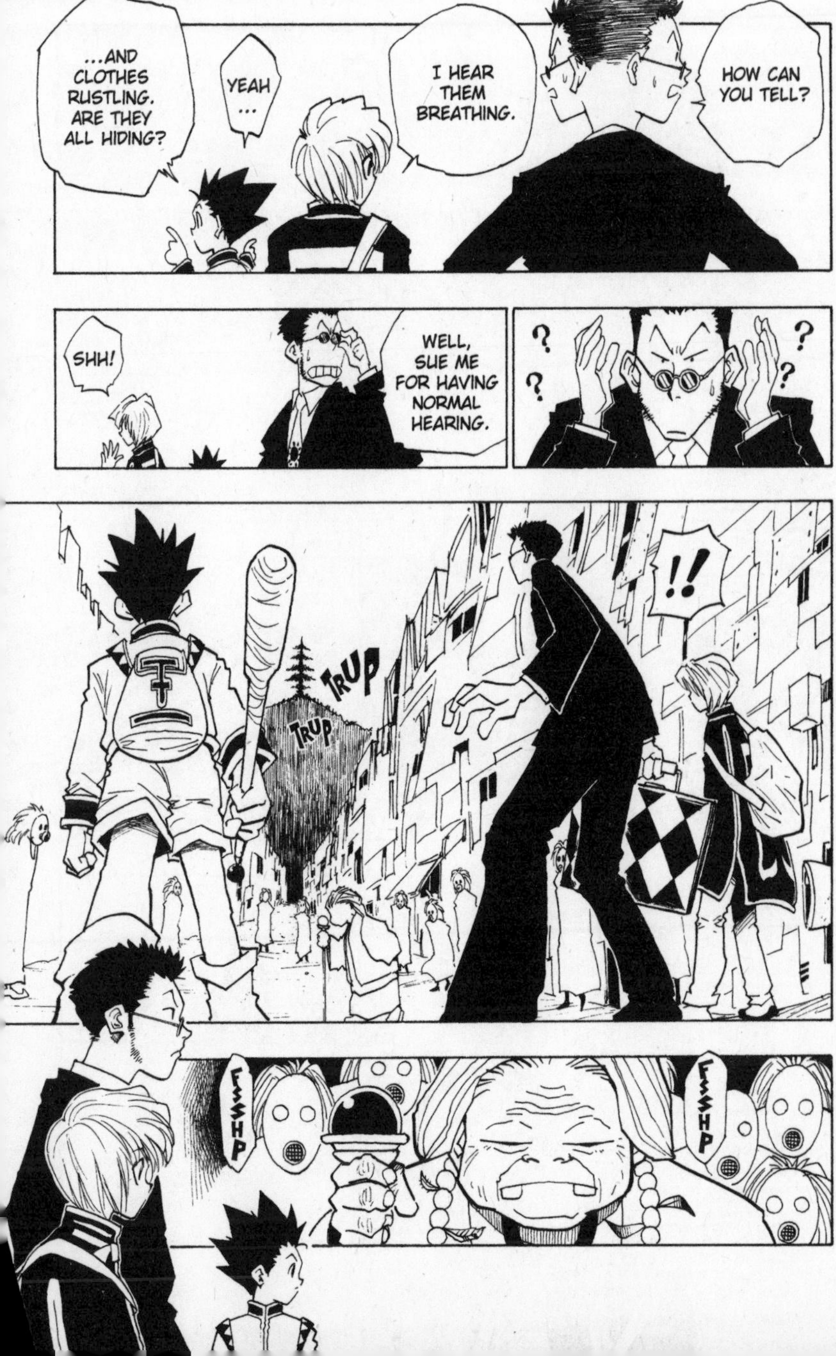
HOW CAN YOU TELL?
I HEAR THEM BREATHING.
YEAH ...
...AND CLOTHES RUSTLING. ARE THEY ALL HIDING?
? ? ? ?
WELL, SUE ME FOR HAVING NORMAL HEARING.
SHH!
!!
TRUP
TRUP
FSSHP
FSSHP

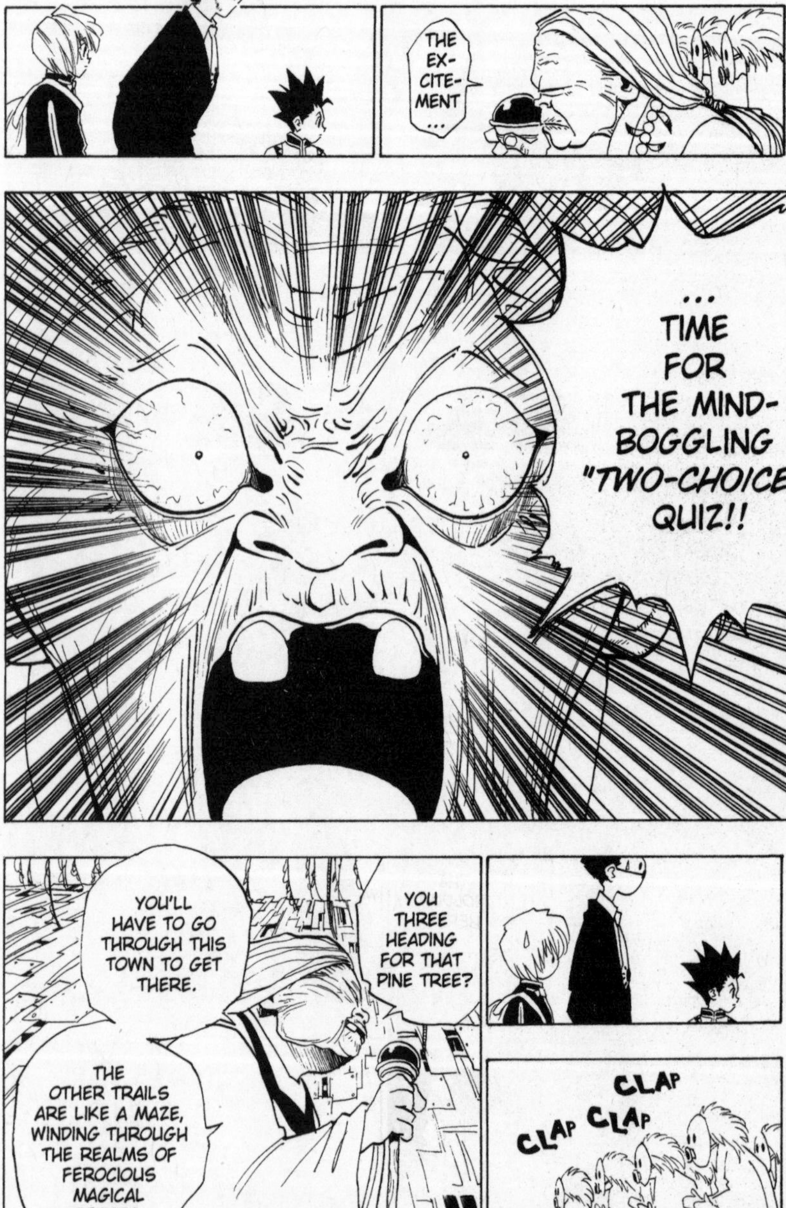
THE EX-CITEMENT...
...TIME FOR THE MIND-BOGGLING "TWO-CHOICE" QUIZ!!
CLAP CLAP CLAP
YOU THREE HEADING FOR THAT PINE TREE?
YOU'LL HAVE TO GO THROUGH THIS TOWN TO GET THERE.
THE OTHER TRAILS ARE LIKE A MAZE, WINDING THROUGH THE REALMS OF FEROCIOUS MAGICAL BEASTS.

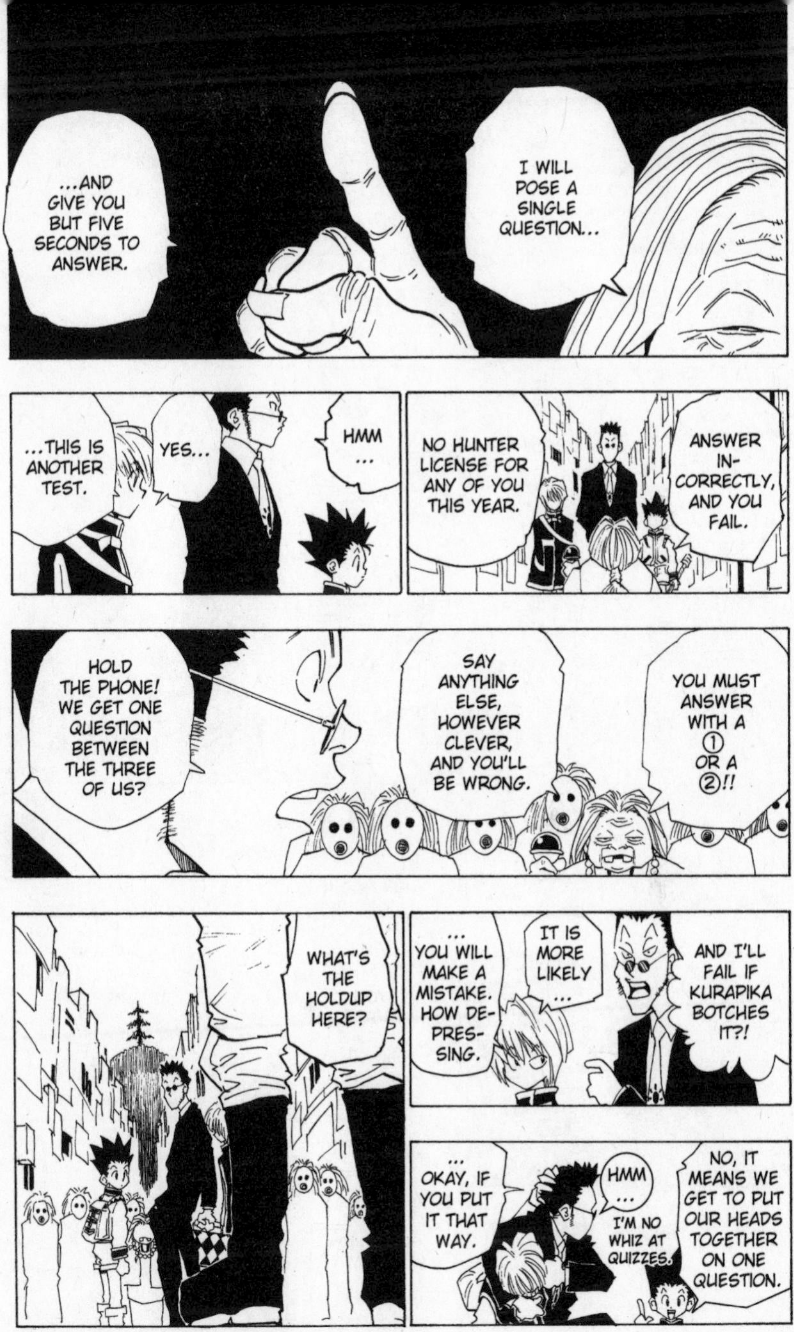
I WILL POSE A SINGLE QUESTION...
...AND GIVE YOU BUT FIVE SECONDS TO ANSWER.
ANSWER IN-CORRECTLY, AND YOU FAIL.
NO HUNTER LICENSE FOR ANY OF YOU THIS YEAR.
HMM ...
YES...
...THIS IS ANOTHER TEST.
YOU MUST ANSWER WITH A ① OR A ②!!
SAY ANYTHING ELSE, HOWEVER CLEVER, AND YOU'LL BE WRONG.
HOLD THE PHONE! WE GET ONE QUESTION BETWEEN THE THREE OF US?
AND I'LL FAIL IF KURAPIKA BOTCHES IT?!
IT IS MORE LIKELY ...
... YOU WILL MAKE A MISTAKE. HOW DEPRESSING.
NO, IT MEANS WE GET TO PUT OUR HEADS TOGETHER ON ONE QUESTION.
HMM ...
I'M NO WHIZ AT QUIZZES.
... OKAY, IF YOU PUT IT THAT WAY.
WHAT'S THE HOLDUP HERE?

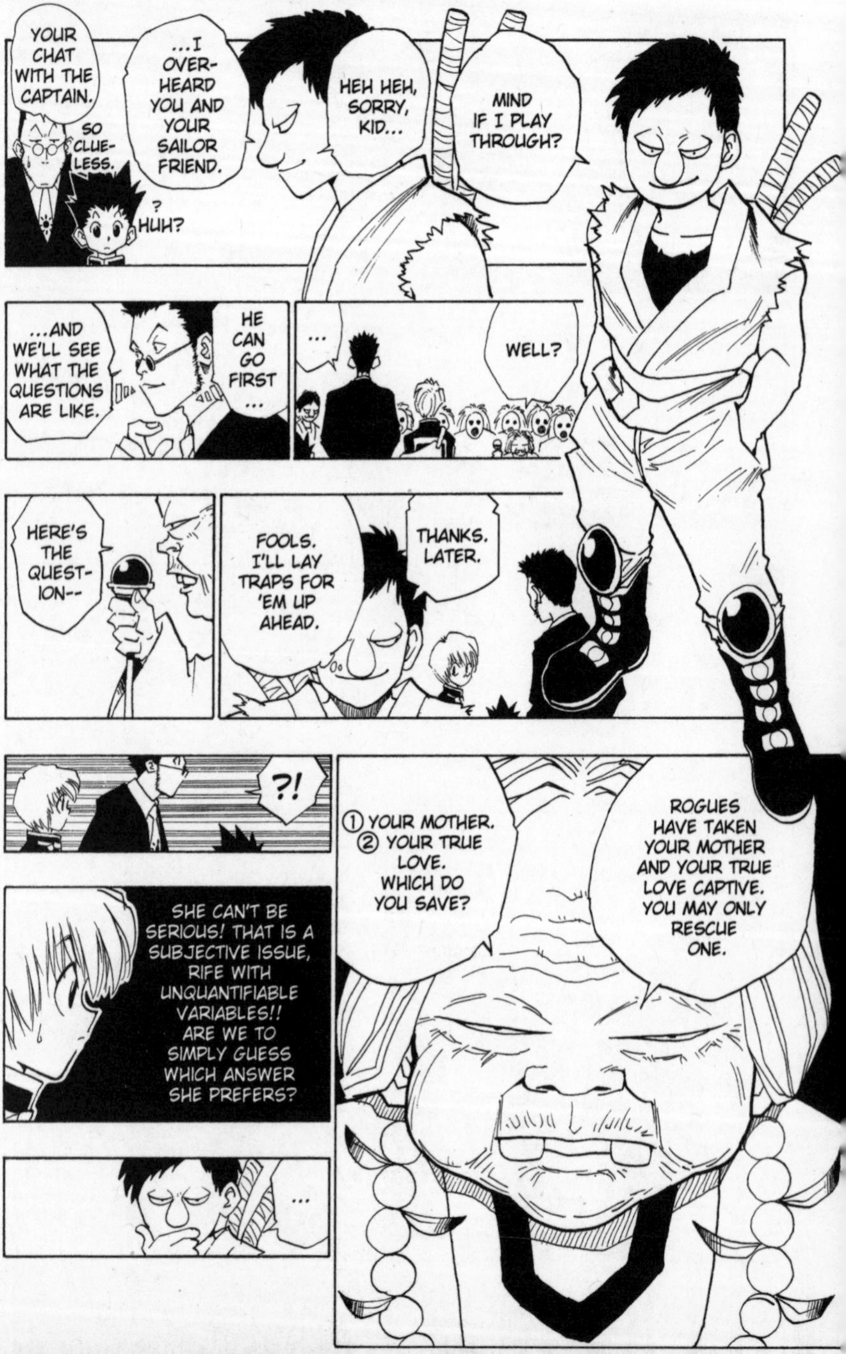
MIND IF I PLAY THROUGH?
HEH HEH, SORRY, KID...
...I OVERHEARD YOU AND YOUR SAILOR FRIEND.
YOUR CHAT WITH THE CAPTAIN.
SO CLUELESS.
? HUH?
WELL?
...
HE CAN GO FIRST ...
...AND WE'LL SEE WHAT THE QUESTIONS ARE LIKE.
THANKS. LATER.
FOOLS. I'LL LAY TRAPS FOR 'EM UP AHEAD.
HERE'S THE QUESTION--
ROGUES HAVE TAKEN YOUR MOTHER AND YOUR TRUE LOVE CAPTIVE. YOU MAY ONLY RESCUE ONE.
① YOUR MOTHER. ② YOUR TRUE LOVE. WHICH DO YOU SAVE?
?!
SHE CAN'T BE SERIOUS! THAT IS A SUBJECTIVE ISSUE, RIFE WITH UNQUANTIFIABLE VARIABLES!! ARE WE TO SIMPLY GUESS WHICH ANSWER SHE PREFERS?
...

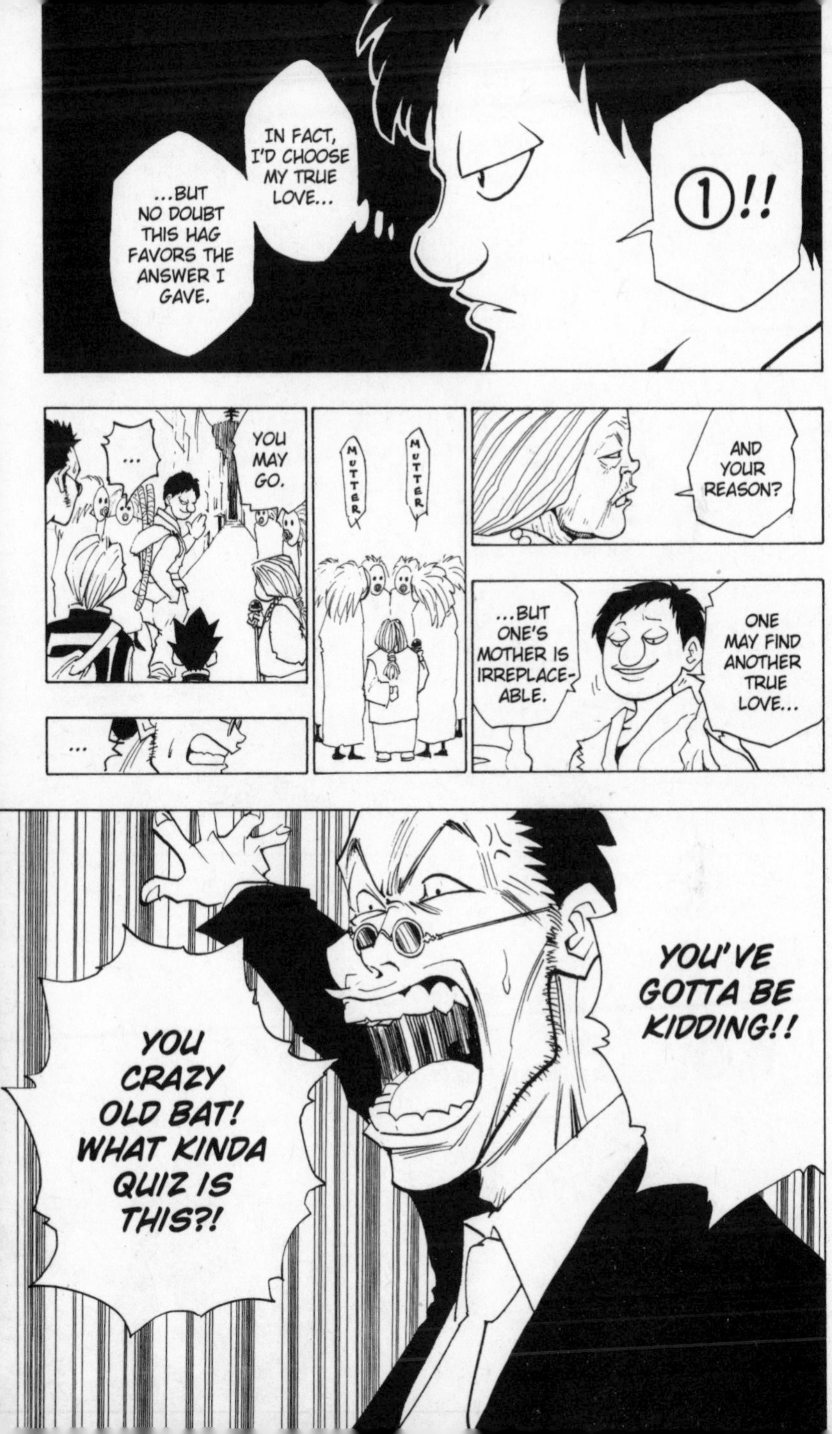
①!!
IN FACT, I'D CHOOSE MY TRUE LOVE...
...BUT NO DOUBT THIS HAG FAVORS THE ANSWER I GAVE.
AND YOUR REASON?
ONE MAY FIND ANOTHER TRUE LOVE...
...BUT ONE'S MOTHER IS IRREPLACE-ABLE.
MUTTER
MUTTER
YOU MAY GO.
...
...
YOU'VE GOTTA BE KIDDING!!
YOU CRAZY OLD BAT! WHAT KINDA QUIZ IS THIS?!

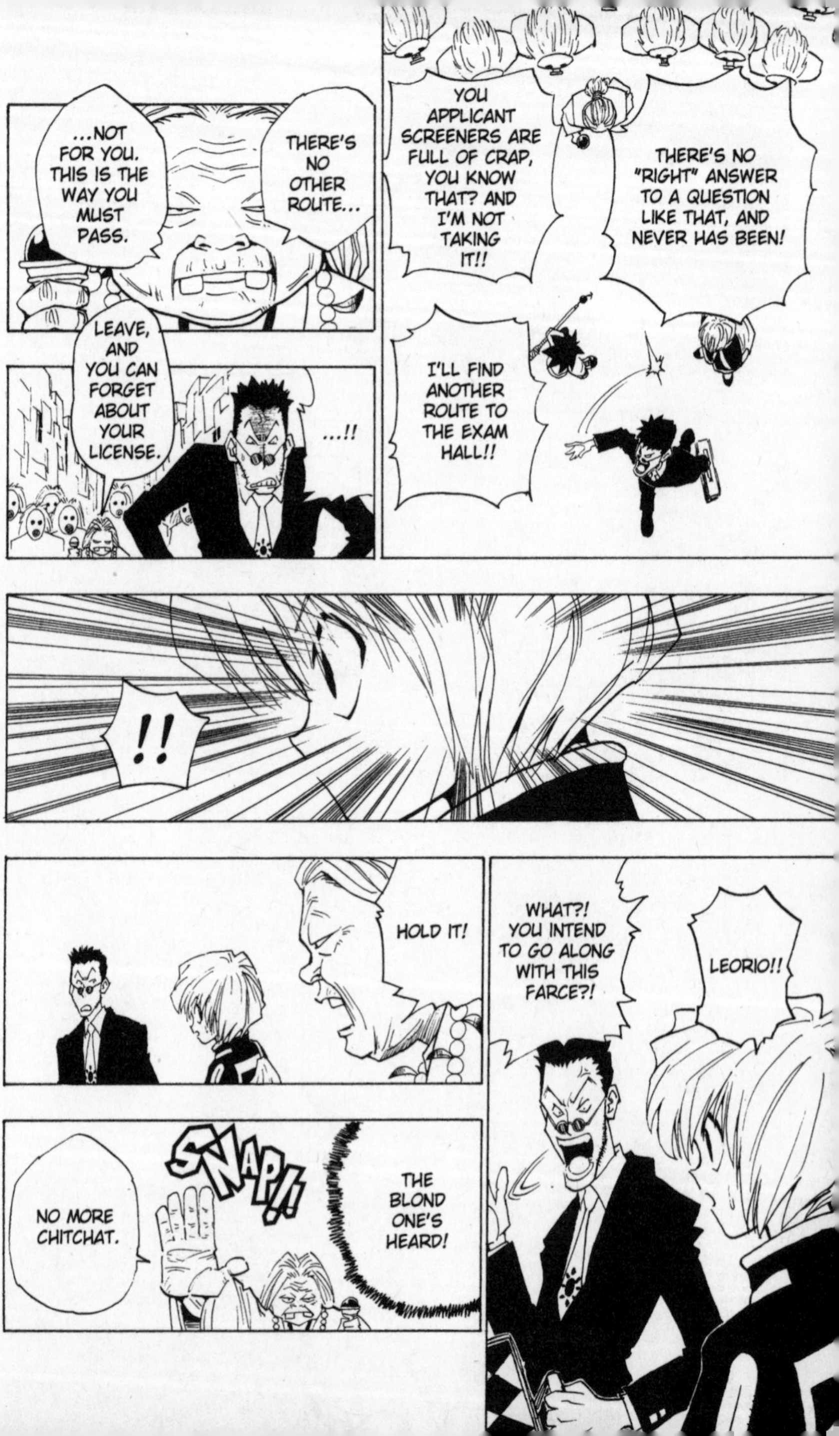
YOU APPLICANT SCREENERS ARE FULL OF CRAP, YOU KNOW THAT? AND I'M NOT TAKING IT!!
THERE'S NO "RIGHT" ANSWER TO A QUESTION LIKE THAT, AND NEVER HAS BEEN!
I'LL FIND ANOTHER ROUTE TO THE EXAM HALL!!
THERE'S NO OTHER ROUTE...
...NOT FOR YOU. THIS IS THE WAY YOU MUST PASS.
...!!
LEAVE, AND YOU CAN FORGET ABOUT YOUR LICENSE.
!!
LEORIO!!
WHAT?! YOU INTEND TO GO ALONG WITH THIS FARCE?!
HOLD IT!
THE BLOND ONE'S HEARD!
SNAP!!
NO MORE CHITCHAT.

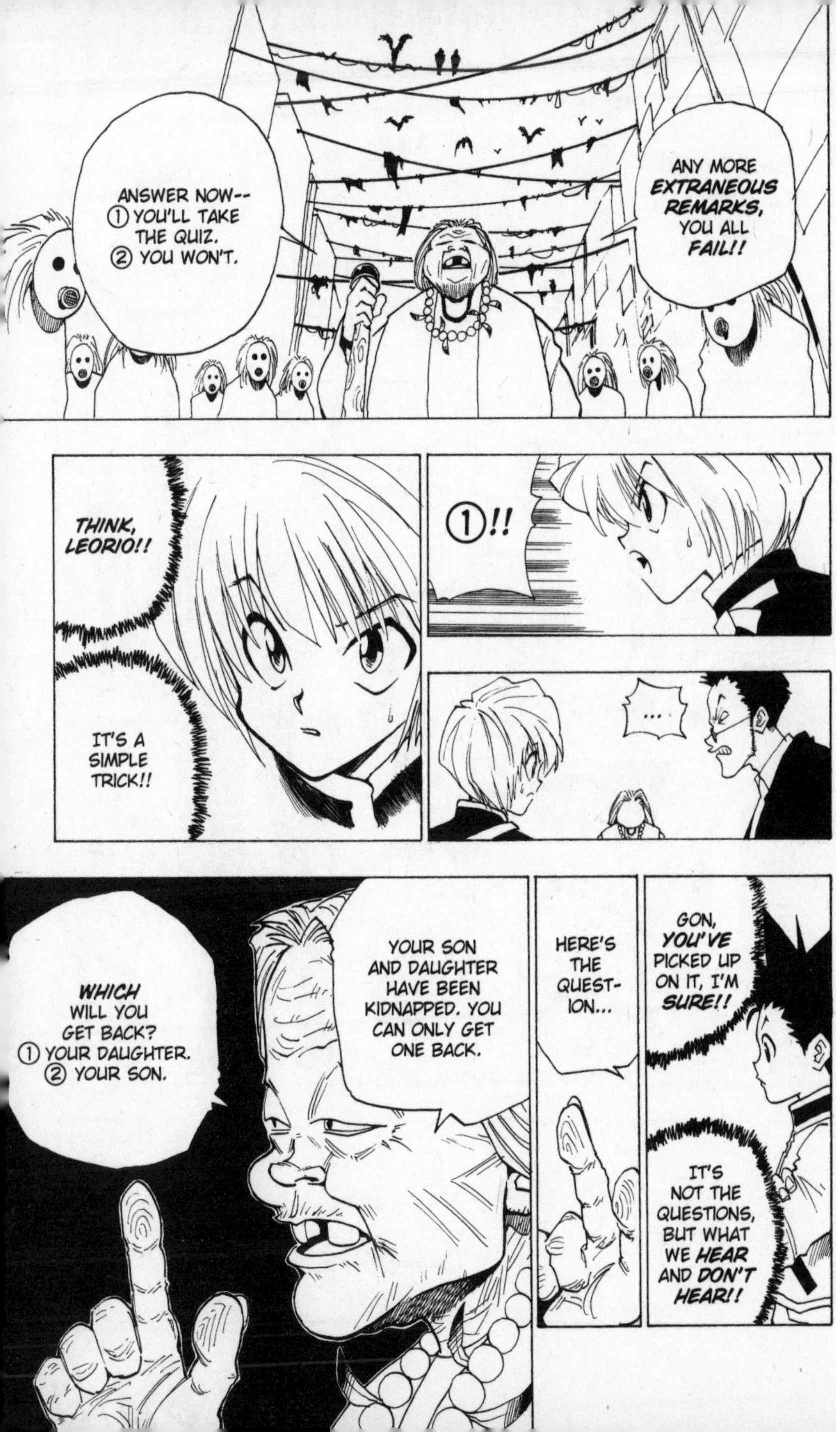
ANY MORE EXTRANEOUS REMARKS, YOU ALL FAIL!!
ANSWER NOW-- ① YOU'LL TAKE THE QUIZ. ② YOU WON'T.
①!!
...
THINK, LEORIO!!
IT'S A SIMPLE TRICK!!
GON, YOU'VE PICKED UP ON IT, I'M SURE!!
IT'S NOT THE QUESTIONS, BUT WHAT WE HEAR AND DON'T HEAR!!
HERE'S THE QUEST-ION...
YOUR SON AND DAUGHTER HAVE BEEN KIDNAPPED. YOU CAN ONLY GET ONE BACK.
WHICH WILL YOU GET BACK? ① YOUR DAUGHTER. ② YOUR SON.

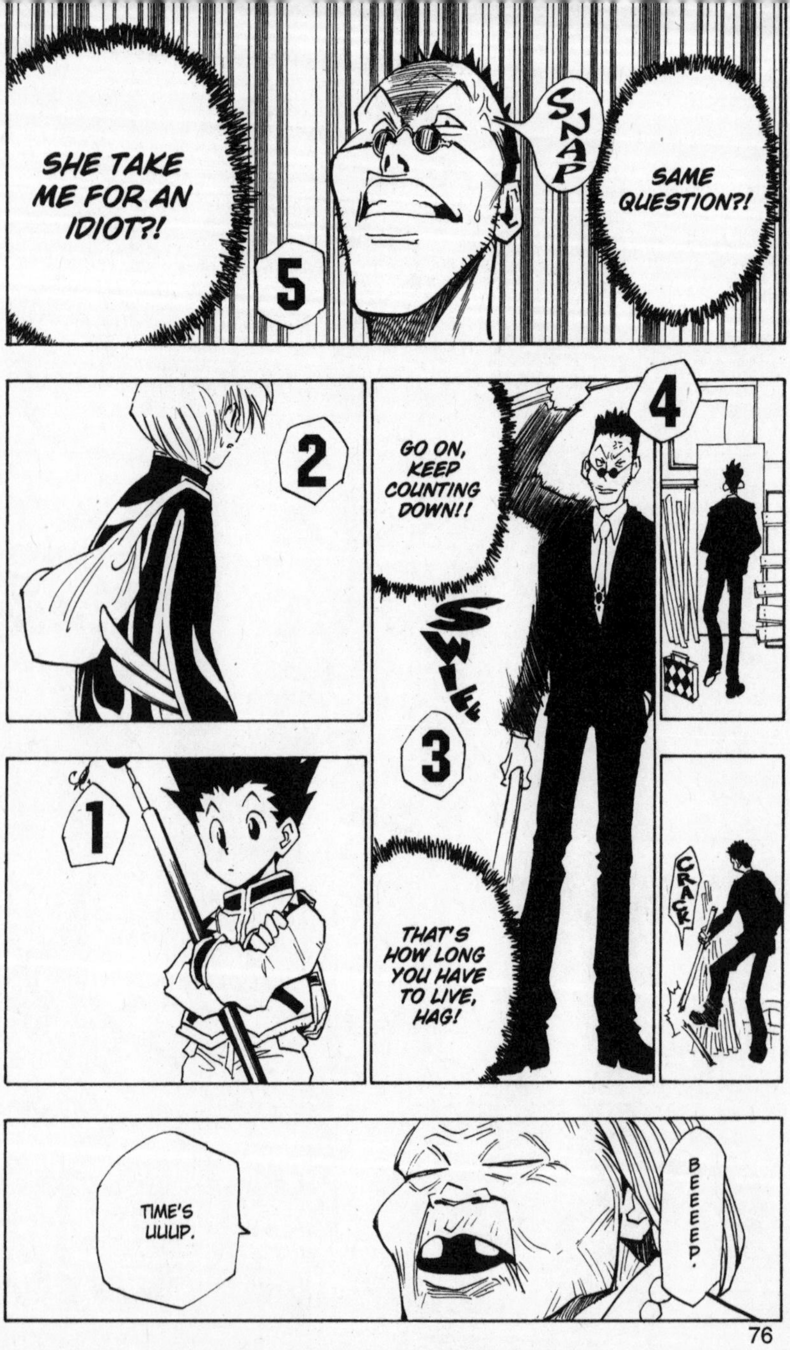
SNAP
SAME QUESTION?!
SHE TAKE ME FOR AN IDIOT?!
5
4
CRACK
GO ON, KEEP COUNTING DOWN!!
SWIFF
3
THAT'S HOW LONG YOU HAVE TO LIVE, HAG!
2
1
BEEEEEP.
TIME'S UUUP.

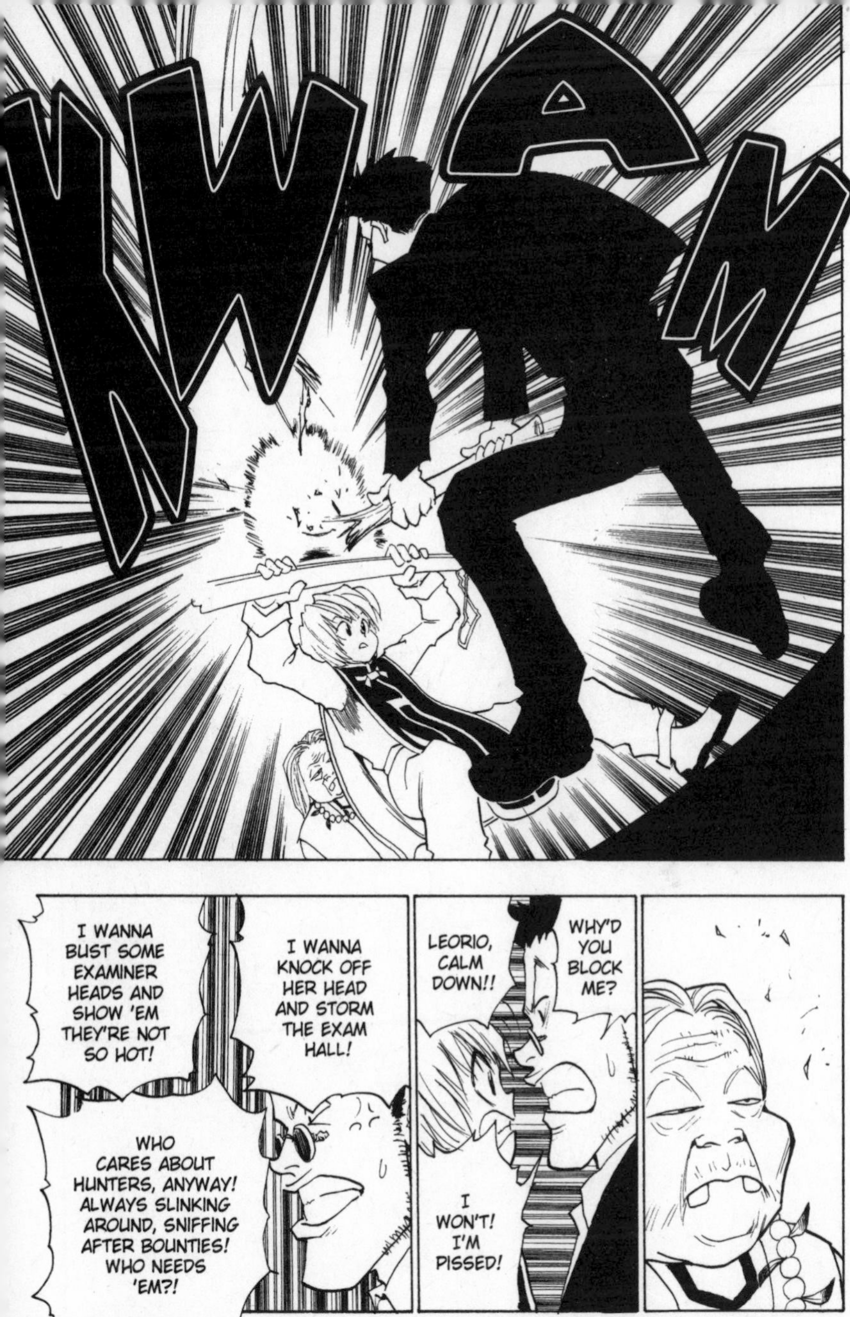
WHY'D YOU BLOCK ME?
LEORIO, CALM DOWN!!
I WON'T! I'M PISSED!
I WANNA KNOCK OFF HER HEAD AND STORM THE EXAM HALL!
I WANNA BUST SOME EXAMINER HEADS AND SHOW 'EM THEY'RE NOT SO HOT!
WHO CARES ABOUT HUNTERS, ANYWAY! ALWAYS SLINKING AROUND, SNIFFING AFTER BOUNTIES! WHO NEEDS 'EM?!

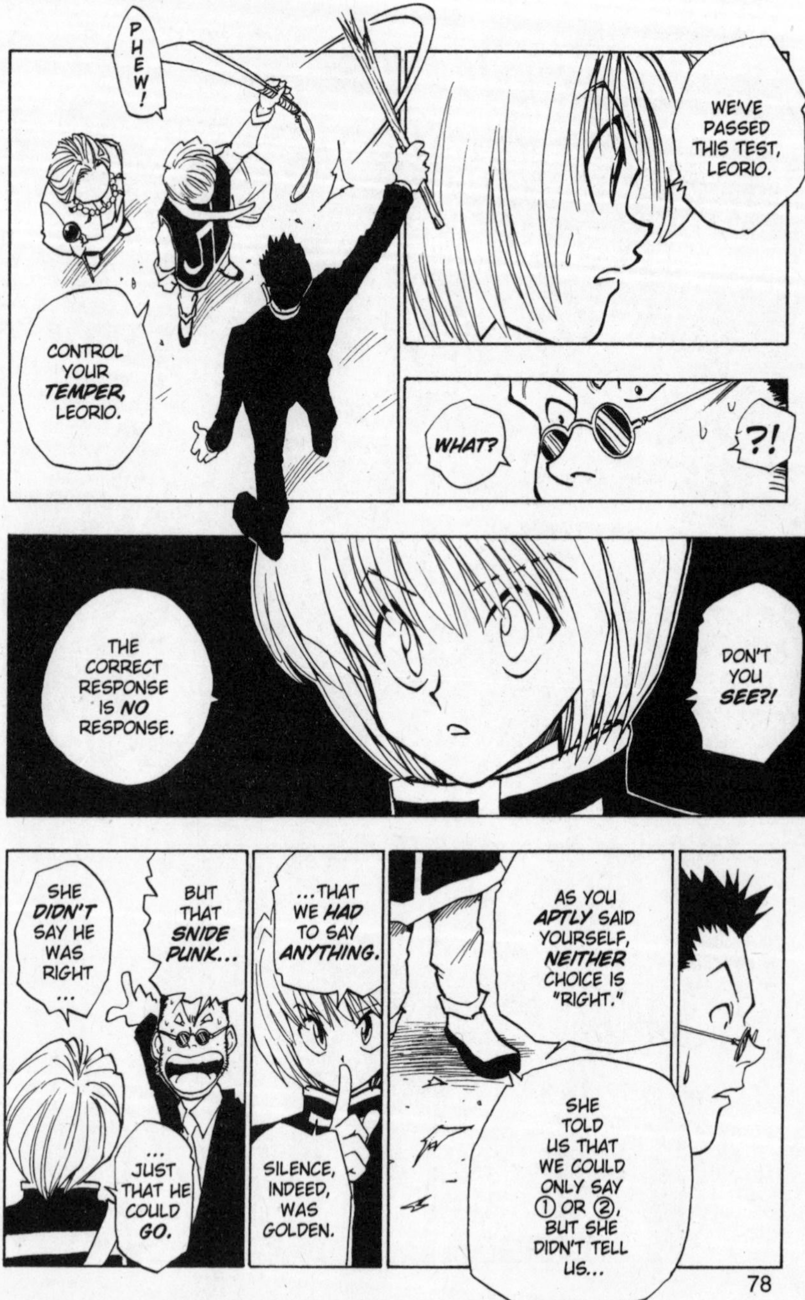
WE'VE PASSED THIS TEST, LEORIO.
?!
WHAT?
PHEW!
CONTROL YOUR TEMPER, LEORIO.
DON'T YOU SEE?!
THE CORRECT RESPONSE IS NO RESPONSE.
AS YOU APTLY SAID YOURSELF, NEITHER CHOICE IS "RIGHT."
SHE TOLD US THAT WE COULD ONLY SAY ① OR ②, BUT SHE DIDN'T TELL US...
...THAT WE HAD TO SAY ANYTHING.
SILENCE, INDEED, WAS GOLDEN.
BUT THAT SNIDE PUNK...
SHE DIDN'T SAY HE WAS RIGHT ...
... JUST THAT HE COULD GO.

READ THIS WAY

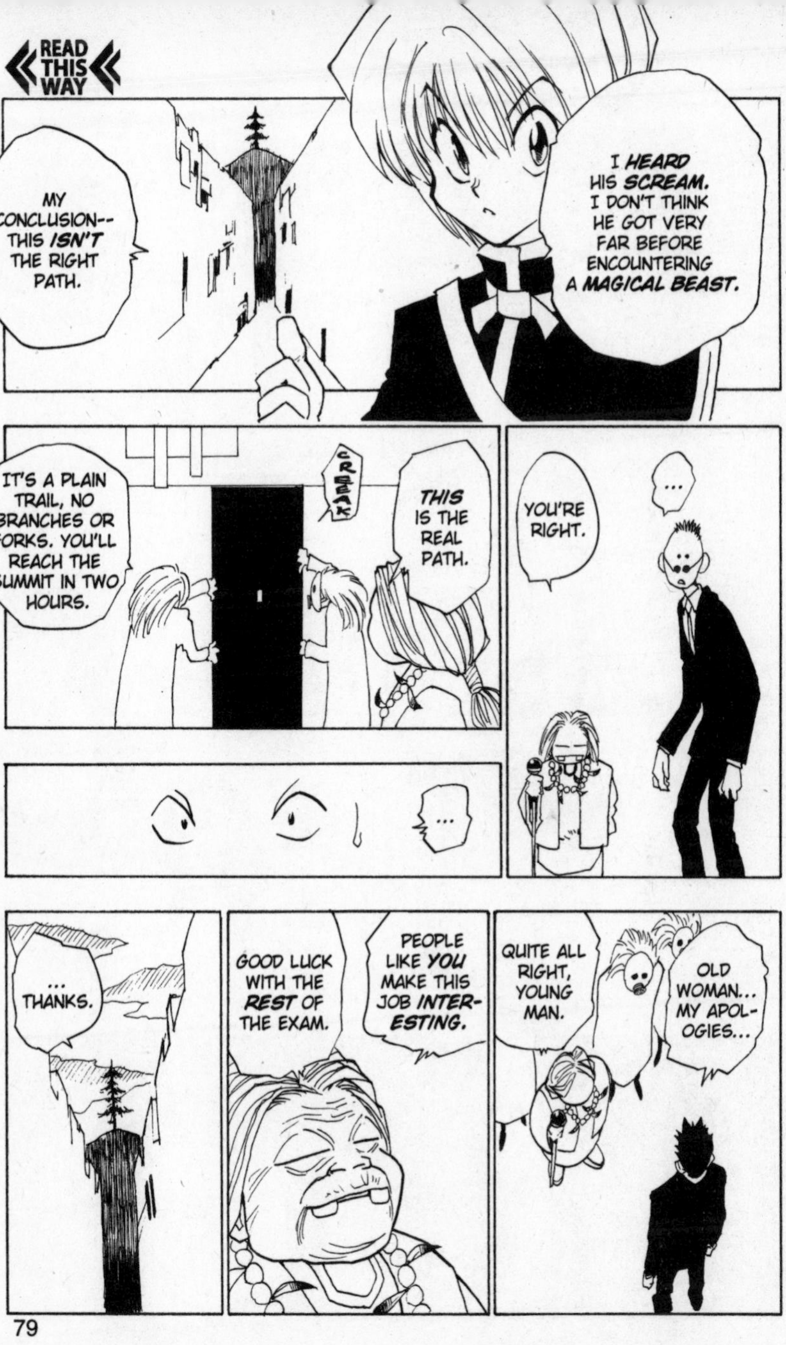
I HEARD HIS SCREAM. I DON'T THINK HE GOT VERY FAR BEFORE ENCOUNTERING A MAGICAL BEAST.
MY CONCLUSION-- THIS ISN'T THE RIGHT PATH.
...
YOU'RE RIGHT.
THIS IS THE REAL PATH.
CREAK
IT'S A PLAIN TRAIL, NO BRANCHES OR FORKS. YOU'LL REACH THE SUMMIT IN TWO HOURS.
...
OLD WOMAN... MY APOLOGIES...
QUITE ALL RIGHT, YOUNG MAN.
PEOPLE LIKE YOU MAKE THIS JOB INTERESTING.
GOOD LUCK WITH THE REST OF THE EXAM.
... THANKS.

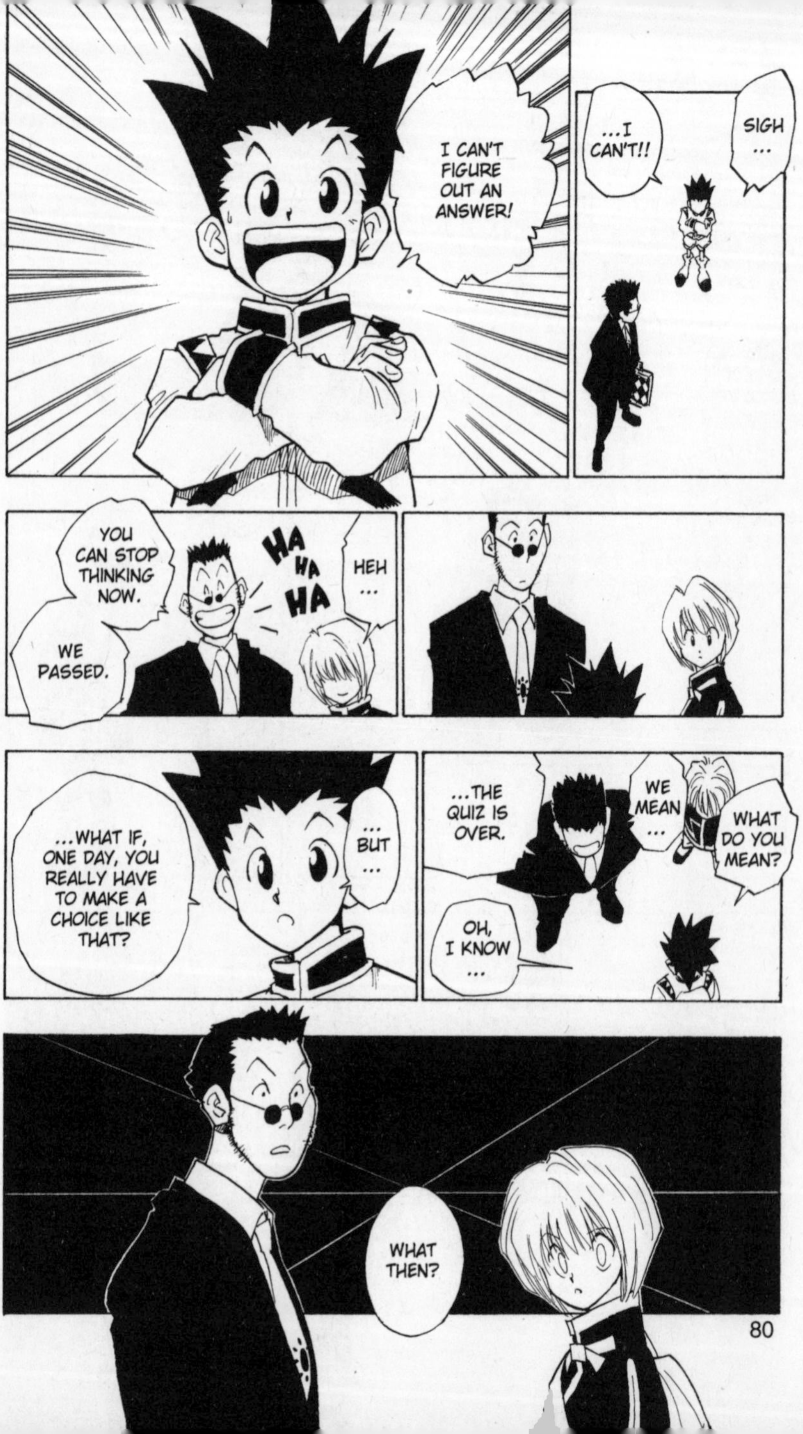
SIGH ...
...I CAN'T!!
I CAN'T FIGURE OUT AN ANSWER!
HEH ...
HA HA HA
YOU CAN STOP THINKING NOW.
WE PASSED.
WHAT DO YOU MEAN?
WE MEAN ...
...THE QUIZ IS OVER.
OH, I KNOW ...
... BUT ...
...WHAT IF, ONE DAY, YOU REALLY HAVE TO MAKE A CHOICE LIKE THAT?
WHAT THEN?

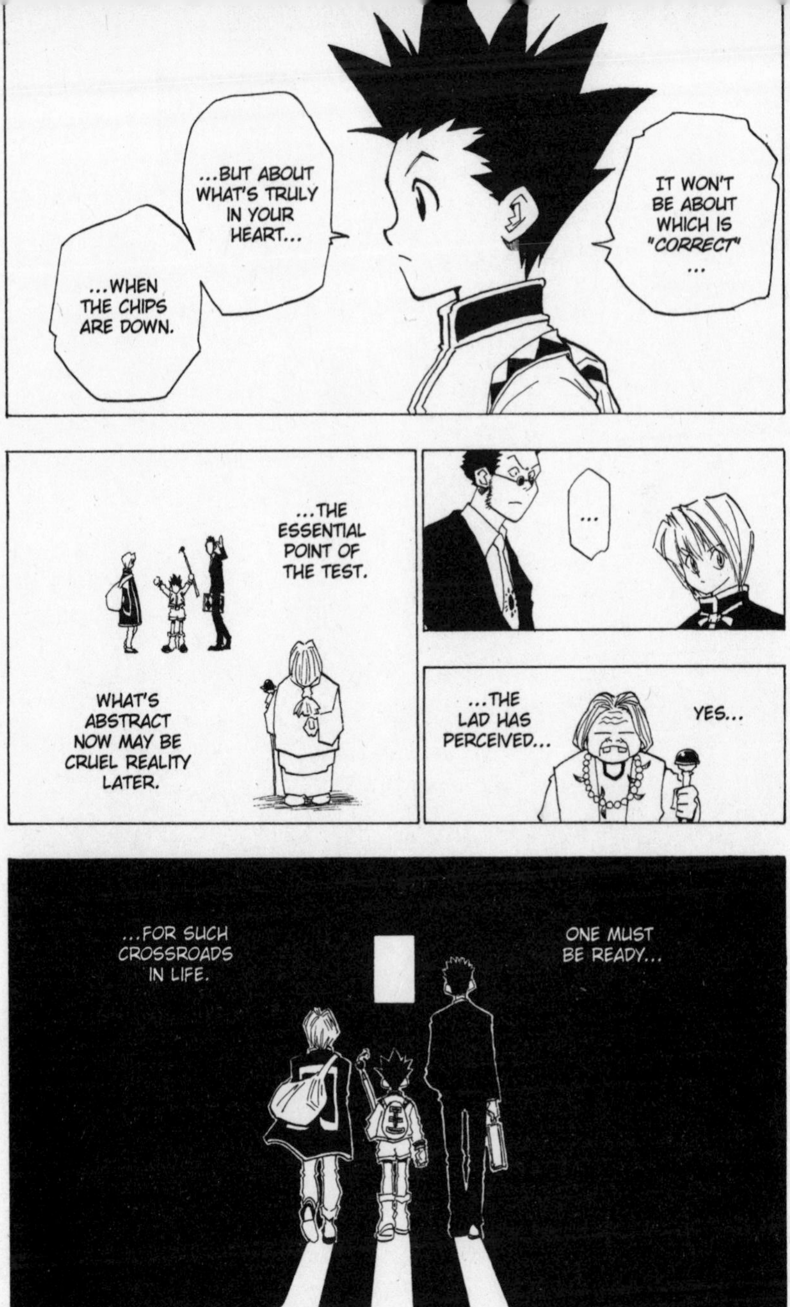
IT WON'T BE ABOUT WHICH IS "CORRECT" ...
...BUT ABOUT WHAT'S TRULY IN YOUR HEART...
...WHEN THE CHIPS ARE DOWN.
...
YES...
...THE LAD HAS PERCEIVED...
...THE ESSENTIAL POINT OF THE TEST.
WHAT'S ABSTRACT NOW MAY BE CRUEL REALITY LATER.
ONE MUST BE READY...
...FOR SUCH CROSSROADS IN LIFE.

Leorio

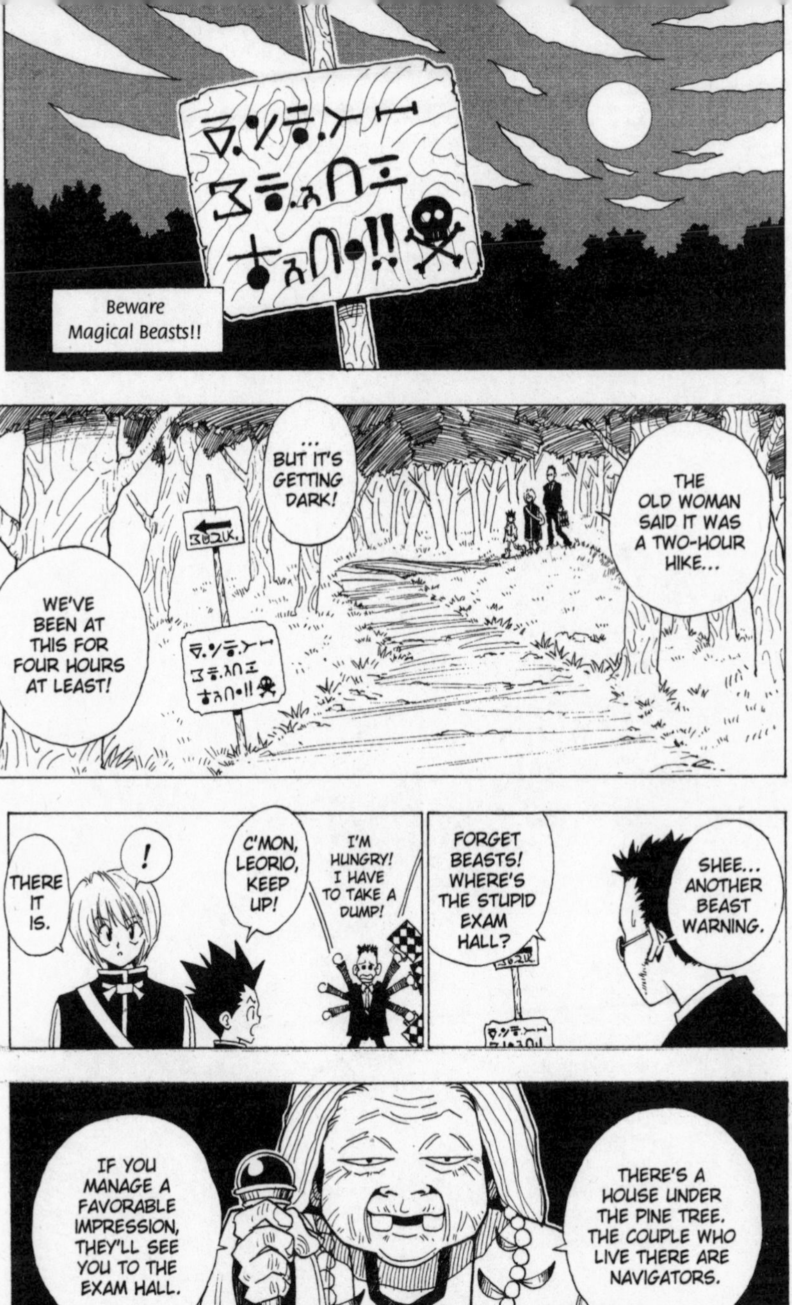
Beware Magical Beasts!!
THE OLD WOMAN SAID IT WAS A TWO-HOUR HIKE...
... BUT IT'S GETTING DARK!
WE'VE BEEN AT THIS FOR FOUR HOURS AT LEAST!
SHEE... ANOTHER BEAST WARNING.
FORGET BEASTS! WHERE'S THE STUPID EXAM HALL?
I'M HUNGRY! I HAVE TO TAKE A DUMP!
C'MON, LEORIO, KEEP UP!
!
THERE IT IS.
THERE'S A HOUSE UNDER THE PINE TREE. THE COUPLE WHO LIVE THERE ARE NAVIGATORS.
IF YOU MANAGE A FAVORABLE IMPRESSION, THEY'LL SEE YOU TO THE EXAM HALL.

Chapter 4
Kiriko: Wicked Magical Vulpes

Chapter 4
Kiriko: Wicked Magical Vulpes

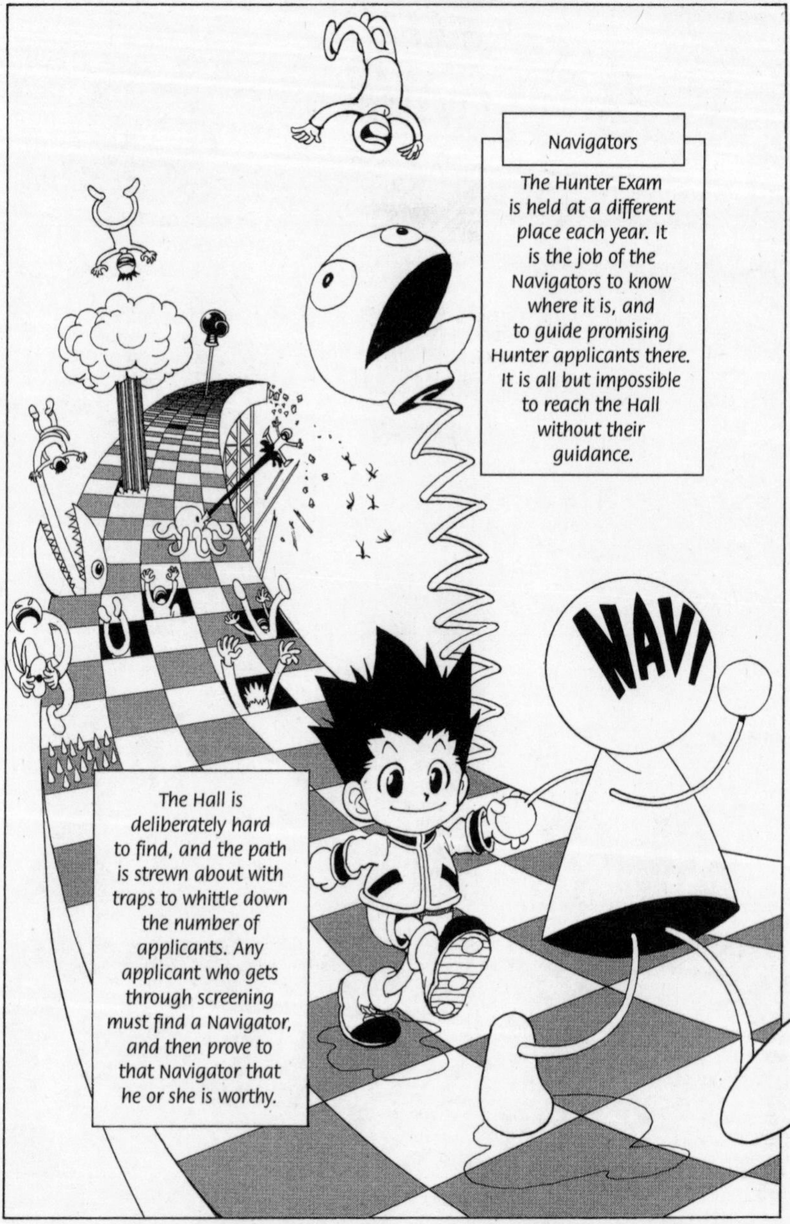
Navigators
The Hunter Exam is held at a different place each year. It is the job of the Navigators to know where it is, and to guide promising Hunter applicants there. It is all but impossible to reach the Hall without their guidance.
NAVI
The Hall is deliberately hard to find, and the path is strewn about with traps to whittle down the number of applicants. Any applicant who gets through screening must find a Navigator, and then prove to that Navigator that he or she is worthy.

READ THIS WAY

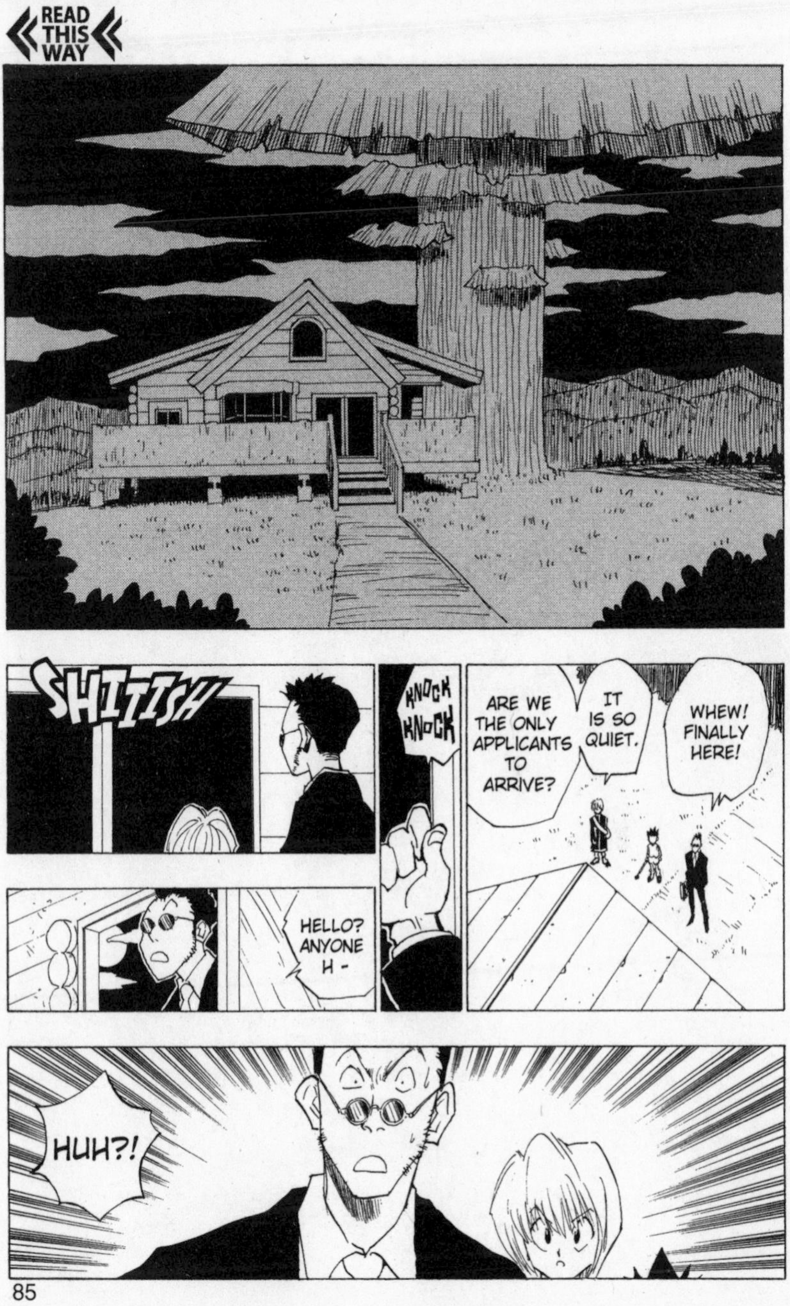
WHEW! FINALLY HERE!
IT IS SO QUIET.
ARE WE THE ONLY APPLICANTS TO ARRIVE?
KNOCK KNOCK
SHIIISH
HELLO? ANYONE H -
HUH?!

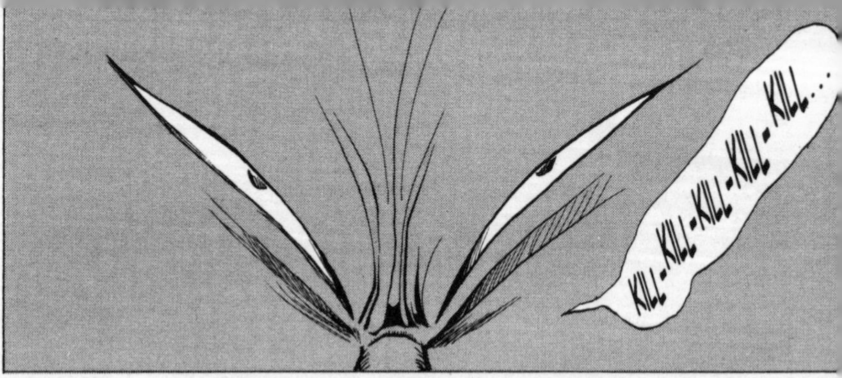
KILL-KILL-KILL-KILL-KILL...
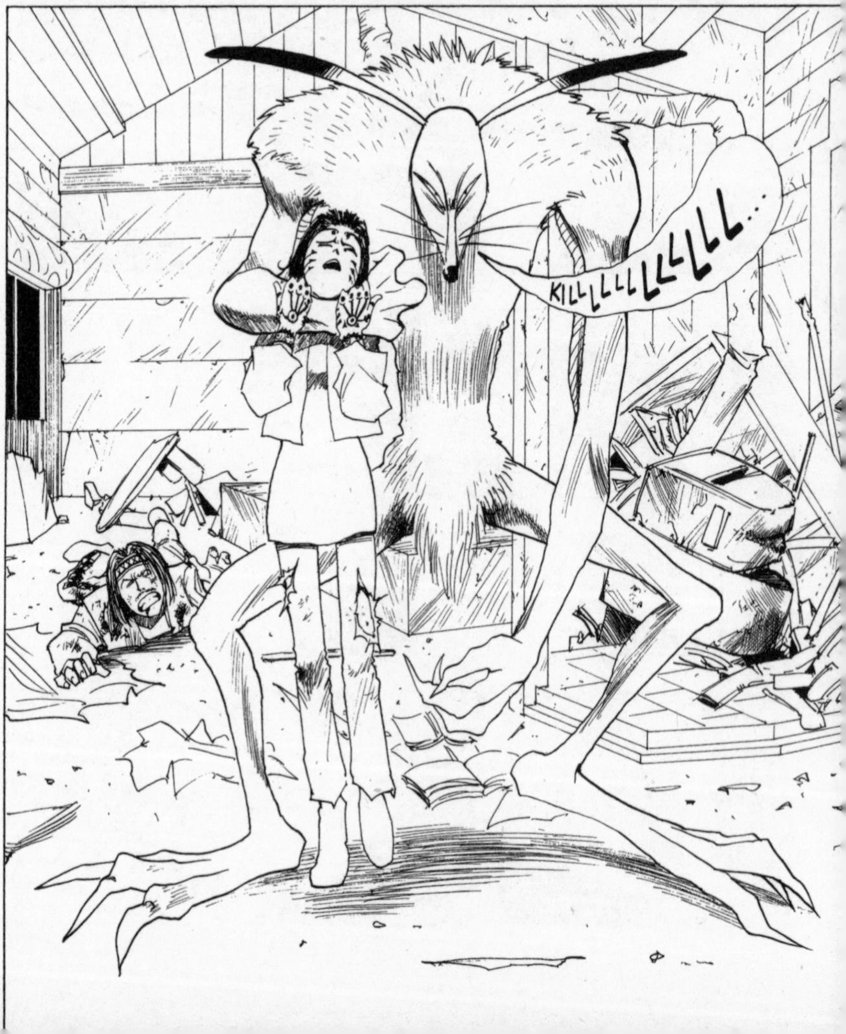
KILLLLLLLLLL...

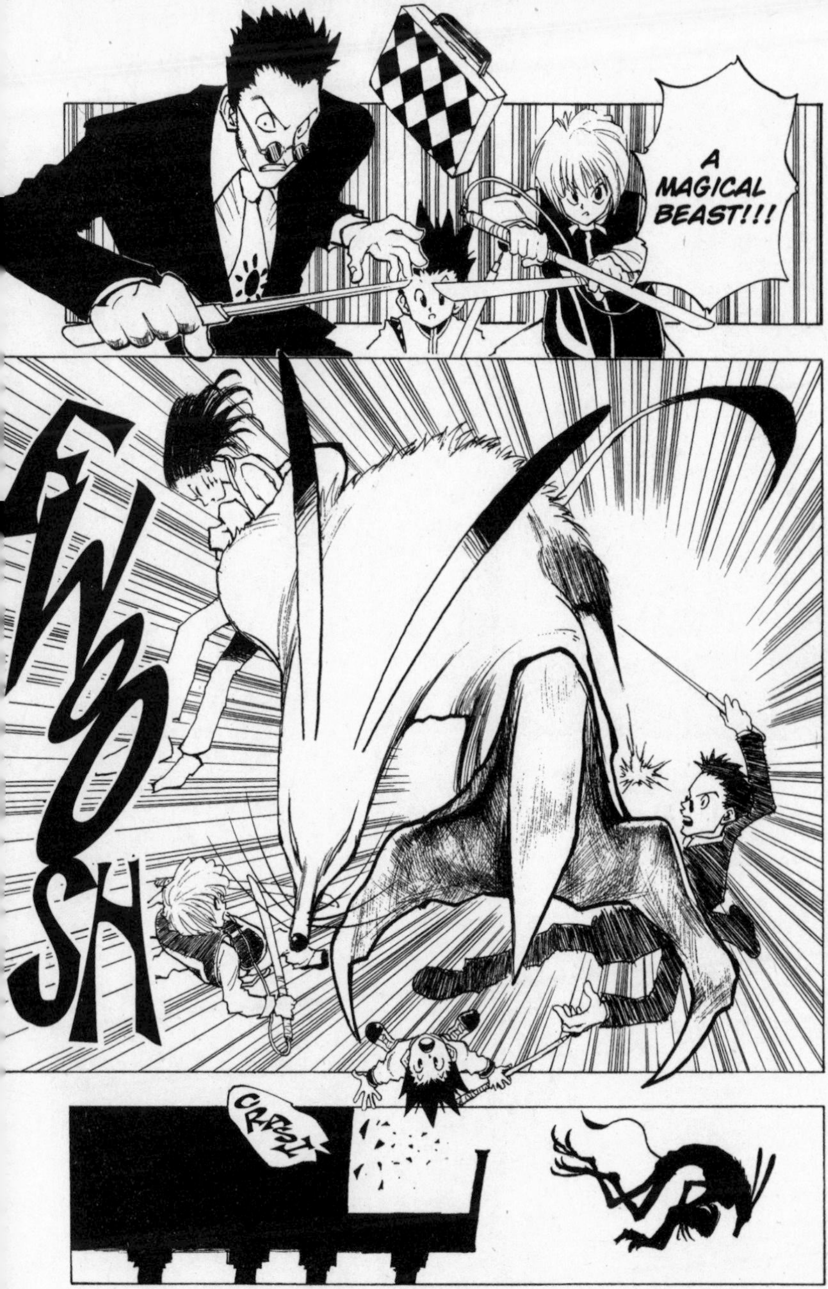
A MAGICAL BEAST!!!
FWOOSH
CRASH

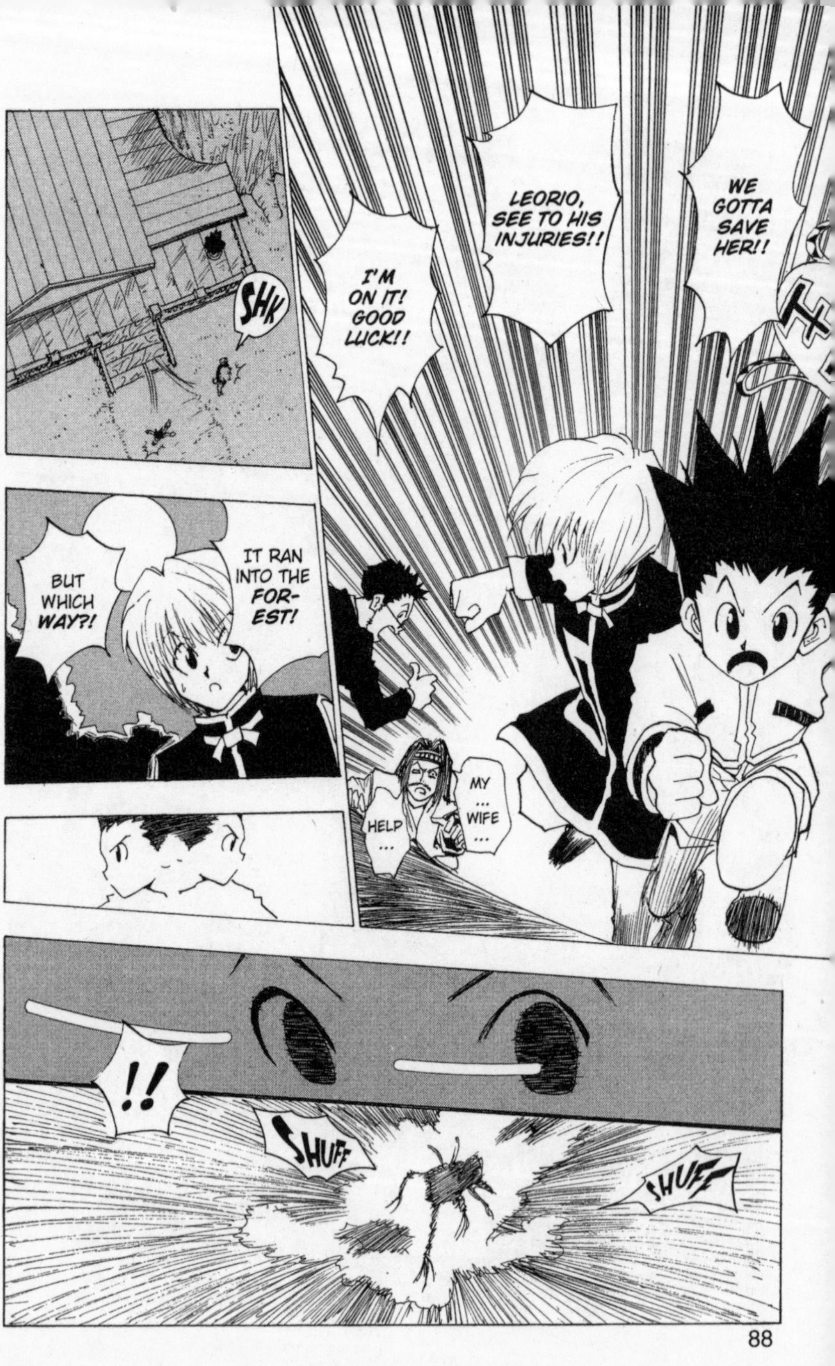
WE GOTTA SAVE HER!!
LEORIO, SEE TO HIS INJURIES!!
I'M ON IT! GOOD LUCK!!
MY ... WIFE ...
HELP ...
SHK
IT RAN INTO THE FOR- EST!
BUT WHICH WAY?!
!!
SHUFF
SHUFF

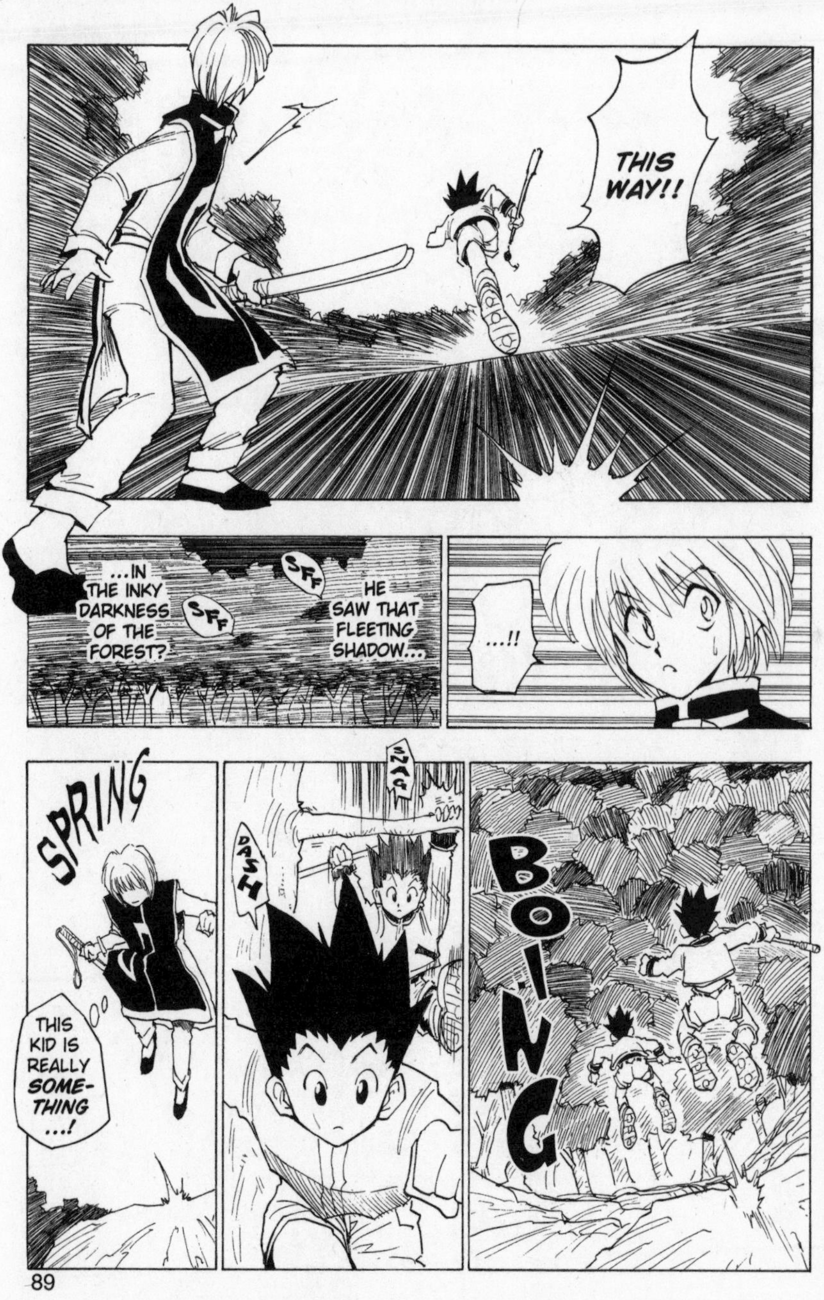
THIS WAY!!
...!!
HE SAW THAT FLEETING SHADOW...
SFF
SFF
...IN THE INKY DARKNESS OF THE FOREST?
BOING
SNAG
DASH
SPRING
THIS KID IS REALLY SOMETHING...!

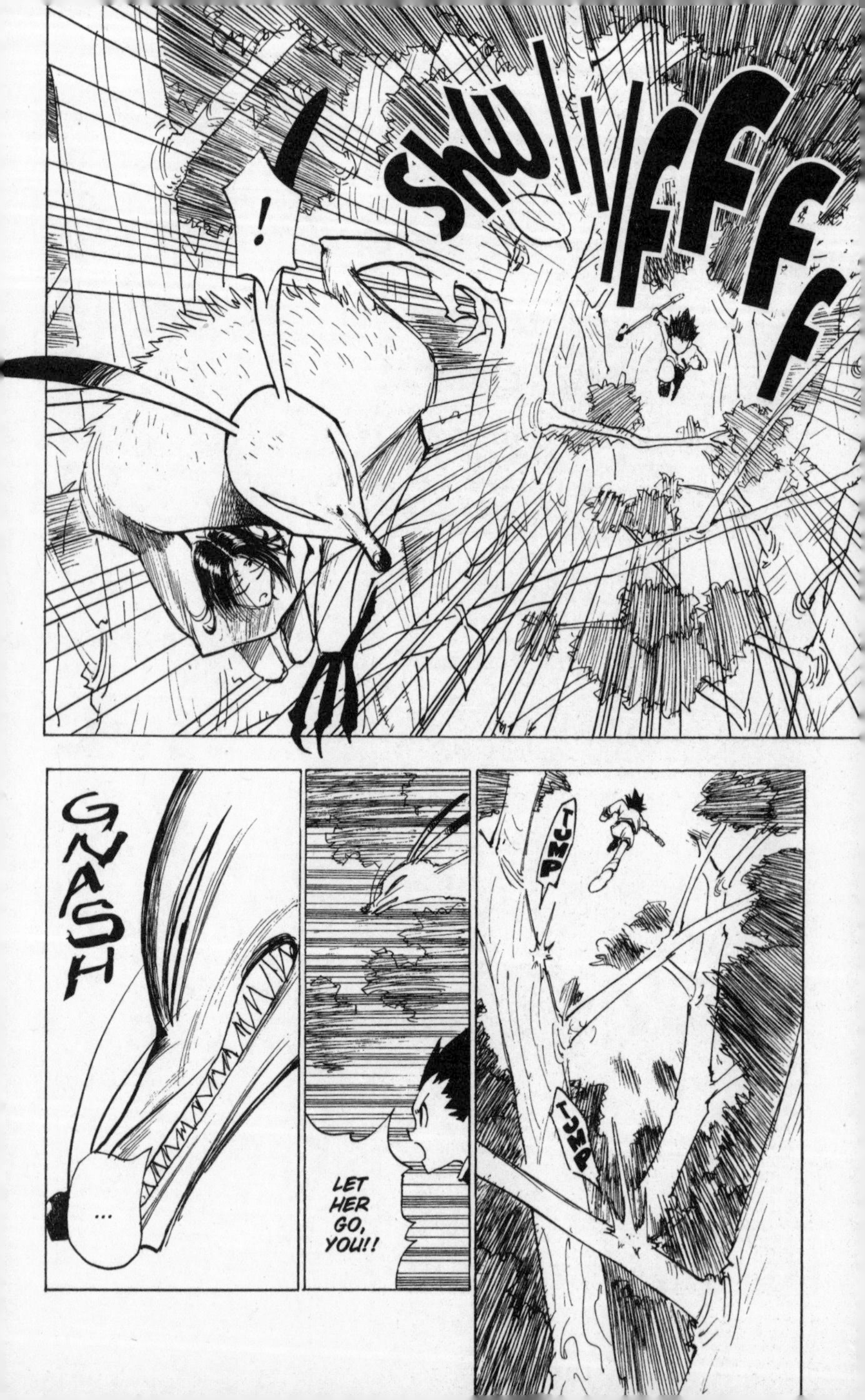

!
SHWIFFFF
TUMP
TUMP
LET HER GO, YOU!!
GNASH
...

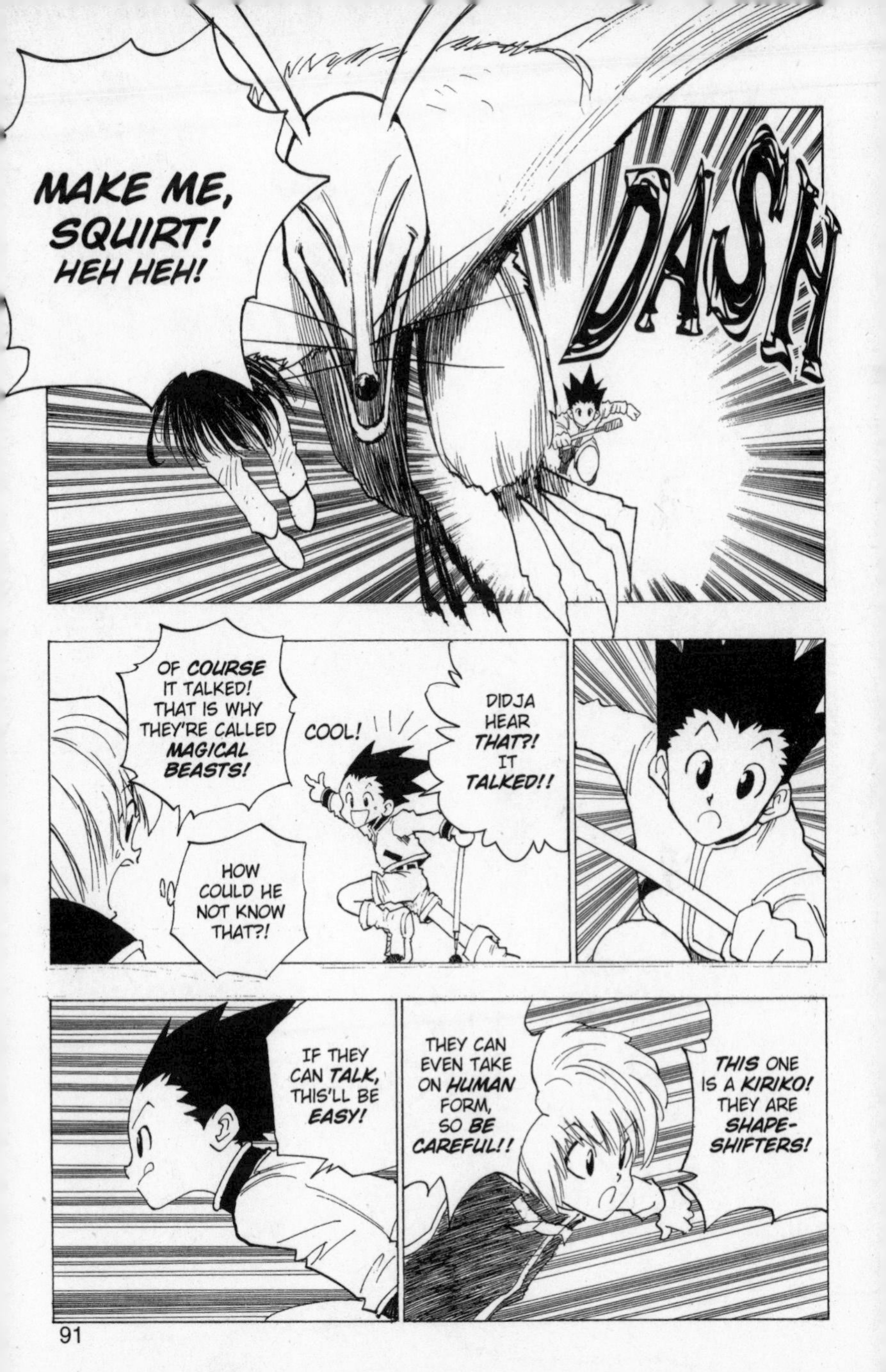
MAKE ME, SQUIRT! HEH HEH!
DASH
DIDJA HEAR THAT?! IT TALKED!!
COOL!
OF COURSE IT TALKED! THAT IS WHY THEY'RE CALLED MAGICAL BEASTS!
HOW COULD HE NOT KNOW THAT?!
THIS ONE IS A KIRIKO! THEY ARE SHAPE-SHIFTERS!
THEY CAN EVEN TAKE ON HUMAN FORM, SO BE CAREFUL!!
IF THEY CAN TALK, THIS'LL BE EASY!

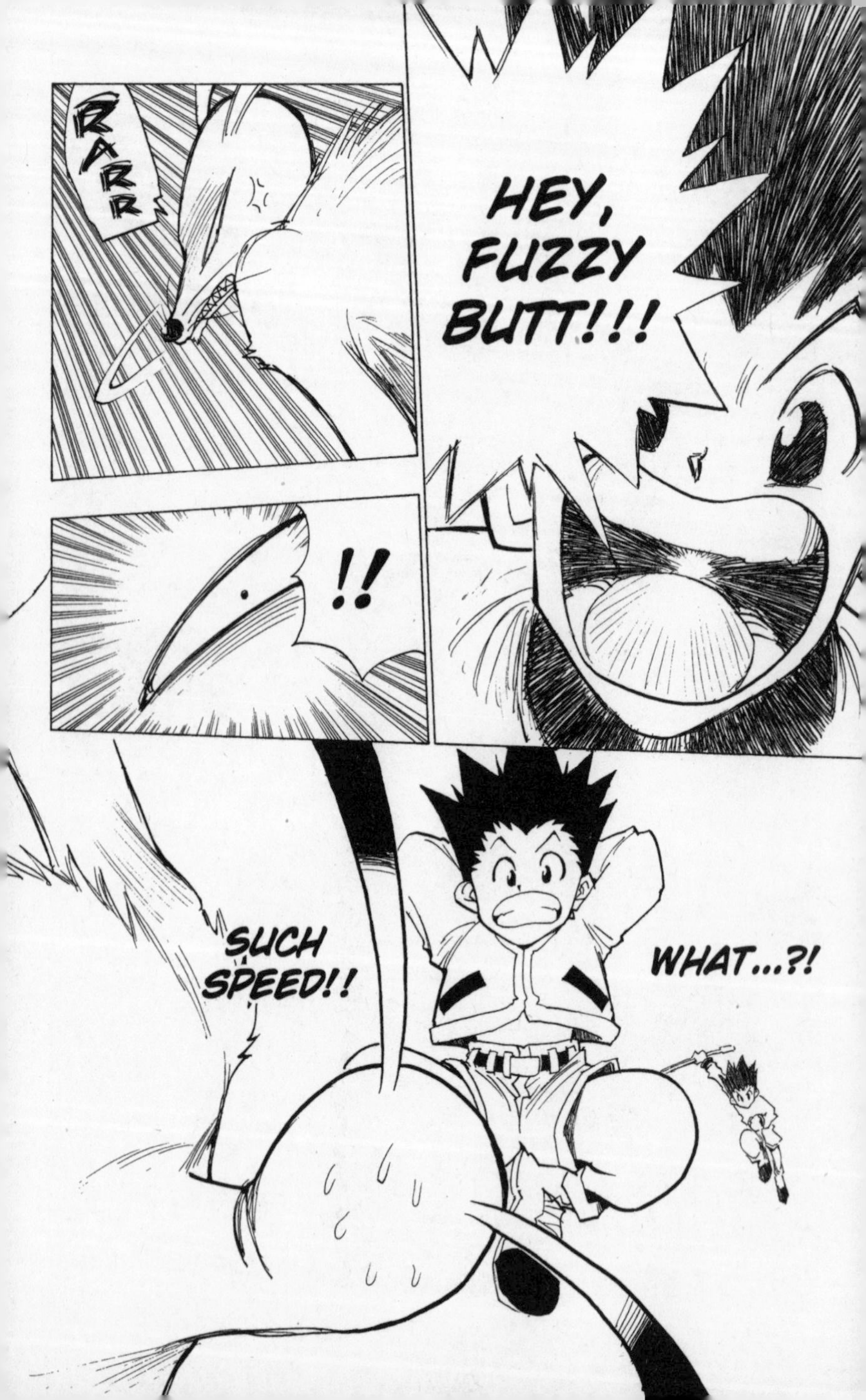
HEY, FUZZY BUTT!!!
RARR
!!
WHAT...?!
SUCH SPEED!!

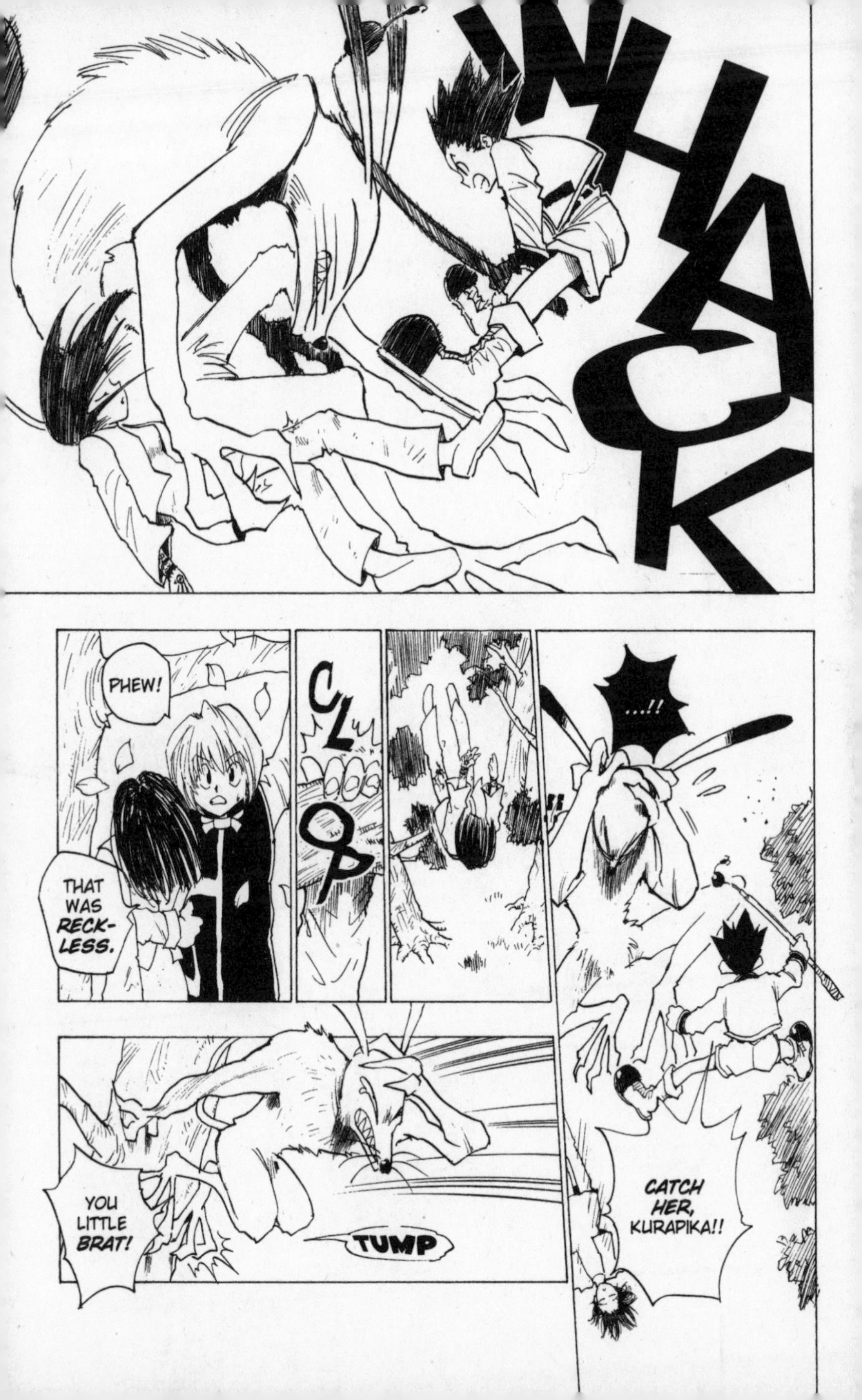
WHACK
...!!
CATCH HER, KURAPIKA!!
CLOP
PHEW!
THAT WAS RECKLESS.
TUMP
YOU LITTLE BRAT!

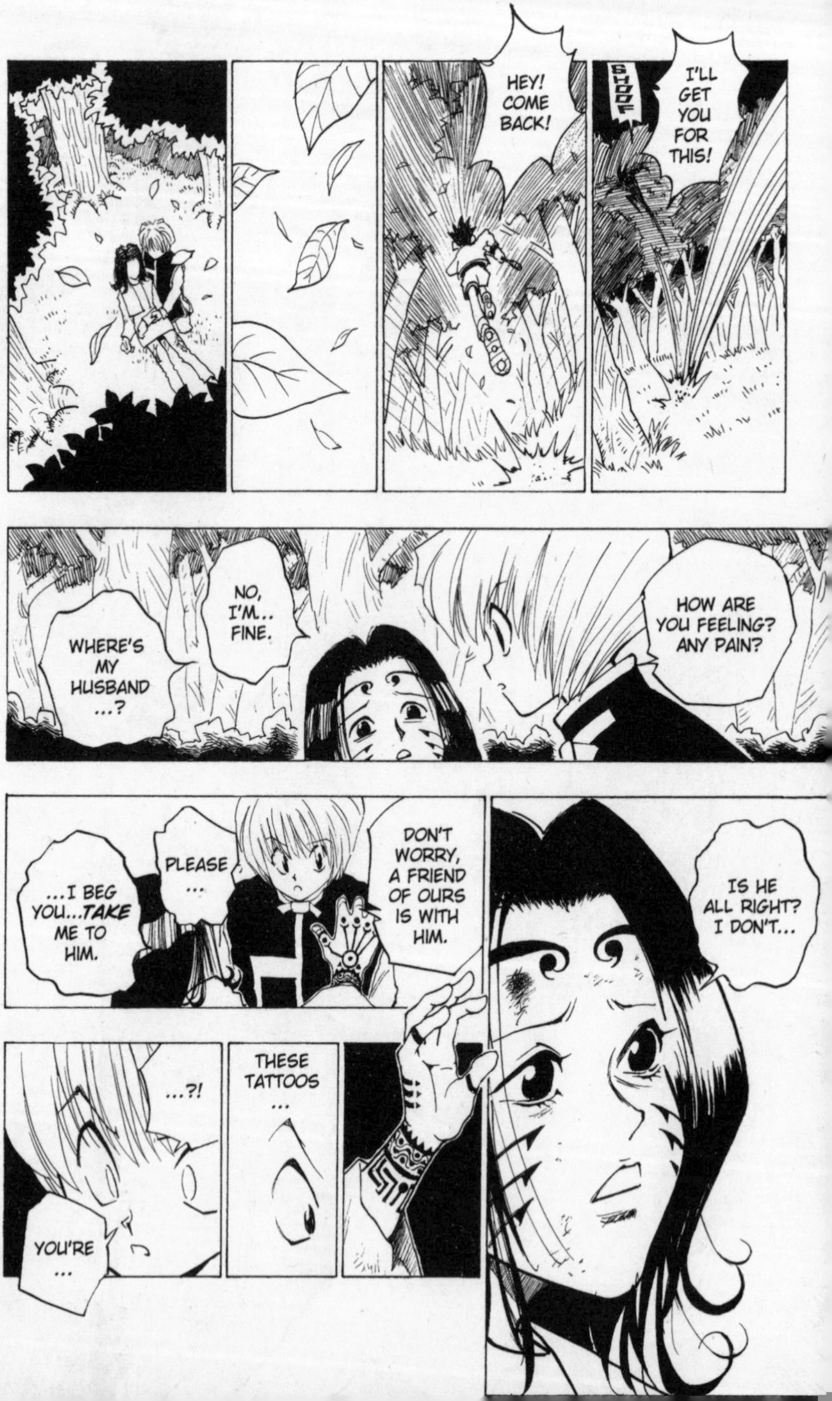
SHOOF
I'LL GET YOU FOR THIS!
HEY! COME BACK!
HOW ARE YOU FEELING? ANY PAIN?
NO, I'M... FINE.
WHERE'S MY HUSBAND ...?
IS HE ALL RIGHT? I DON'T...
DON'T WORRY, A FRIEND OF OURS IS WITH HIM.
PLEASE ...
...I BEG YOU...*TAKE* ME TO HIM.
THESE TATTOOS ...
...?!
YOU'RE ...

READ THIS WAY

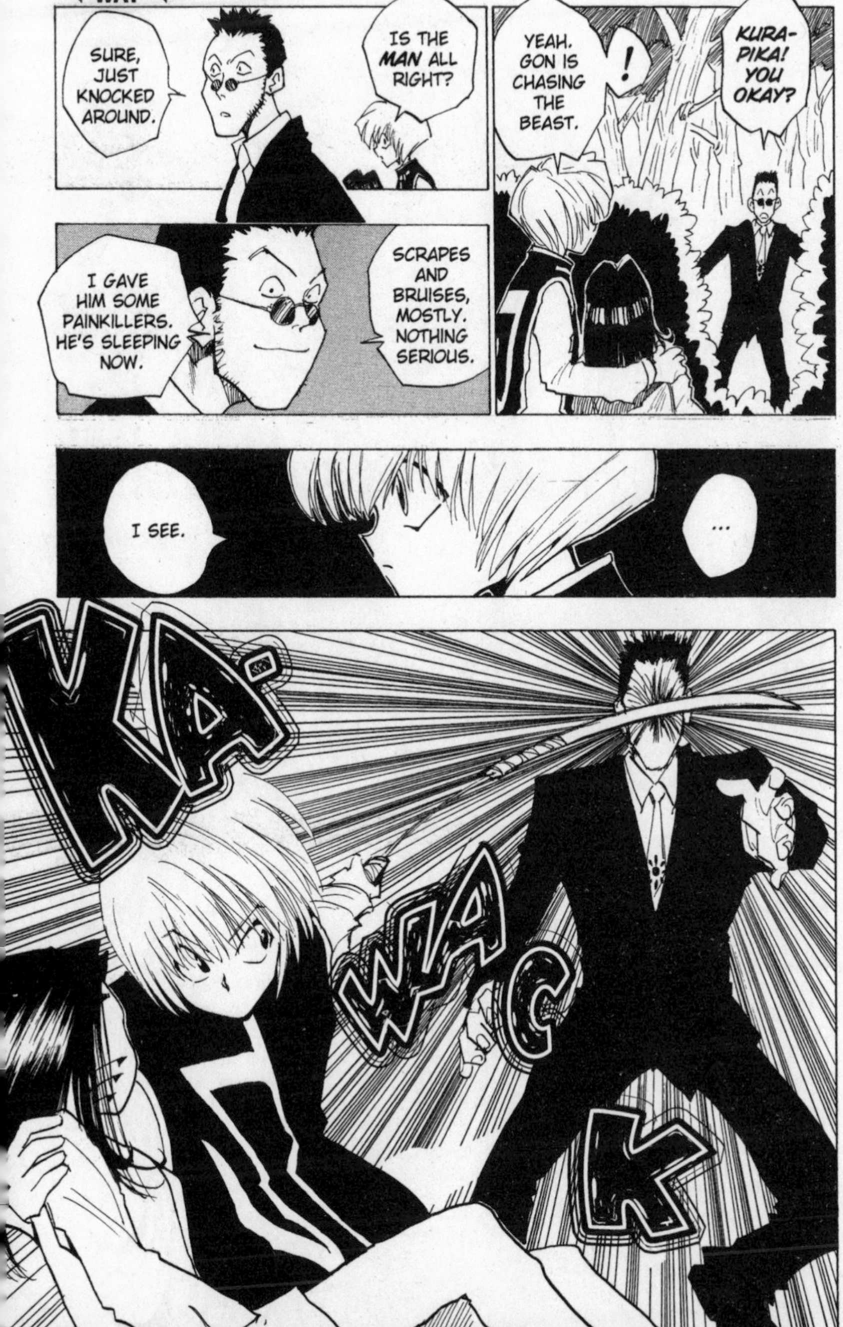
KURA-PIKA! YOU OKAY?
!
YEAH. GON IS CHASING THE BEAST.
IS THE MAN ALL RIGHT?
SURE, JUST KNOCKED AROUND.
SCRAPES AND BRUISES, MOSTLY. NOTHING SERIOUS.
I GAVE HIM SOME PAINKILLERS. HE'S SLEEPING NOW.
...
I SEE.
WA
WACK

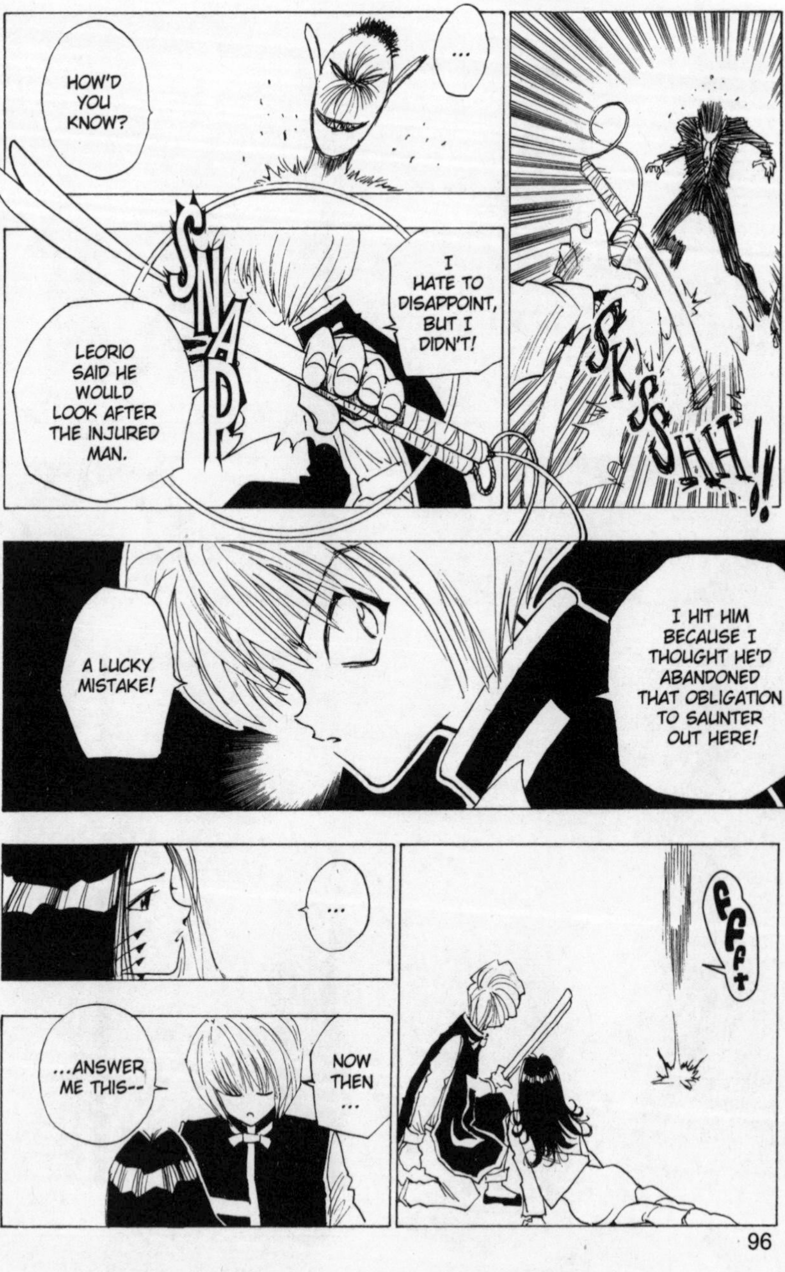
SKSSHH!!
...
HOW'D YOU KNOW?
I HATE TO DISAPPOINT, BUT I DIDN'T!
LEORIO SAID HE WOULD LOOK AFTER THE INJURED MAN.
SNAP
I HIT HIM BECAUSE I THOUGHT HE'D ABANDONED THAT OBLIGATION TO SAUNTER OUT HERE!
A LUCKY MISTAKE!
fft
...
NOW THEN ...
...ANSWER ME THIS--

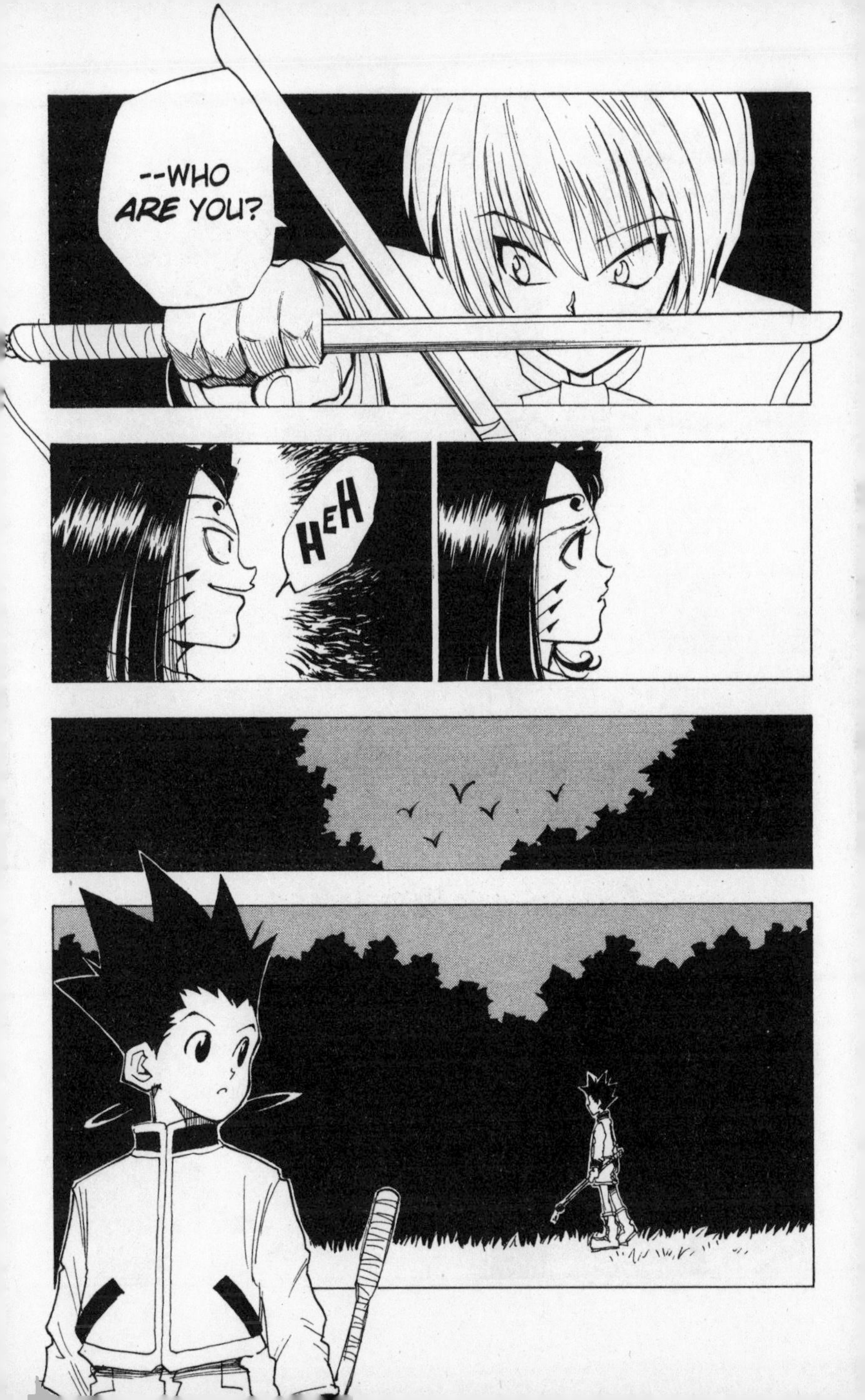
--WHO ARE YOU?
HEH

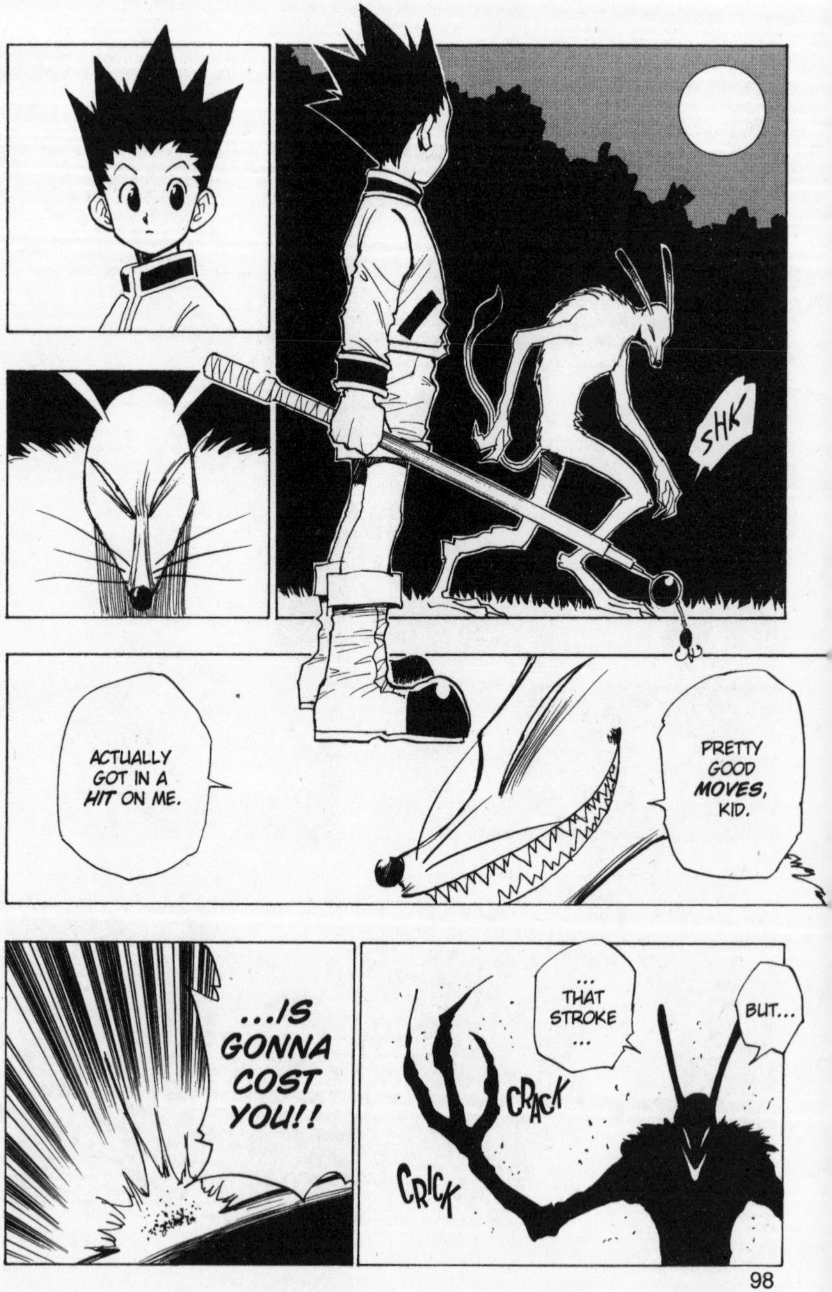
SHK
PRETTY GOOD MOVES, KID.
ACTUALLY GOT IN A HIT ON ME.
BUT...
... THAT STROKE ...
CRACK
CRICK
...IS GONNA COST YOU!!

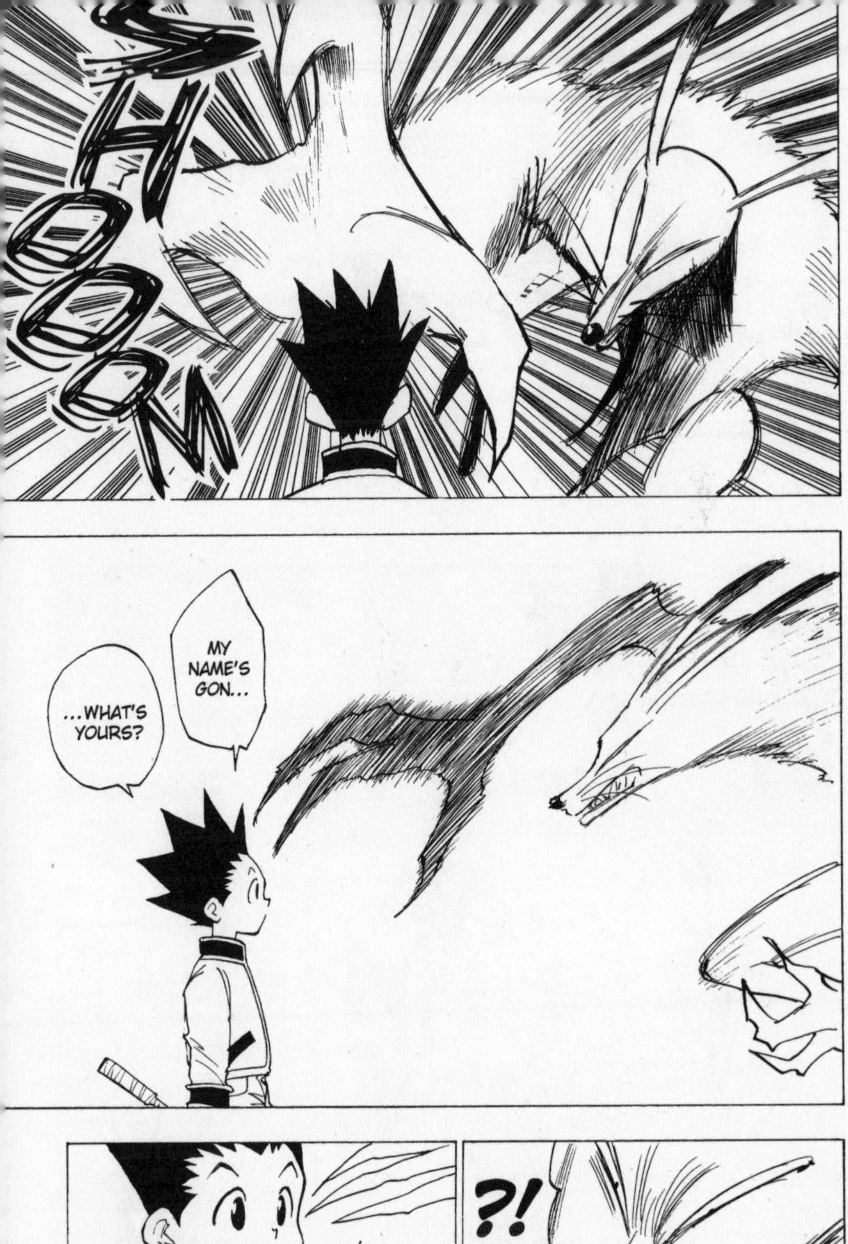
WHOOOM
MY NAME'S GON...
...WHAT'S YOURS?
?!
SCREEE

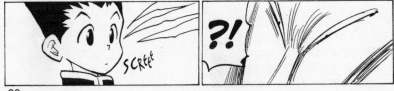

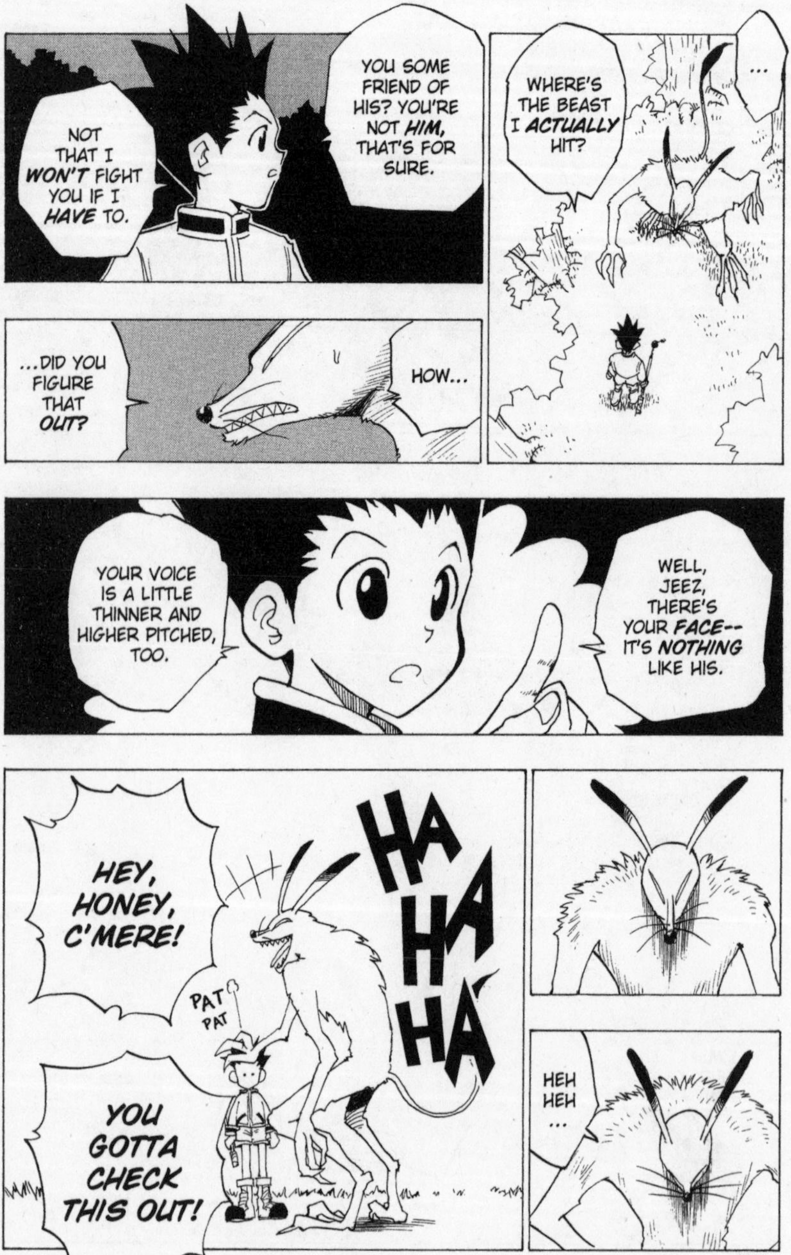
...
WHERE'S THE BEAST I ACTUALLY HIT?
YOU SOME FRIEND OF HIS? YOU'RE NOT HIM, THAT'S FOR SURE.
NOT THAT I WON'T FIGHT YOU IF I HAVE TO.
HOW...
...DID YOU FIGURE THAT OUT?
WELL, JEEZ, THERE'S YOUR FACE-- IT'S NOTHING LIKE HIS.
YOUR VOICE IS A LITTLE THINNER AND HIGHER PITCHED, TOO.
HEH HEH ...
HA HA HA HA
HEY, HONEY, C'MERE!
PAT PAT
YOU GOTTA CHECK THIS OUT!

READ THIS WAY

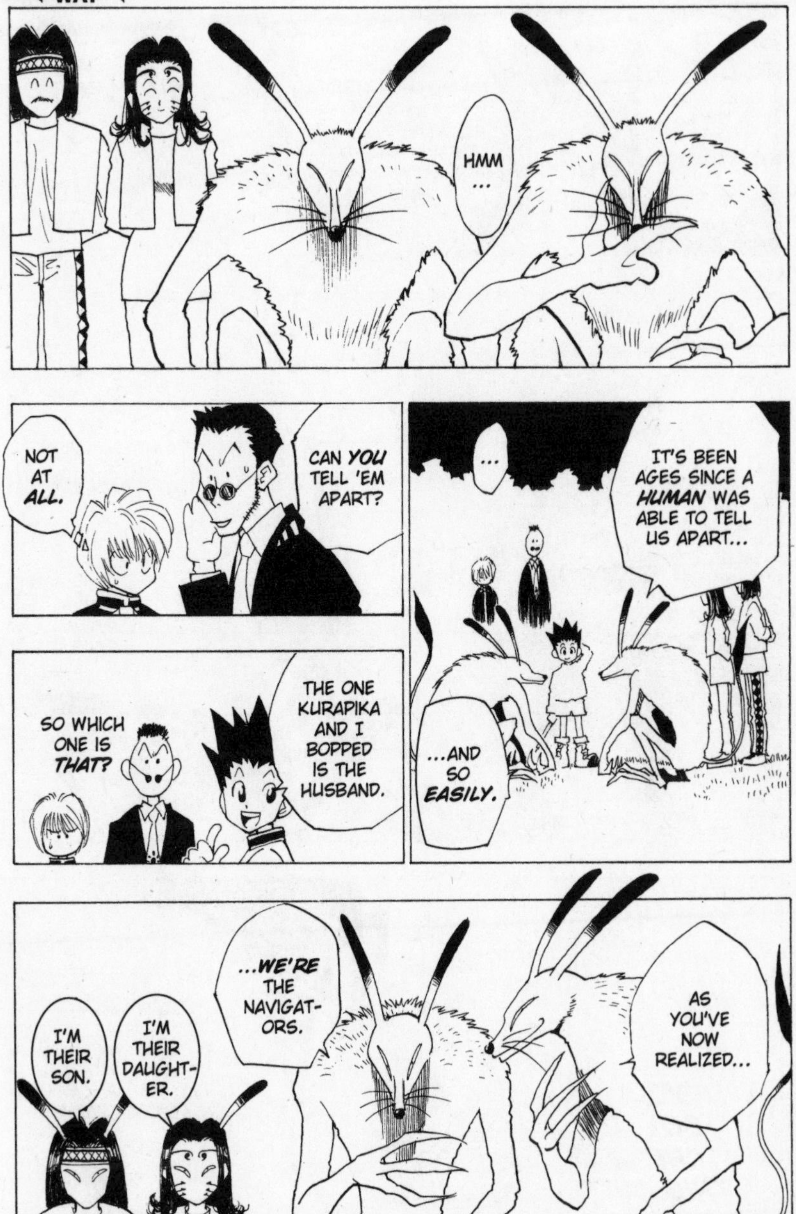

HMM ...
...
IT'S BEEN AGES SINCE A *HUMAN* WAS ABLE TO TELL US APART...
...AND SO *EASILY.*
CAN *YOU* TELL 'EM APART?
NOT AT *ALL.*
THE ONE KURAPIKA AND I BOPPED IS THE HUSBAND.
SO WHICH ONE IS *THAT?*
AS YOU'VE NOW REALIZED...
...*WE'RE* THE NAVIGAT-ORS.
I'M THEIR DAUGHT-ER.
I'M THEIR SON.

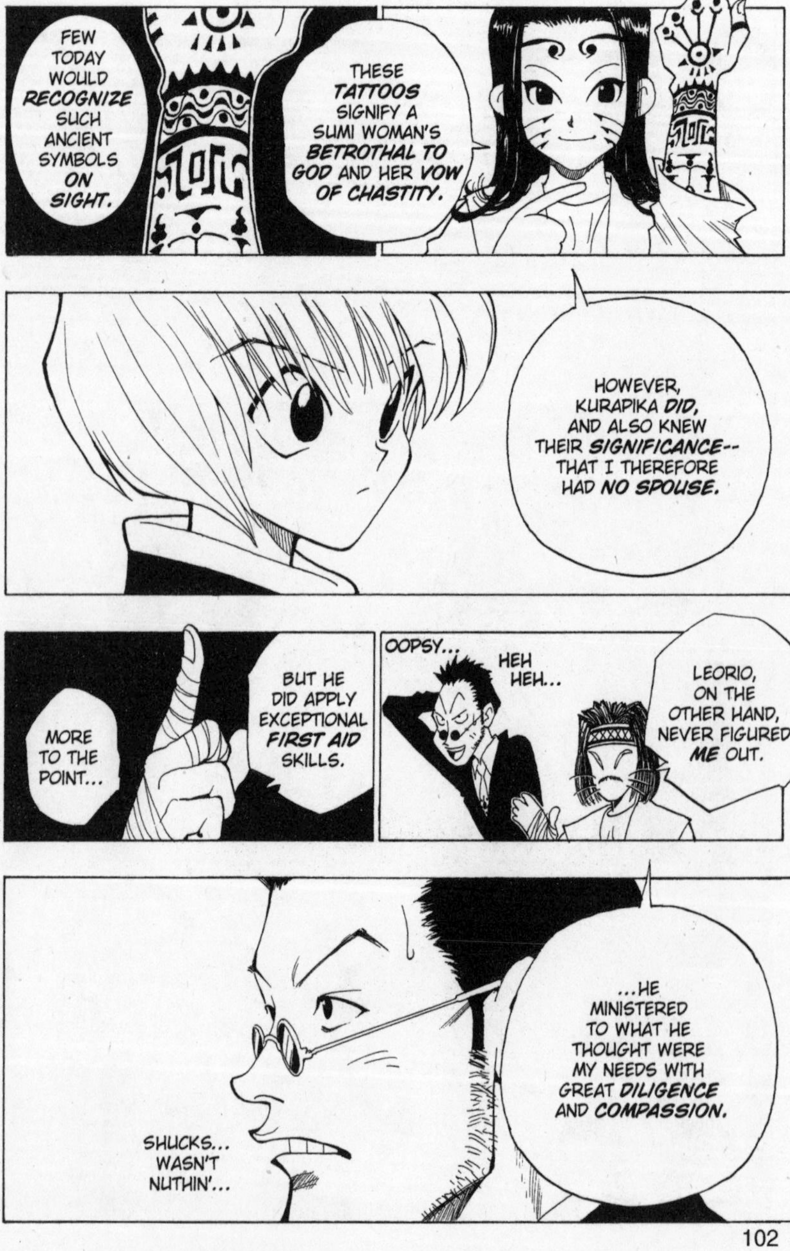
THESE TATTOOS SIGNIFY A SUMI WOMAN'S BETROTHAL TO GOD AND HER VOW OF CHASTITY.
FEW TODAY WOULD RECOGNIZE SUCH ANCIENT SYMBOLS ON SIGHT.
HOWEVER, KURAPIKA DID, AND ALSO KNEW THEIR SIGNIFICANCE-- THAT I THEREFORE HAD NO SPOUSE.
LEORIO, ON THE OTHER HAND, NEVER FIGURED ME OUT.
HEH HEH...
OOPSY...
BUT HE DID APPLY EXCEPTIONAL FIRST AID SKILLS.
MORE TO THE POINT...
...HE MINISTERED TO WHAT HE THOUGHT WERE MY NEEDS WITH GREAT DILIGENCE AND COMPASSION.
SHUCKS... WASN'T NUTHIN'...

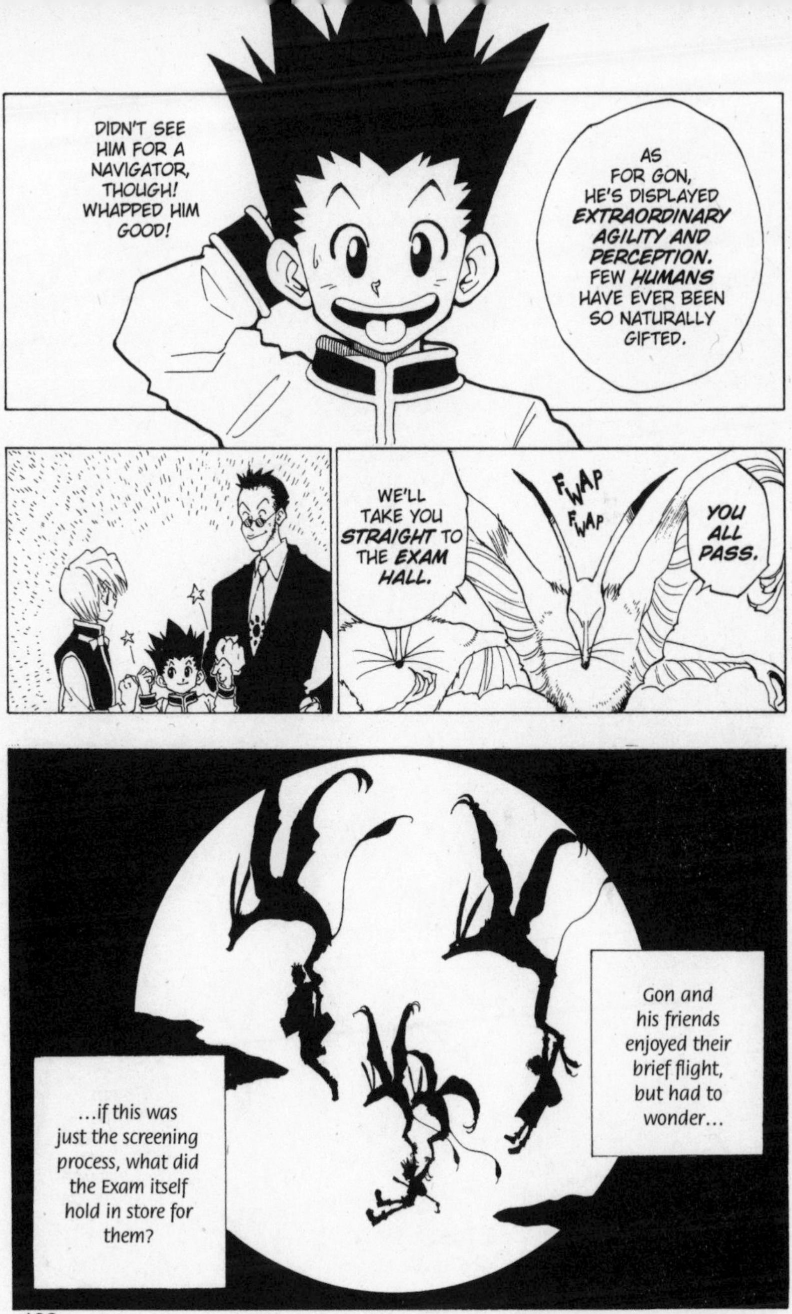
AS FOR GON, HE'S DISPLAYED **EXTRAORDINARY AGILITY AND PERCEPTION.** FEW **HUMANS** HAVE EVER BEEN SO NATURALLY GIFTED.
DIDN'T SEE HIM FOR A NAVIGATOR, THOUGH! WHAPPED HIM GOOD!
YOU ALL PASS.
FWAP
FWAP
WE'LL TAKE YOU **STRAIGHT** TO THE **EXAM HALL.**
Gon and his friends enjoyed their brief flight, but had to wonder…
…if this was just the screening process, what did the Exam itself hold in store for them?

Hisoka

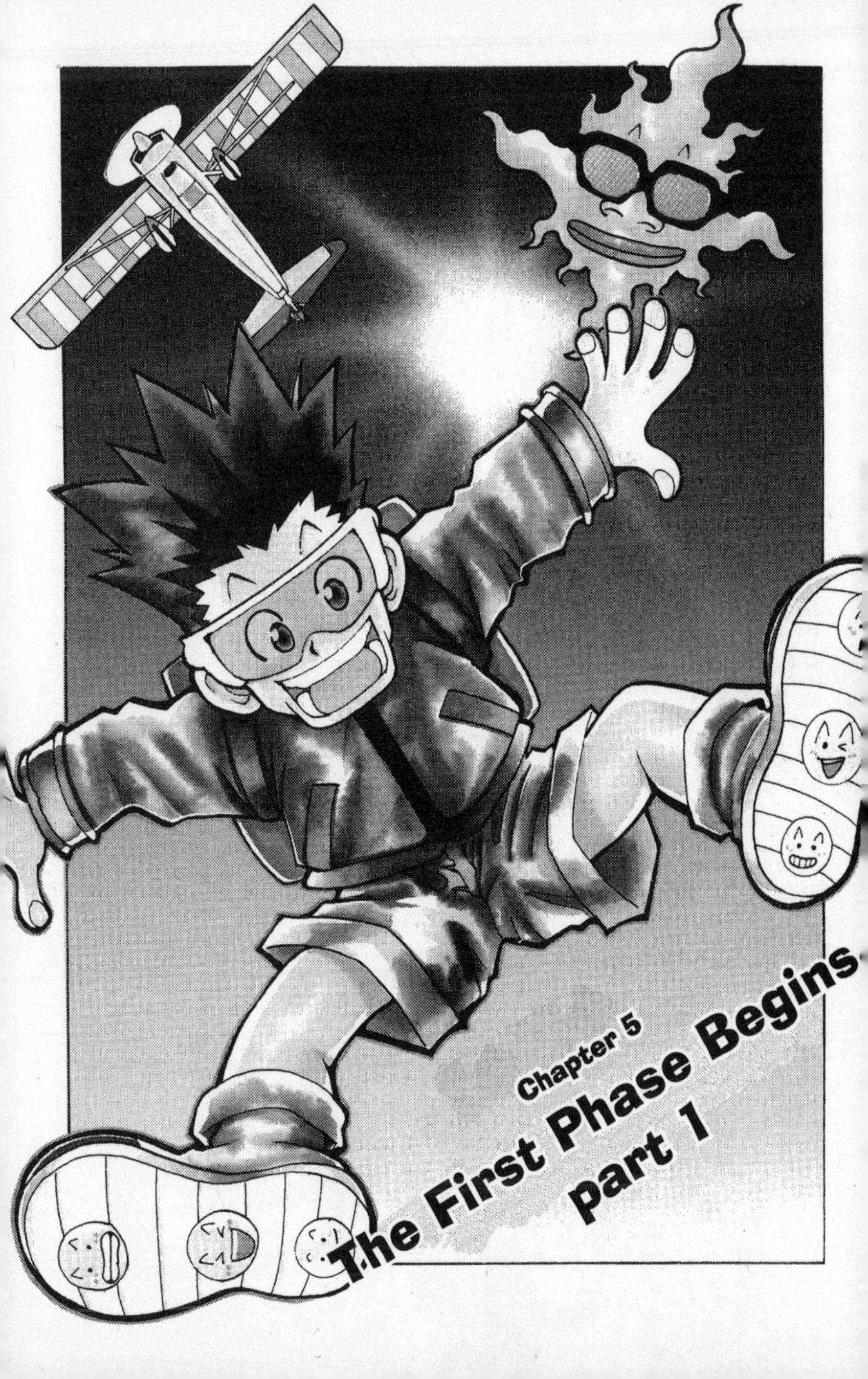
Chapter 5
The First Phase Begins
part 1

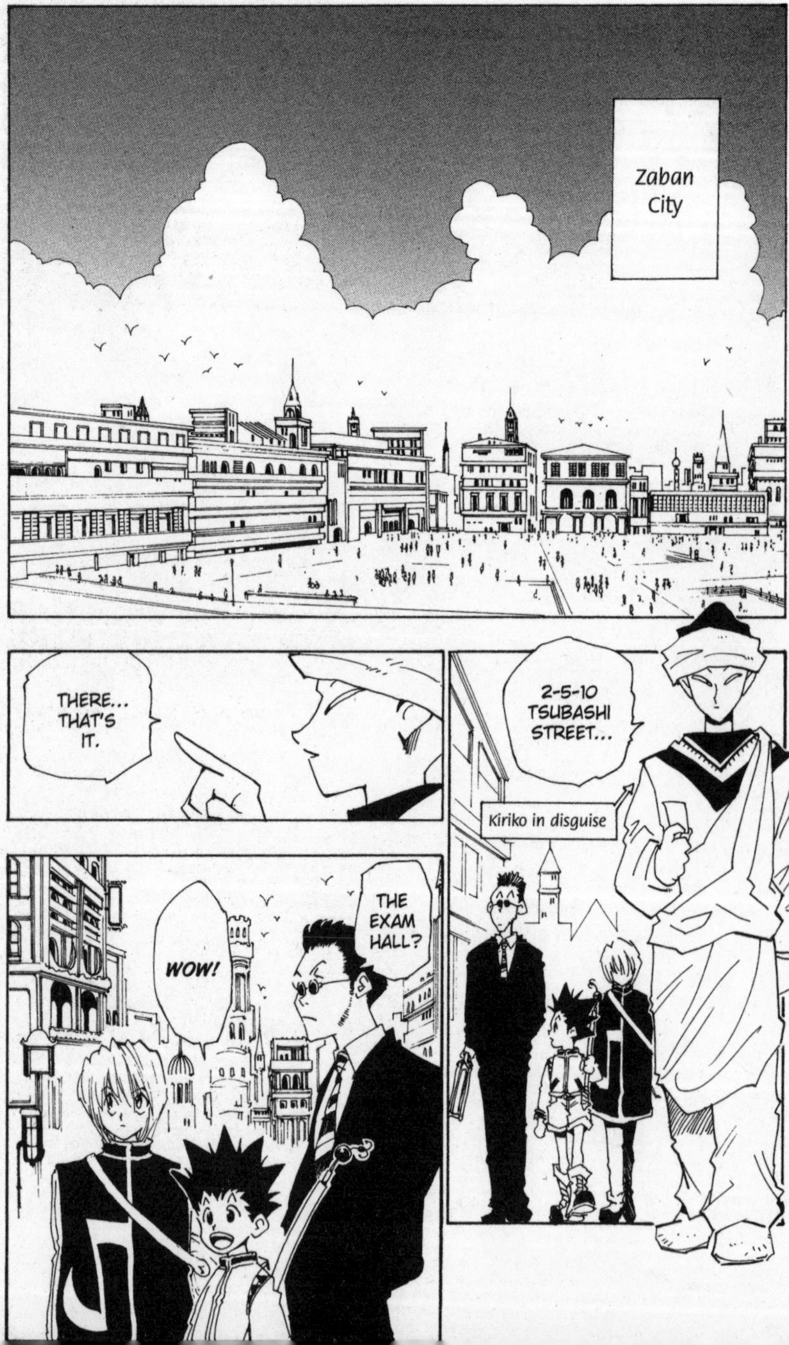
Zaban City
2-5-10 TSUBASHI STREET...
Kiriko in disguise
THERE... THAT'S IT.
THE EXAM HALL?
WOW!

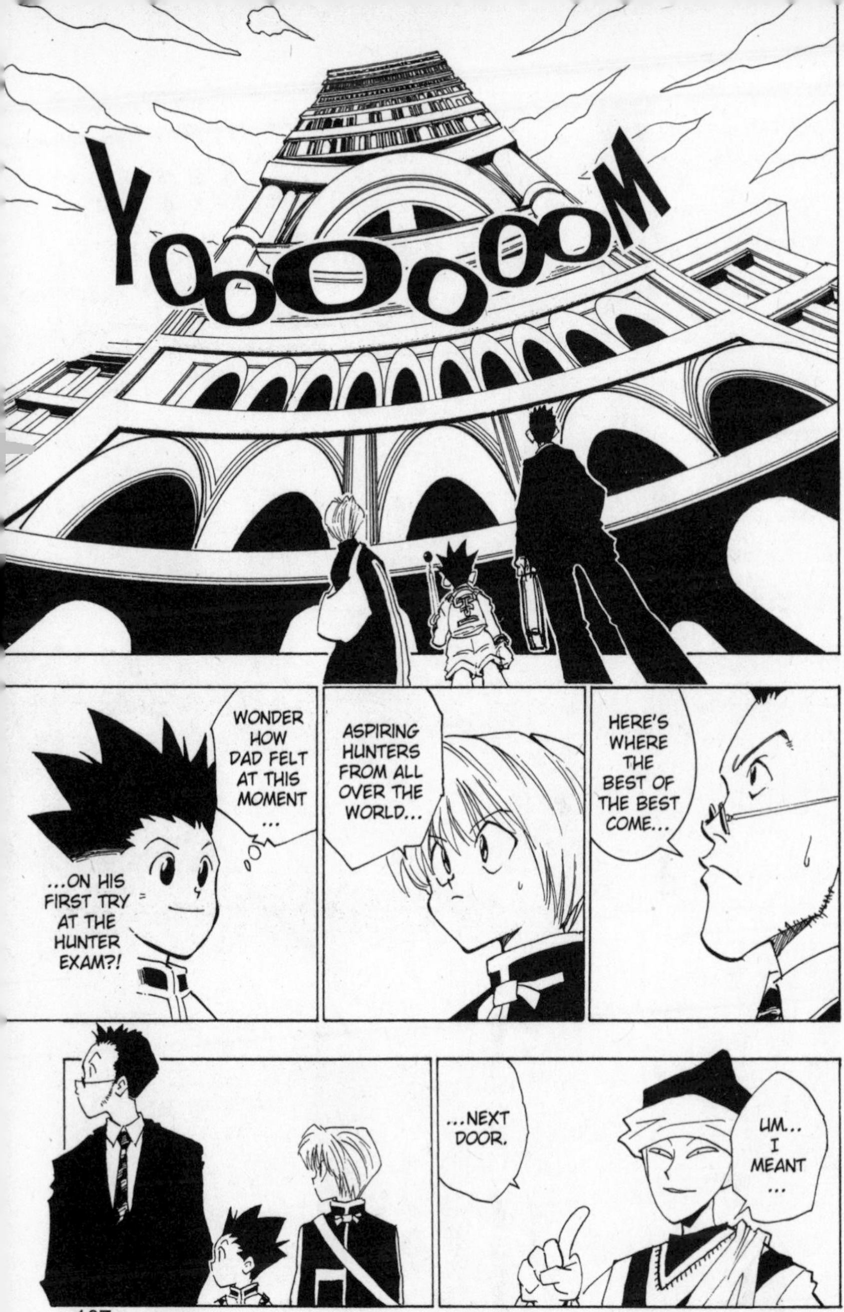
YOOOOOOM
HERE'S WHERE THE BEST OF THE BEST COME...
ASPIRING HUNTERS FROM ALL OVER THE WORLD...
WONDER HOW DAD FELT AT THIS MOMENT ...
...ON HIS FIRST TRY AT THE HUNTER EXAM?!
UM... I MEANT ...
...NEXT DOOR.

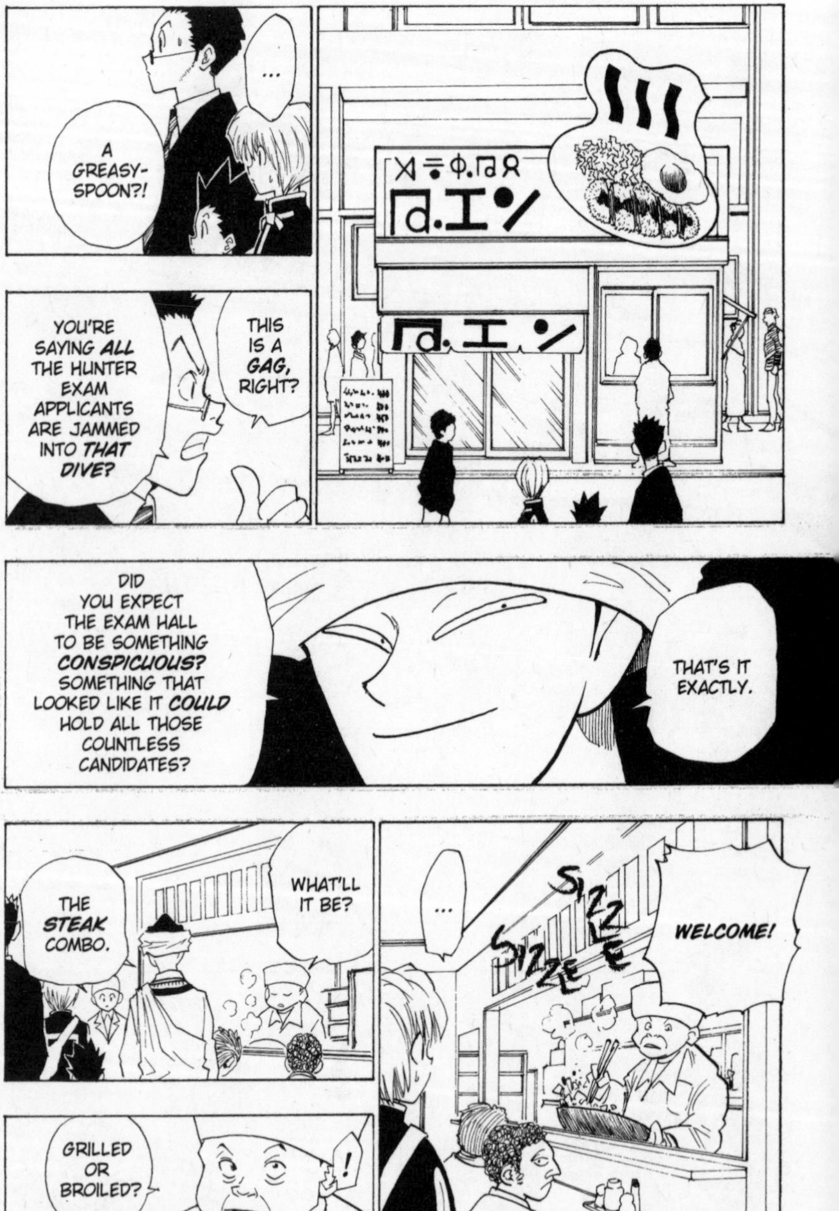
...
A GREASY-SPOON?!
THIS IS A GAG, RIGHT?
YOU'RE SAYING ALL THE HUNTER EXAM APPLICANTS ARE JAMMED INTO THAT DIVE?
DID YOU EXPECT THE EXAM HALL TO BE SOMETHING CONSPICUOUS? SOMETHING THAT LOOKED LIKE IT COULD HOLD ALL THOSE COUNTLESS CANDIDATES?
THAT'S IT EXACTLY.
WELCOME!
SIZZLE
SIZZLE
...
WHAT'LL IT BE?
THE STEAK COMBO.
!
GRILLED OR BROILED?

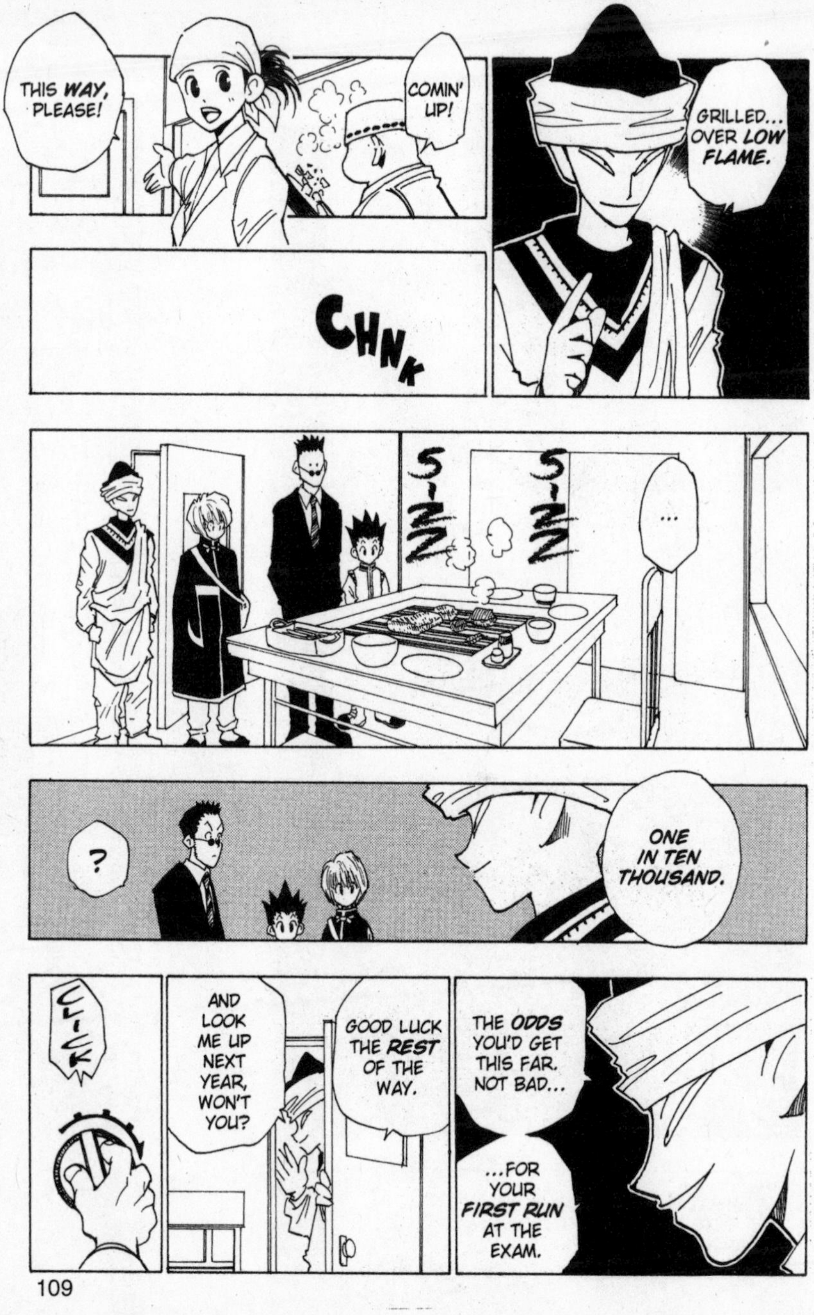
GRILLED... OVER LOW FLAME.
COMIN' UP!
THIS WAY, PLEASE!
CHNK
SIZZ
SIZZ
...
ONE IN TEN THOUSAND.
?
THE ODDS YOU'D GET THIS FAR. NOT BAD...
...FOR YOUR FIRST RUN AT THE EXAM.
GOOD LUCK THE REST OF THE WAY.
AND LOOK ME UP NEXT YEAR, WON'T YOU?
CLICK

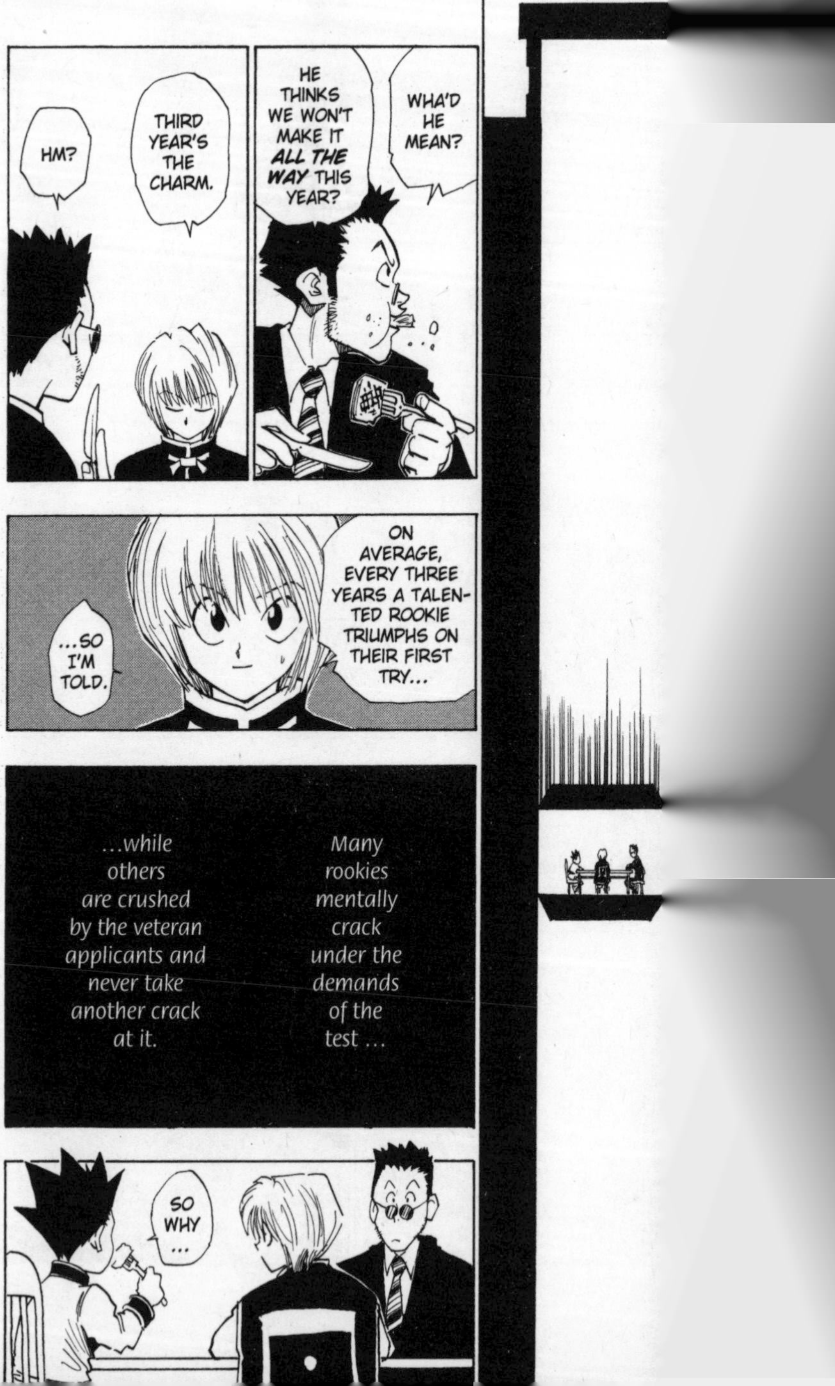
WHA'D HE MEAN?
HE THINKS WE WON'T MAKE IT ALL THE WAY THIS YEAR?
THIRD YEAR'S THE CHARM.
HM?
ON AVERAGE, EVERY THREE YEARS A TALENTED ROOKIE TRIUMPHS ON THEIR FIRST TRY...
...SO I'M TOLD.
Many rookies mentally crack under the demands of the test ...
...while others are crushed by the veteran applicants and never take another crack at it.
SO WHY ...

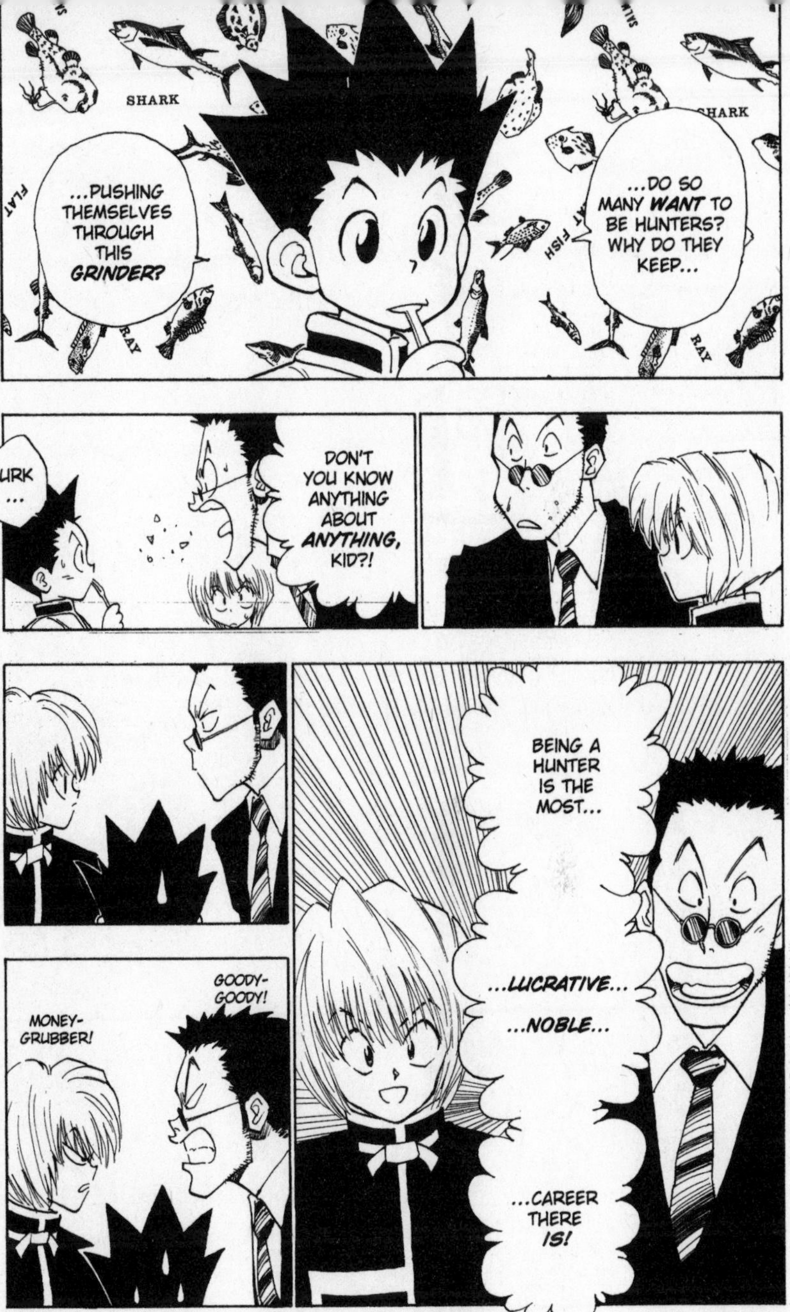
...DO SO MANY *WANT* TO BE HUNTERS? WHY DO THEY KEEP...
SHARK
FLAT FISH
RAY
...PUSHING THEMSELVES THROUGH THIS *GRINDER?*
SHARK
RAY
DON'T YOU KNOW ANYTHING ABOUT *ANYTHING,* KID?!
URK...
BEING A HUNTER IS THE MOST...
...LUCRATIVE...
...NOBLE...
...CAREER THERE *IS!*
GOODY-GOODY!
MONEY-GRUBBER!

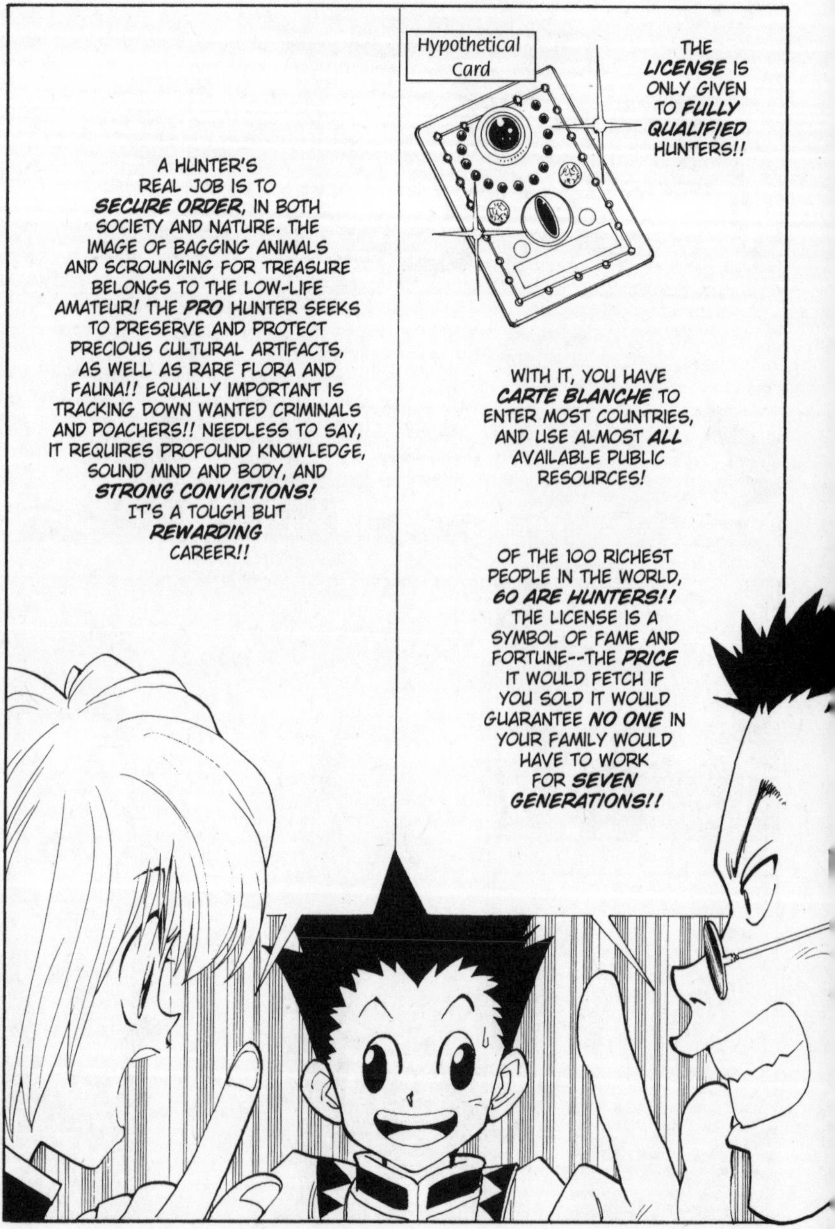
Hypothetical Card
THE LICENSE IS ONLY GIVEN TO FULLY QUALIFIED HUNTERS!!
WITH IT, YOU HAVE CARTE BLANCHE TO ENTER MOST COUNTRIES, AND USE ALMOST ALL AVAILABLE PUBLIC RESOURCES!
OF THE 100 RICHEST PEOPLE IN THE WORLD, 60 ARE HUNTERS!! THE LICENSE IS A SYMBOL OF FAME AND FORTUNE--THE PRICE IT WOULD FETCH IF YOU SOLD IT WOULD GUARANTEE NO ONE IN YOUR FAMILY WOULD HAVE TO WORK FOR SEVEN GENERATIONS!!
A HUNTER'S REAL JOB IS TO SECURE ORDER, IN BOTH SOCIETY AND NATURE. THE IMAGE OF BAGGING ANIMALS AND SCROUNGING FOR TREASURE BELONGS TO THE LOW-LIFE AMATEUR! THE PRO HUNTER SEEKS TO PRESERVE AND PROTECT PRECIOUS CULTURAL ARTIFACTS, AS WELL AS RARE FLORA AND FAUNA!! EQUALLY IMPORTANT IS TRACKING DOWN WANTED CRIMINALS AND POACHERS!! NEEDLESS TO SAY, IT REQUIRES PROFOUND KNOWLEDGE, SOUND MIND AND BODY, AND STRONG CONVICTIONS! IT'S A TOUGH BUT REWARDING CAREER!!

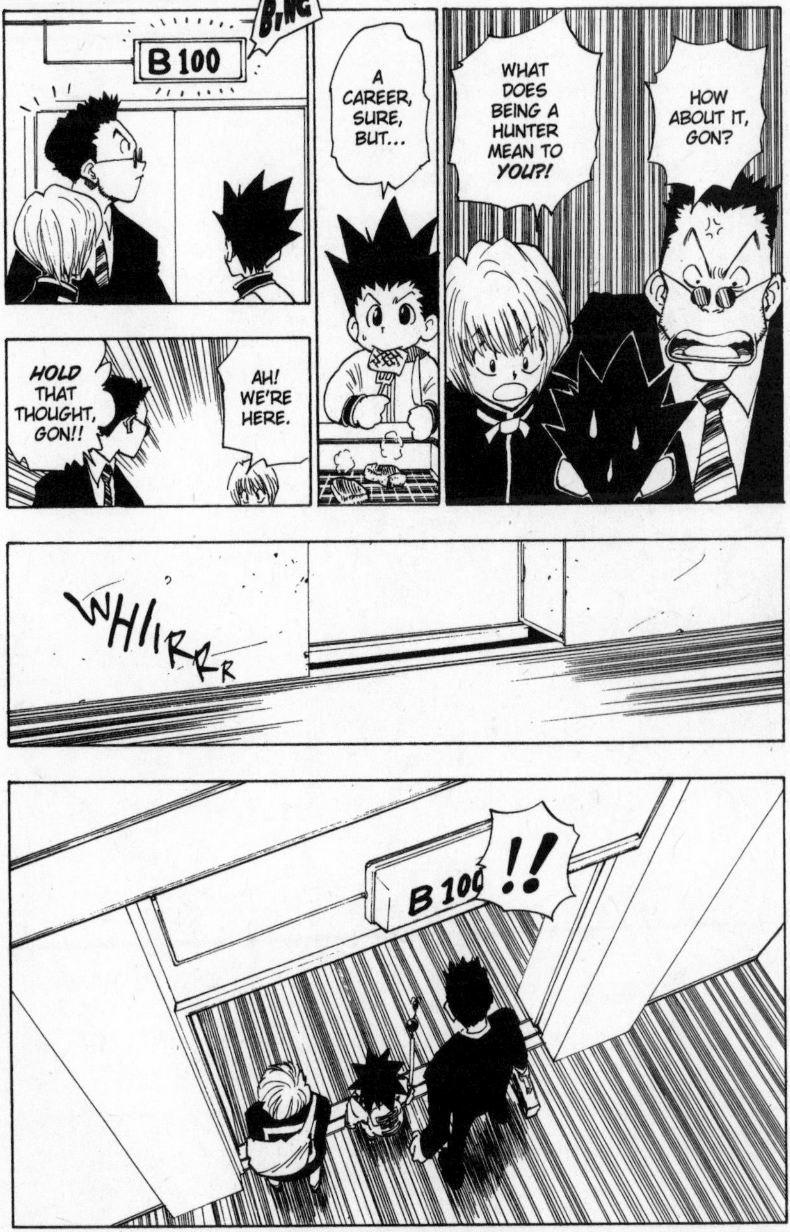
HOW ABOUT IT, GON?
WHAT DOES BEING A HUNTER MEAN TO *YOU*?!
A CAREER, SURE, BUT...
B 100
BING
AH! WE'RE HERE.
HOLD THAT THOUGHT, GON!!
WHIIRRR
B 100
!!

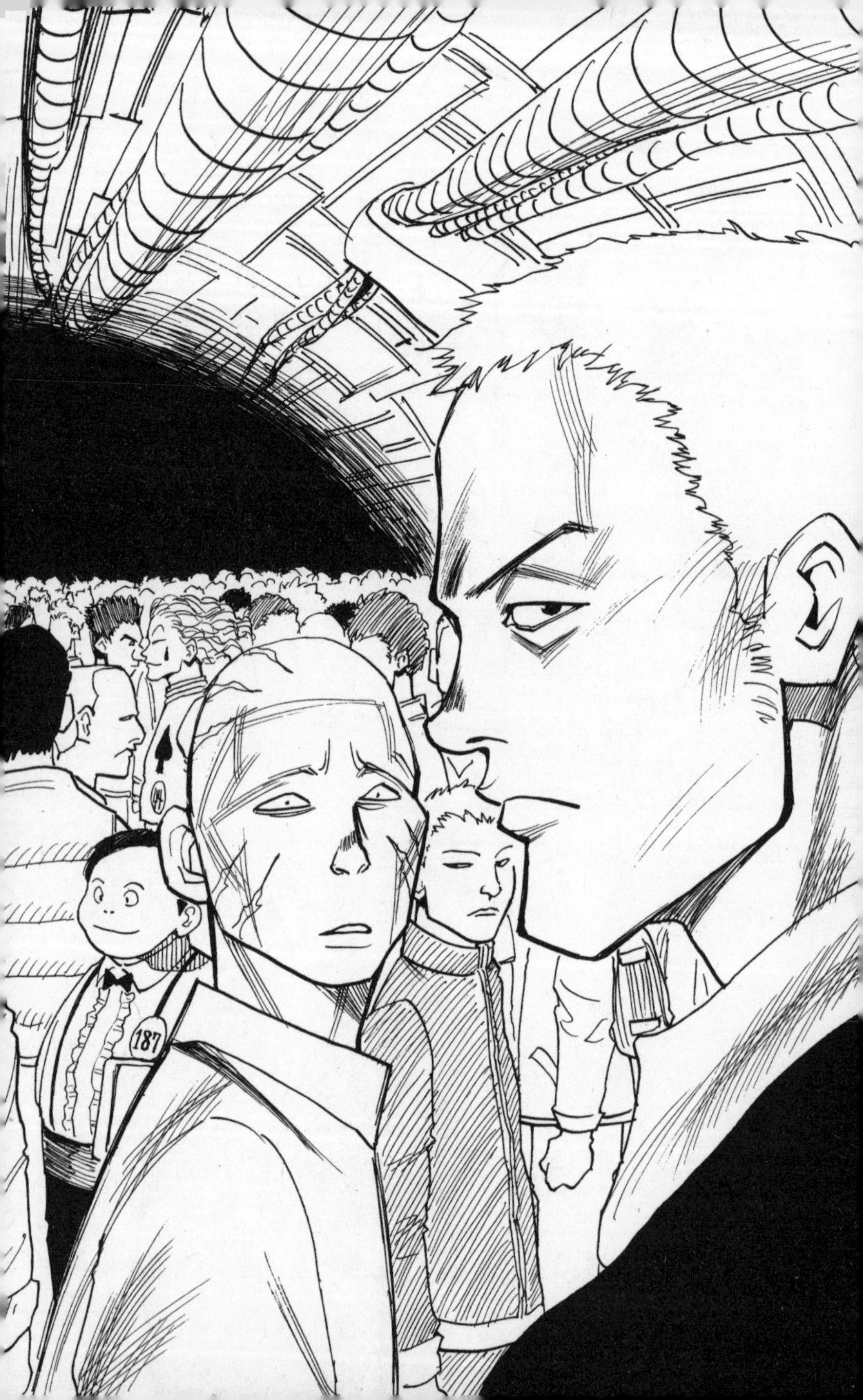
187

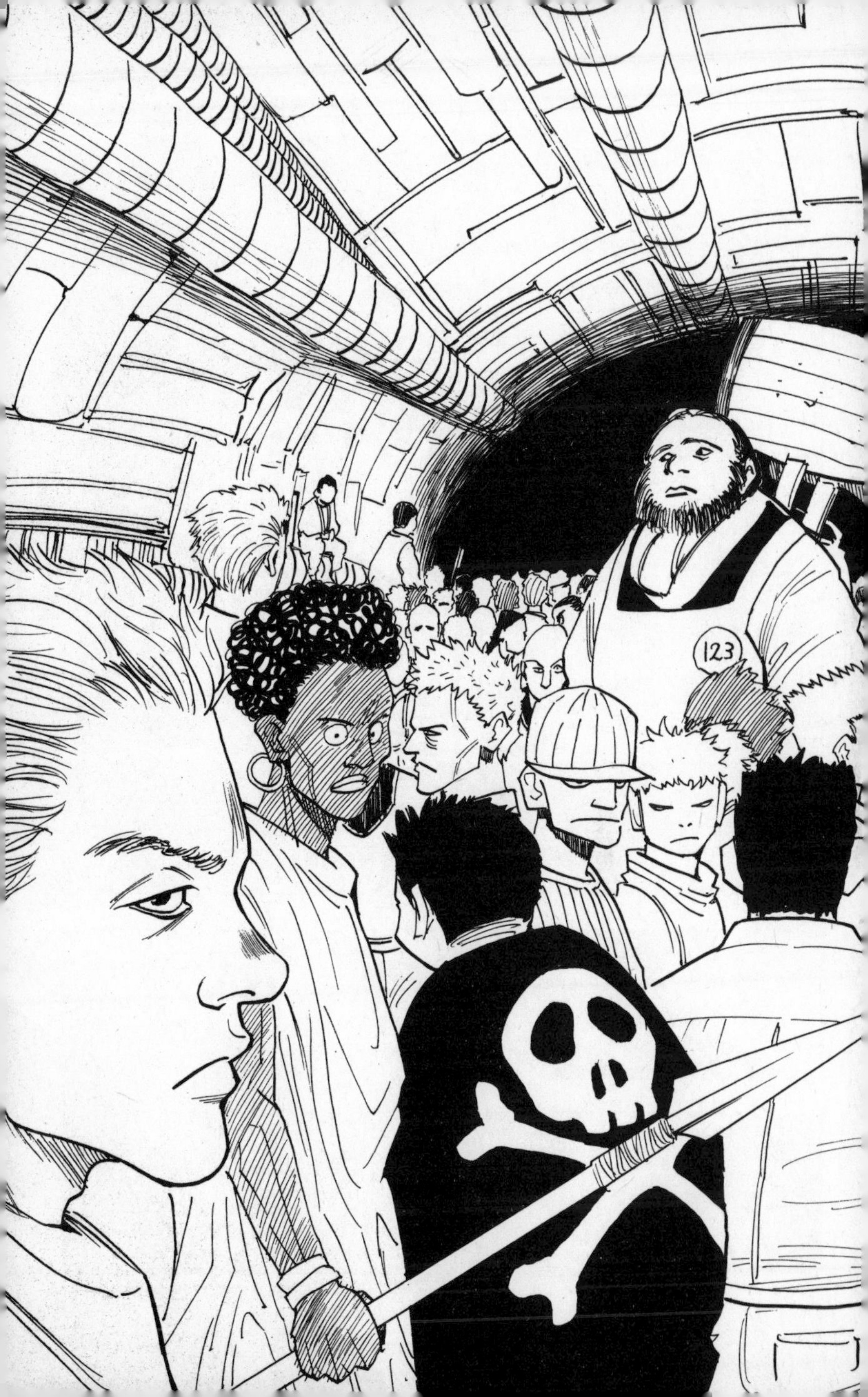
123

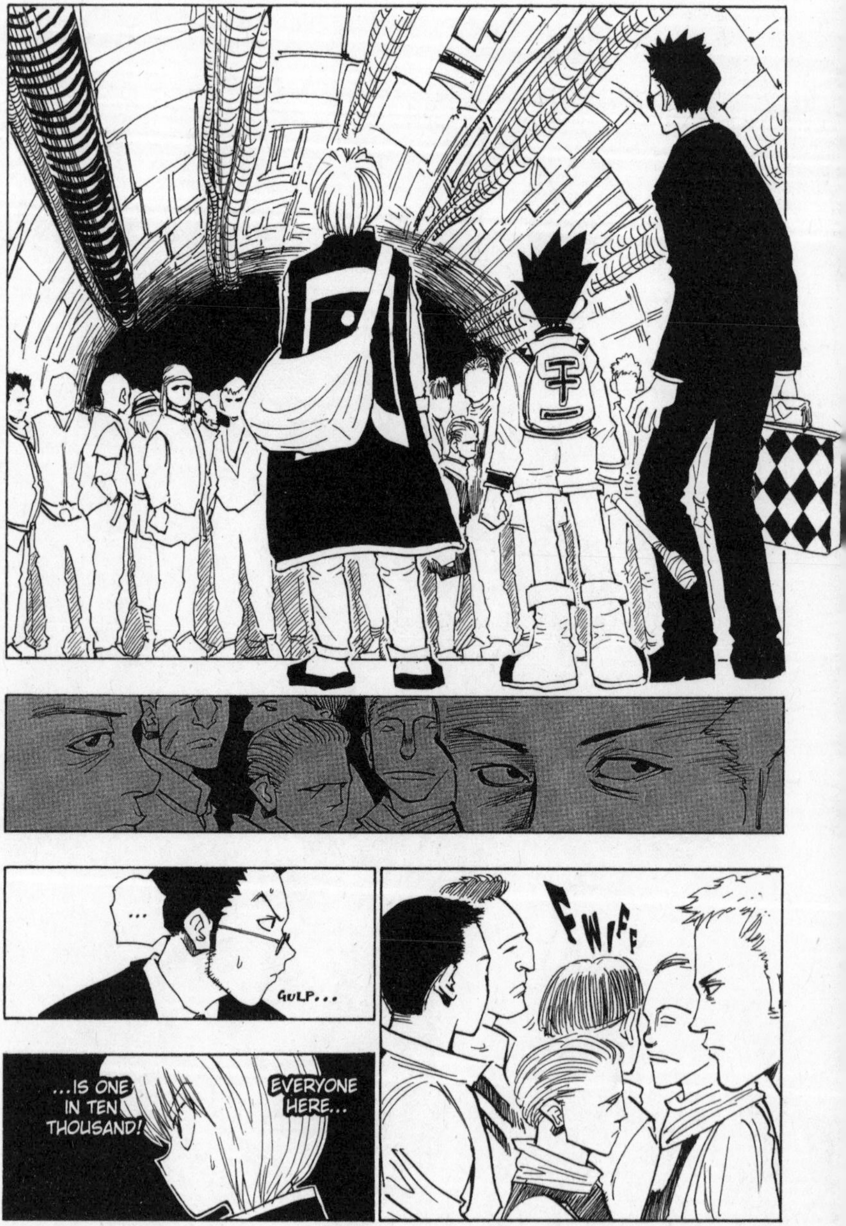
SWIFF
...
GULP...
EVERYONE HERE...
...IS ONE IN TEN THOUSAND!

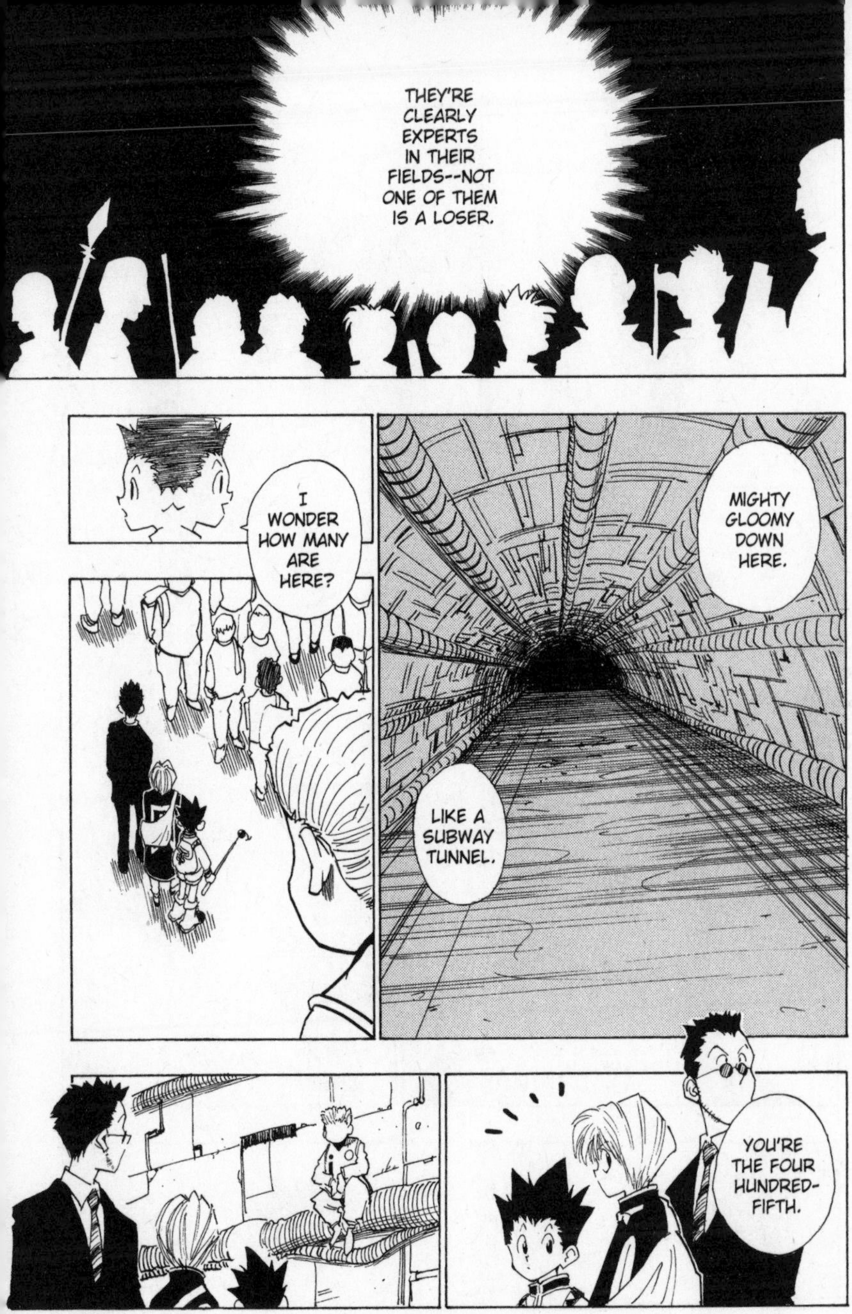
THEY'RE CLEARLY EXPERTS IN THEIR FIELDS--NOT ONE OF THEM IS A LOSER.
MIGHTY GLOOMY DOWN HERE.
LIKE A SUBWAY TUNNEL.
I WONDER HOW MANY ARE HERE?
YOU'RE THE FOUR HUNDRED-FIFTH.

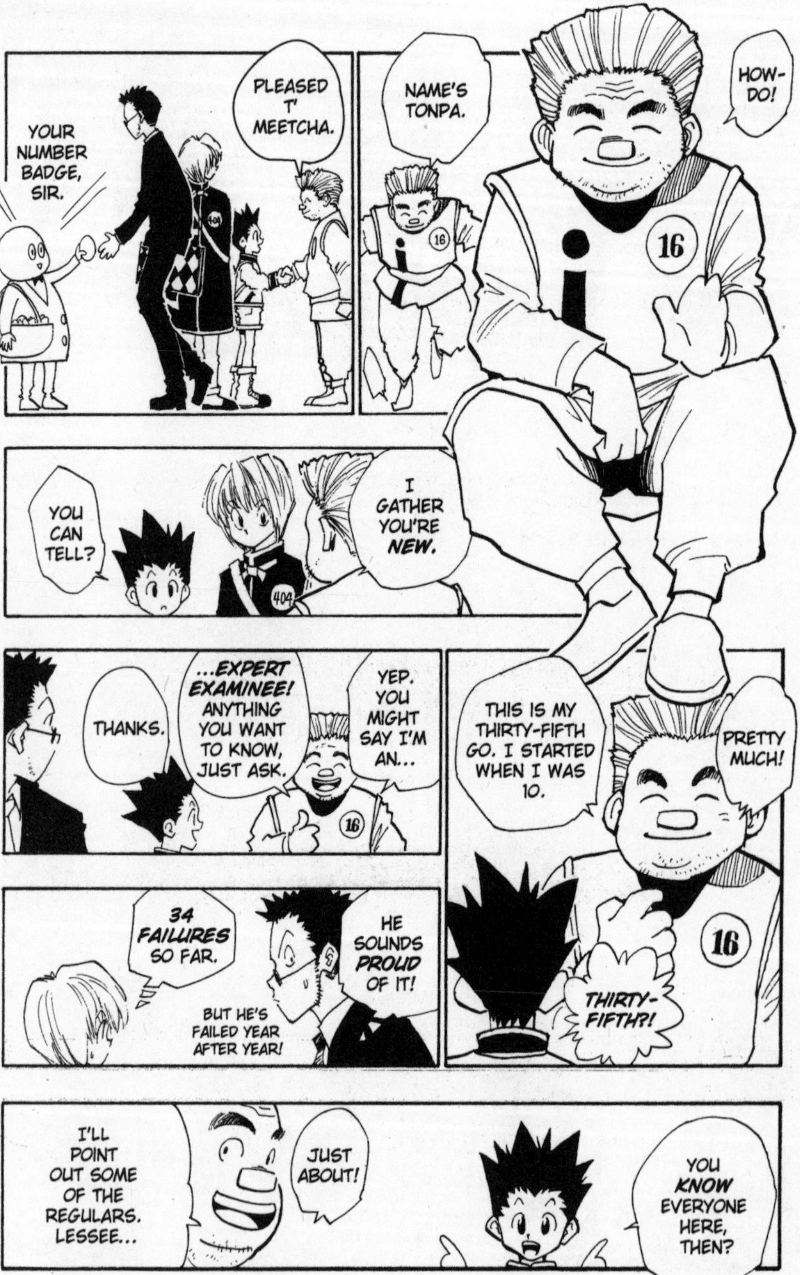
HOW-DO!
NAME'S TONPA.
PLEASED T' MEETCHA.
YOUR NUMBER BADGE, SIR.
404
I GATHER YOU'RE *NEW.*
YOU CAN TELL?
PRETTY MUCH!
THIS IS MY THIRTY-FIFTH GO. I STARTED WHEN I WAS 10.
THIRTY-FIFTH?!
YEP. YOU MIGHT SAY I'M AN...
...EXPERT EXAMINEE! ANYTHING YOU WANT TO KNOW, JUST ASK.
THANKS.
HE SOUNDS *PROUD* OF IT!
34 FAILURES SO FAR.
BUT HE'S FAILED YEAR AFTER YEAR!
YOU *KNOW* EVERYONE HERE, THEN?
JUST ABOUT!
I'LL POINT OUT SOME OF THE REGULARS. LESSEE...

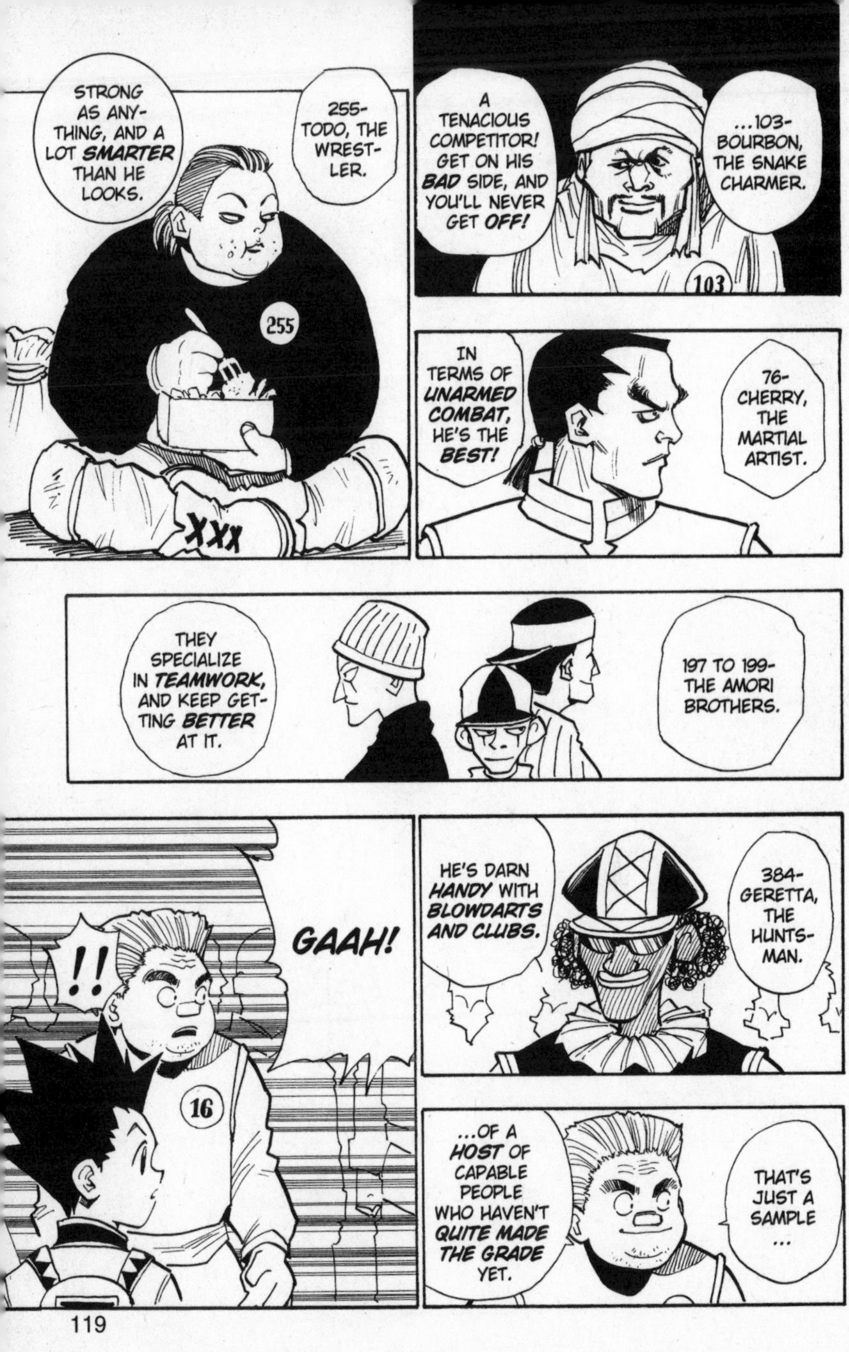
...103- BOURBON, THE SNAKE CHARMER.
A TENACIOUS COMPETITOR! GET ON HIS BAD SIDE, AND YOU'LL NEVER GET OFF!
103
76- CHERRY, THE MARTIAL ARTIST.
IN TERMS OF UNARMED COMBAT, HE'S THE BEST!
255- TODO, THE WRESTLER.
STRONG AS ANYTHING, AND A LOT SMARTER THAN HE LOOKS.
255
XXX
197 TO 199- THE AMORI BROTHERS.
THEY SPECIALIZE IN TEAMWORK, AND KEEP GETTING BETTER AT IT.
384- GERETTA, THE HUNTSMAN.
HE'S DARN HANDY WITH BLOWDARTS AND CLUBS.
THAT'S JUST A SAMPLE...
...OF A HOST OF CAPABLE PEOPLE WHO HAVEN'T QUITE MADE THE GRADE YET.
GAAH!
!!
16

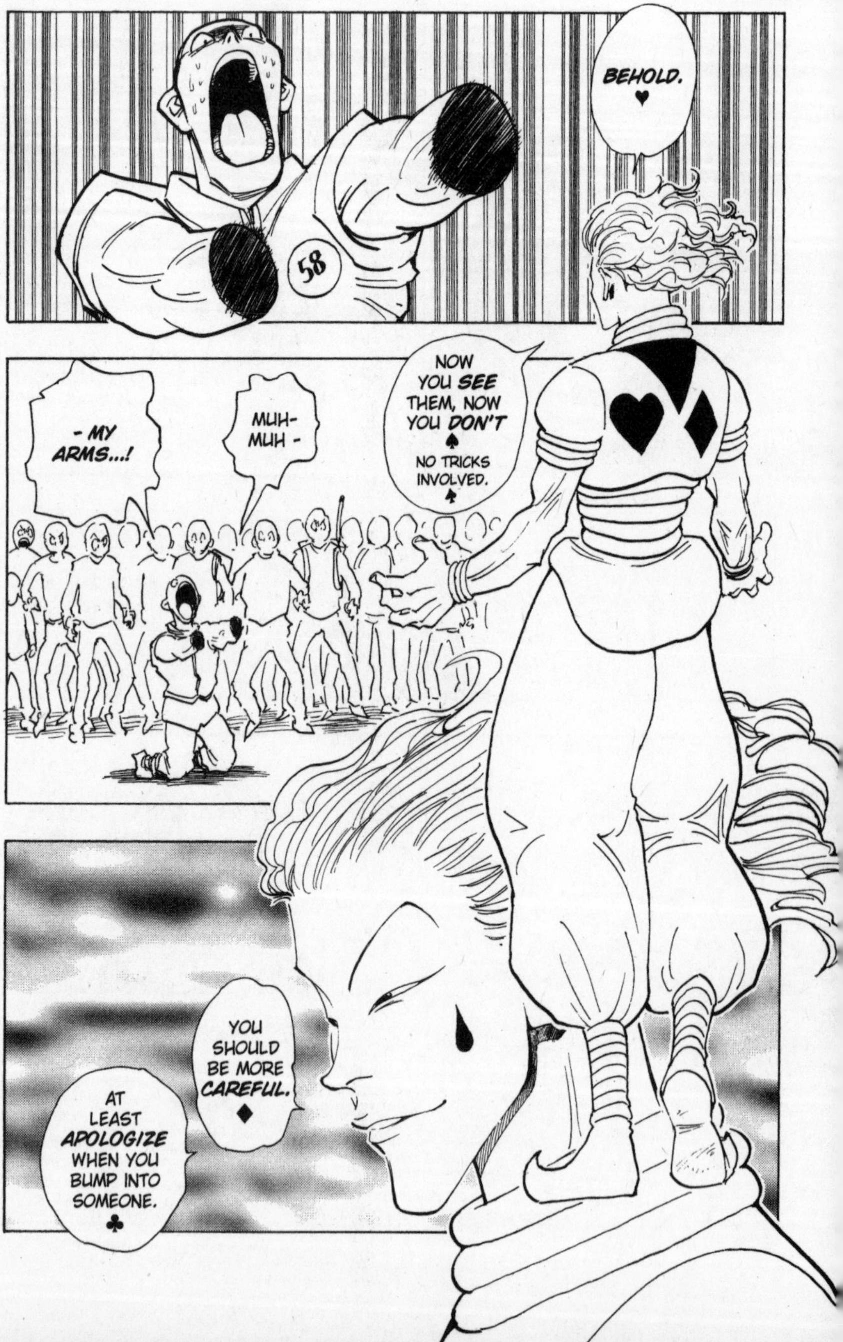

BEHOLD. ♥
58
NOW YOU SEE THEM, NOW YOU DON'T ♠ NO TRICKS INVOLVED. ♠
MUH-MUH -
- MY ARMS...!
YOU SHOULD BE MORE CAREFUL. ♦
AT LEAST APOLOGIZE WHEN YOU BUMP INTO SOMEONE. ♣

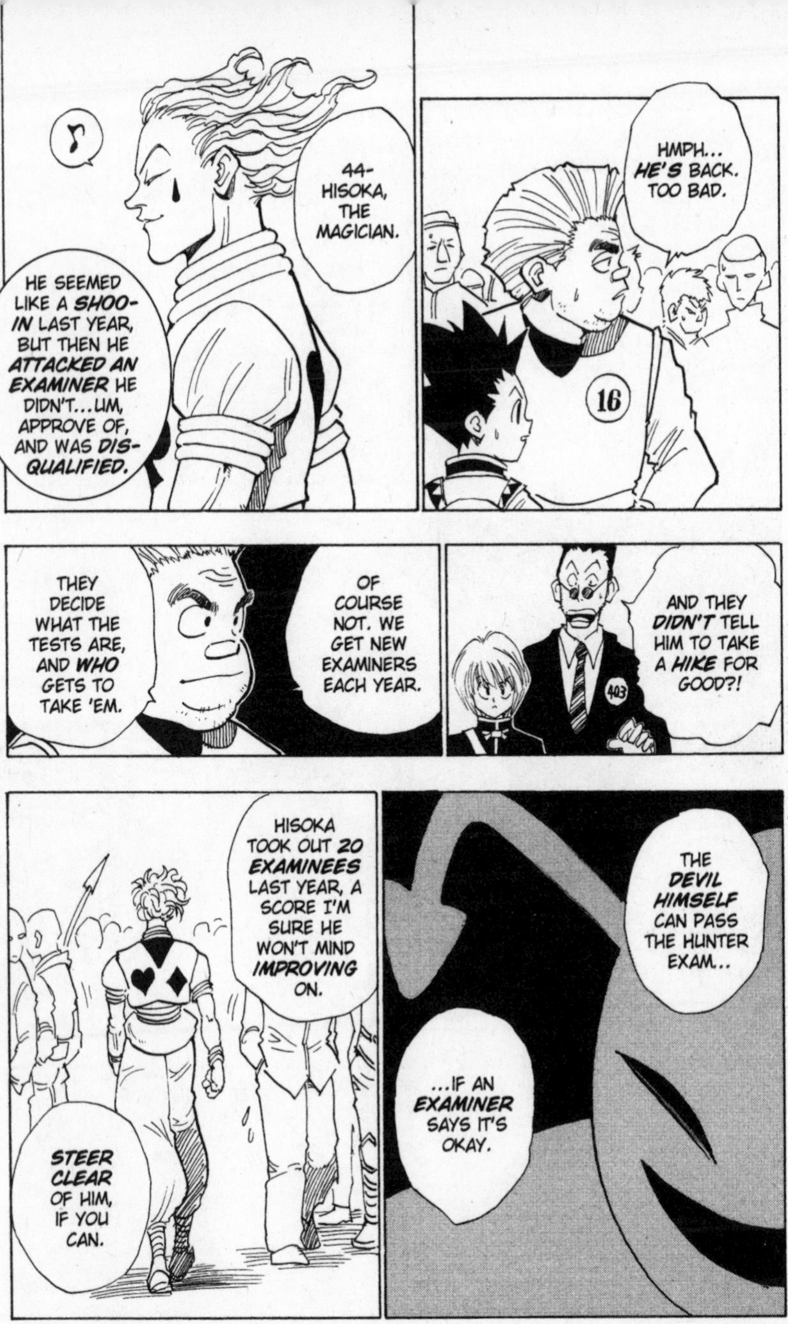
HMPH... HE'S BACK. TOO BAD.
16
44- HISOKA, THE MAGICIAN.
HE SEEMED LIKE A SHOO-IN LAST YEAR, BUT THEN HE ATTACKED AN EXAMINER HE DIDN'T...UM, APPROVE OF, AND WAS DIS-QUALIFIED.
AND THEY DIDN'T TELL HIM TO TAKE A HIKE FOR GOOD?!
403
OF COURSE NOT. WE GET NEW EXAMINERS EACH YEAR.
THEY DECIDE WHAT THE TESTS ARE, AND WHO GETS TO TAKE 'EM.
THE DEVIL HIMSELF CAN PASS THE HUNTER EXAM...
...IF AN EXAMINER SAYS IT'S OKAY.
HISOKA TOOK OUT 20 EXAMINEES LAST YEAR, A SCORE I'M SURE HE WON'T MIND IMPROVING ON.
STEER CLEAR OF HIM, IF YOU CAN.

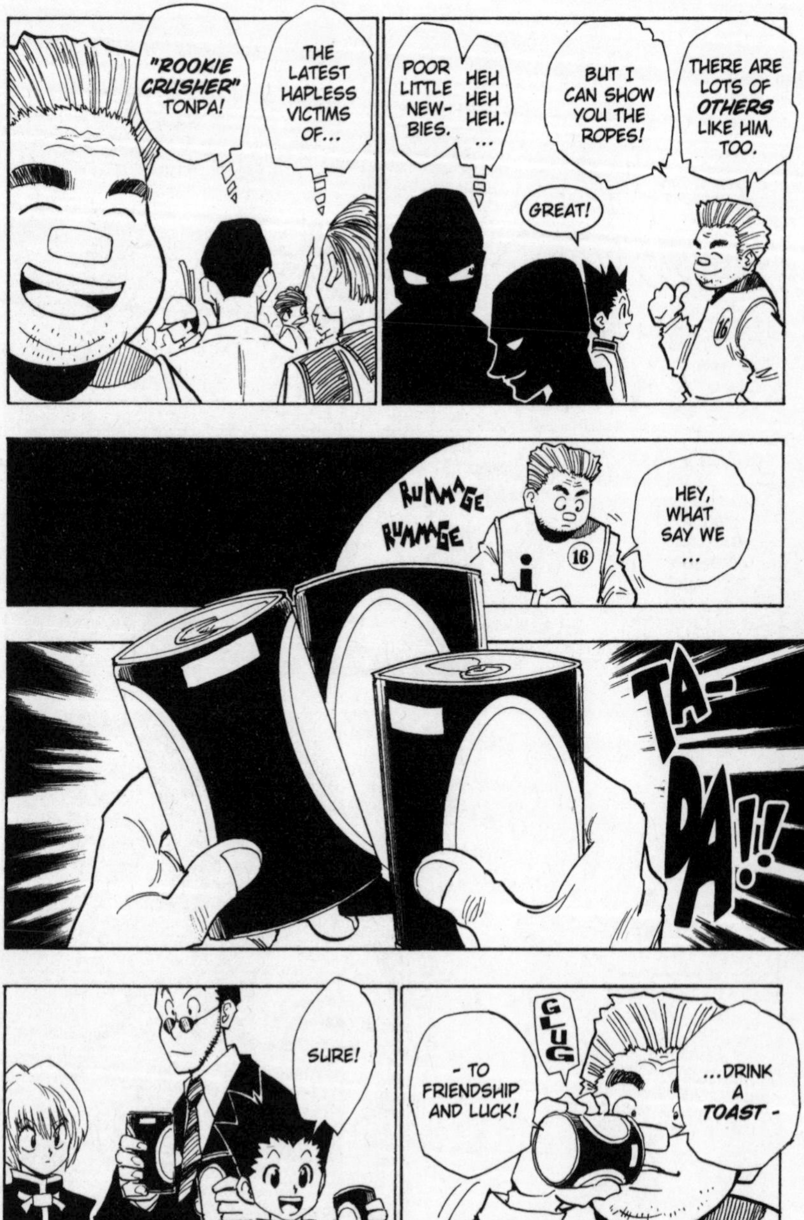
THERE ARE LOTS OF OTHERS LIKE HIM, TOO.
BUT I CAN SHOW YOU THE ROPES!
GREAT!
HEH HEH HEH. ...
POOR LITTLE NEW-BIES.
THE LATEST HAPLESS VICTIMS OF...
"ROOKIE CRUSHER" TONPA!
HEY, WHAT SAY WE ...
RUMMAGE
RUMMAGE
TA-DA!!!
...DRINK A TOAST -
GLUG
- TO FRIENDSHIP AND LUCK!
SURE!

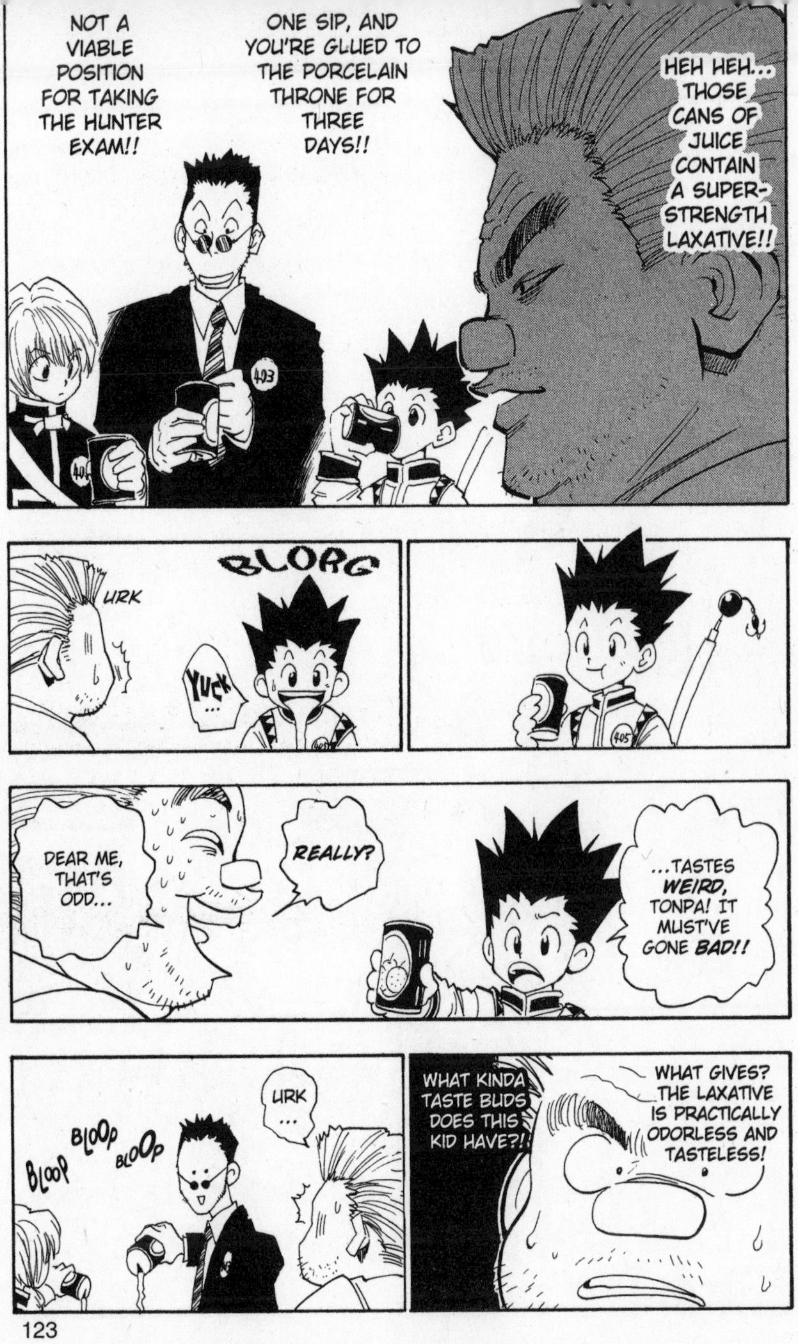
HEH HEH... THOSE CANS OF JUICE CONTAIN A SUPER-STRENGTH LAXATIVE!!
ONE SIP, AND YOU'RE GLUED TO THE PORCELAIN THRONE FOR THREE DAYS!!
NOT A VIABLE POSITION FOR TAKING THE HUNTER EXAM!!
BLORG
URK
YUCK ...
...TASTES WEIRD, TONPA! IT MUST'VE GONE BAD!!
REALLY?
DEAR ME, THAT'S ODD...
WHAT GIVES? THE LAXATIVE IS PRACTICALLY ODORLESS AND TASTELESS!
WHAT KINDA TASTE BUDS DOES THIS KID HAVE?!
URK ...
BLOOP
BLOOP
BLOOP

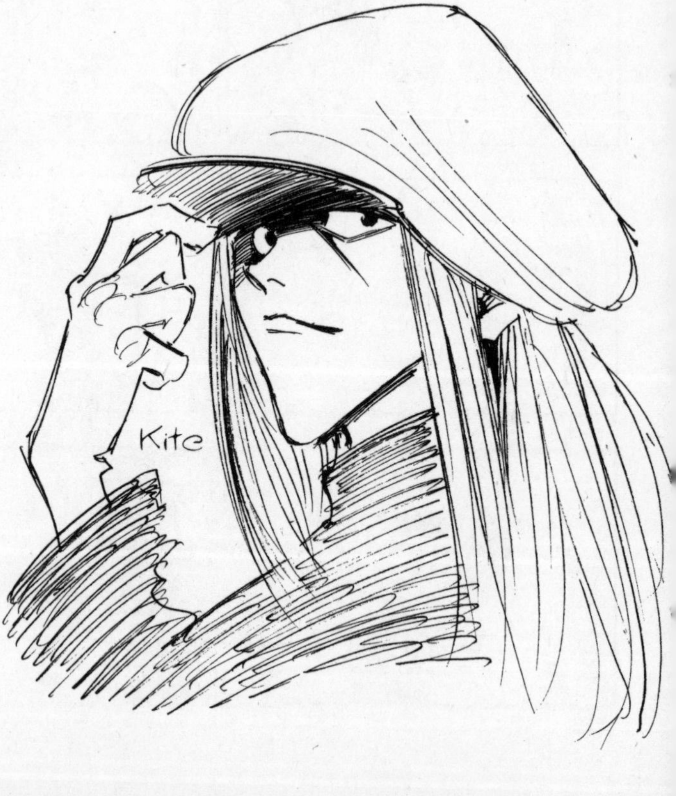
Kite

Chapter 6
The First Phase Begins, part 2

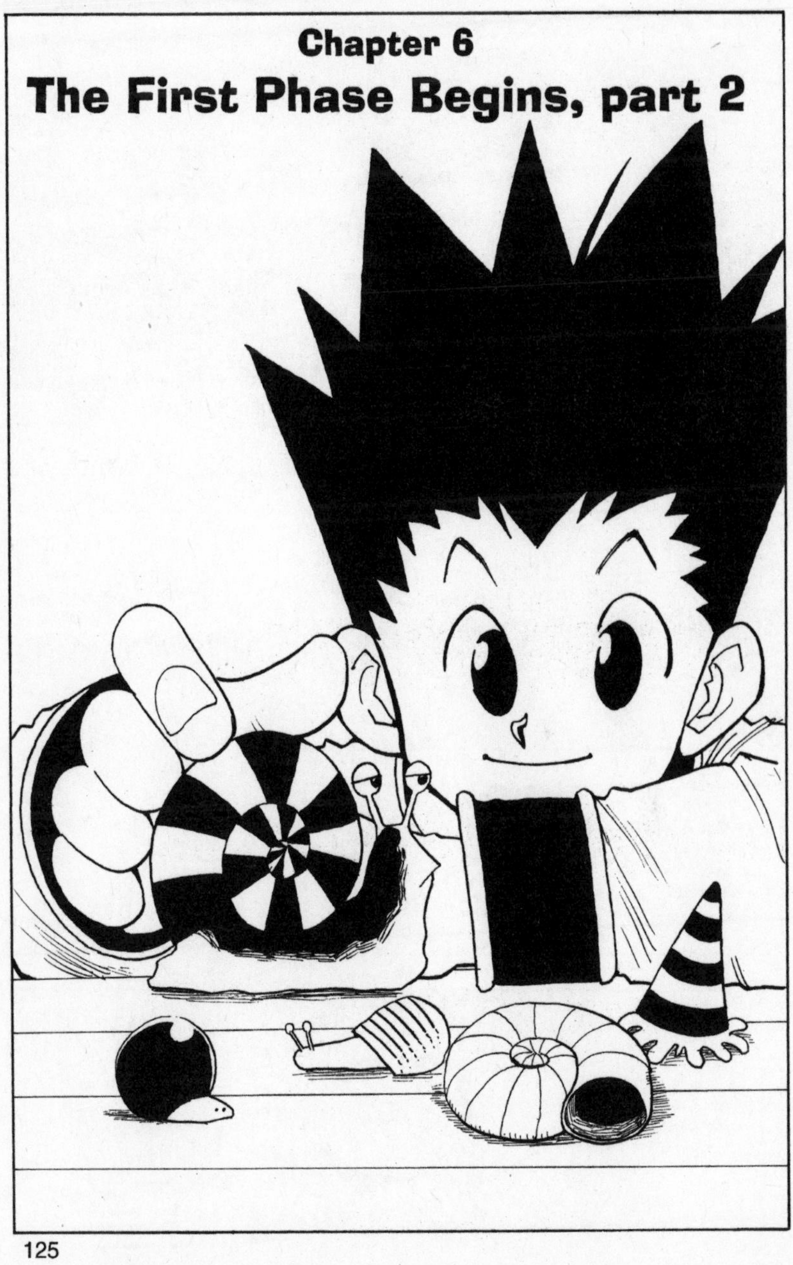

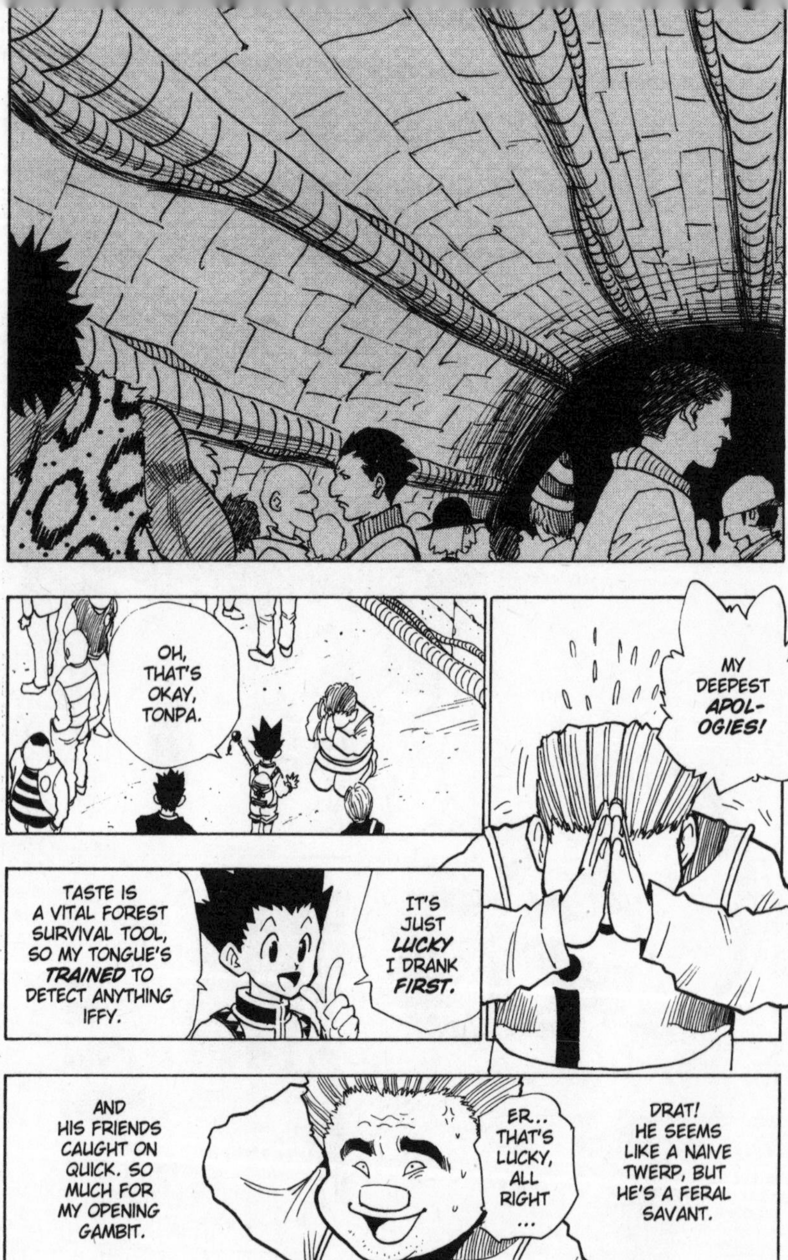
MY DEEPEST APOLOGIES!
OH, THAT'S OKAY, TONPA.
IT'S JUST LUCKY I DRANK FIRST.
TASTE IS A VITAL FOREST SURVIVAL TOOL, SO MY TONGUE'S TRAINED TO DETECT ANYTHING IFFY.
DRAT! HE SEEMS LIKE A NAIVE TWERP, BUT HE'S A FERAL SAVANT.
ER.. THAT'S LUCKY, ALL RIGHT ...
AND HIS FRIENDS CAUGHT ON QUICK. SO MUCH FOR MY OPENING GAMBIT.

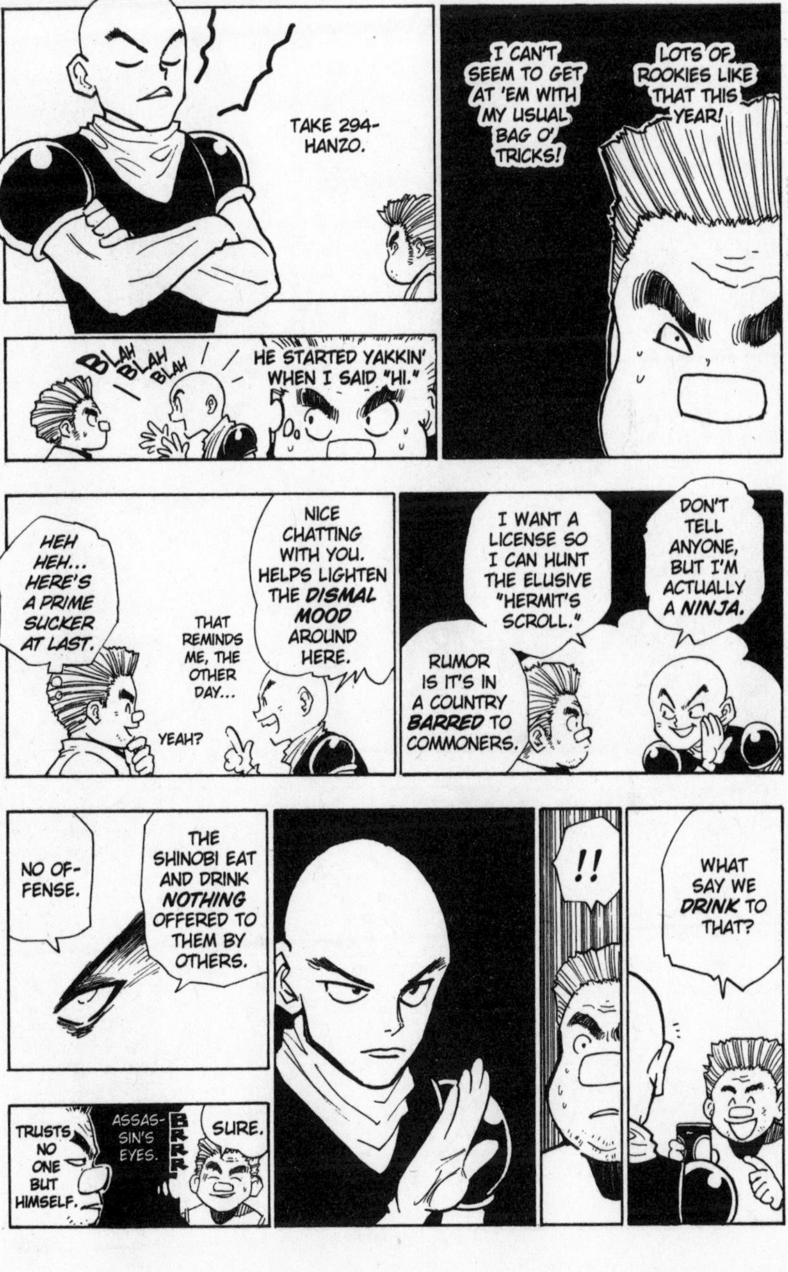
LOTS OF ROOKIES LIKE THAT THIS YEAR!
I CAN'T SEEM TO GET AT 'EM WITH MY USUAL BAG O' TRICKS!
TAKE 294-HANZO.
HE STARTED YAKKIN' WHEN I SAID "HI."
BLAH BLAH BLAH
DON'T TELL ANYONE, BUT I'M ACTUALLY A NINJA.
I WANT A LICENSE SO I CAN HUNT THE ELUSIVE "HERMIT'S SCROLL."
RUMOR IS IT'S IN A COUNTRY BARRED TO COMMONERS.
NICE CHATTING WITH YOU. HELPS LIGHTEN THE DISMAL MOOD AROUND HERE.
THAT REMINDS ME, THE OTHER DAY...
HEH HEH... HERE'S A PRIME SUCKER AT LAST.
YEAH?
WHAT SAY WE DRINK TO THAT?
!!
THE SHINOBI EAT AND DRINK NOTHING OFFERED TO THEM BY OTHERS.
NO OF-FENSE.
SURE.
BRRR
ASSAS-SIN'S EYES.
TRUSTS NO ONE BUT HIMSELF.

AS FOR 187-NICHOLAS...
TAP TAP
ONE MOMENT, PLEASE.
"TONPA"...
AH...YOU'RE ON YOUR THIRTY-FIFTH ATTEMPT. THAT'S THE SECOND HIGHEST NUMBER OF TRIES BY ANYONE.
YOU DO, HOWEVER, HOLD THE RECORD FOR CONSECUTIVE TRIES AT 30. PRETTY IMPRESSIVE.
YOU MAKE A GOOD SHOWING EVERY TIME, BUT YOU GET TOO CAUGHT UP IN WHITTLING DOWN THE NEWBIE FACTION TO MAKE THE CUT.
THAT'S HOW YOU EARNED THE SOBRIQUET...
..."ROOKIE CRUSHER." THEREFORE, I'LL DECLINE YOUR OVERTURES.
AND THEN THERE'S 301...
...WHO'S JUST TOO CREEPY! I DECIDED TO TAKE A PASS.
KLAGGA KLAGGA KLAGGA KLAGGA

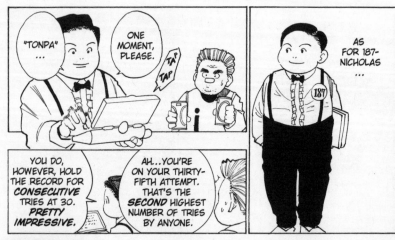

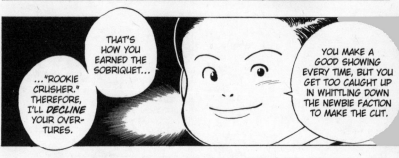

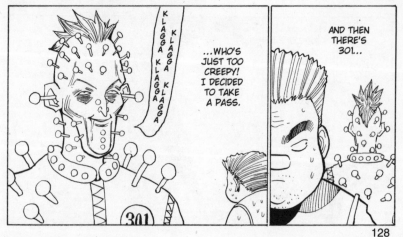

READ THIS WAY

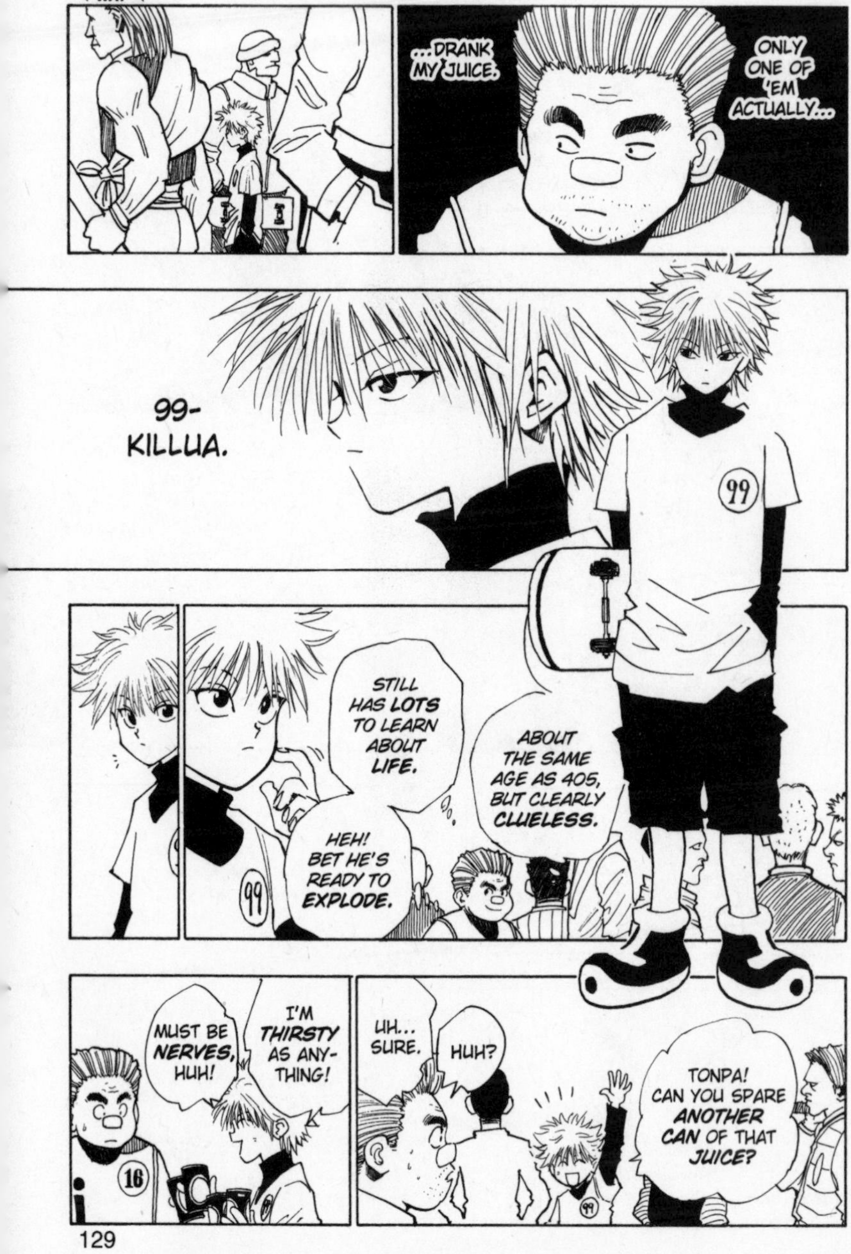

ONLY ONE OF 'EM ACTUALLY...
...DRANK MY JUICE.
99-
KILLUA.
ABOUT THE SAME AGE AS 405, BUT CLEARLY CLUELESS.
STILL HAS LOTS TO LEARN ABOUT LIFE.
HEH! BET HE'S READY TO EXPLODE.
TONPA! CAN YOU SPARE ANOTHER CAN OF THAT JUICE?
HUH?
UH... SURE.
I'M THIRSTY AS ANYTHING!
MUST BE NERVES, HUH!

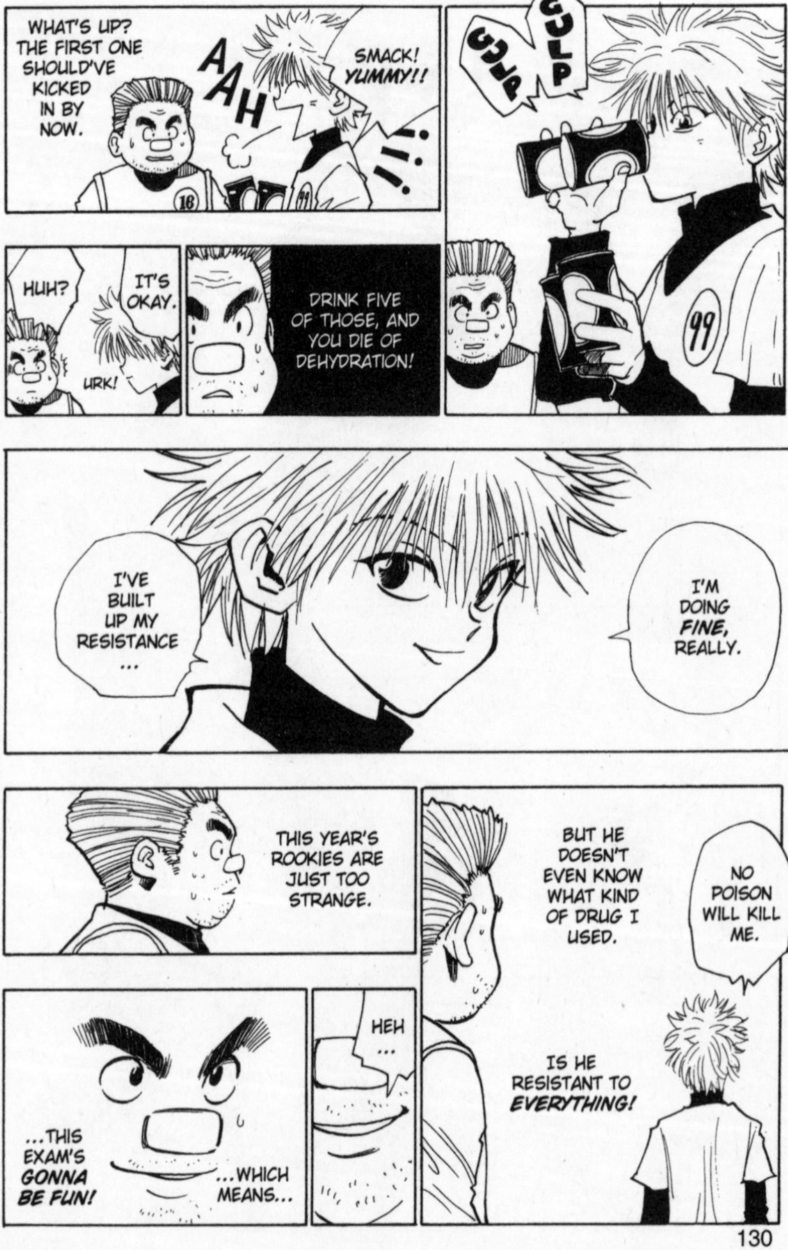
GULP
GULP
SMACK! YUMMY!!
AAH
!!
WHAT'S UP? THE FIRST ONE SHOULD'VE KICKED IN BY NOW.
DRINK FIVE OF THOSE, AND YOU DIE OF DEHYDRATION!
IT'S OKAY.
HUH?
URK!
I'M DOING FINE, REALLY.
I'VE BUILT UP MY RESISTANCE...
NO POISON WILL KILL ME.
BUT HE DOESN'T EVEN KNOW WHAT KIND OF DRUG I USED.
IS HE RESISTANT TO EVERYTHING!
THIS YEAR'S ROOKIES ARE JUST TOO STRANGE.
HEH...
...WHICH MEANS...
...THIS EXAM'S GONNA BE FUN!

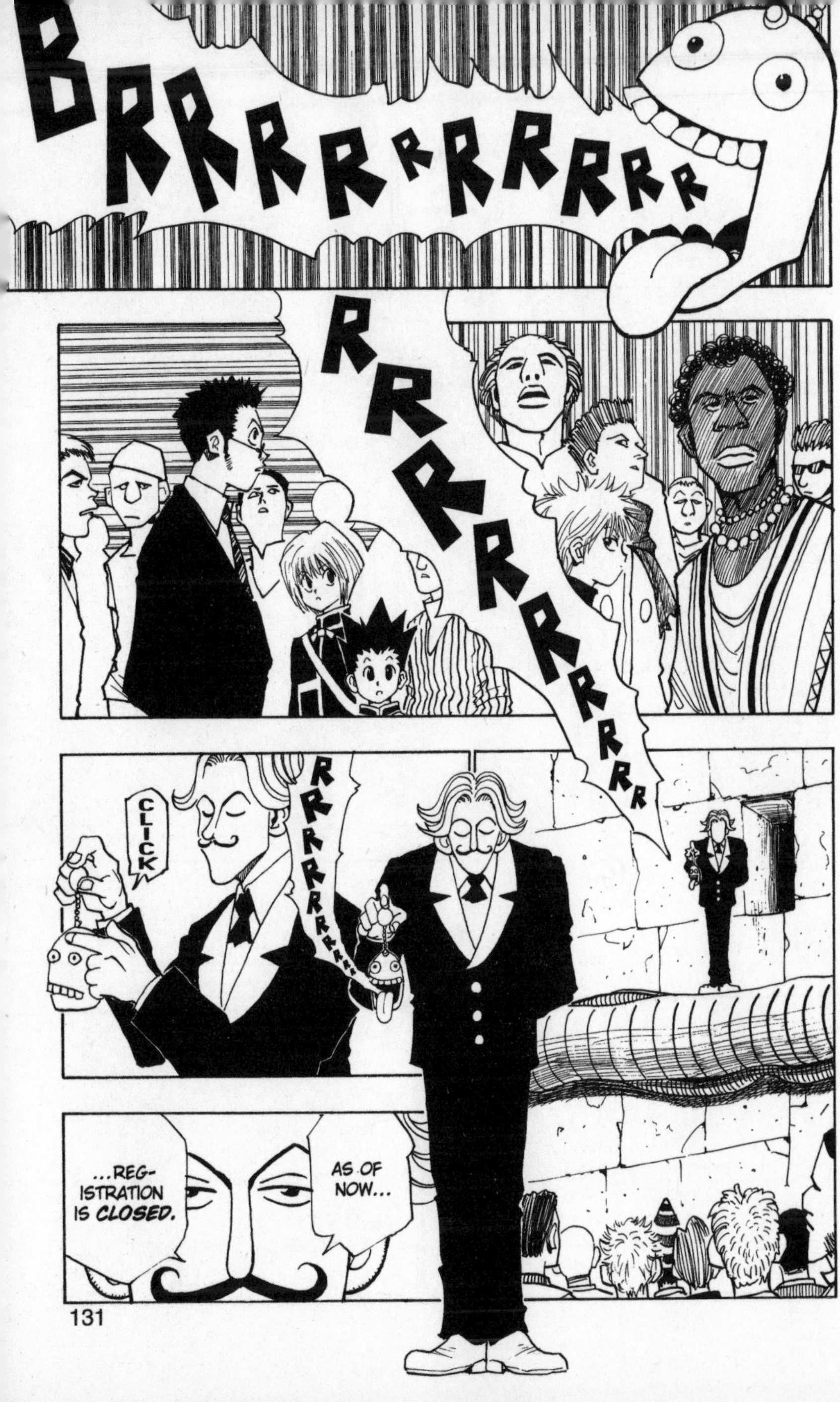
BRRRRRRRRRRR
RRRRRRRRRR
CLICK
RRRRRRRRRR
AS OF NOW...
...REGISTRATION IS CLOSED.

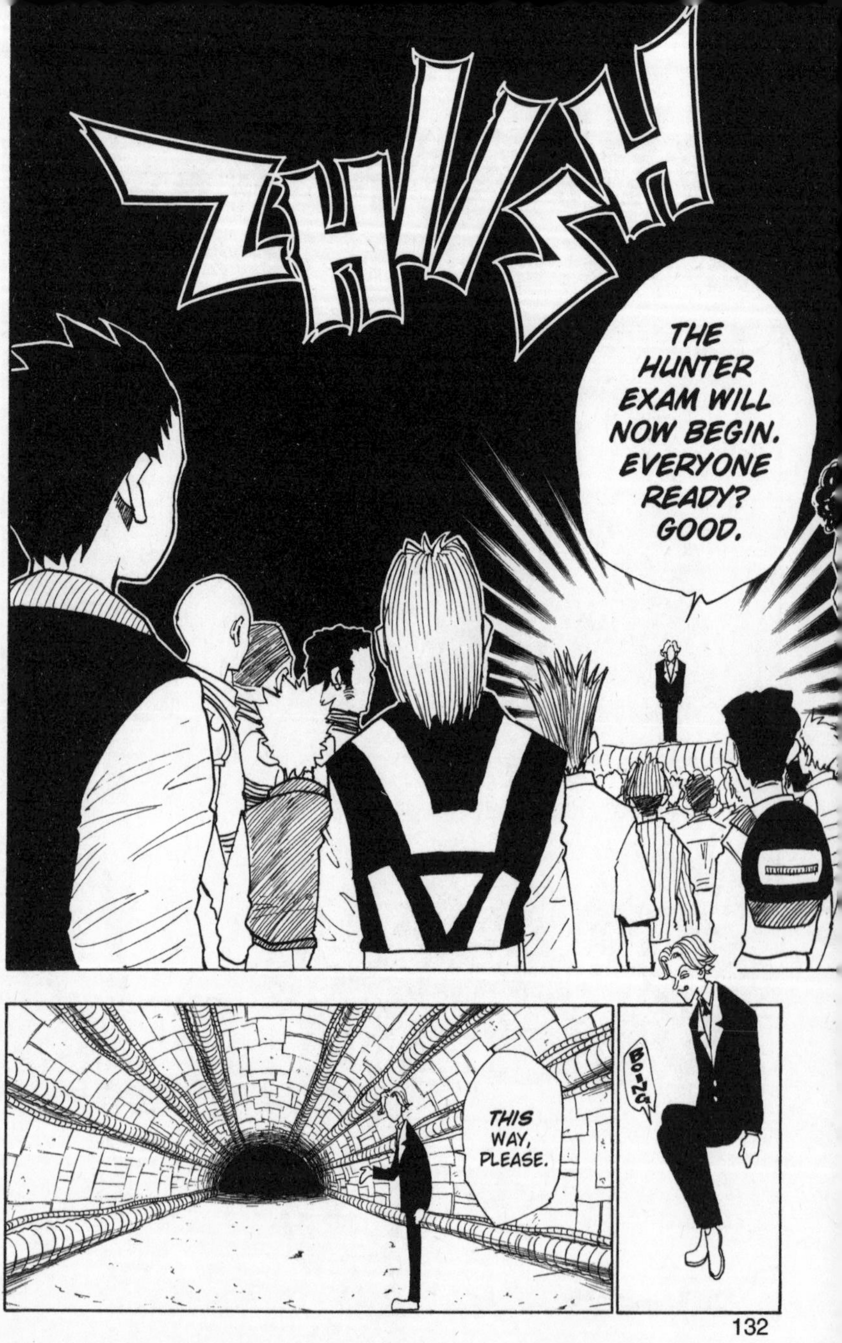
ZHISH
THE HUNTER EXAM WILL NOW BEGIN. EVERYONE READY? GOOD.
BOING
THIS WAY, PLEASE.

JUST SO THERE'S NO MISTAKE...
TUP
TUP
TUP
...THE HUNTER EXAM IS VERY RIGOROUS. IF YOU LACK THE NECESSARY ABILITY--TOO BAD. IF YOU'RE UNLUCKY--AGAIN, TOO BAD.
AND EXAMINEES ARE NOT ABOVE SABOTAGING EACH OTHER, AS YOU SAW.
IF YOU'RE OKAY WITH THAT...
...THEN YOU'RE WELCOME TO CONTINUE.
TROOP
TROOP
SHUFF SHUFF
TROOP
TROOP
TROOP
TROOP

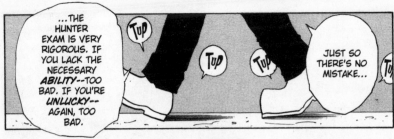

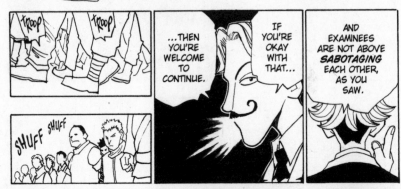

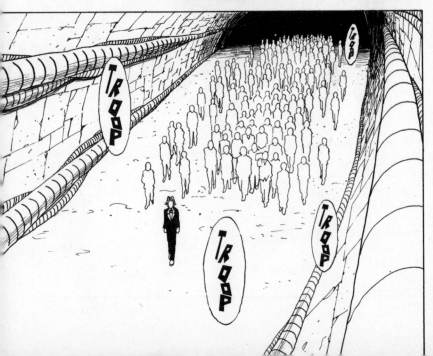

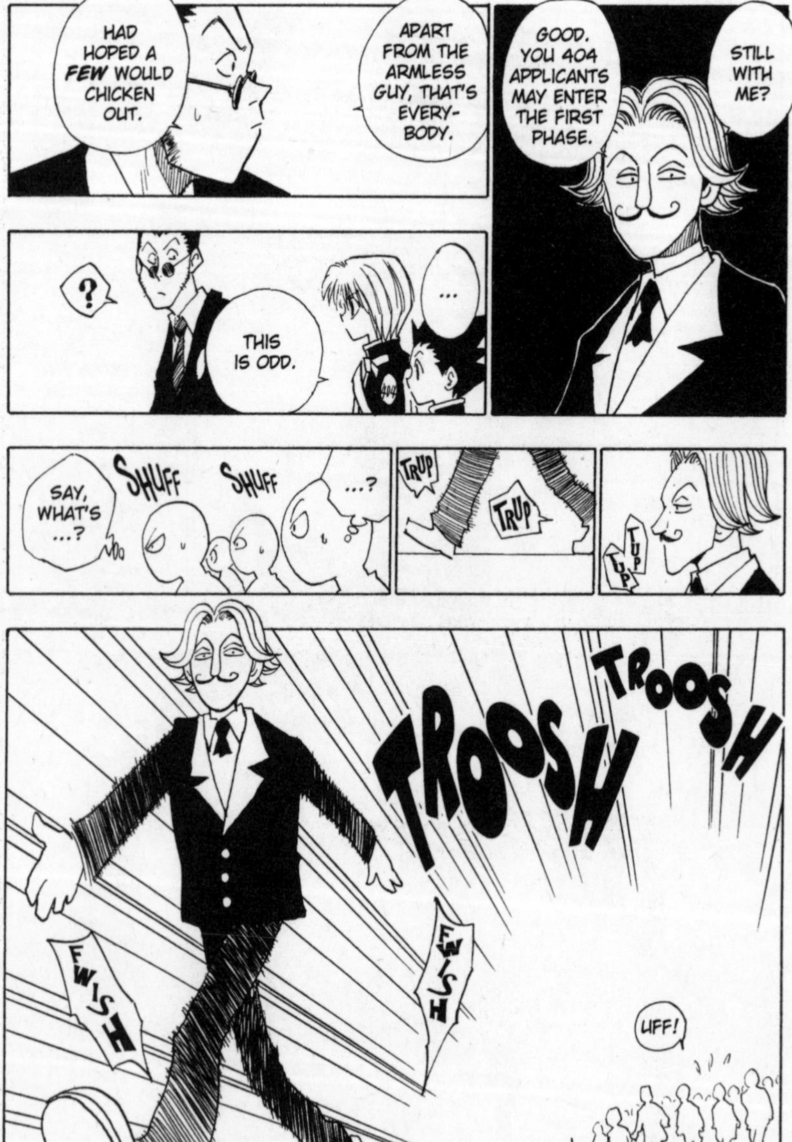
STILL WITH ME?
GOOD. YOU 404 APPLICANTS MAY ENTER THE FIRST PHASE.
APART FROM THE ARMLESS GUY, THAT'S EVERY-BODY.
HAD HOPED A FEW WOULD CHICKEN OUT.
...
THIS IS ODD.
?
TUP
TUP
TRUP
TRUP
...?
SHUFF
SHUFF
SAY, WHAT'S ...?
TROOSH
TROOSH
FWISH
UFF!
FWISH

READ THIS WAY

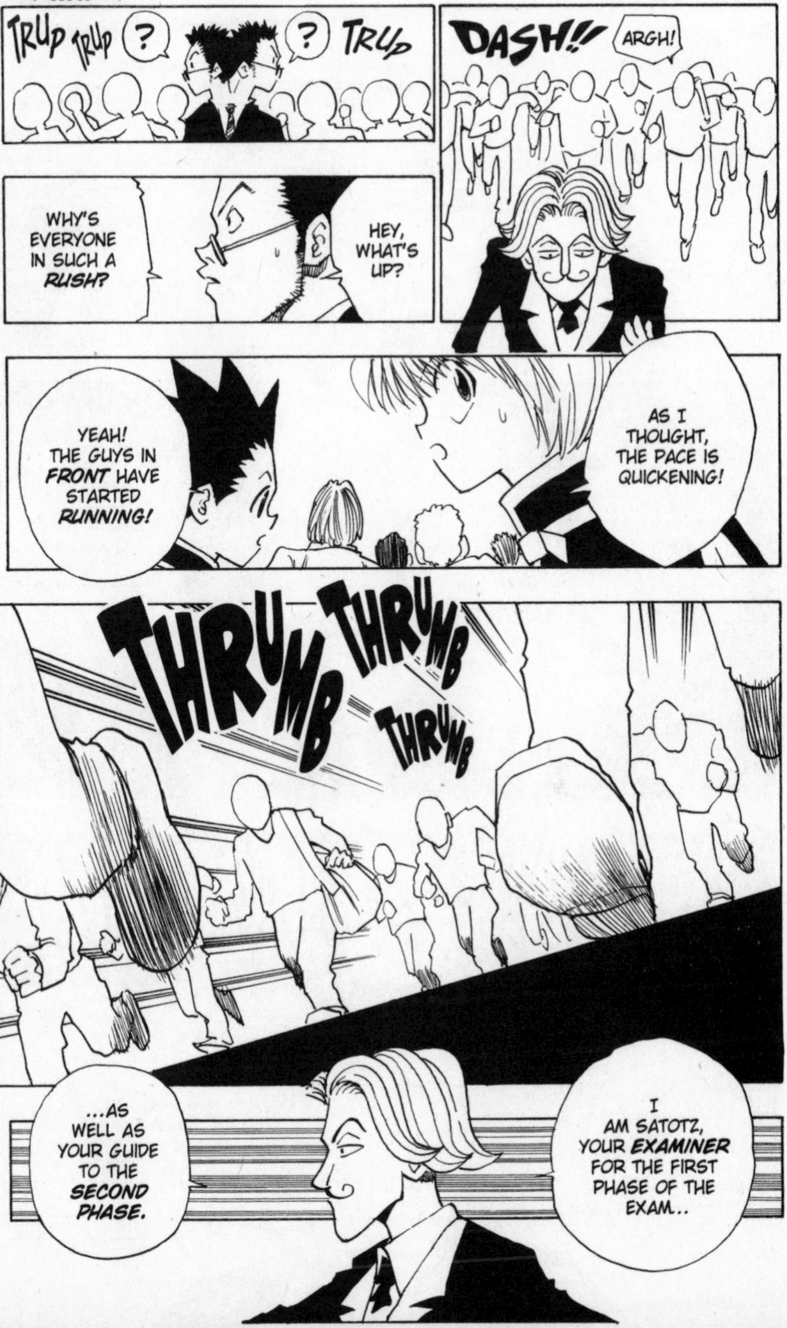
DASH!!
ARGH!
TRUP
?
?
TRUP
TRUP
HEY, WHAT'S UP?
WHY'S EVERYONE IN SUCH A *RUSH?*
AS I THOUGHT, THE PACE IS QUICKENING!
YEAH! THE GUYS IN *FRONT* HAVE STARTED *RUNNING!*
THRUMB THRUMB THRUMB THRUMB
I AM SATOTZ, YOUR *EXAMINER* FOR THE FIRST PHASE OF THE EXAM...
...AS WELL AS YOUR GUIDE TO THE *SECOND PHASE.*

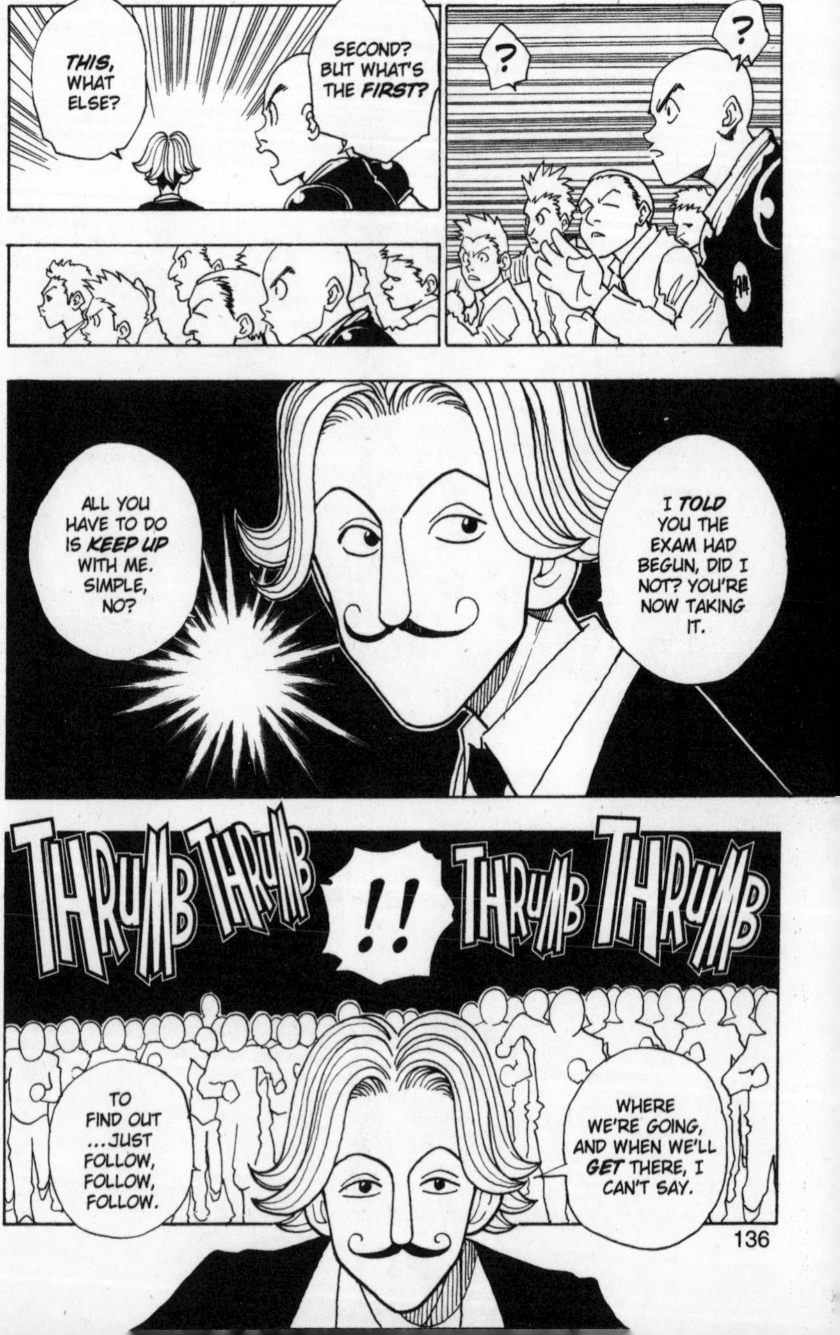
?
?
SECOND? BUT WHAT'S THE FIRST?
THIS, WHAT ELSE?
I TOLD YOU THE EXAM HAD BEGUN, DID I NOT? YOU'RE NOW TAKING IT.
ALL YOU HAVE TO DO IS KEEP UP WITH ME. SIMPLE, NO?
THRUMB THRUMB
!!
THRUMB THRUMB
WHERE WE'RE GOING, AND WHEN WE'LL GET THERE, I CAN'T SAY.
TO FIND OUT ...JUST FOLLOW, FOLLOW, FOLLOW.

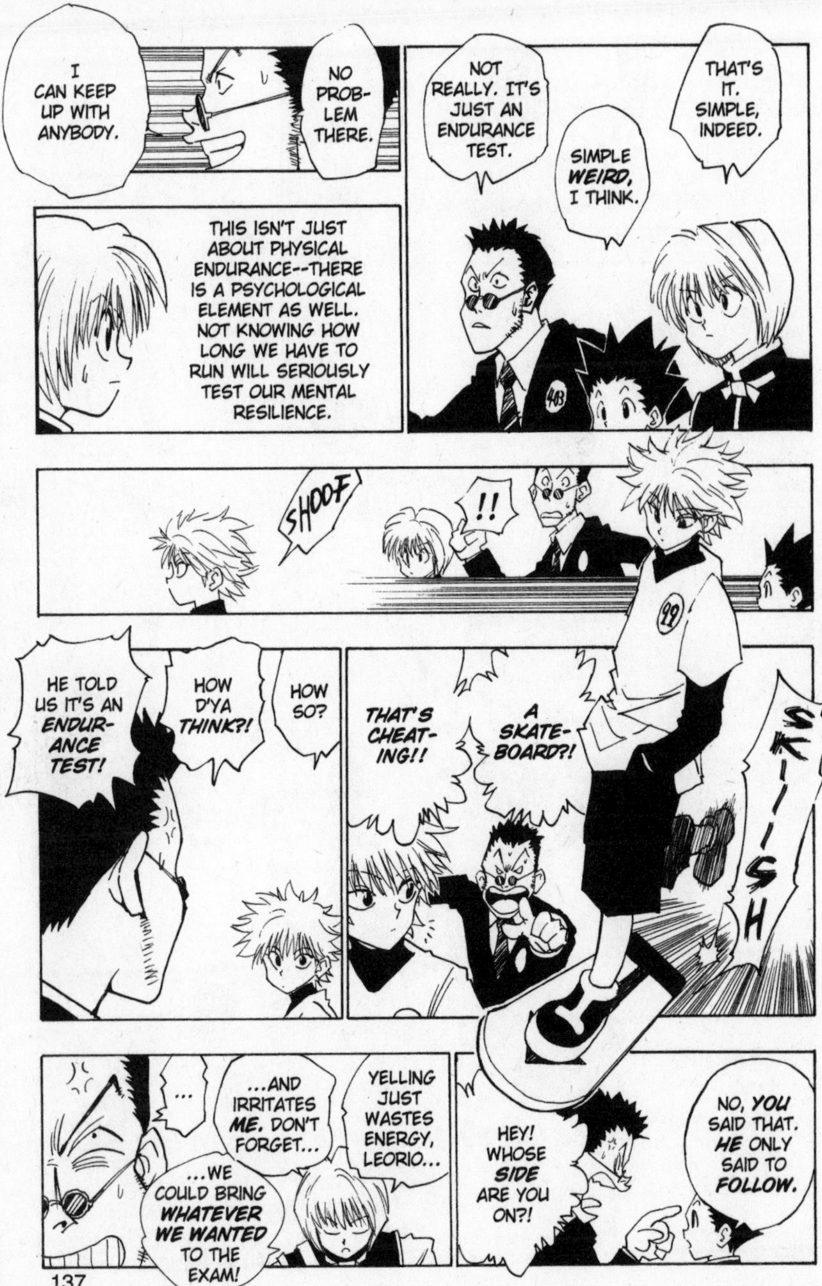
THAT'S IT. SIMPLE, INDEED.
NOT REALLY. IT'S JUST AN ENDURANCE TEST.
SIMPLE WEIRD, I THINK.
NO PROB-LEM THERE.
I CAN KEEP UP WITH ANYBODY.
THIS ISN'T JUST ABOUT PHYSICAL ENDURANCE--THERE IS A PSYCHOLOGICAL ELEMENT AS WELL. NOT KNOWING HOW LONG WE HAVE TO RUN WILL SERIOUSLY TEST OUR MENTAL RESILIENCE.
SHOOF
!!
SKIISH
A SKATE-BOARD?!
THAT'S CHEAT-ING!!
HOW SO?
HOW D'YA THINK?!
HE TOLD US IT'S AN ENDUR-ANCE TEST!
NO, YOU SAID THAT. HE ONLY SAID TO FOLLOW.
HEY! WHOSE SIDE ARE YOU ON?!
YELLING JUST WASTES ENERGY, LEORIO...
...AND IRRITATES ME. DON'T FORGET...
...WE COULD BRING WHATEVER WE WANTED TO THE EXAM!
...

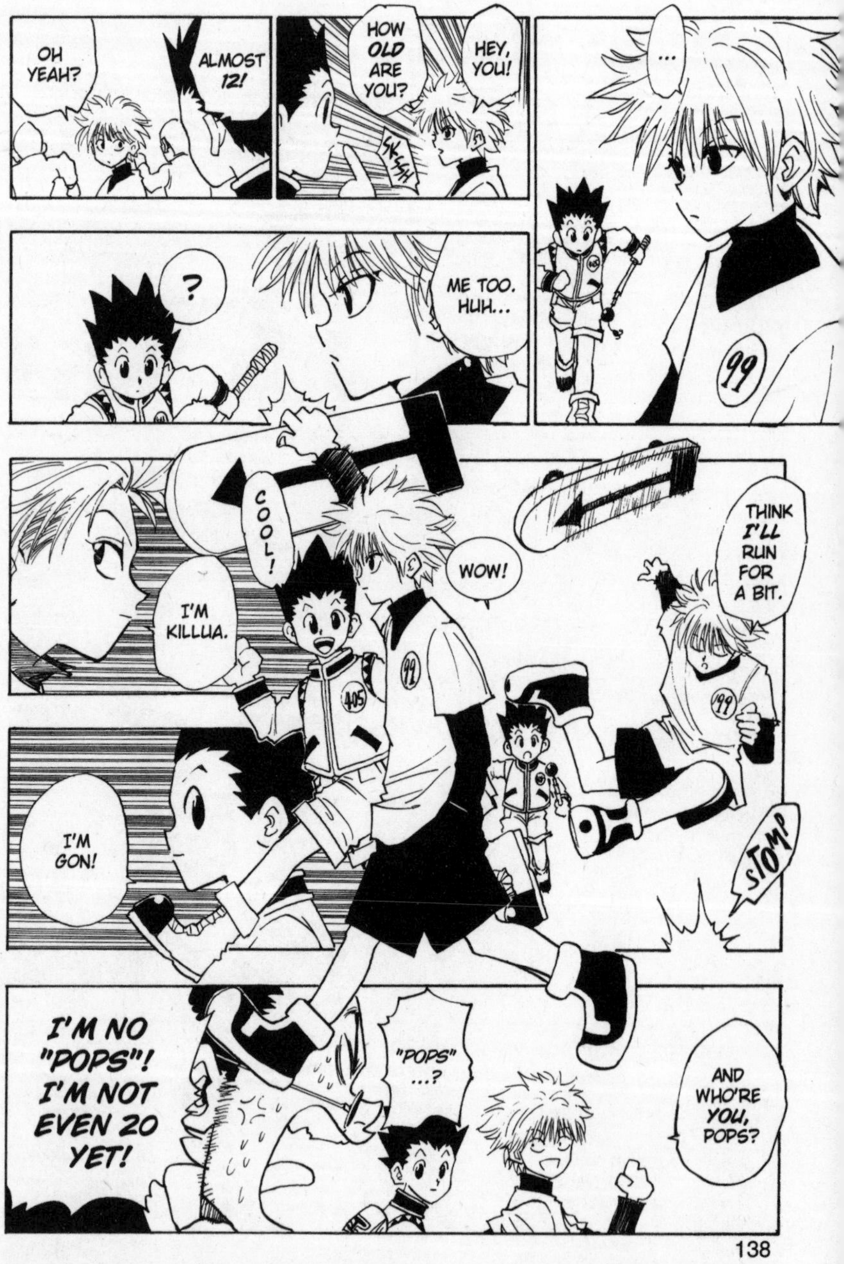
...
HEY, YOU!
HOW OLD ARE YOU?
SKSSH
ALMOST 12!
OH YEAH?
ME TOO. HUH...
?
THINK I'LL RUN FOR A BIT.
STOMP
WOW!
COOL!
I'M KILLUA.
I'M GON!
AND WHO'RE YOU, POPS?
"POPS" ...?
I'M NO "POPS"! I'M NOT EVEN 20 YET!

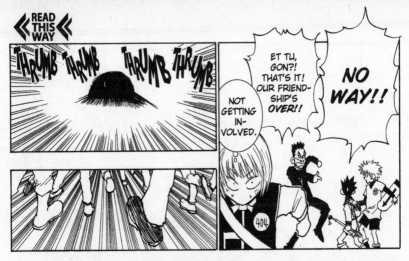

READ THIS WAY
NO WAY!!
ET TU, GON?! THAT'S IT! OUR FRIEND-SHIP'S OVER!!
NOT GETTING IN-VOLVED.
THRUMB THRUMB THRUMB THRUMB
404
BEEN RUNNING ABOUT... THREE HOURS.
WE MUST HAVE COVERED NEARLY 40KM AT THIS PACE.
SOME MUST HAVE DROPPED OUT BY NOW...
THRUMB THRUMB THRU

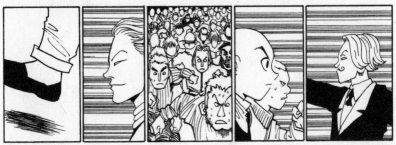

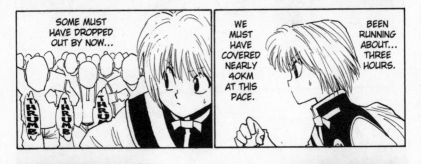

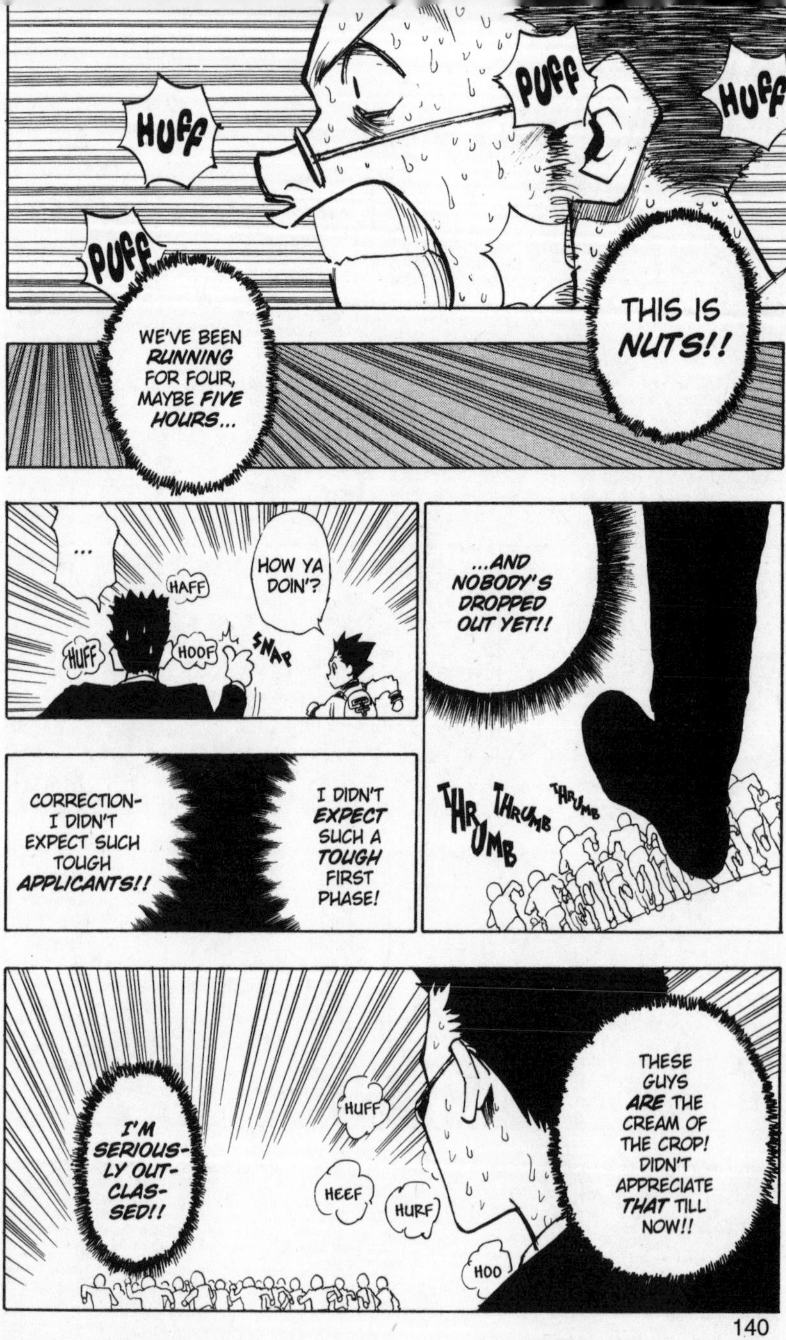
HUFF
PUFF
HUFF
PUFF
THIS IS NUTS!!
WE'VE BEEN RUNNING FOR FOUR, MAYBE FIVE HOURS...
...AND NOBODY'S DROPPED OUT YET!!
THRUMB THRUMB THRUMB
HOW YA DOIN'?
SNAP
HOOF
HAFF
HUFF
...
I DIDN'T EXPECT SUCH A TOUGH FIRST PHASE!
CORRECTION- I DIDN'T EXPECT SUCH TOUGH APPLICANTS!!
THESE GUYS ARE THE CREAM OF THE CROP! DIDN'T APPRECIATE THAT TILL NOW!!
HUFF
HURF
HEEF
HOO
I'M SERIOUS-LY OUT-CLAS-SED!!

READ THIS WAY

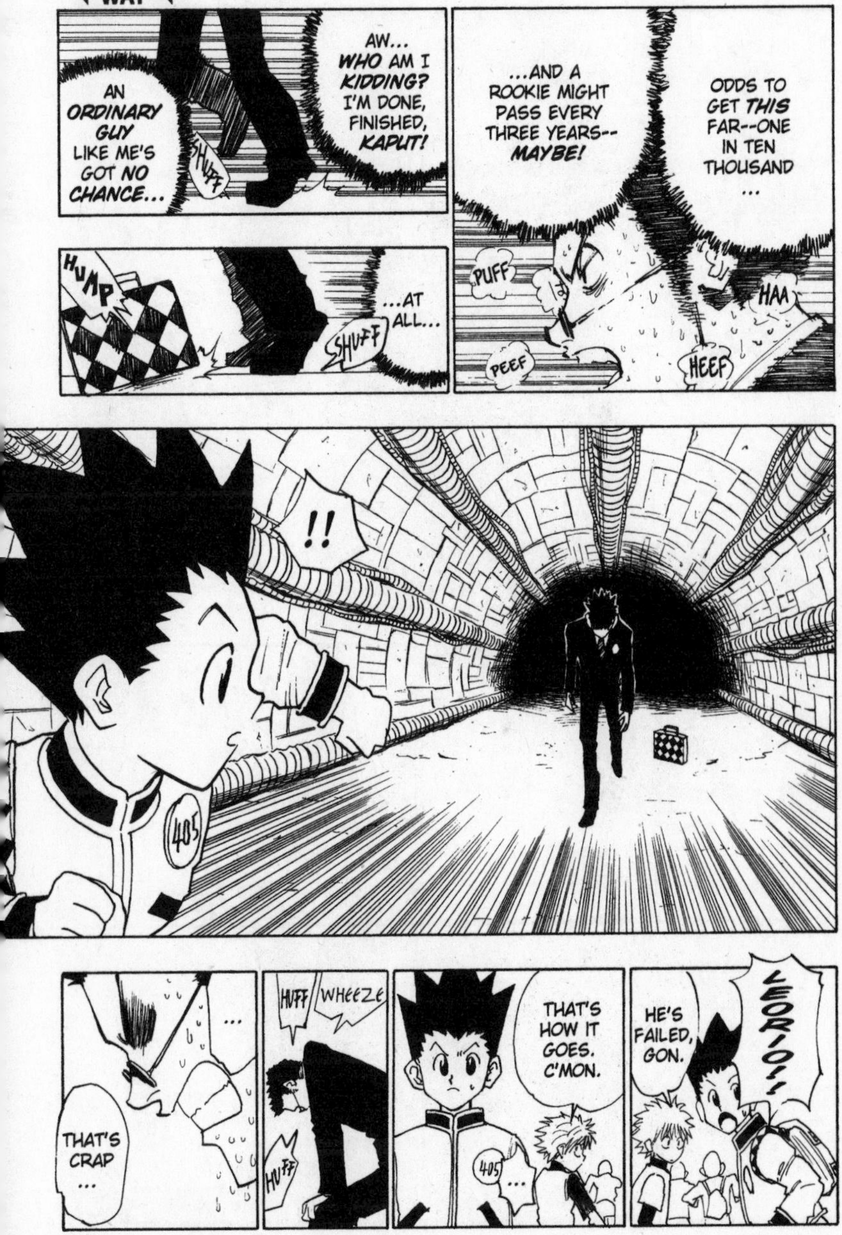
ODDS TO GET THIS FAR--ONE IN TEN THOUSAND ...
...AND A ROOKIE MIGHT PASS EVERY THREE YEARS--MAYBE!
HAA
PUFF
HEEF
PEEF
AW... WHO AM I KIDDING? I'M DONE, FINISHED, KAPUT!
SHUFF
AN ORDINARY GUY LIKE ME'S GOT NO CHANCE...
...AT ALL...
SHUFF
HUMP
!!
LEORIO!!
HE'S FAILED, GON.
THAT'S HOW IT GOES. C'MON.
...
WHEEZE
HUFF
HUFF
...
THAT'S CRAP ...

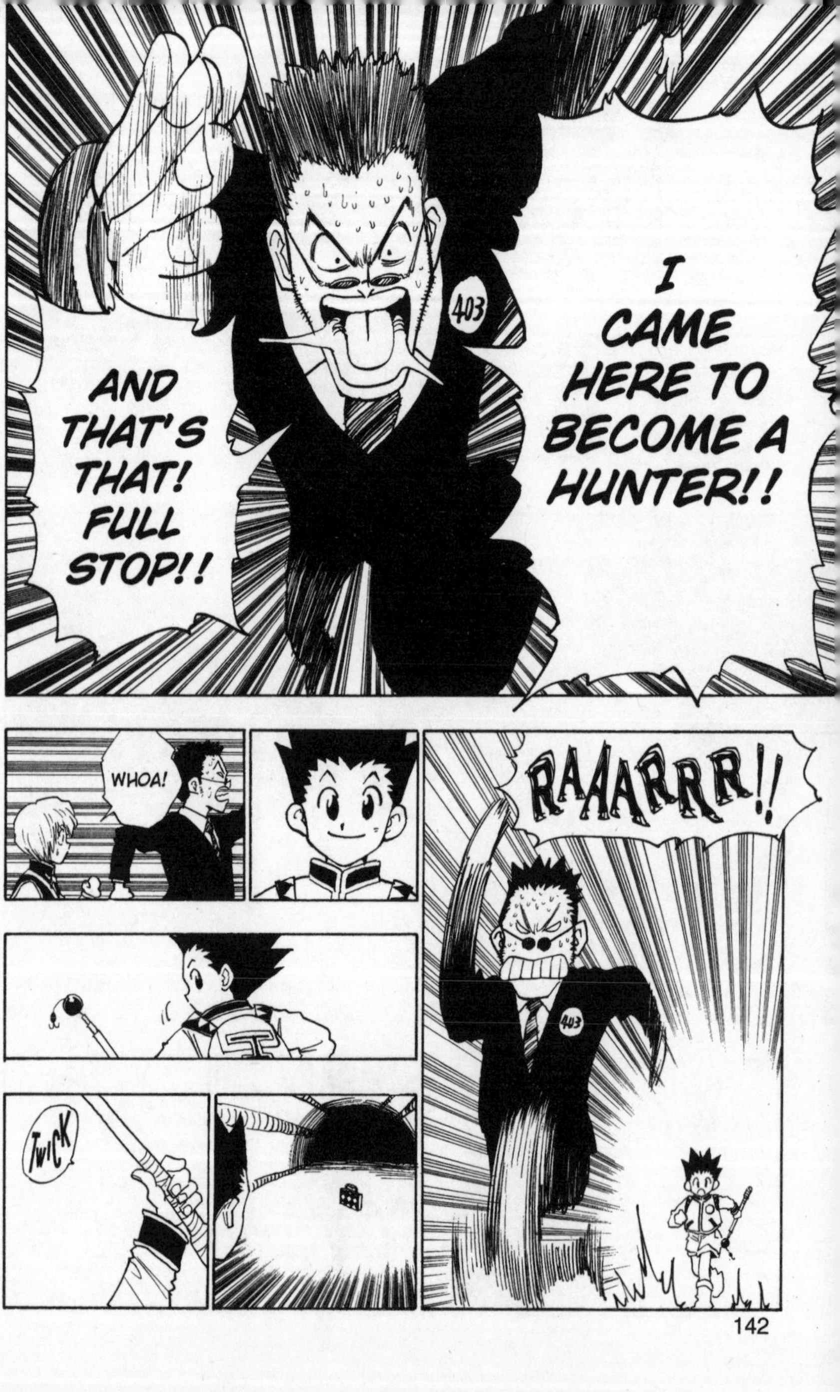
I CAME HERE TO BECOME A HUNTER!!
AND THAT'S THAT! FULL STOP!!
RAAARRRR!!
WHOA!
TWICK

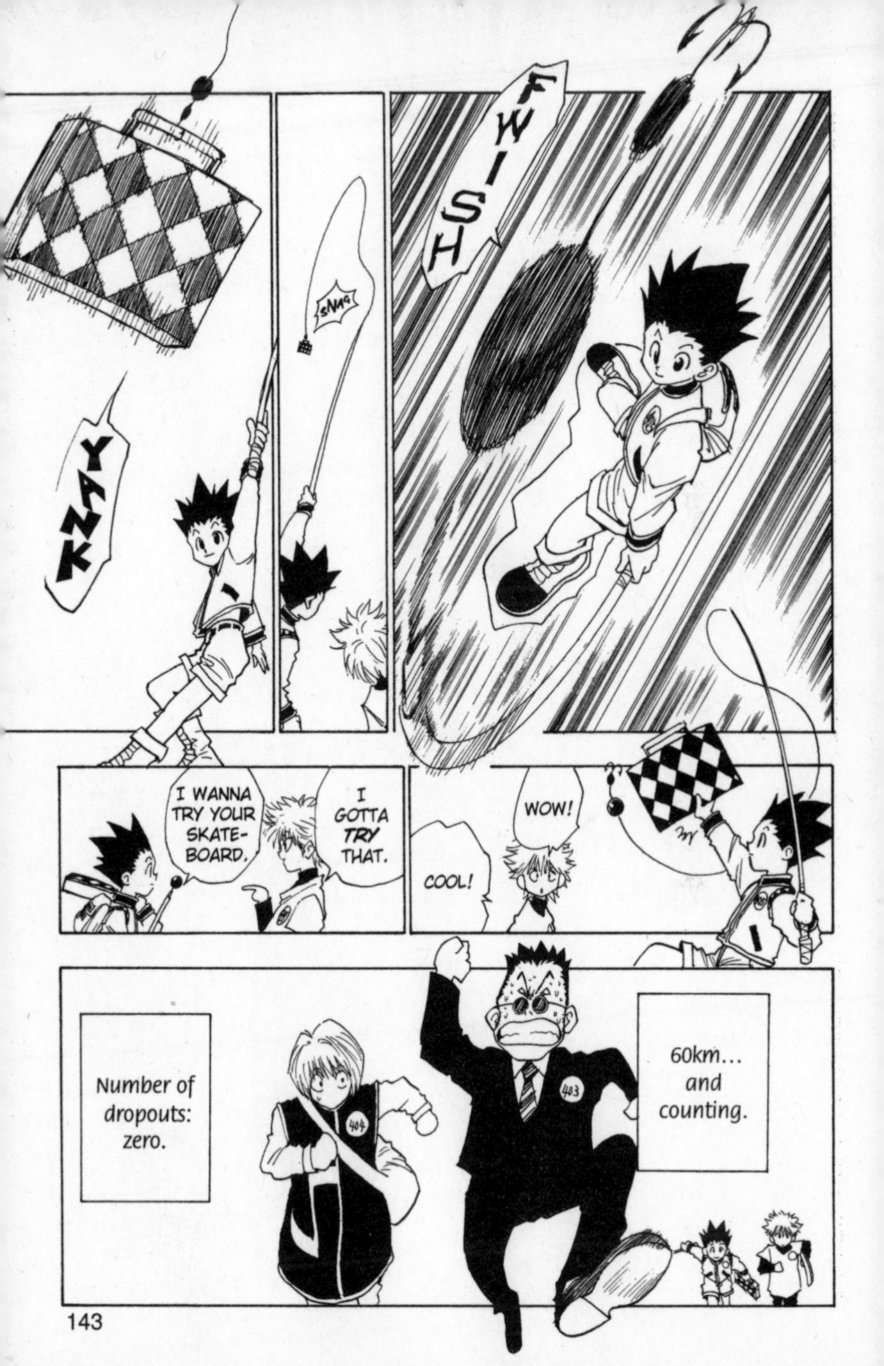
FWISH
sNAG
YANK
WOW!
COOL!
I GOTTA TRY THAT.
I WANNA TRY YOUR SKATE-BOARD.
60km… and counting.
Number of dropouts: zero.

Killua

Chapter 7
Respective Reasons

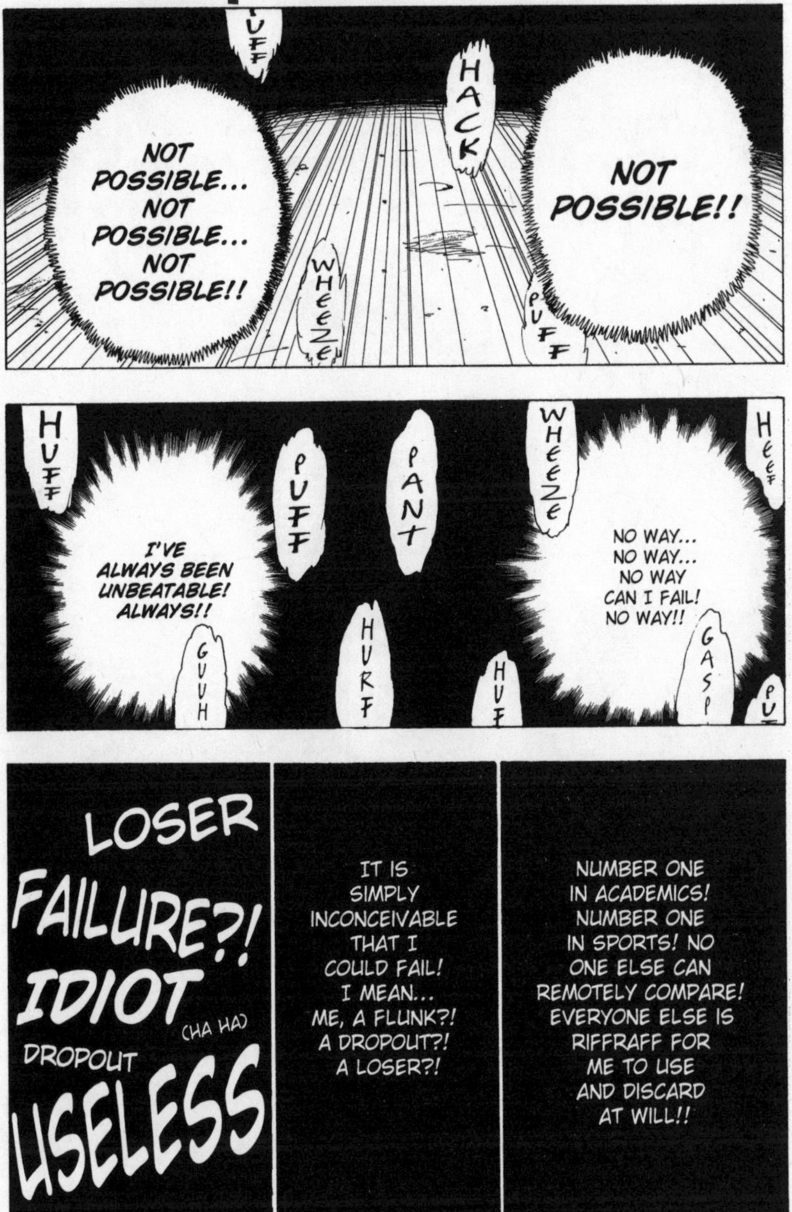
NOT POSSIBLE!!
HACK
PUFF
UFF
NOT POSSIBLE... NOT POSSIBLE... NOT POSSIBLE!!
WHEEZE
HEEF
WHEEZE
NO WAY... NO WAY... NO WAY CAN I FAIL! NO WAY!!
GASP
PU
PANT
PUFF
HUFF
HURF
HUF
I'VE ALWAYS BEEN UNBEATABLE! ALWAYS!!
GUUH
NUMBER ONE IN ACADEMICS! NUMBER ONE IN SPORTS! NO ONE ELSE CAN REMOTELY COMPARE! EVERYONE ELSE IS RIFFRAFF FOR ME TO USE AND DISCARD AT WILL!!
IT IS SIMPLY INCONCEIVABLE THAT I COULD FAIL! I MEAN... ME, A FLUNK?! A DROPOUT?! A LOSER?!
LOSER
FAILURE?!
IDIOT
(HA HA)
DROPOUT
USELESS

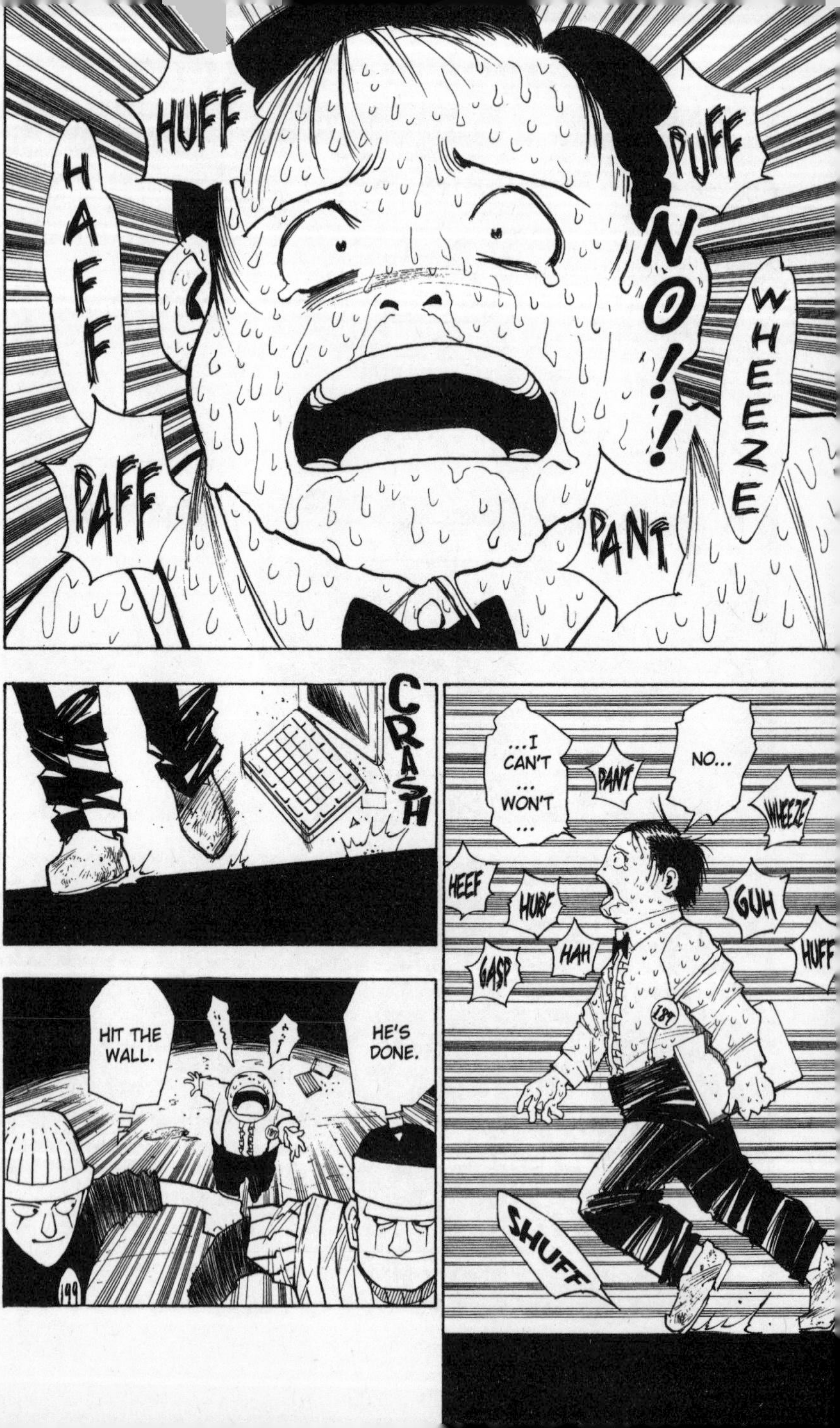
WHEEZE
PUFF
NO!!!
HUFF
HAFF
PANT
PAFF
NO...
WHEEZE
PANT
...I CAN'T ... WON'T ...
GUH
HUFF
HURF
HAH
HEEF
GASP
SHUFF
CRASH
HE'S DONE.
HIT THE WALL.

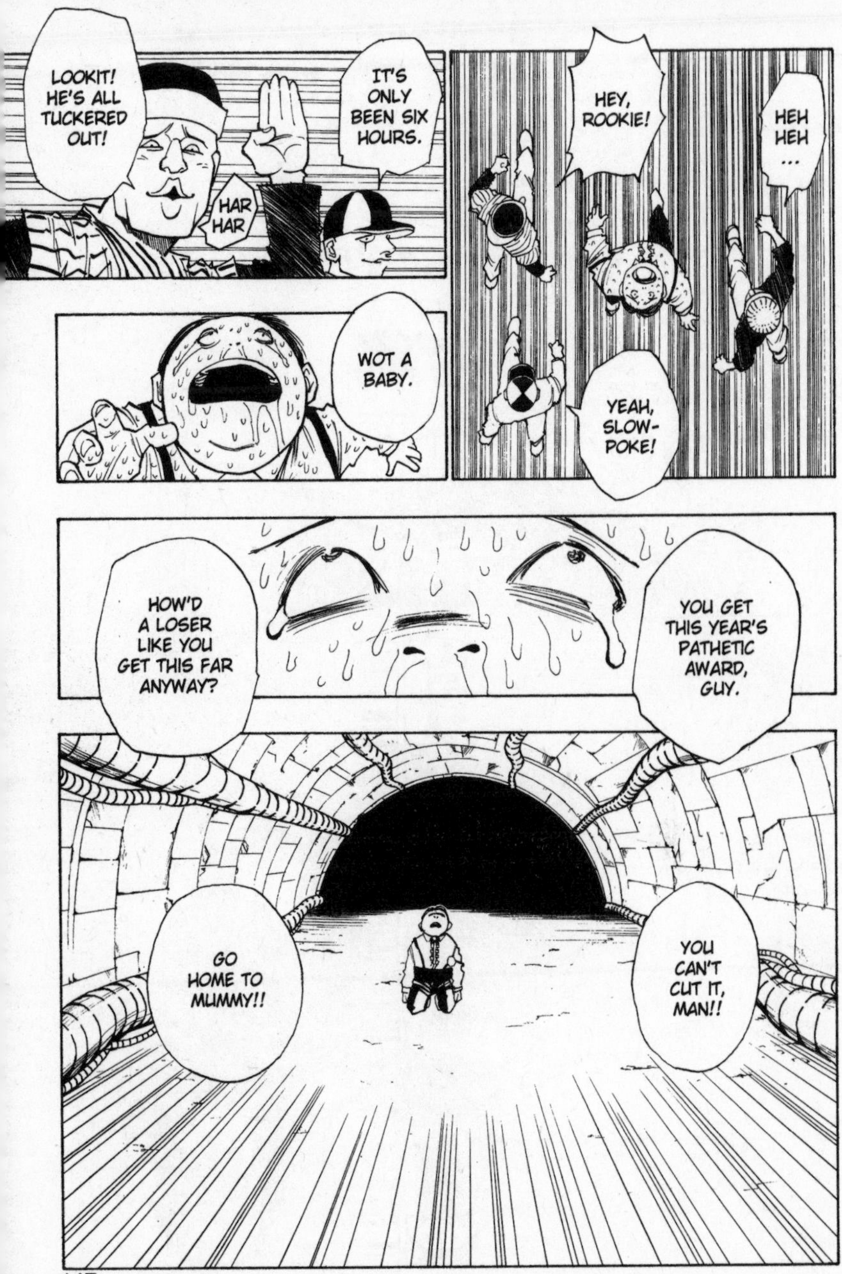
HEH HEH ...
HEY, ROOKIE!
YEAH, SLOW-POKE!
LOOKIT! HE'S ALL TUCKERED OUT!
IT'S ONLY BEEN SIX HOURS.
HAR HAR
WOT A BABY.
YOU GET THIS YEAR'S PATHETIC AWARD, GUY.
HOW'D A LOSER LIKE YOU GET THIS FAR ANYWAY?
YOU CAN'T CUT IT, MAN!!
GO HOME TO MUMMY!!

Chapter 7
Respective Reasons

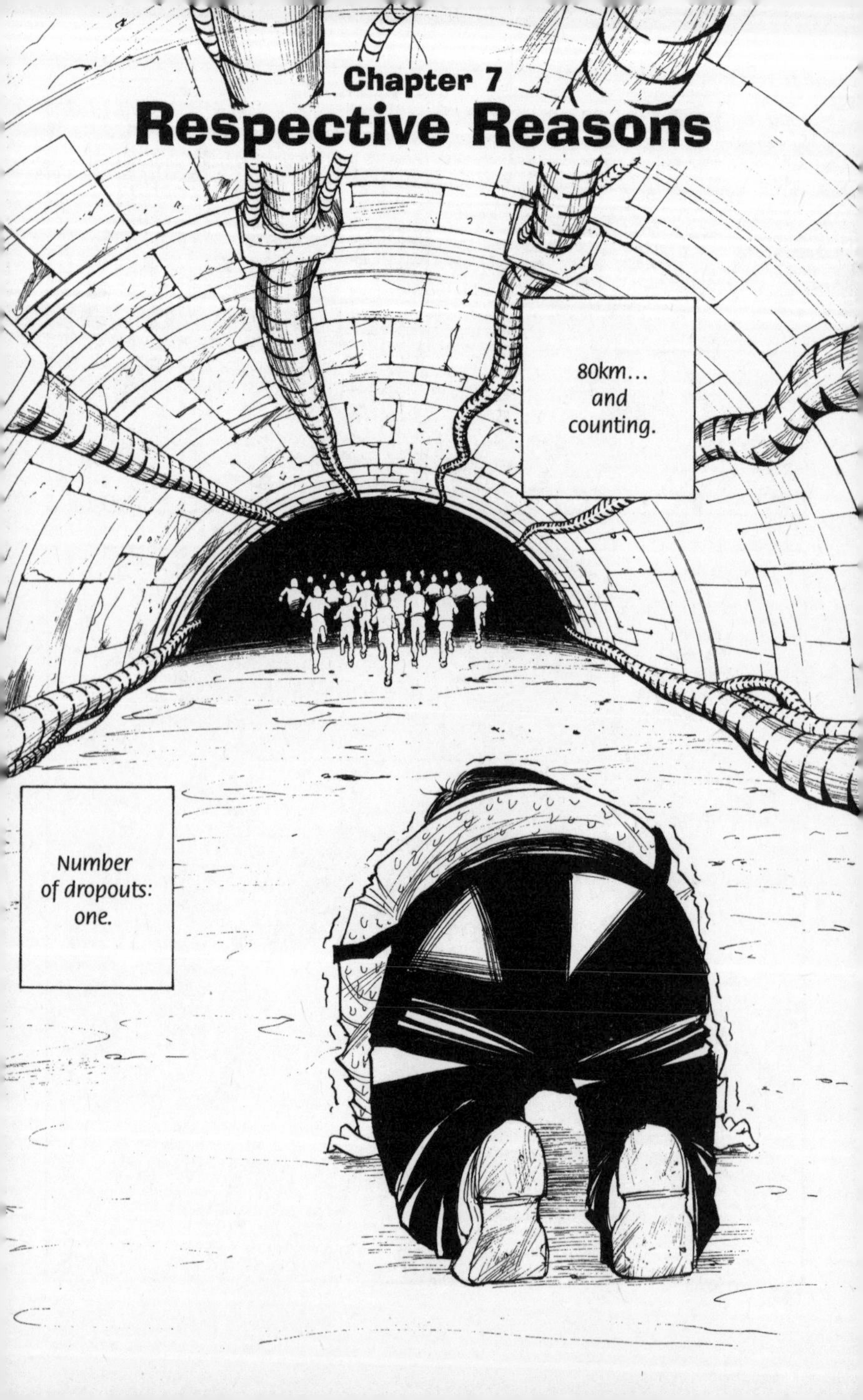
80km… and counting.
Number of dropouts: one.

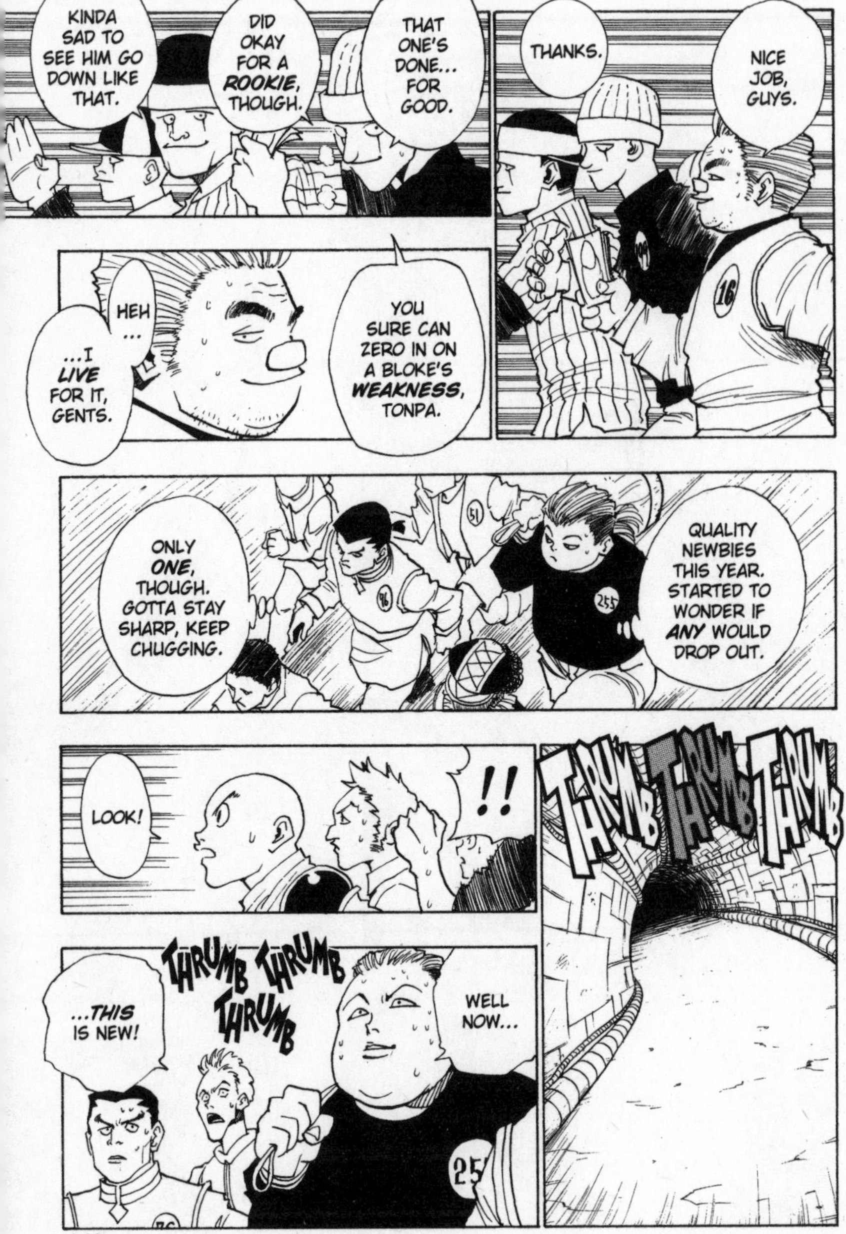

NICE JOB, GUYS.
THANKS.
THAT ONE'S DONE... FOR GOOD.
DID OKAY FOR A *ROOKIE*, THOUGH.
KINDA SAD TO SEE HIM GO DOWN LIKE THAT.
YOU SURE CAN ZERO IN ON A BLOKE'S *WEAKNESS*, TONPA.
HEH...
...I *LIVE* FOR IT, GENTS.
QUALITY NEWBIES THIS YEAR. STARTED TO WONDER IF *ANY* WOULD DROP OUT.
ONLY *ONE*, THOUGH. GOTTA STAY SHARP, KEEP CHUGGING.
THRUMB THRUMB THRUMB
!!
LOOK!
WELL NOW...
THRUMB THRUMB THRUMB
...*THIS* IS NEW!

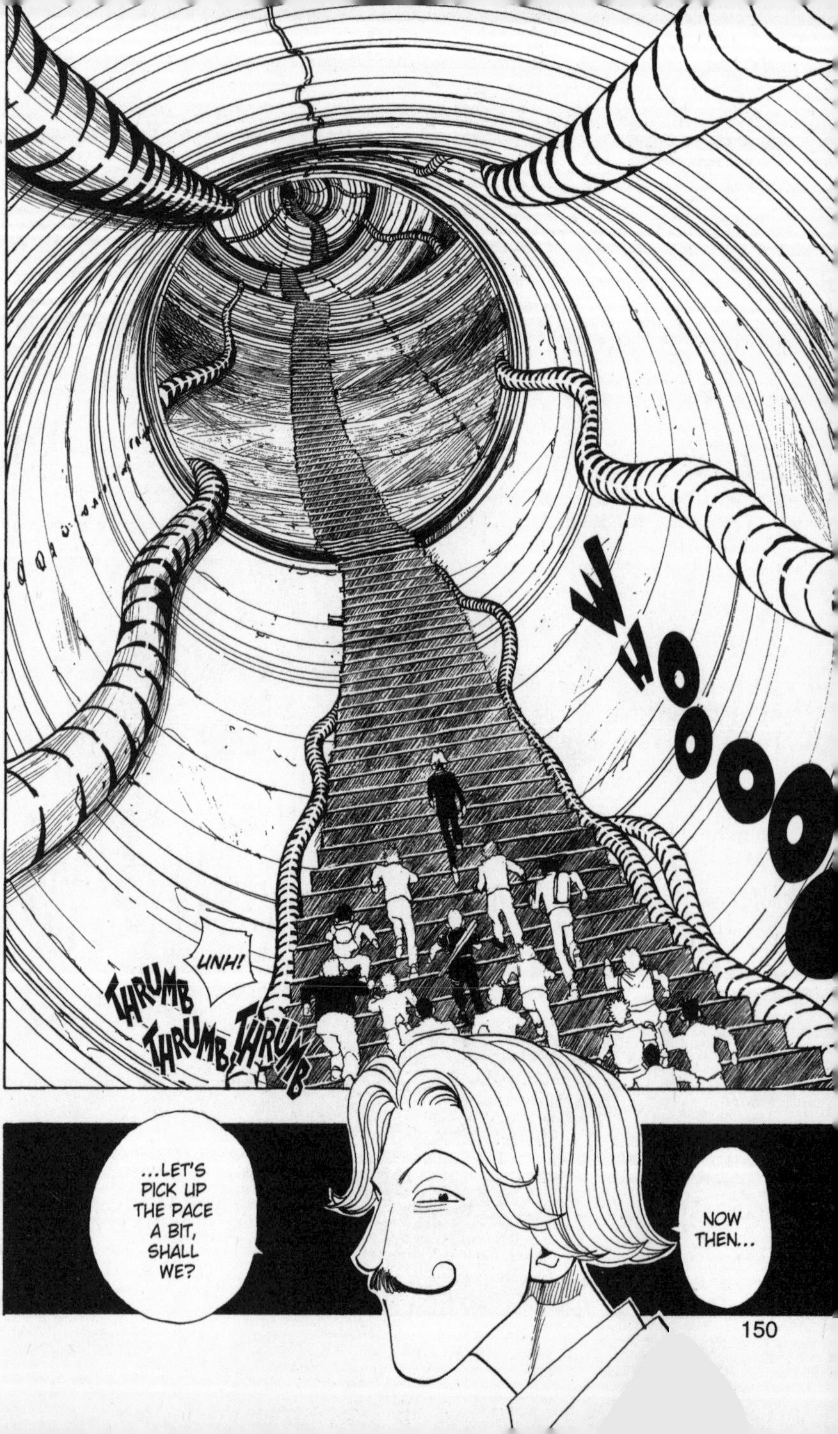
WHOOOOO
UNH!
THRUMB THRUMB THRUMB
NOW THEN...
...LET'S PICK UP THE PACE A BIT, SHALL WE?

READ THIS WAY

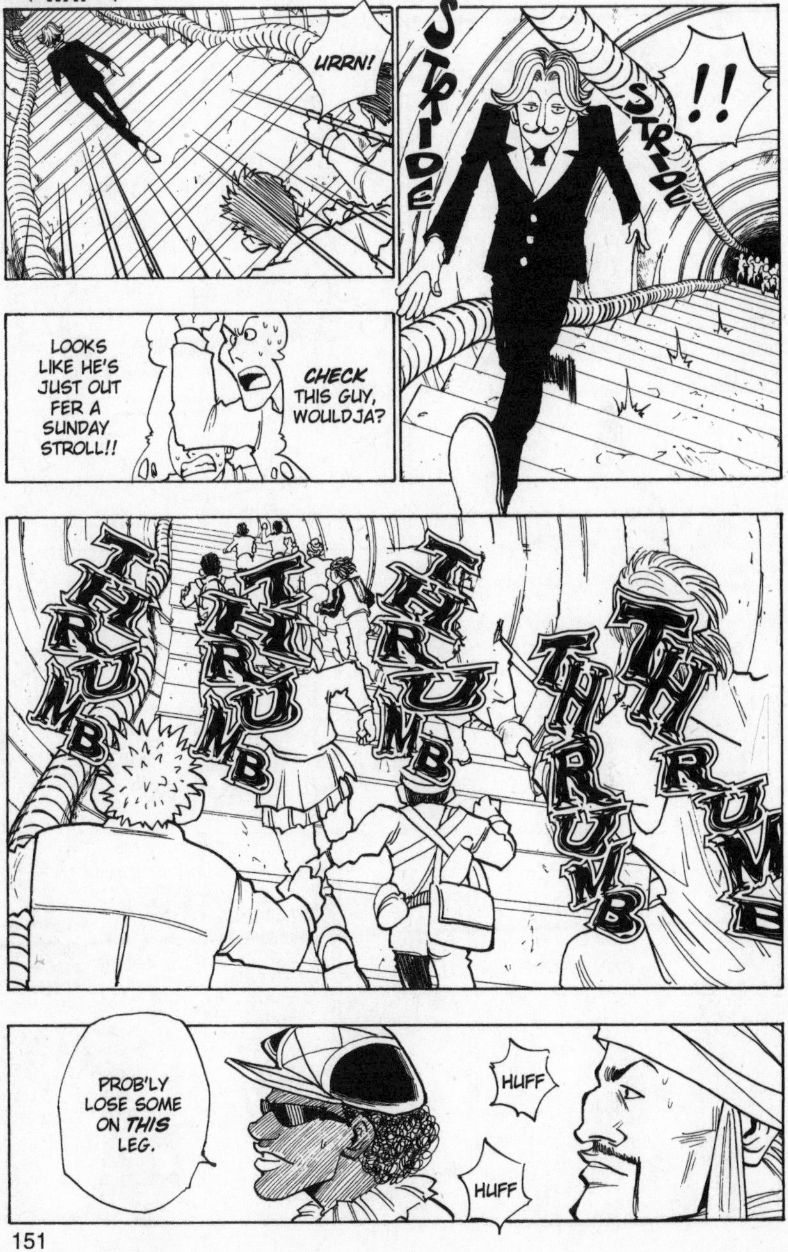

STRIDE
STRIDE
!!
URRN!
CHECK THIS GUY, WOULDJA?
LOOKS LIKE HE'S JUST OUT FER A SUNDAY STROLL!!
THRUMB
THRUMB
THRUMB
THRUMB
THRUMB
HUFF
HUFF
PROB'LY LOSE SOME ON THIS LEG.

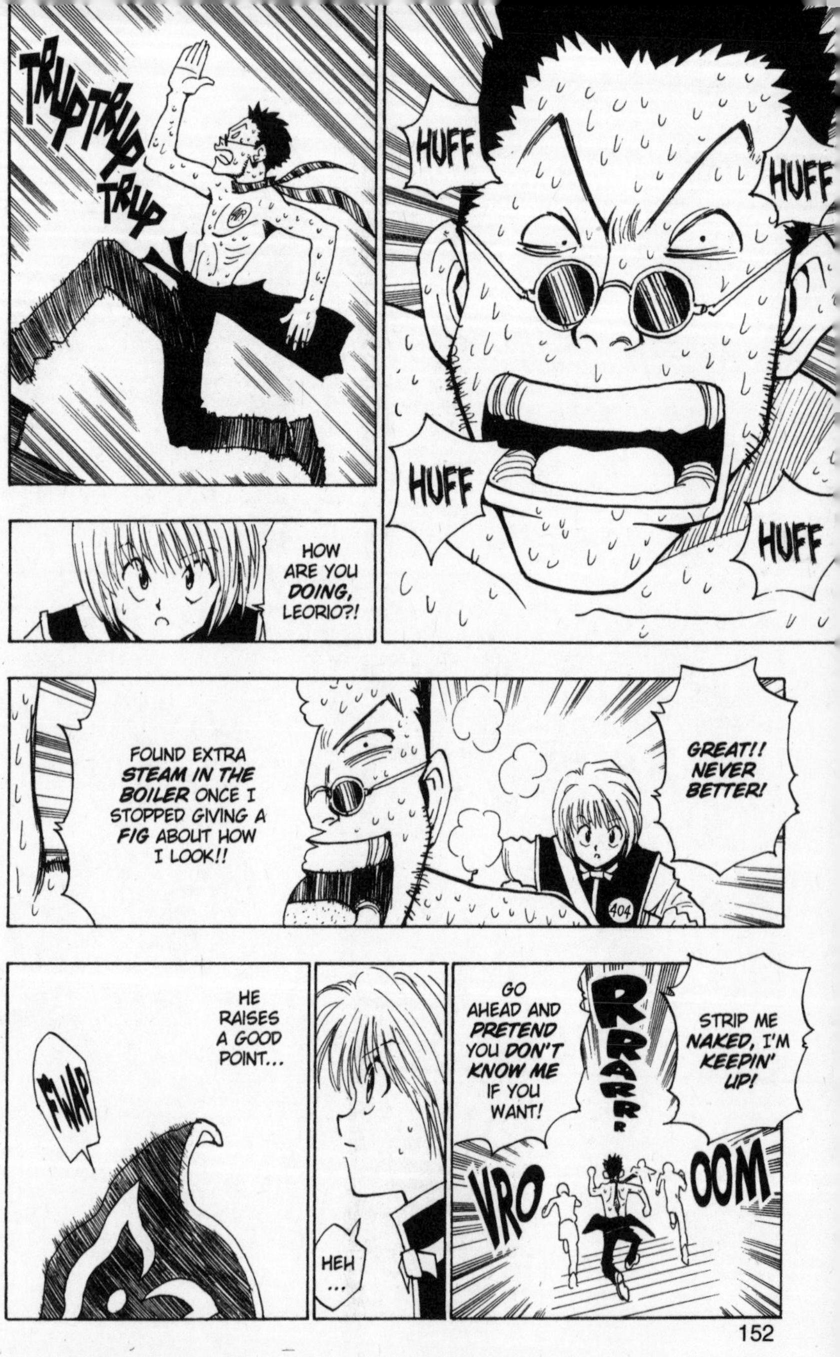
HUFF
HUFF
HUFF
HUFF
TRUPTRUP
TRUP
HOW ARE YOU *DOING*, LEORIO?!
GREAT!! NEVER BETTER!
FOUND EXTRA *STEAM IN THE BOILER* ONCE I STOPPED GIVING A *FIG* ABOUT HOW I LOOK!!
STRIP ME *NAKED*, I'M *KEEPIN' UP!*
RRARR
GO AHEAD AND *PRETEND* YOU *DON'T KNOW ME* IF YOU WANT!
VRO
OOM
HEH ...
HE RAISES A GOOD POINT...
FWAP

READ THIS WAY

TRUP
TRUP
TRUP
MAY I ASK YOU SOMETHING?
SAVE YER ENERGY FOR *RUNNIN'*, NOT CHITCHAT!
IS IT REALLY *MONEY* YOU'RE AFTER?
!
I BET NOT.
I'VE ONLY KNOWN YOU FOR A FEW DAYS, AND IT'S TRUE THAT...
...YOU'RE AN INDISCREET FOOL...
REALLY!
...
...BUT AS *SHALLOW* AS YOU SAY? I THINK NOT!
I'VE MET PEOPLE MOTIVATED ONLY BY MONEY, AND THEY *DON'T* SHOW THIS KIND OF *DEDICATION.*
HMPH!
FAT LOT *YOU* KNOW.
THE SCARLET EYES.
TRUP
TRUP
TRUP
TRUP
?

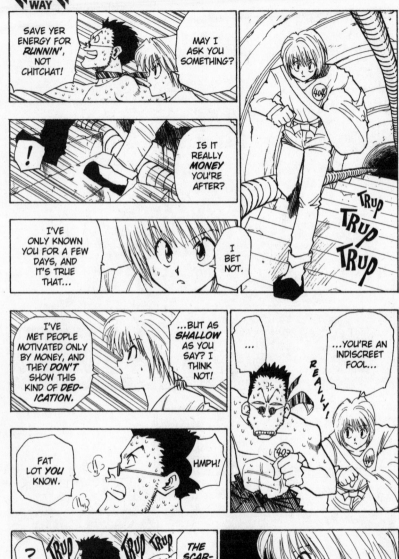

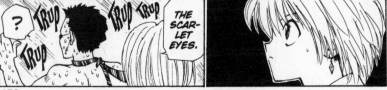

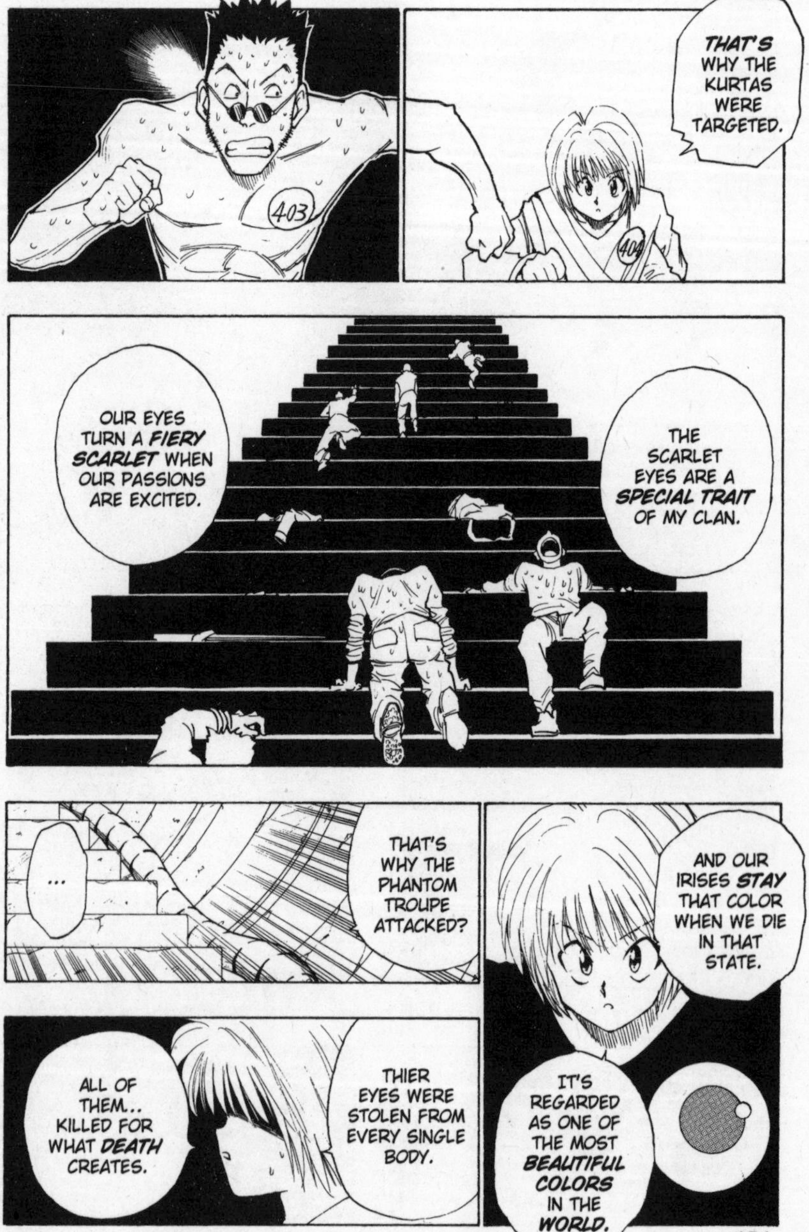
THAT'S WHY THE KURTAS WERE TARGETED.
THE SCARLET EYES ARE A SPECIAL TRAIT OF MY CLAN.
OUR EYES TURN A FIERY SCARLET WHEN OUR PASSIONS ARE EXCITED.
AND OUR IRISES STAY THAT COLOR WHEN WE DIE IN THAT STATE.
IT'S REGARDED AS ONE OF THE MOST BEAUTIFUL COLORS IN THE WORLD.
THAT'S WHY THE PHANTOM TROUPE ATTACKED?
...
THIER EYES WERE STOLEN FROM EVERY SINGLE BODY.
ALL OF THEM... KILLED FOR WHAT DEATH CREATES.

READ THIS WAY

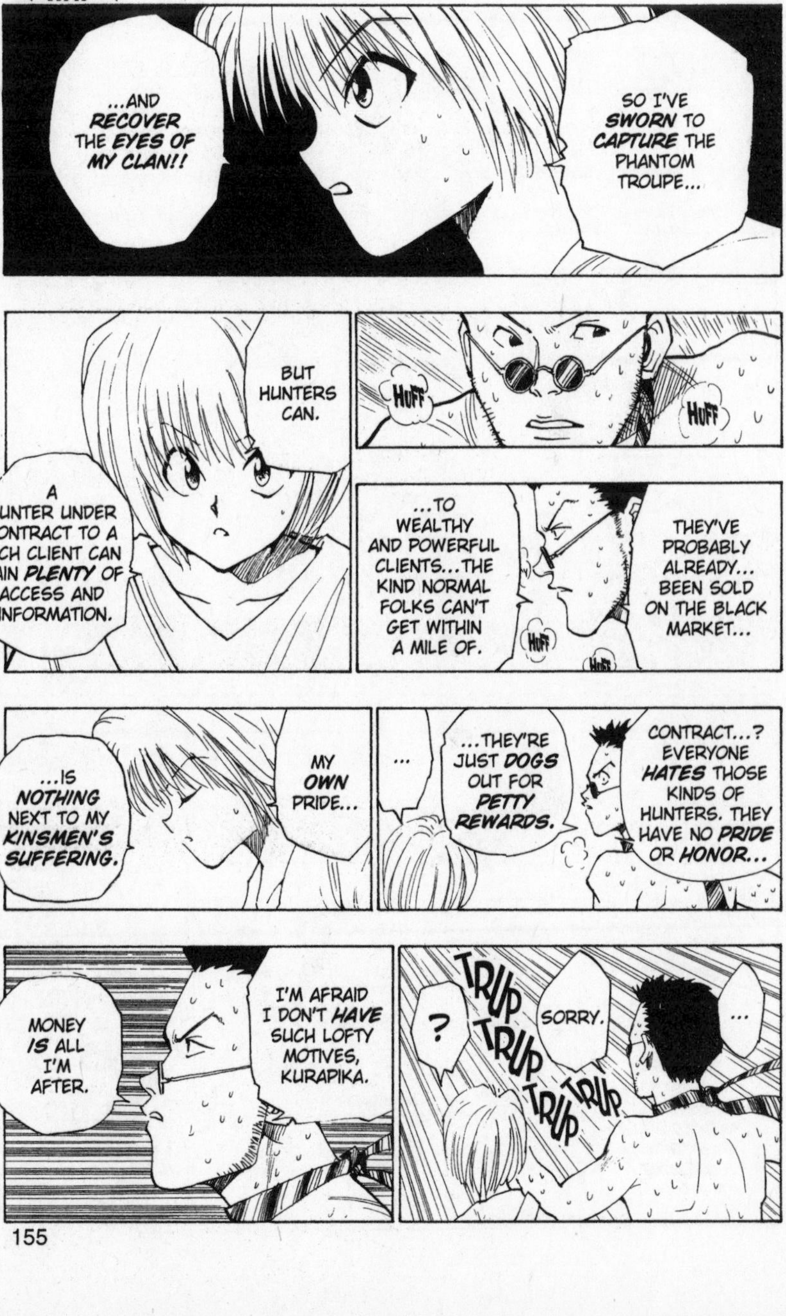
SO I'VE SWORN TO CAPTURE THE PHANTOM TROUPE...
...AND RECOVER THE EYES OF MY CLAN!!
HUFF
HUFF
THEY'VE PROBABLY ALREADY... BEEN SOLD ON THE BLACK MARKET...
...TO WEALTHY AND POWERFUL CLIENTS...THE KIND NORMAL FOLKS CAN'T GET WITHIN A MILE OF.
HUFF
BUT HUNTERS CAN.
A HUNTER UNDER CONTRACT TO A RICH CLIENT CAN GAIN PLENTY OF ACCESS AND INFORMATION.
CONTRACT...? EVERYONE HATES THOSE KINDS OF HUNTERS. THEY HAVE NO PRIDE OR HONOR...
...THEY'RE JUST DOGS OUT FOR PETTY REWARDS.
...
MY OWN PRIDE...
...IS NOTHING NEXT TO MY KINSMEN'S SUFFERING.
...
SORRY.
TRUP TRUP TRUP TRUP TRUP
?
I'M AFRAID I DON'T HAVE SUCH LOFTY MOTIVES, KURAPIKA.
MONEY IS ALL I'M AFTER.

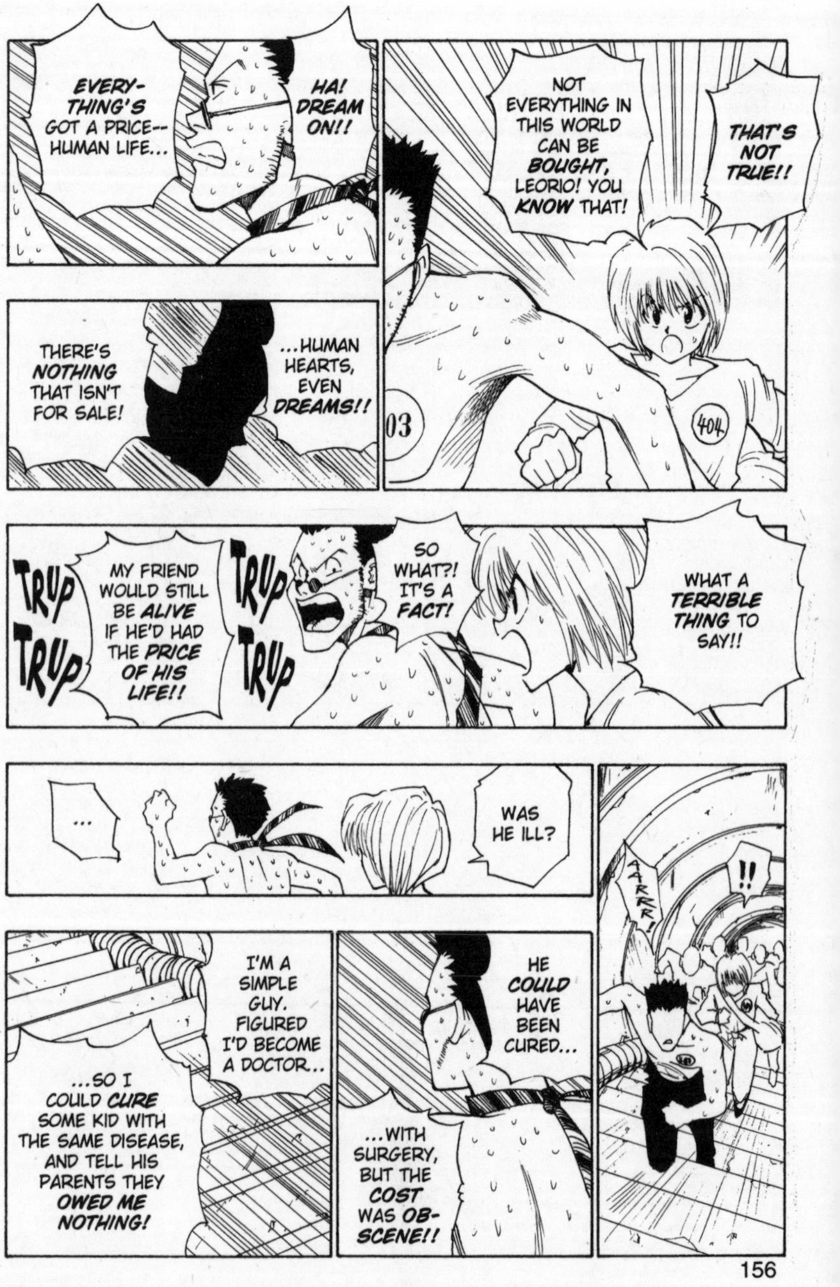
THAT'S NOT TRUE!!
NOT EVERYTHING IN THIS WORLD CAN BE BOUGHT, LEORIO! YOU KNOW THAT!
HA! DREAM ON!!
EVERY-THING'S GOT A PRICE-- HUMAN LIFE...
...HUMAN HEARTS, EVEN DREAMS!!
THERE'S NOTHING THAT ISN'T FOR SALE!
WHAT A TERRIBLE THING TO SAY!!
SO WHAT?! IT'S A FACT!
TRUP TRUP
MY FRIEND WOULD STILL BE ALIVE IF HE'D HAD THE PRICE OF HIS LIFE!!
TRUP TRUP
!!
AARRR!
WAS HE ILL?
...
HE COULD HAVE BEEN CURED...
...WITH SURGERY, BUT THE COST WAS OB-SCENE!!
I'M A SIMPLE GUY. FIGURED I'D BECOME A DOCTOR...
...SO I COULD CURE SOME KID WITH THE SAME DISEASE, AND TELL HIS PARENTS THEY OWED ME NOTHING!

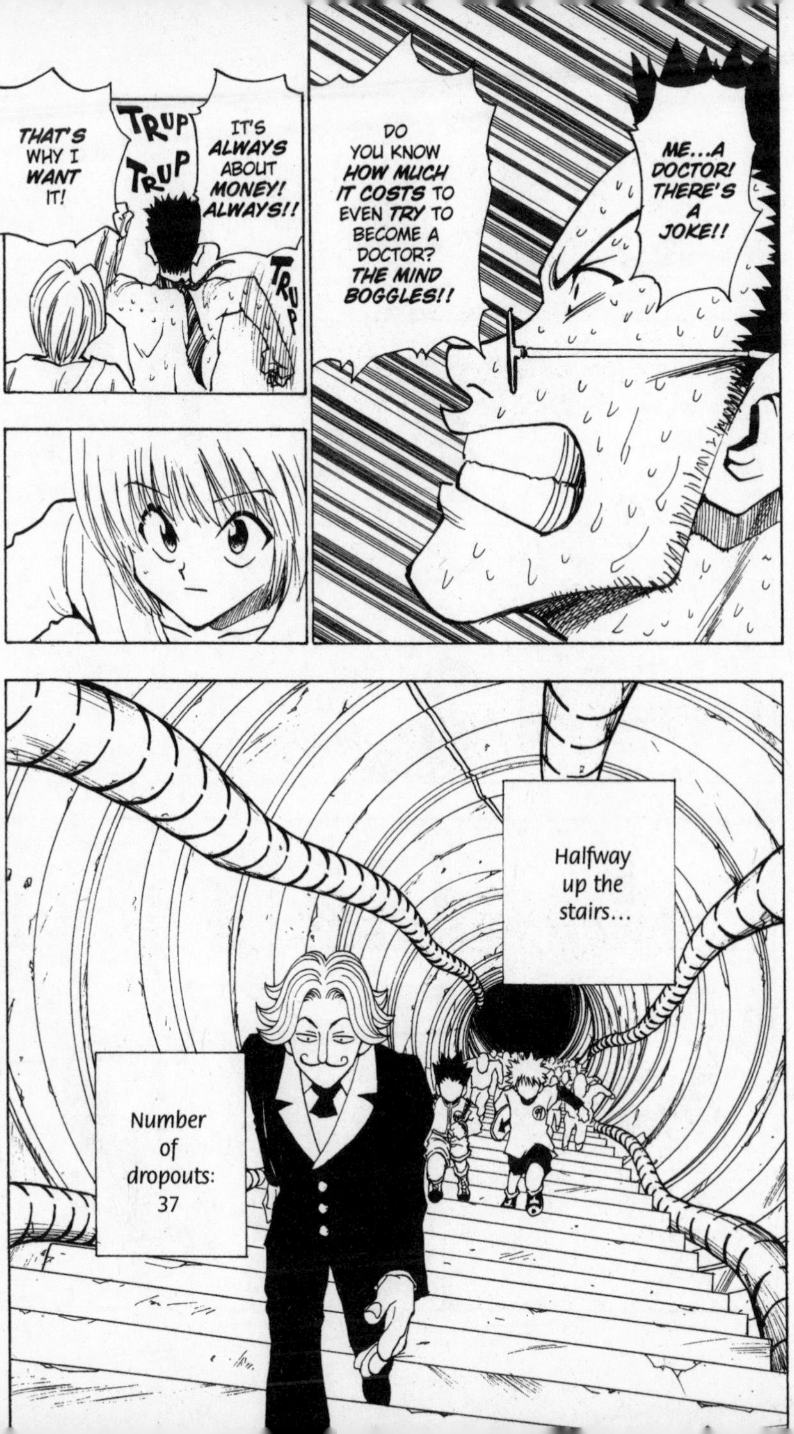
ME...A DOCTOR! THERE'S A JOKE!!
DO YOU KNOW HOW MUCH IT COSTS TO EVEN TRY TO BECOME A DOCTOR? THE MIND BOGGLES!!
TRUP
IT'S ALWAYS ABOUT MONEY! ALWAYS!!
TRUP TRUP
THAT'S WHY I WANT IT!
Halfway up the stairs...
Number of dropouts: 37

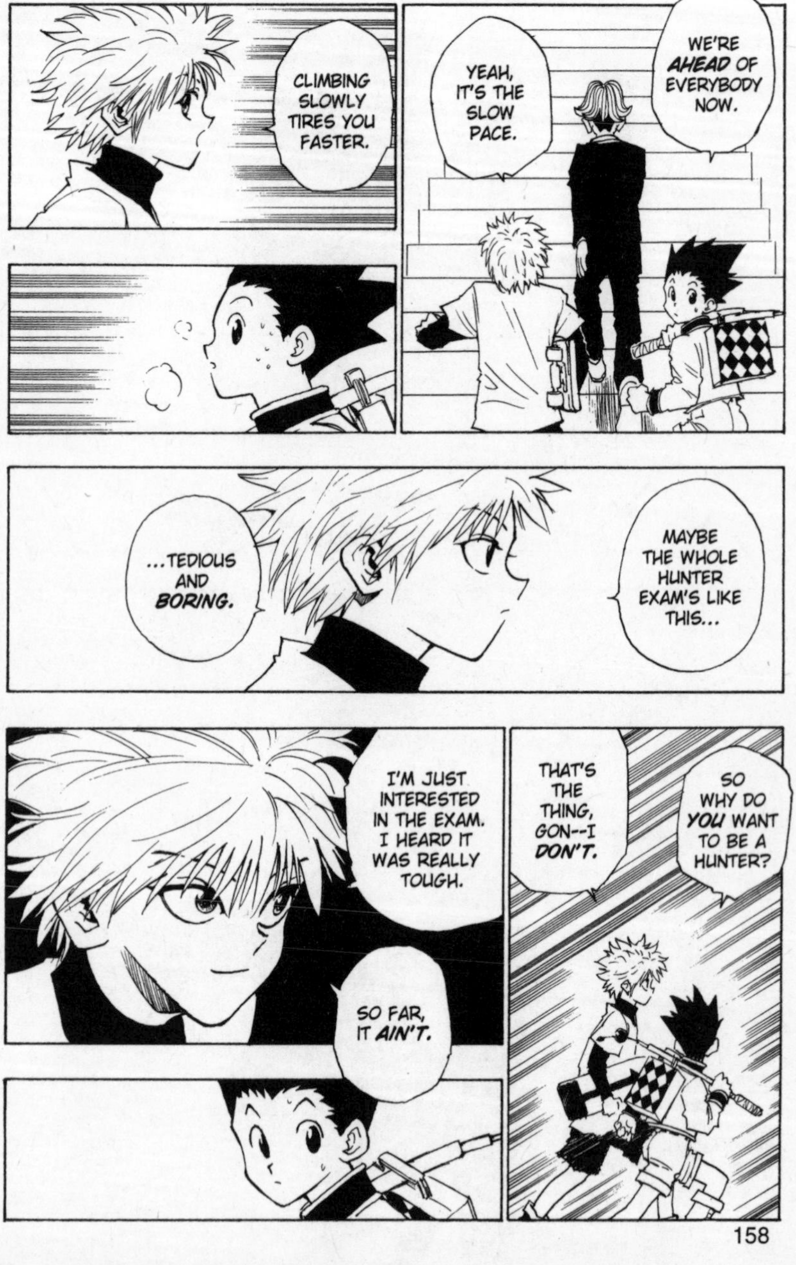
WE'RE AHEAD OF EVERYBODY NOW.
YEAH, IT'S THE SLOW PACE.
CLIMBING SLOWLY TIRES YOU FASTER.
MAYBE THE WHOLE HUNTER EXAM'S LIKE THIS...
...TEDIOUS AND BORING.
SO WHY DO YOU WANT TO BE A HUNTER?
THAT'S THE THING, GON--I DON'T.
I'M JUST INTERESTED IN THE EXAM. I HEARD IT WAS REALLY TOUGH.
SO FAR, IT AIN'T.

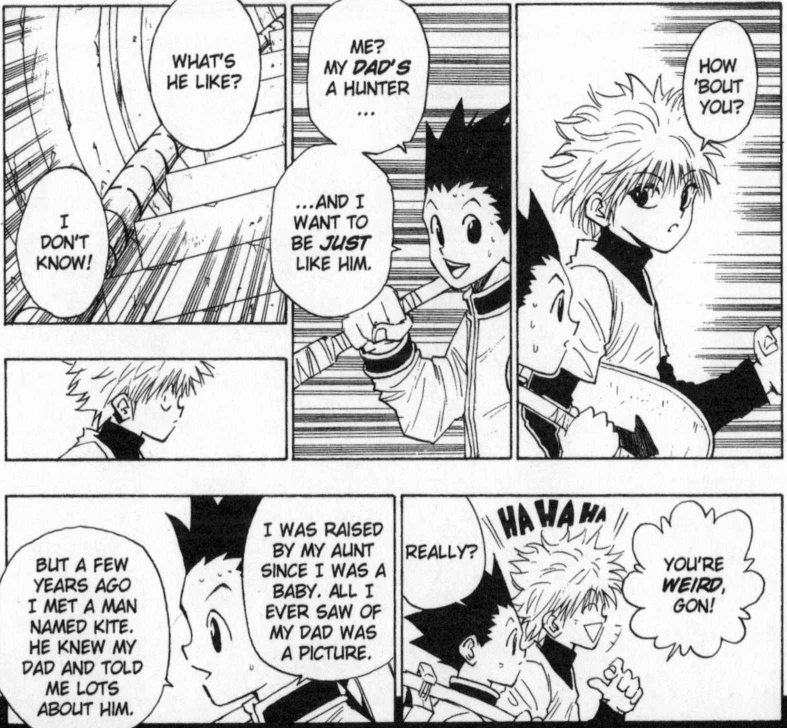
HOW 'BOUT YOU?
ME? MY DAD'S A HUNTER ...
...AND I WANT TO BE JUST LIKE HIM.
WHAT'S HE LIKE?
I DON'T KNOW!
YOU'RE WEIRD, GON!
HA HA HA HA
REALLY?
I WAS RAISED BY MY AUNT SINCE I WAS A BABY. ALL I EVER SAW OF MY DAD WAS A PICTURE.
BUT A FEW YEARS AGO I MET A MAN NAMED KITE. HE KNEW MY DAD AND TOLD ME LOTS ABOUT HIM.

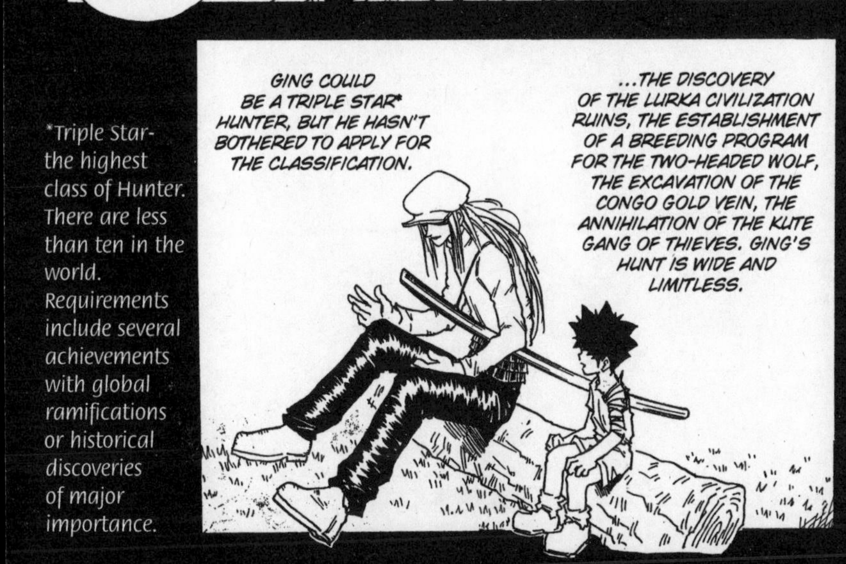
...THE DISCOVERY OF THE LURKA CIVILIZATION RUINS, THE ESTABLISHMENT OF A BREEDING PROGRAM FOR THE TWO-HEADED WOLF, THE EXCAVATION OF THE CONGO GOLD VEIN, THE ANNIHILATION OF THE KUTE GANG OF THIEVES. GING'S HUNT IS WIDE AND LIMITLESS.
GING COULD BE A TRIPLE STAR* HUNTER, BUT HE HASN'T BOTHERED TO APPLY FOR THE CLASSIFICATION.

*Triple Star- the highest class of Hunter. There are less than ten in the world. Requirements include several achievements with global ramifications or historical discoveries of major importance.

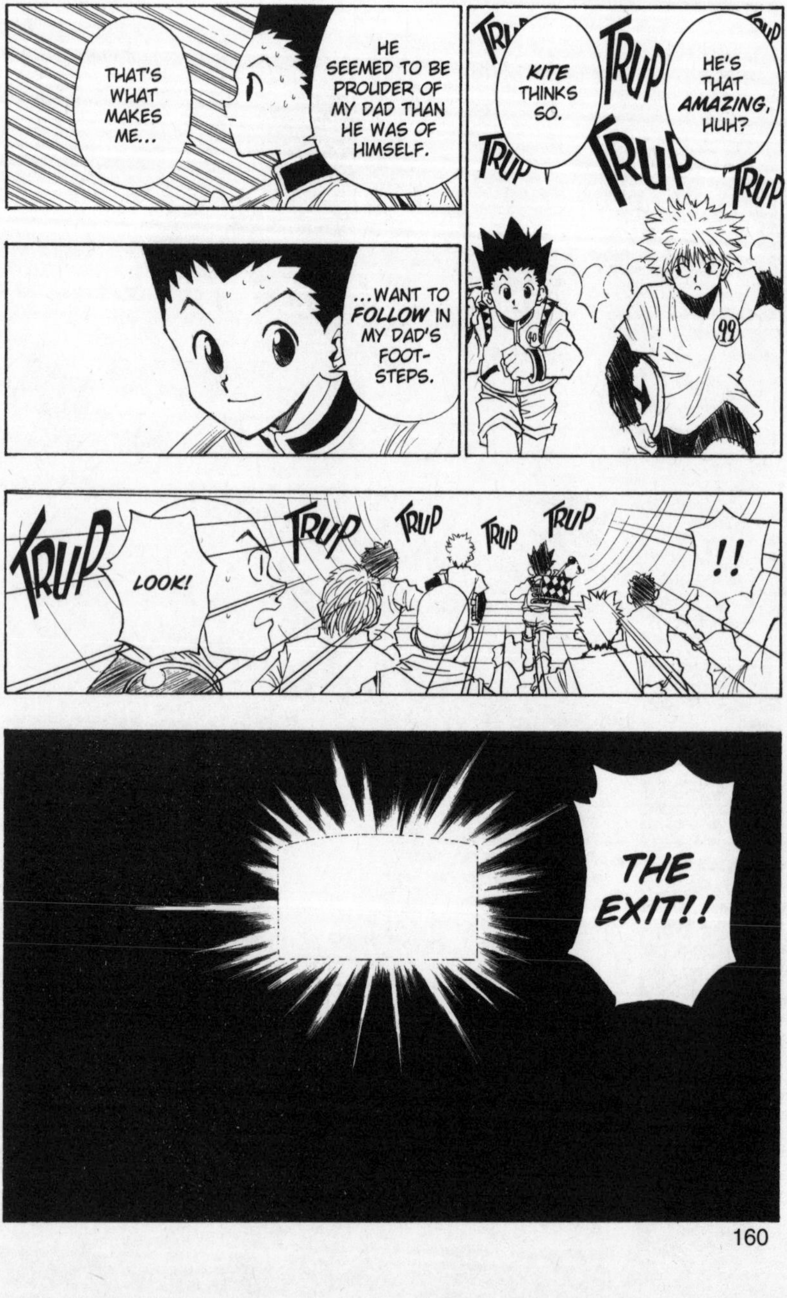
TRUP
HE'S THAT AMAZING, HUH?
KITE THINKS SO.
TRUP
TRUP
TRUP
TRUP
HE SEEMED TO BE PROUDER OF MY DAD THAN HE WAS OF HIMSELF.
THAT'S WHAT MAKES ME...
...WANT TO FOLLOW IN MY DAD'S FOOT-STEPS.
!!
TRUP
TRUP
TRUP
TRUP
LOOK!
TRUP
THE EXIT!!

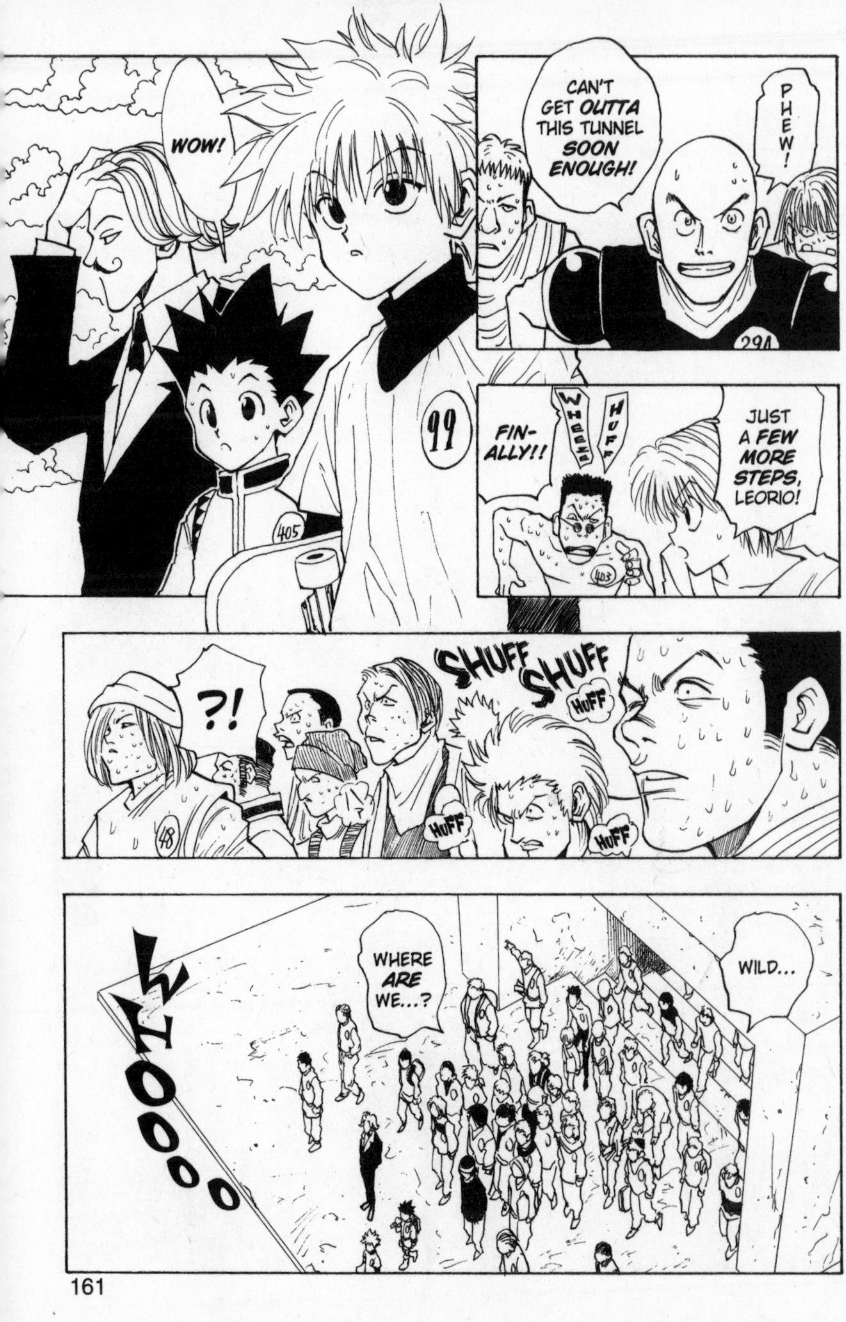
PHEW!
CAN'T GET OUTTA THIS TUNNEL SOON ENOUGH!
JUST A FEW MORE STEPS, LEORIO!
HUFF
WHEEZE
FIN-ALLY!!
WOW!
SHUFF SHUFF
HUFF
HUFF
HUFF
?!
WILD...
WHERE ARE WE...?
WHOOOO

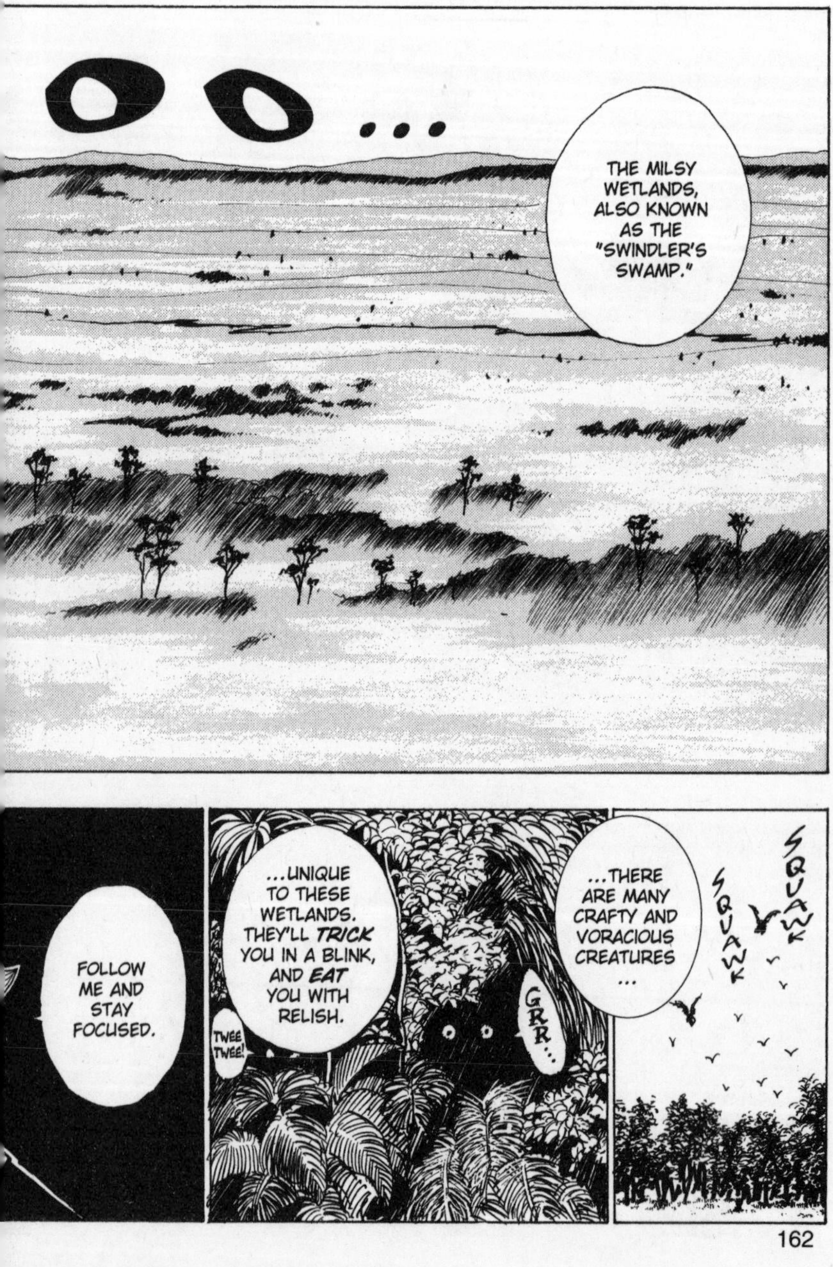
OO...
THE MILSY WETLANDS, ALSO KNOWN AS THE "SWINDLER'S SWAMP."
SQUAWK
SQUAWK
...THERE ARE MANY CRAFTY AND VORACIOUS CREATURES ...
GRR...
...UNIQUE TO THESE WETLANDS. THEY'LL TRICK YOU IN A BLINK, AND EAT YOU WITH RELISH.
TWEE TWEE!
FOLLOW ME AND STAY FOCUSED.

READ THIS WAY

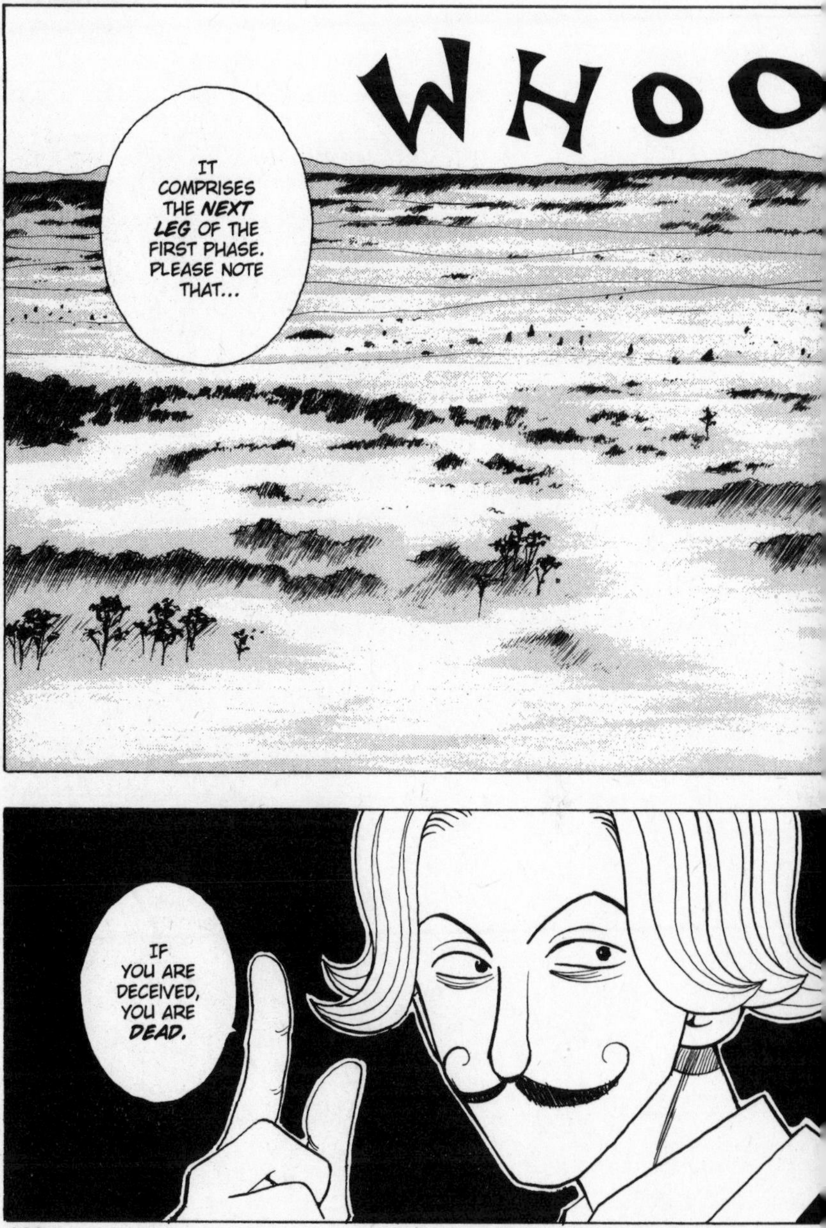
WHOO
IT COMPRISES THE ***NEXT LEG*** OF THE FIRST PHASE. PLEASE NOTE THAT...
IF YOU ARE DECEIVED, YOU ARE ***DEAD.***

Special thanks to
Naoko Takeuchi

She helped me with my
color pages. She's a
great painter, and
her work is
gorgeous.

© Naoko Takeuchi

Chapter 8
The Other Enemy

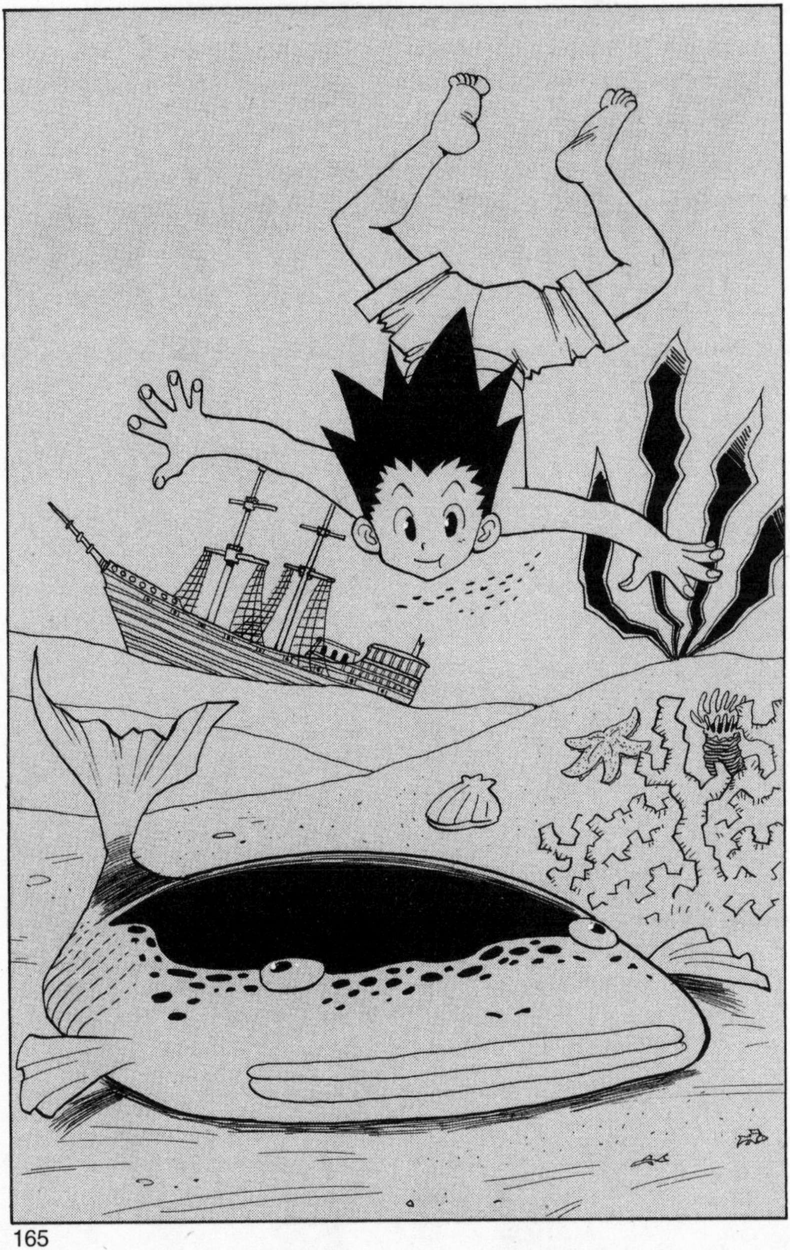

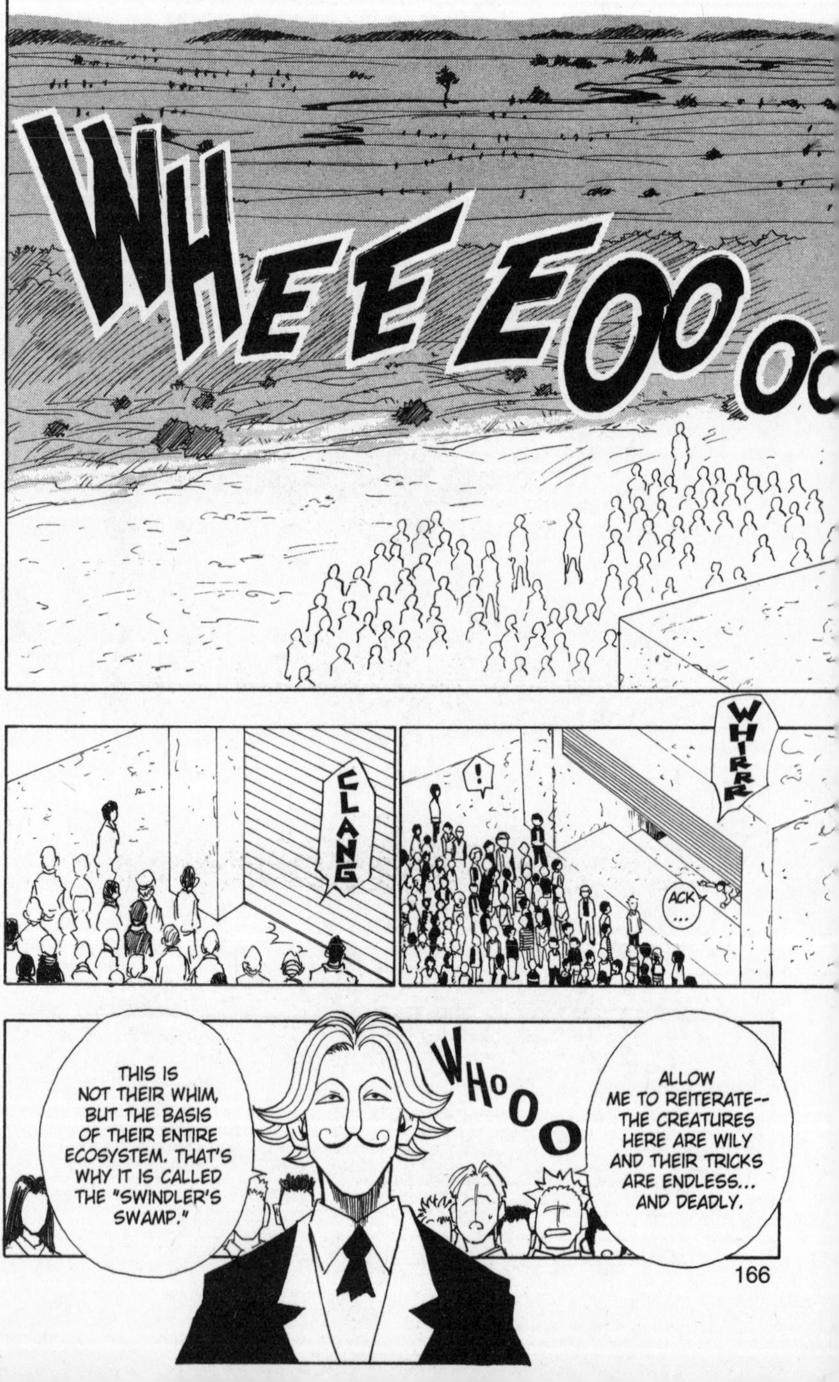
WHEEEOOOO
WHIRRR
!
ACK...
CLANG
ALLOW ME TO REITERATE-- THE CREATURES HERE ARE WILY AND THEIR TRICKS ARE ENDLESS... AND DEADLY.
WHOOOO
THIS IS NOT THEIR WHIM, BUT THE BASIS OF THEIR ENTIRE ECOSYSTEM. THAT'S WHY IT IS CALLED THE "SWINDLER'S SWAMP."

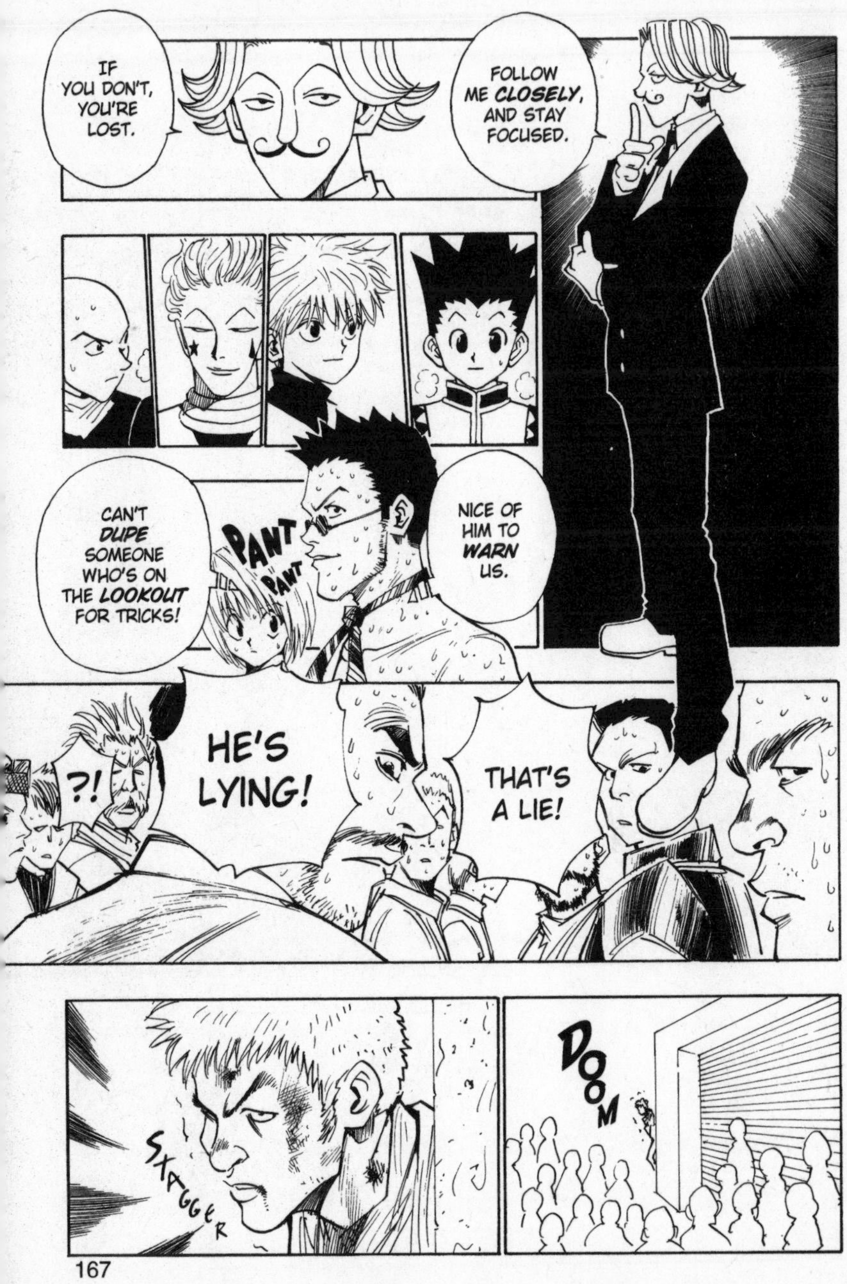
FOLLOW ME CLOSELY, AND STAY FOCUSED.
IF YOU DON'T, YOU'RE LOST.
NICE OF HIM TO WARN US.
PANT PANT
CAN'T DUPE SOMEONE WHO'S ON THE LOOKOUT FOR TRICKS!
THAT'S A LIE!
HE'S LYING!
?!
DOOM
STAGGER

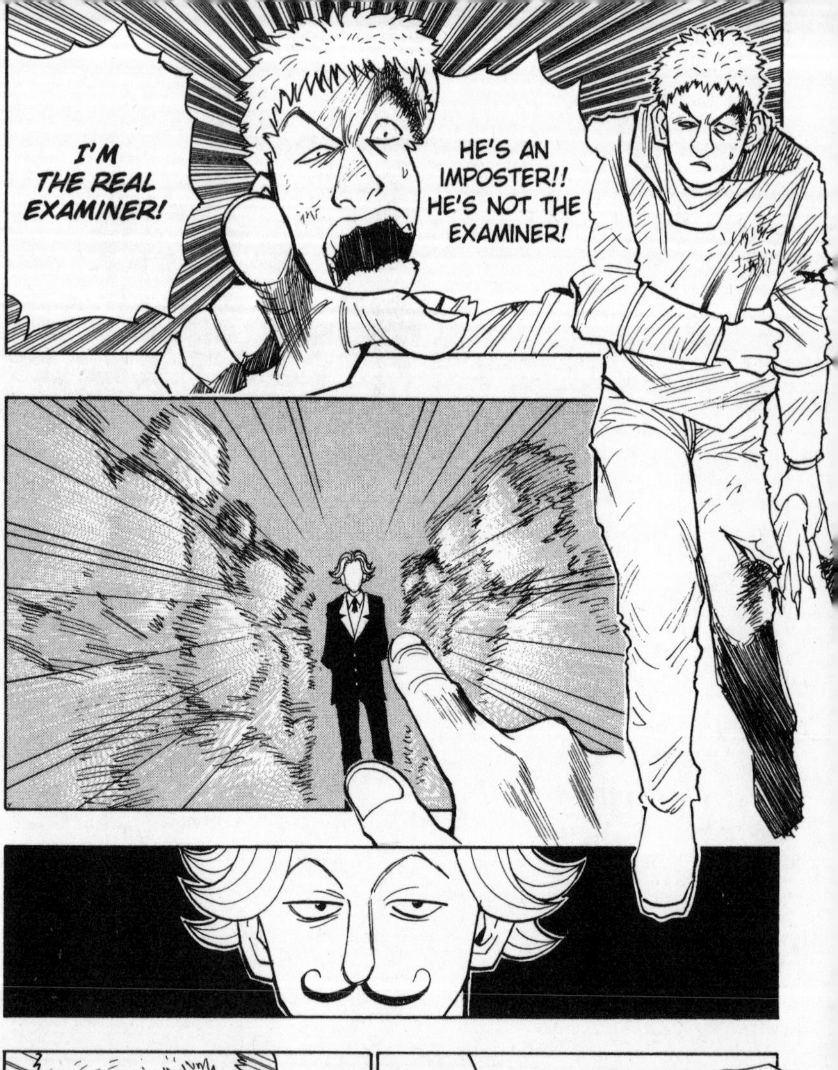
HE'S AN IMPOSTER!! HE'S NOT THE EXAMINER!
I'M THE REAL EXAMINER!
AN IM-POSTER?! BUT...!!
THEN WHO--OR WHAT--IS HE?!
I'LL SHOW YOU!!
FWING

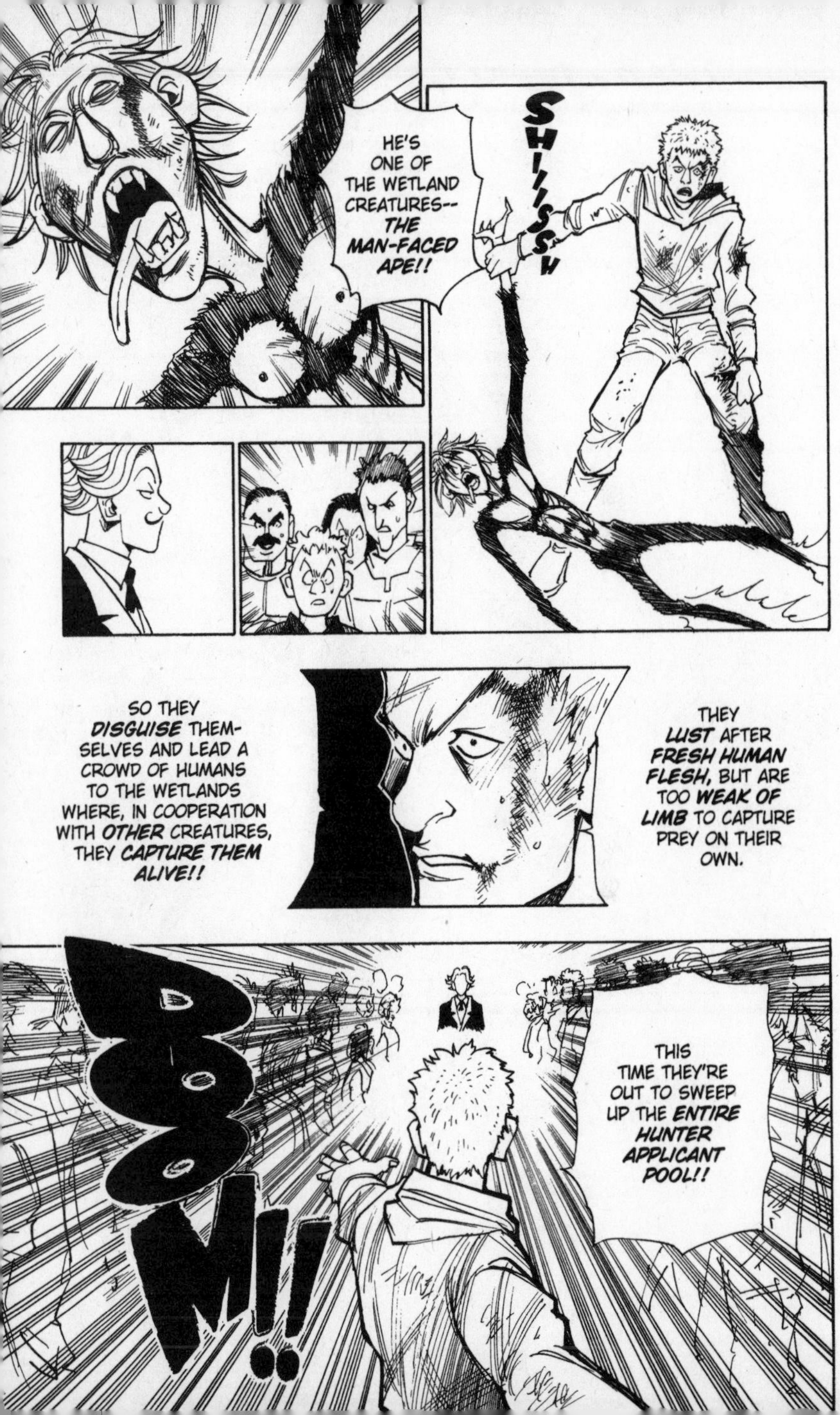
SHIIISSH
HE'S ONE OF THE WETLAND CREATURES-- THE MAN-FACED APE!!
THEY LUST AFTER FRESH HUMAN FLESH, BUT ARE TOO WEAK OF LIMB TO CAPTURE PREY ON THEIR OWN.
SO THEY DISGUISE THEM-SELVES AND LEAD A CROWD OF HUMANS TO THE WETLANDS WHERE, IN COOPERATION WITH OTHER CREATURES, THEY CAPTURE THEM ALIVE!!
THIS TIME THEY'RE OUT TO SWEEP UP THE ENTIRE HUNTER APPLICANT POOL!!
DOOOM!!

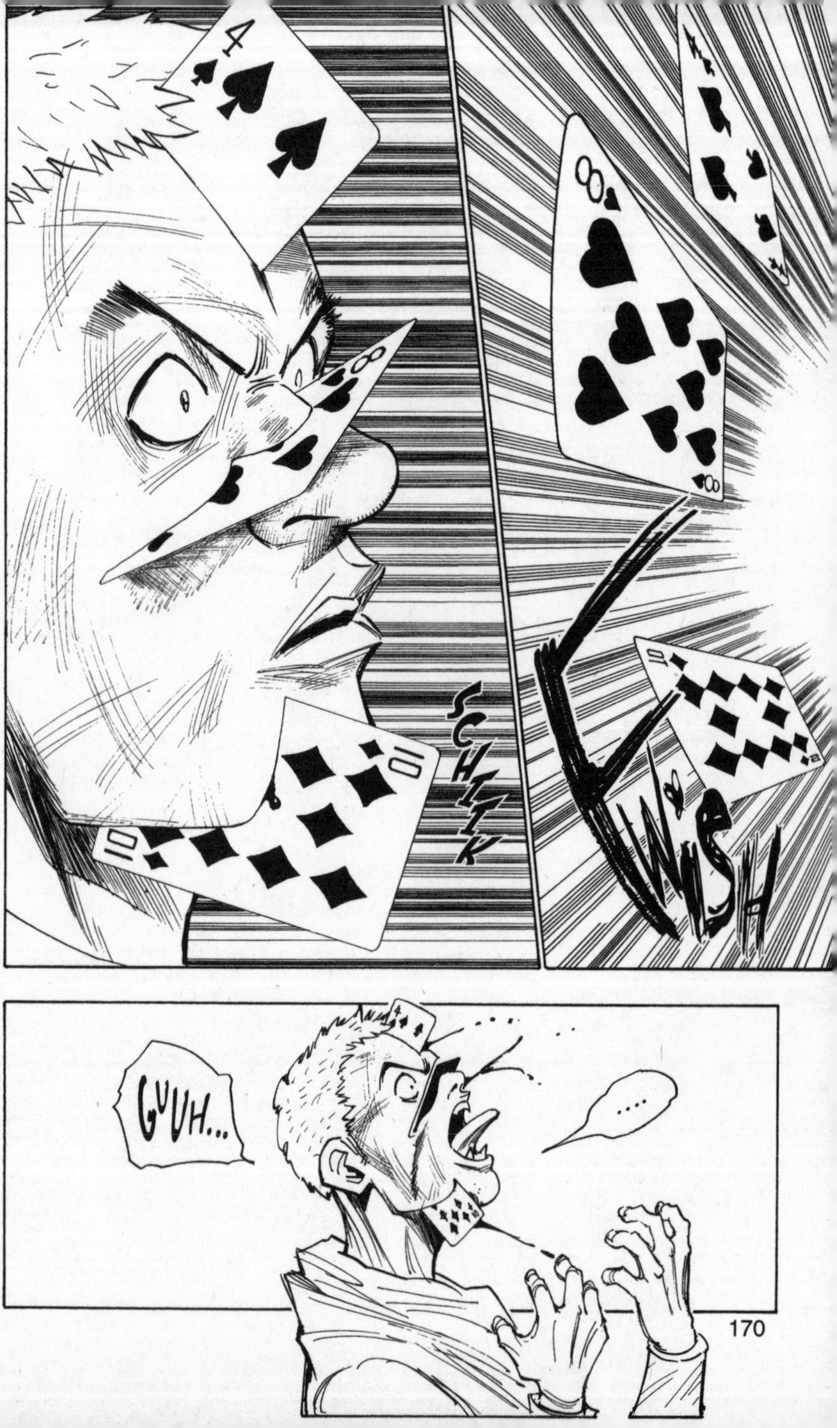
WHSH
SCHIIK
GUUH...
....

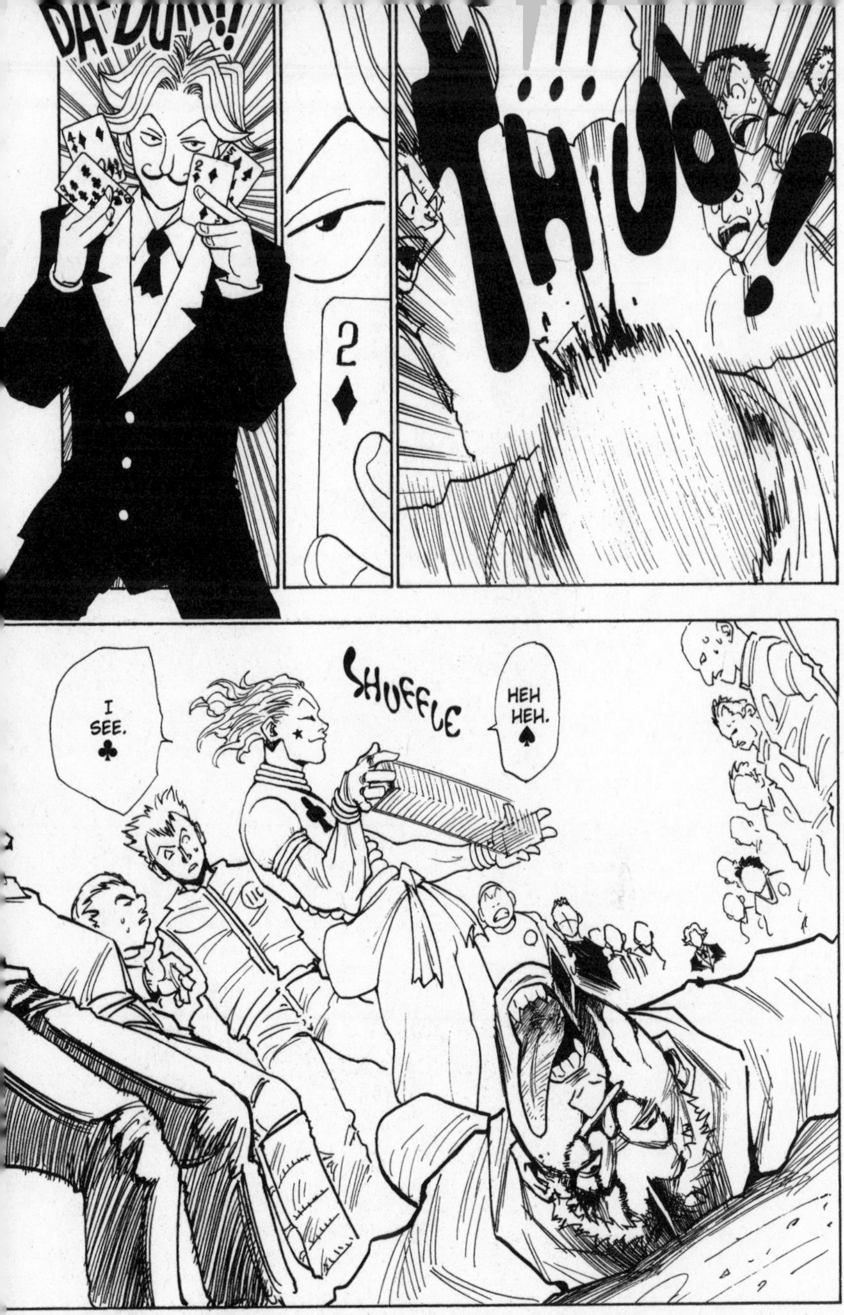
!!
THUD!
DA-DUM!!
HEH HEH. ♠
SHUFFLE
I SEE. ♣

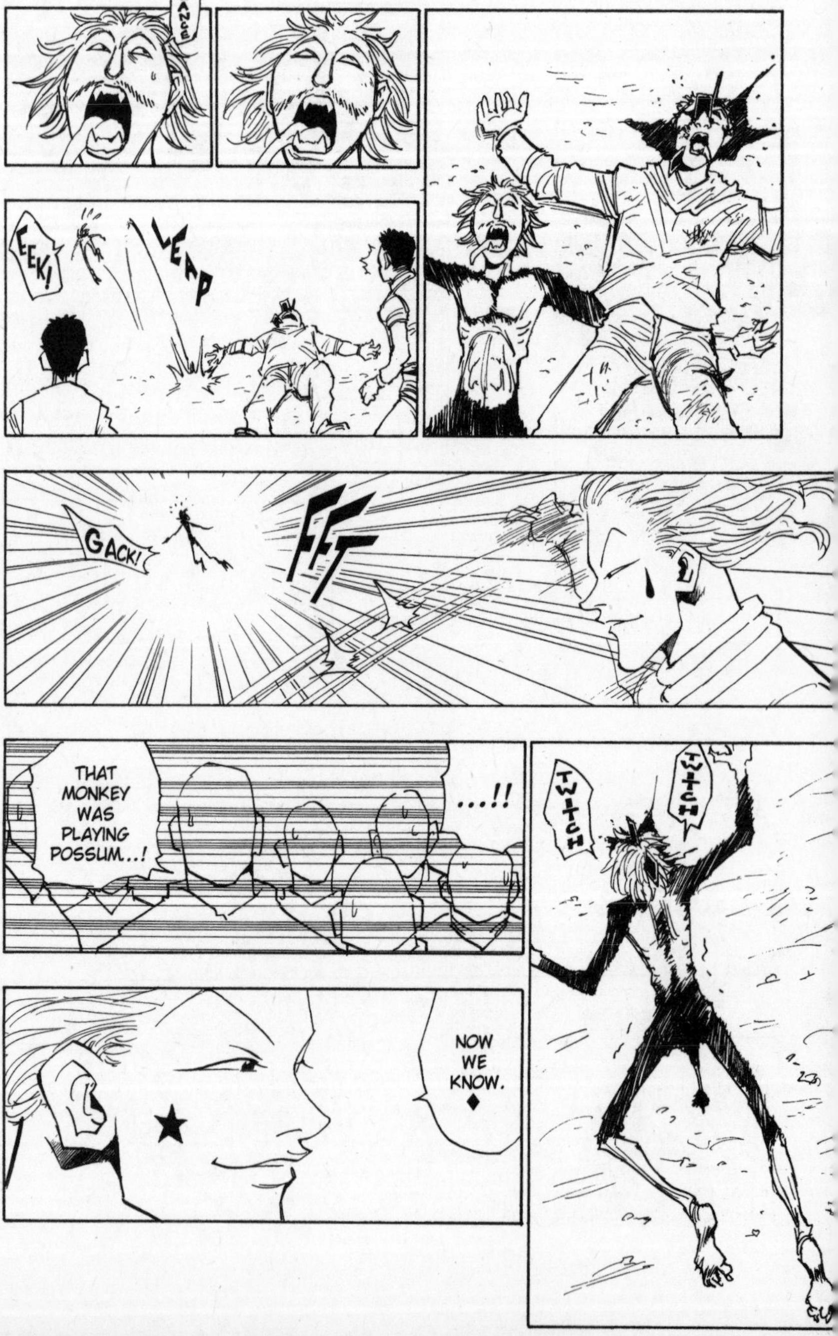
GLANCE
LEAP
EEK!
FFT
GACK!
TWITCH
TWITCH
...!!
THAT MONKEY WAS PLAYING POSSUM...!
NOW WE KNOW. ◆

READ THIS WAY

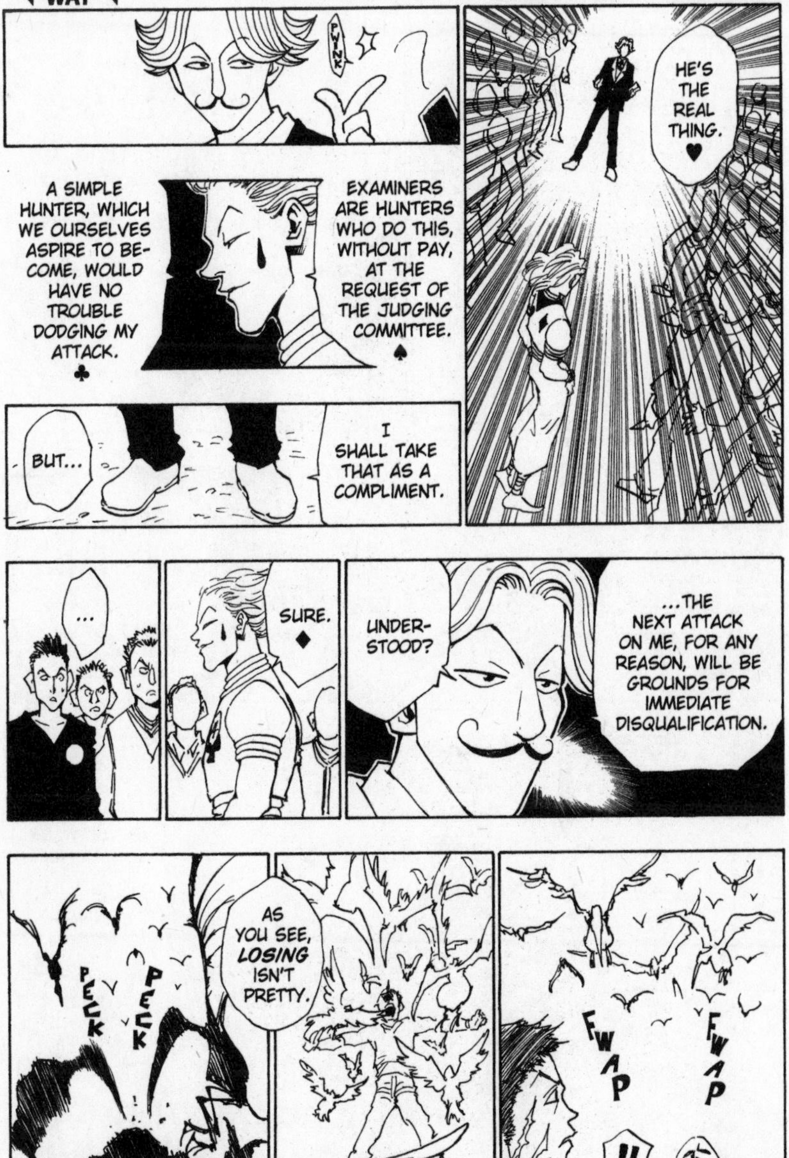
HE'S THE REAL THING. ♥
PWINK
EXAMINERS ARE HUNTERS WHO DO THIS, WITHOUT PAY, AT THE REQUEST OF THE JUDGING COMMITTEE. ♠
A SIMPLE HUNTER, WHICH WE OURSELVES ASPIRE TO BE-COME, WOULD HAVE NO TROUBLE DODGING MY ATTACK. ♣
I SHALL TAKE THAT AS A COMPLIMENT.
BUT...
...THE NEXT ATTACK ON ME, FOR ANY REASON, WILL BE GROUNDS FOR IMMEDIATE DISQUALIFICATION.
UNDER-STOOD?
SURE. ♦
...
FWAP
FWAP
!!
AS YOU SEE, *LOSING* ISN'T PRETTY.
PECK
PECK

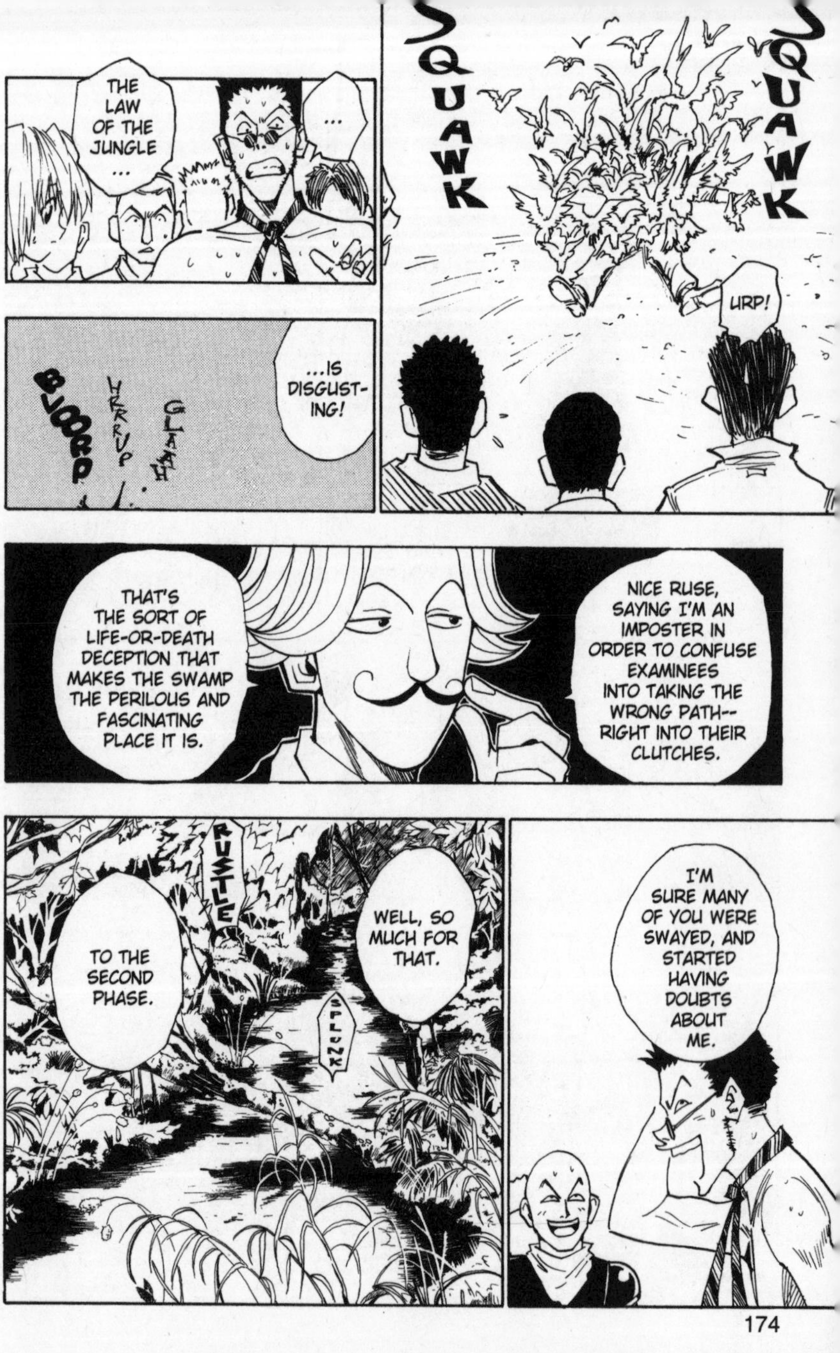
SQUAWK
SQUAWK
URP!
THE LAW OF THE JUNGLE ...
...
...IS DISGUSTING!
BLOORP
HRRRUP
GLAAH
NICE RUSE, SAYING I'M AN IMPOSTER IN ORDER TO CONFUSE EXAMINEES INTO TAKING THE WRONG PATH-- RIGHT INTO THEIR CLUTCHES.
THAT'S THE SORT OF LIFE-OR-DEATH DECEPTION THAT MAKES THE SWAMP THE PERILOUS AND FASCINATING PLACE IT IS.
I'M SURE MANY OF YOU WERE SWAYED, AND STARTED HAVING DOUBTS ABOUT ME.
WELL, SO MUCH FOR THAT.
RUSTLE
TO THE SECOND PHASE.
SPLUNK

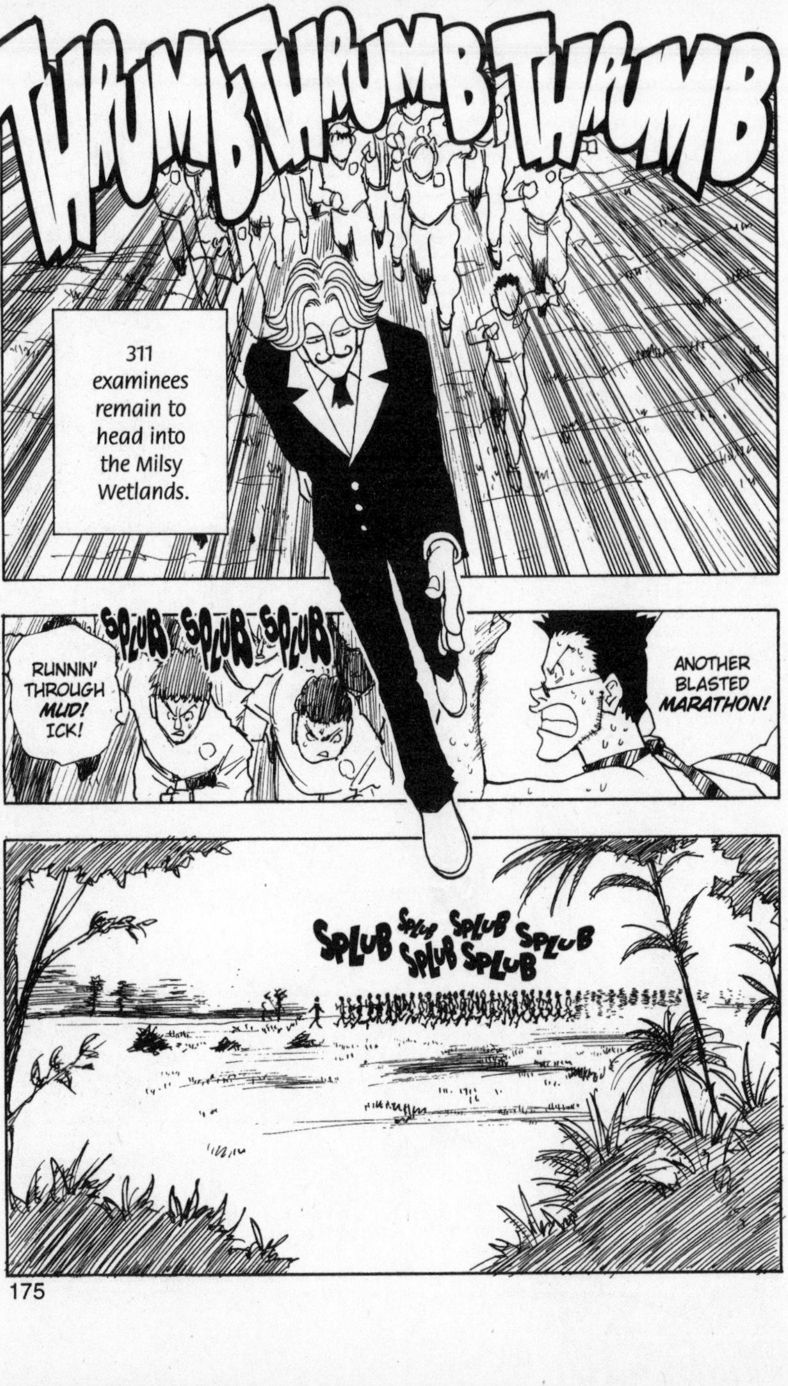
THRUMB THRUMB THRUMB
311 examinees remain to head into the Milsy Wetlands.
ANOTHER BLASTED *MARATHON!*
SPLUB SPLUB SPLUB
RUNNIN' THROUGH *MUD!* ICK!
SPLUB SPLUB SPLUB SPLUB SPLUB SPLUB

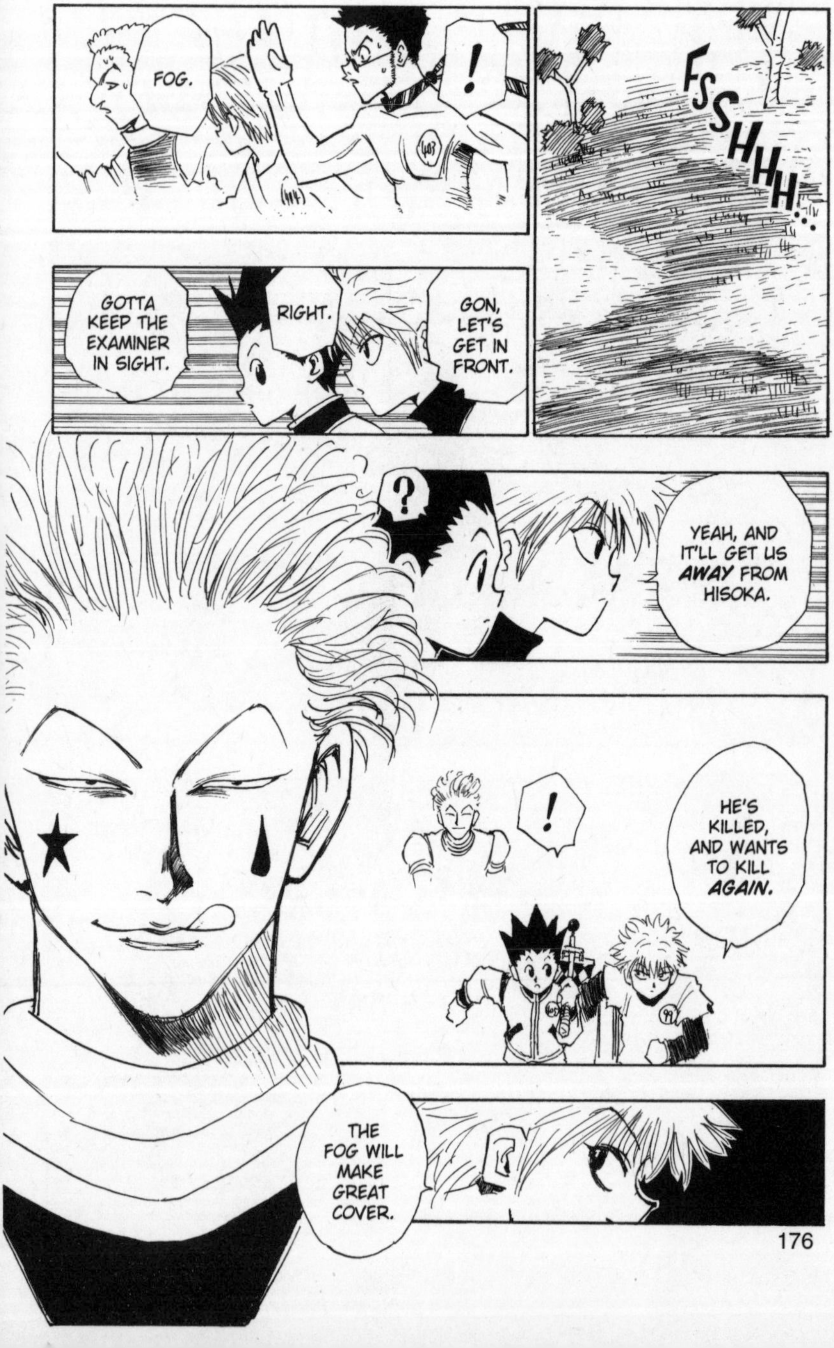
FSSHHH...
!
FOG.
GON, LET'S GET IN FRONT.
RIGHT.
GOTTA KEEP THE EXAMINER IN SIGHT.
YEAH, AND IT'LL GET US *AWAY* FROM HISOKA.
?
HE'S KILLED, AND WANTS TO KILL *AGAIN.*
!
THE FOG WILL MAKE GREAT COVER.

READ THIS WAY

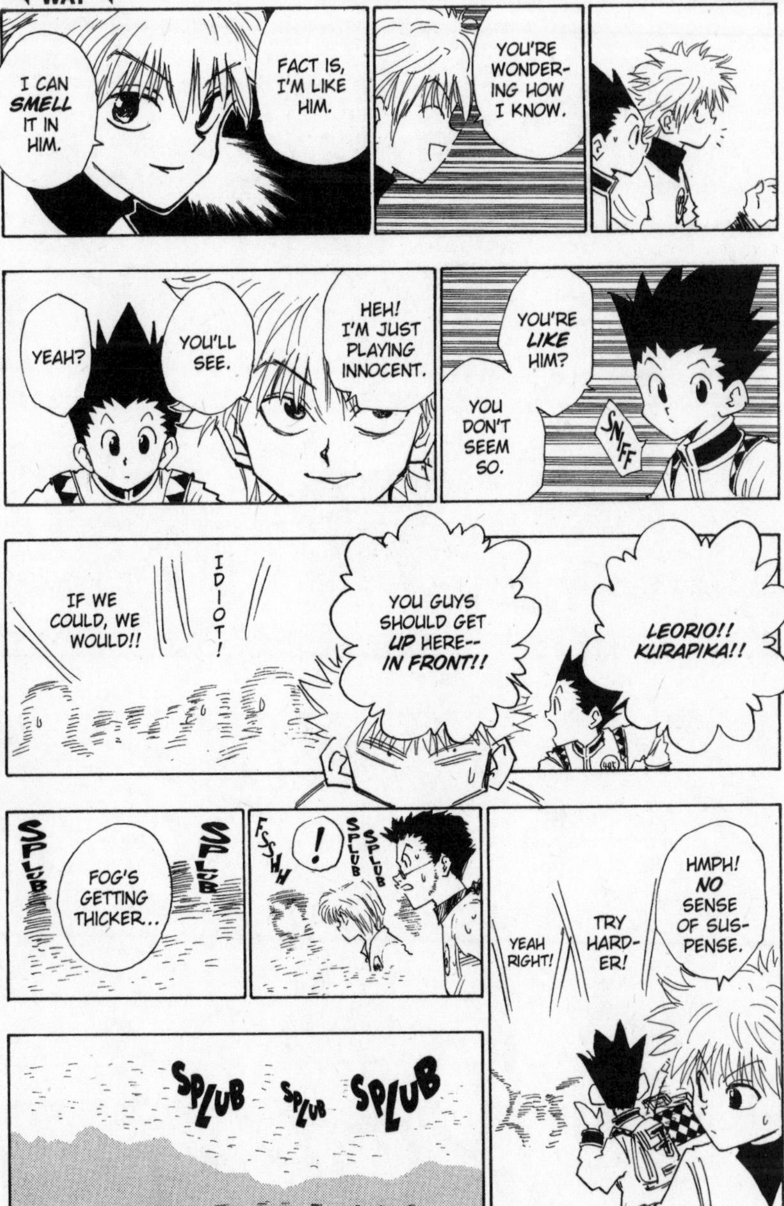

YOU'RE WONDER-ING HOW I KNOW.
FACT IS, I'M LIKE HIM.
I CAN **SMELL** IT IN HIM.
YOU'RE **LIKE** HIM?
YOU DON'T SEEM SO.
SNIFF
HEH! I'M JUST PLAYING INNOCENT.
YOU'LL SEE.
YEAH?
LEORIO!! KURAPIKA!!
YOU GUYS SHOULD GET **UP** HERE-- **IN FRONT!!**
IDIOT!
IF WE COULD, WE WOULD!!
HMPH! **NO** SENSE OF SUS-PENSE.
TRY HARD-ER!
YEAH RIGHT!
FSSHH
!
SPLUB SPLUB
SPLUB
FOG'S GETTING THICKER...
SPLUB
SPLUB SPLUB SPLUB

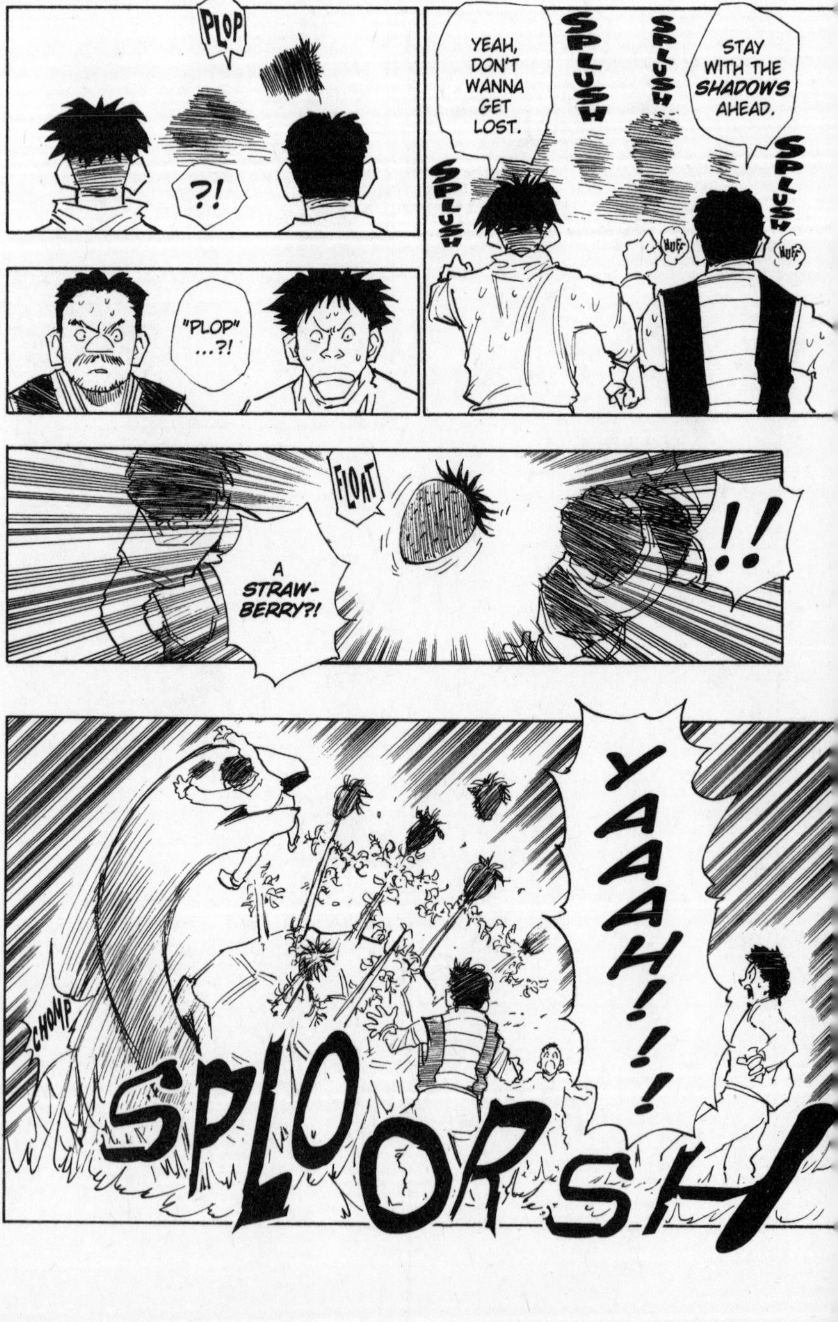
STAY WITH THE SHADOWS AHEAD.
SPLUSH
HUFF
HUFF
SPLUSH
SPLUSH
YEAH, DON'T WANNA GET LOST.
SPLUSH
PLOP
?!
"PLOP" ...?!
!!
FLOAT
A STRAW-BERRY?!
YAAAH!!!!
SPLOORSH
CHOMP

READ THIS WAY

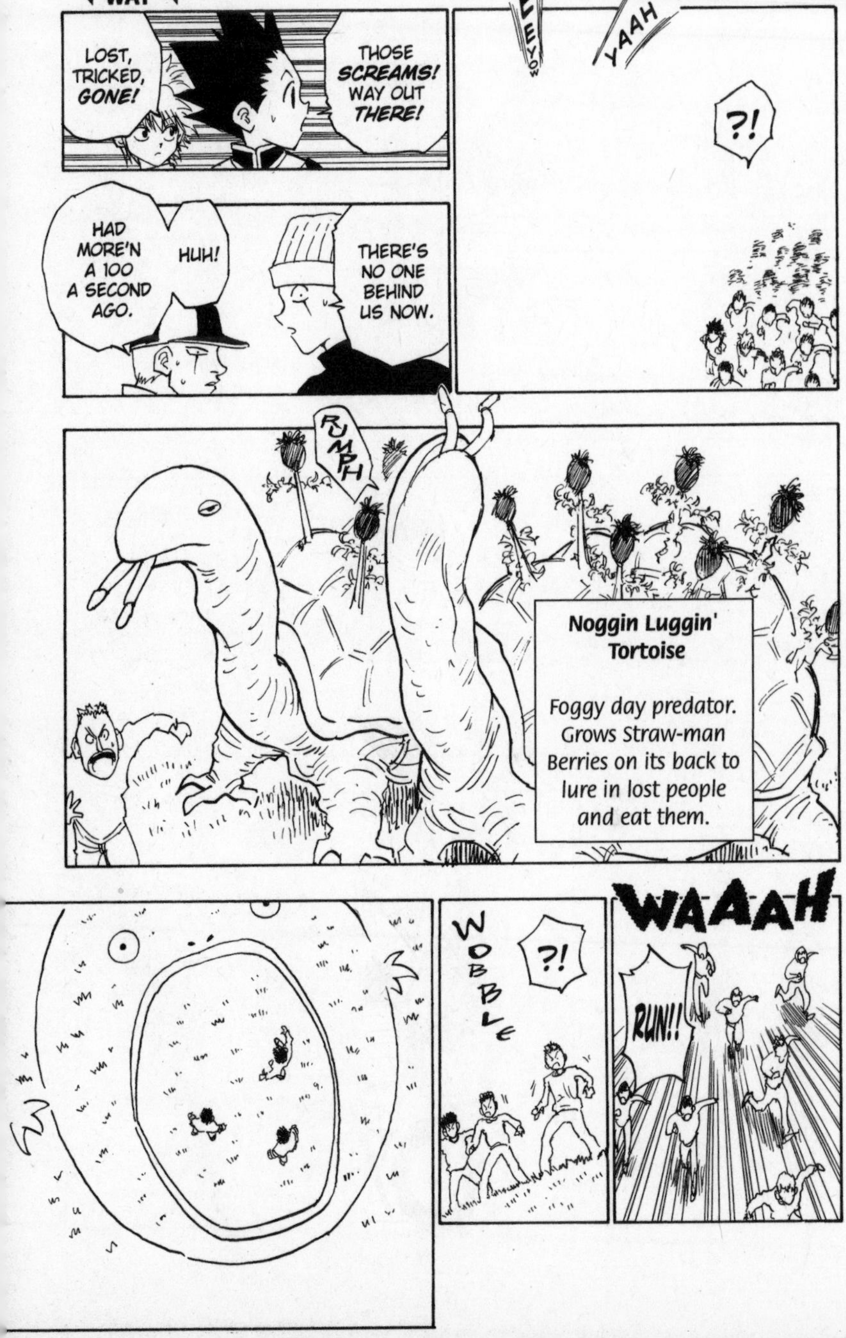

EEYOW
YAAH
?!
THOSE SCREAMS! WAY OUT THERE!
LOST, TRICKED, GONE!
THERE'S NO ONE BEHIND US NOW.
HUH!
HAD MORE'N A 100 A SECOND AGO.
RUMPH
Noggin Luggin' Tortoise
Foggy day predator. Grows Straw-man Berries on its back to lure in lost people and eat them.
WAAAH
RUN!!
?!
WOBBLE

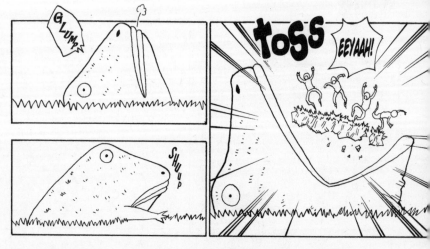

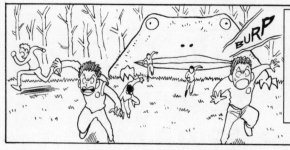

EEYAAH!
TOSS
GLUMP
SHUUUP
BURP
Frog-in-Waiting
Extremely slow moving. It hides itself underground, waiting patiently for prey to pass over its open mouth.
THIS WAY! SAFE HERE! SAFE!!
AAAH
Ruse Raven
Croaks lies that lure people into deadly traps, then feeds on the bodies.
KA-BOOM
Claymore Mushroom
Explodes when stepped on. Propagates by spreading spores on its immobilized prey.
Hypnosis Butterfly
Its pattern of flight puts prey to sleep, which makes live food for its larvae.

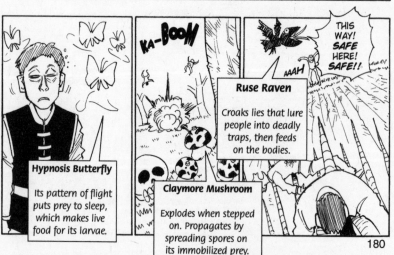

READ THIS WAY

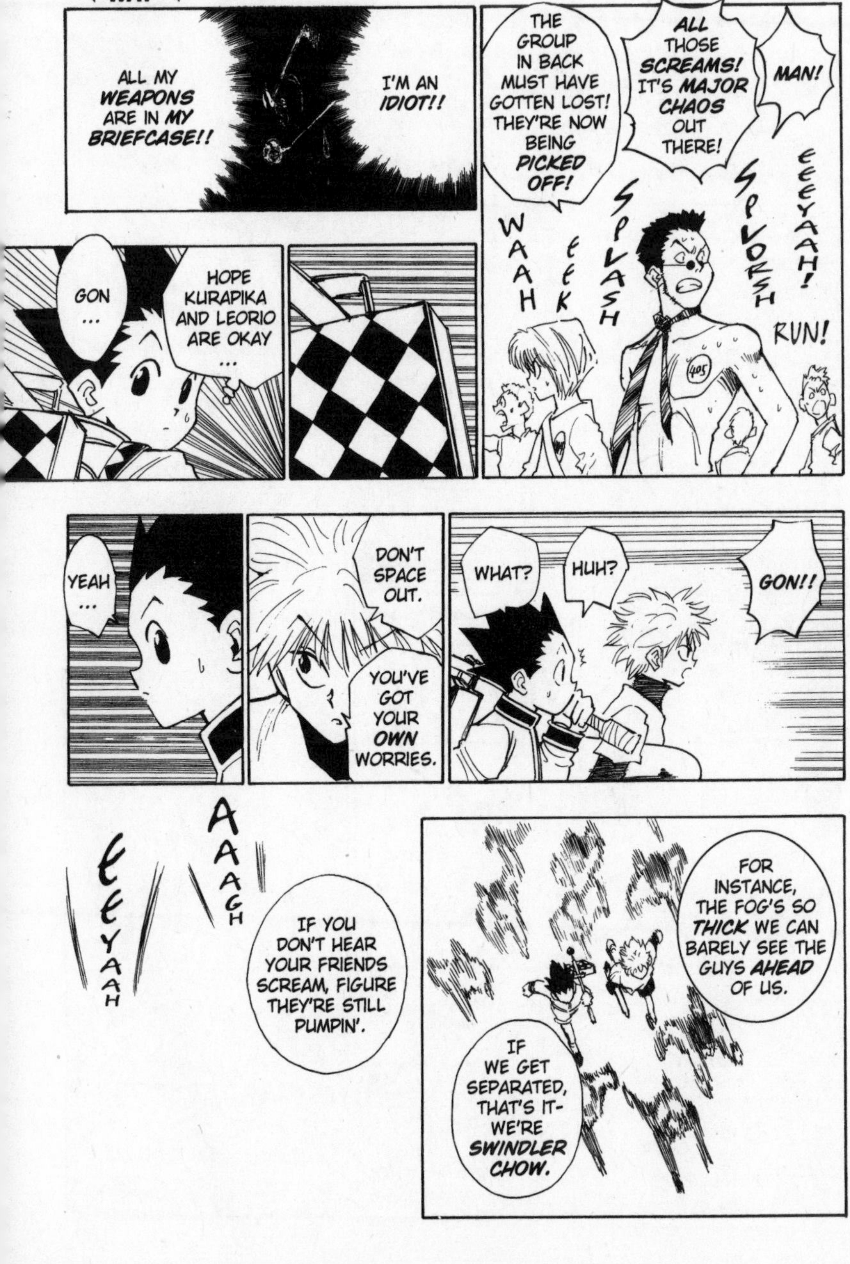
MAN!
ALL THOSE SCREAMS! IT'S MAJOR CHAOS OUT THERE!
THE GROUP IN BACK MUST HAVE GOTTEN LOST! THEY'RE NOW BEING PICKED OFF!
EEEYAAAH!
SPLORSH
RUN!
SPLASH
EEK
WAAH
I'M AN IDIOT!!
ALL MY WEAPONS ARE IN MY BRIEFCASE!!
HOPE KURAPIKA AND LEORIO ARE OKAY ...
GON ...
GON!!
HUH?
WHAT?
DON'T SPACE OUT.
YOU'VE GOT YOUR OWN WORRIES.
YEAH ...
FOR INSTANCE, THE FOG'S SO THICK WE CAN BARELY SEE THE GUYS AHEAD OF US.
IF WE GET SEPARATED, THAT'S IT- WE'RE SWINDLER CHOW.
IF YOU DON'T HEAR YOUR FRIENDS SCREAM, FIGURE THEY'RE STILL PUMPIN'.
AAAAGH
EEEYAAAH

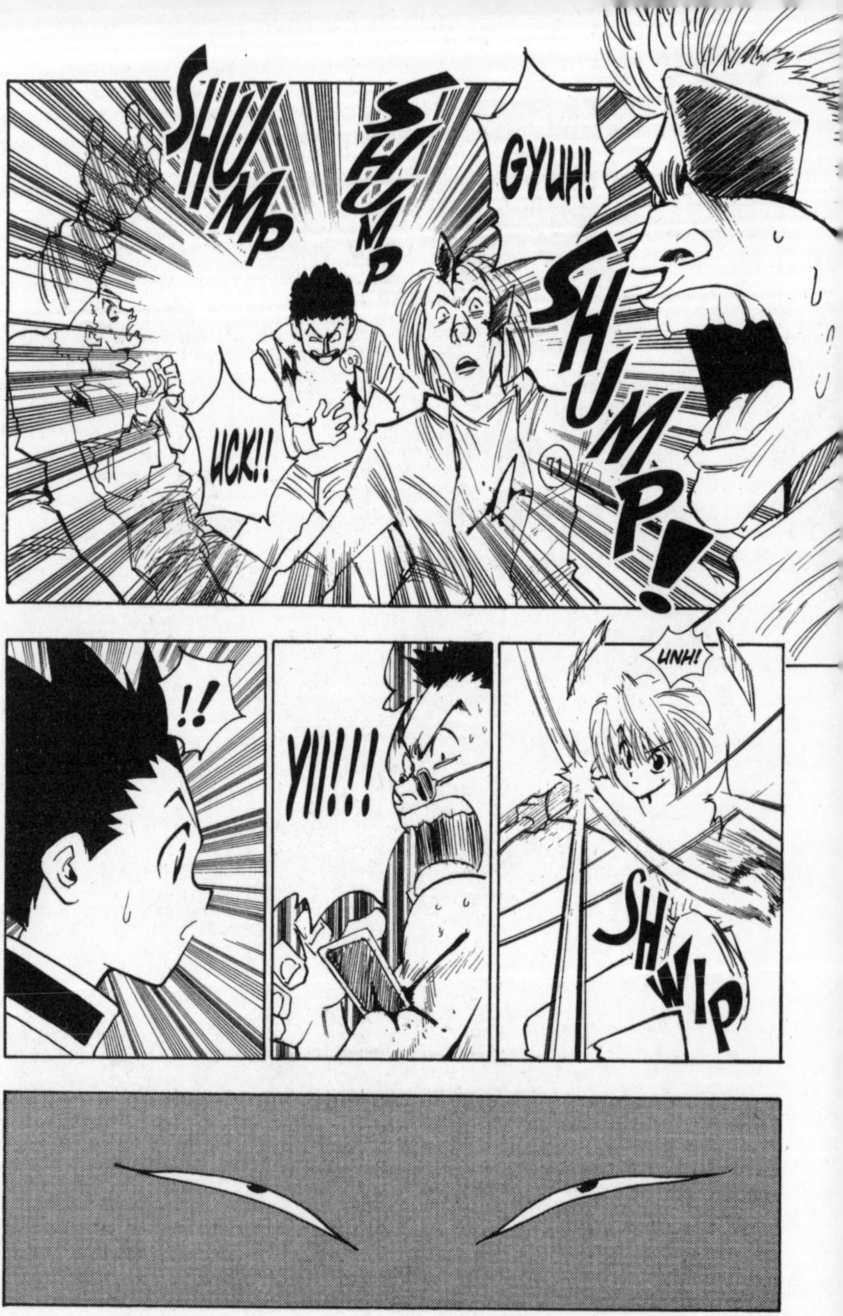
SHUMP!!
GYUH!
SHUMP
UCK!!
SHUMP
UNH!
SHWIP
YIII!!!
!!

READ THIS WAY

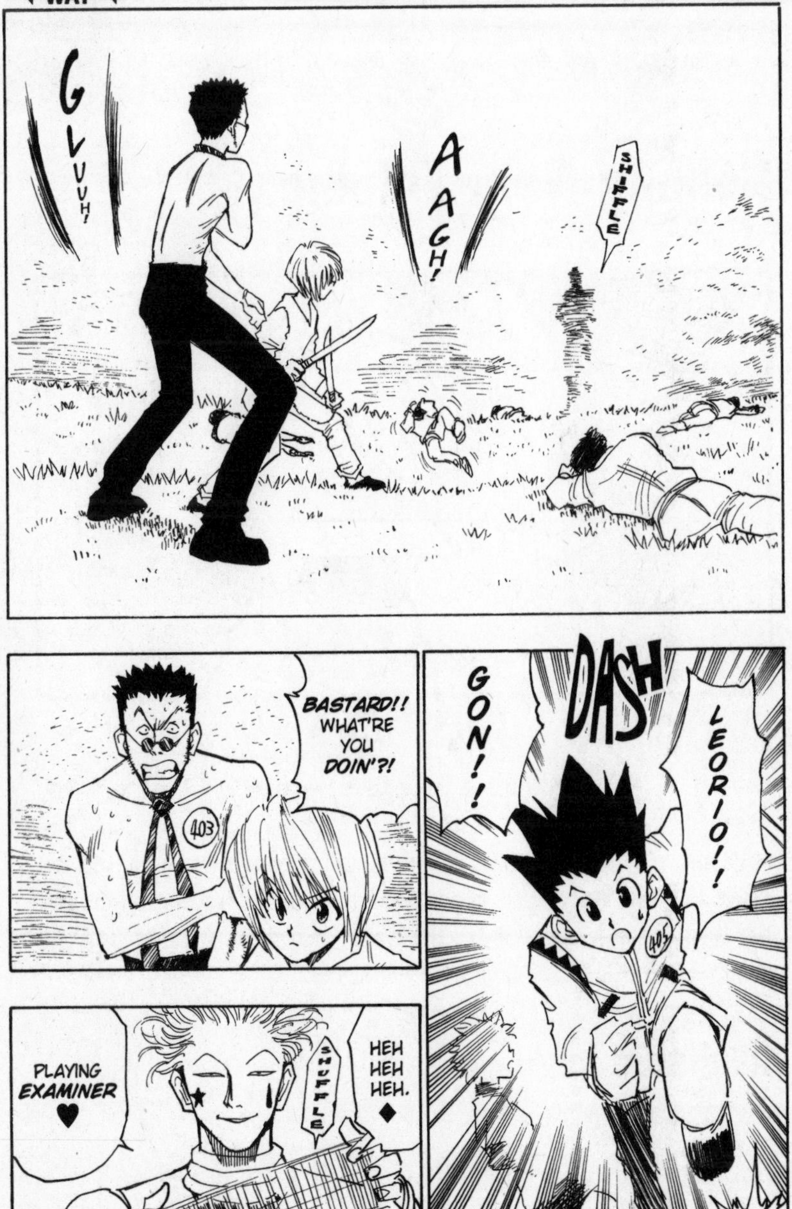
SHIFFLE
AAAGH!
GLUUUH!
LEORIO!!
DASH
GON!!
BASTARD!! WHAT'RE YOU DOIN'?!
HEH HEH HEH. ♦
SHUFFLE
PLAYING EXAMINER ♥

Coming Next Volume...

Gon and his friends Leorio and Kurapika finally make it to the Exam Hall, where they run into some trouble with Hisoka, a fellow applicant. The tests prove to be both inventive and daunting as the would-be Hunters strive to prove their mettle in a kitchen stadium and a tower maze. Can the team make it past the trouble waiting for them at the end of the tower test?

Available now!